Rethinking Facticity

SUNY series in Contemporary Continental Philosophy
Dennis J. Schmidt, editor

Rethinking Facticity

Edited by

François Raffoul
Eric Sean Nelson

State University of New York Press

Published by
State University of New York Press, Albany

Printed in the United States of America

For information, contact State University of New York Press, Albany, NY
www.sunypress.edu

Production by Kelli W. LeRoux
Marketing by Anne M. Valentine

Library of Congress Cataloging-in-Publication Data

Rethinking facticity / edited by François Raffoul, Eric Sean Nelson.
p. cm. — (SUNY series in contemporary continental philosophy ; 214)
Includes bibliographical references and index.
ISBN 978-0-7914-7365-8 (hardcover : alk. paper)
1. Phenomenology. I. Raffoul, François, 1960– II. Nelson, Eric Sean, 1968–

B829.5.R48 2008
110—dc22 2007033408

10 9 8 7 6 5 4 3 2 1

Contents

Acknowledgments

Editing an anthology is, to be sure, a cooperative endeavor and we are indeed indebted to the many individuals who have contributed to the realization of this project. We would like to especially express our appreciation to Alice Frye for her generosity and encouragement and Mélida Badilla for her unfailing support and infectious spirit. We are grateful to Jeanne Marie Kusina and Andrea Conque Johnson for their comments on and editorial assistance with the manuscript. We wish to thank Jane Bunker, Dennis Schmidt, and the editors and staff at SUNY Press who have helped make this book possible. We are also grateful to Troy Mellon for her editorial help at a crucial juncture in the preparation of the manuscript.

All chapters are previously unpublished except for Giorgio Agamben, "The Passion of Facticity." It is reprinted with the permission of Stanford University Press from Giorgio Agamben, *Potentialities: Collected Essays in Philosophy* (Stanford: Stanford University Press, 1999), 185–204.

Translation credits: Daniel Heller-Roazen translated Giorgio Agamben, "The Passion of Facticity." François Raffoul and David Pettigrew translated Jean-Luc Nancy, "The Being-with of the Being-There." Robert Vallier translated Jacob Rogozinski, "The Chiasm and the Remainder (How Does Touching Touch Itself?)."

Introduction

François Raffoul and Eric Sean Nelson

The ambition of this volume is to rethink the significance of facticity in its historical context and reflect on its contemporary relevance. This collection takes as its point of departure the young Martin Heidegger's remark that "a philosophical interpretation which has seen the main issue in philosophy, namely, facticity, is (insofar as it is genuine) factical and specifically philosophical-factical."[1] If it is the case that facticity is the horizon of philosophizing, and that philosophy is itself rooted in facticity, then facticity cannot be "reduced" through some idealistic or transcendental intellectual operation. Nor can facticity be overcome by a transcendent freedom, as Sartre at times implied, if facticity is a condition of that freedom. These considerations suggest the need to acknowledge both the question of facticity and the provocation that its pursuit offers for thinking today—once the dreams of various idealisms, Platonisms, and transcendences can no longer regulate the work of thought.

If facticity is the origin of sense, it then needs to be confronted not only as a point of departure of philosophy but also as its element. In this sense, the very object of philosophy is facticity, including its own factical origins. Despite the recognition of the importance of facticity in hermeneutics and phenomenology, it has not yet received the attention it warrants. It has too often remained unquestioned and in the background. The aspiration of this anthology is, consequently, to explore the ways in which facticity can emerge from its concealment and relative neglect so as to become a resource for thought and how more radical interpretations of facticity can be articulated from out of this context.

The term "facticity" began to assume its contemporary meaning in the late-nineteenth-century debate between Neo-Kantianism and what has been retrospectively called "life-philosophy" (*Lebensphilosophie*). Whereas the first sought to exclude facticity as irrationality from philosophy, the second celebrated it in embracing the particularity and "facticity of life." This debate influenced—and was itself transformed in—Husserl's phenomenology and Heidegger's early project of a "hermeneutics of facticity," traces of which still inform later works such as "A Dialogue on Language." The ongoing publication and translation of Husserl's research manuscripts, as well as the publication of Heidegger's *Ontology—The Hermeneutics of Facticity* and other early writings, allows for a renewed and more rigorous attention to this facet of phenomenology as well as its radicalization in contemporary thought.

TOWARD A GENEALOGY OF FACTICITY

The word *fact* has a long lineage, originating with the Roman *factum*, which is not an assertion about nature, but primarily associated with human activity and production. The early modern Italian philosopher Giambattista Vico continued to use the word in this sense in the principle of *verum factum* ("the true is the made"). This sense of fact as human doing and making is still at work in German Idealism, especially in Fichte, for whom *factum* is still to be understood in relation to action (*Tat*), and in Marxism. Yet this "production model" was already falling into eclipse. Since the world was traditionally understood as a product of God's doing and making, *factum* had already become associated with objective truths about the world and—through modern secularization—the empirical facts that are the data of modern scientific inquiry. Other meanings besides action and the factuality of empirical data are associated with "fact" during this period, even the possibility of a transcendental facticity in Kant's grounding of morality in a transcendental fact of reason that cannot be demonstrated by reasoning but forces itself upon us.[2] Despite the emergence and dominance of empiricism and positivism, and thus the model of empirical factuality, the words *fact* and *facticity* have retained a wealth of meaning that should be kept in mind in interpreting their significance in twentieth-century European thought.

The articles gathered in this volume show that the concept of facticity has undergone crucial transformations and has been "reinvented" and given unprecedented meanings in the last century. Facticity designates a kind of "fact" that has not been previously thematized in the history of philosophy. Although clearly contrasted with transcendental ideality and normative validity, it nonetheless does not designate empirical "factuality," a fact of nature, or an ontic occurrence. It points to another kind of fact, one that falls out of and subverts the transcendental/empirical duality. It is a fact that, as Jean-Luc Nancy wrote, is "undiscernibly and simultaneously empirical and transcendental, material and ideational, physical and spiritual," an "unprecedented fact of reason that would manifest at once the bare outline of a logic and the thickness of a flesh."[3]

In the hermeneutical "life-philosophy" of Wilhelm Dilthey, such a fact is identified with the resistance of the world to consciousness and will. Dilthey, however, still used the word *Tatsächlichkeit* to refer to both the facticity of life (i.e., its resistance and unfathomability) and the factuality of the sciences (i.e., the givenness of "facts" that call forth analysis and explanation).[4] Whereas Neo-Kantians such as Rickert and the Husserl of the *Logos* essay[5] perceived such facticity as a danger to the very idea of philosophy as rigorous science, Husserl soon after began to unfold in other writings, many only recently published, a phenomenology of facticity. In Husserl's phenomenology, facticity represents the passivity and alterity that resists reduction, dimensions traditionally neglected in modern idealism. Whereas his mature phenomenology has often been taken to task for its Cartesian, subjectivistic (idealistic and solipsistic) orientation, the recent publication of Husserl's research manuscripts has compelled commentators to reevaluate this traditional reading and give greater attention to the dimension of facticity and historicity in Husserl's thinking in order to engage issues of passivity, alterity, and the ethical within subjectivity. Heidegger articulates facticity as the fact of the thrownness of existence itself in its essentially finite constitution and individuation. Such facticity cannot be reduced to and challenges the transcendental, logical, and constitutive conditions of transcendental philosophies. From Heidegger's early project of a "hermeneutics of facticity" to his reflection on transcendence and freedom in the late 1920s, it is Dasein's own finitude that calls forth interpretation and individuation and, as a number of essays in this volume show, an ethical as well as a philosophical response.

Maurice Merleau-Ponty famously proposed that phenomenology is not only a philosophy of essences, "But phenomenology is also a philosophy which places essences back into existence, and does not expect to arrive at an understanding of man and the world from any starting point other than that of their 'facticity.'"[6] Merleau-Ponty's turn to facticity raises multiple questions: What does it mean to take facticity as the starting point of understanding "man" and "world"? What does a phenomenology of facticity signify given that facticity still remains obscure and given the theoretical primacy of ideality, universality, and validity? Can facticity be a basis for philosophy even though it radically undermines foundations by indicating the multiplicity, singularity, and alterity of the life and existence from which philosophy is born?

Merleau-Ponty articulated the facticity of embodiment and flesh from *The Phenomenology of Perception* to its crystallization in *The Visible and the Invisible* via texts of seminars such as *La nature*, translated by Robert Vallier. The stress on facticity, or the need to resituate the origin of thought in the factical site of the lived body, orients a rethinking of reflection and philosophy in its relation to nonphilosophy. If the lived body is indeed the origin of thought, then the task of philosophy can only be to reflect such original perception, that is, to bring into language the mute experience of the perceptual world, to make the implicit explicit. There is therefore no philosophical reflection or proper realm of thought independent of the chiasm between perception and philosophical reflection, each engaging the other. Once brought back to its factical soil from which it springs, reflection loses its pretense to independence or autonomy as well as its presumption of accessing an idealized objective realm. It is not a matter of departing from all reflection in order to be lost in the supposed immediacy of life. For Merleau-Ponty, it is a question of reflecting on reflection, of a "hyper-reflection" that would contrast with the absolute reflection of modern idealism in the sense that philosophy would recognize its birthplace in facticity, in a radically nonintellectual origin. Philosophy loses in this recognition its—not so innocent—illusion that it can have a transcendent overview of the world and life. Instead it assumes its finitude—as a vision happening from the invisible, bordered by invisibility—and responsibility for its finitude. Merleau-Ponty shows how there can be no truth without facticity and that facticity transforms the very concept and understanding of truth.

In the works of Jacques Derrida, we find the thought that *différance*, and the work and possibility of sense, are never grounded in a "transcendental signified," but operate in an immanent process (albeit in a disrupted and aporetic way), engaging us into a rethinking of materiality and materialism understood in a radically nonmetaphysical way as an effect of *différance*.[7] We are here called to a thought of a trace and of an expropriation or ex-appropriation that defers any metaphysical dream of full presence and appropriation. From a deepening of this perspective, Giorgio Agamben underscores how facticity entails an irreducible element of non-originarity, and therefore of nonpropriety. The improper is the very mark of finitude. The emphasis on facticity—

with its senses of opacity, singularity, concreteness, factuality, finitude, and expropriation—could be seen as a challenge to the values and ideals of modernity, and its model of the absoluteness and transparency of subjectivity. More precisely, does facticity not challenge the very possibility of a free self-assumption of subjectivity, a freedom that posits and constructs itself, since it represents precisely what I cannot in principle appropriate? In each case, facticity represents a challenge to the identitarian and totalizing dreams of a full appropriation in thought or in practice—whether in contemporary theoretical philosophy, transcendental idealism, traditional metaphysics, or in conventional modes of thinking. Thus, for instance, Jean-Luc Nancy's rethinking of the facticity of existence as signifying that existence is without essence, the essence-less itself, challenges the construction and imposition of such idealities. For Nancy, facticity means exposure, the "in-common" of factical and singular existences exposed to one another, and so is a fact that challenges conventional understandings of identity and demands a rethinking of traditional categories.

Yet facticity should not be simply approached as a negative phenomenon marking the limits and impossibility of projects of meaning, foundation, intelligibility, and appropriation. Such an account continues to govern the work of Jürgen Habermas, whose distinction between *Faktizität* (facticity) und *Geltung* (validity) remains within the logic of the Neo-Kantian bifurcation of the concrete particularity of factuality (systems and institutions) and universal normative ideality.[8] The task then is not to reiterate and reify this negativity but conceive of these limits—or "edges," as Edward Casey invites us to consider them in his essay—as truly opening the space of the world and of our ethical coexistence as ungrounded freedom.

In his recent book, *The Creation of the World or Globalization*,[9] Jean-Luc Nancy insists that the world manifests a radical absence of (theological) ground and foundation, a withdrawal that constitutes the world as a *fact*. Nancy goes so far as to equate the emergence of the world as such and as fact with a "de-theologization." He identifies "world-formation" (*mondialisation*, which is not to be confused with *globalization*)—i.e., the immanent structure of the world and the fact that the world only refers to itself and never to another world (the postulate of onto-theology)—as a "detheologization" (CW, 51). The meaning or sense of the world is not transcendent to that world but radically immanent to it. It lies in the world's own self-creation, the world making sense of itself. The world makes sense without any reference to an outside of the world (an essence). This is why one could follow Nancy in thinking that the making sense of the world is taking place from an absence of the given—a creation *ex nihilo*, coming from nothing, and going into nothing[10]—that allows us to conceive of the world as fact. Such a fact appears as a nothing-of-given and as without-reason. Recalling Heidegger's *Principle of Reason*, where it is said that "neither reason nor ground support the world" (cited in CW, 120, n.20), Nancy proposes that the world is a *fact* and only a fact—even if it is a singular fact, not being itself a fact *within* the world, but the fact *of* the world, the fact of itself as world. It is the fact of a "mystery," the mystery of an accidental, errant, or wandering existence (according to Wittgenstein, what is mystical is the *fact* that the world is). It is an absolute fact absolutely deprived of relation to an "other" world beyond this one. The world is a fact without cause and without reason. It is consequently, according to Nancy, "a fact without reason or end, and it is our fact" (CW, 45). We are thus called, in this thought of the world as absolute immanence, to take on its facticity without reason—as well as its non-sense—or rather the fact that its sense only lies in such a fact: "To think it is to think this factuality, which implies not referring it to a meaning capable of appropriating it, but to placing in it, in its truth as a fact, all possible meaning" (CW, 45). The world is without reason; it is to itself its entire possible reason. The world is a significance without a foundation in reason or, as Nancy writes suggestively, a "resonance without reason" (CW, 47).

This fact, without reason of the world, opens a *praxis*, an inhabiting, and an ethics. Nancy explains that if the world is not to be a land of exile—or what he describes as an "unworld" (*immonde*), i.e., the contrary of the world as it becomes increasingly inhabitable—then the world must be the place of a possible dwelling, a place to inhabit. More precisely, it is the place of a possible taking-place, where there is a genuine place, one in which things can genuinely *take place* in the world. The world is the place of any possible taking-place, the opening of space-time, the dimension where everything can take place. The world as fact is a place and a dimension to inhabit, where to coexist. Further, thinking together the stance of the world and the originary sense of *ethos* as dwelling, Nancy shows how the world as fact is also a *praxis*. The sense of the world is not given a priori. Our coexistence in the world is not given nor is it able to rely on any substantial basis. Unable to rely on any given, the world can only rely on itself. That is to say, the world suddenly appears from nothing . . . from itself: there lies its facticity, as well as its finitude. The sense of the world, not given, is to create, because: "The withdrawal of any given thus forms the heart of a thinking of creation" (CW, 69). The world, resting on nothing, is to invent meaning in an original *praxis*: "[M]eaning is always in *praxis*" (CW, 54). It is never established as a given, fulfilled or achieved. It is to be made and enacted. Being itself, as it is always "being without given," has the meaning of an act, of a making. It is in this sense that there is a world only for those who inhabit it. It is a place for a proper taking-place and dwelling, because to take-place is not simply to occur but to properly arrive and happen. This properness indicates the ethical dimension of the world, an originary ethics of being-of-the-world. However, such an ethics, as Nelson shows in his essay on "The Ethics of Facticity," needs to be situated and rooted in facticity.

Heidegger reveals in *Being and Time* the constituting role of facticity, understood as thrownness, in his thinking of ethical responsibility beyond any doctrinal ethics. Facticity seems at first a principle of inappropriability at the heart of his analytic of Dasein, a veritable challenge to the very possibility of responsible agency and a free self-assumption of subjectivity in responsibility, since facticity indicates not only what I am not responsible for but also precisely what I cannot possibly appropriate. Facticity, it would seem, would represent the impossibility of ethics and responsibility. Whereas Sartre attempted at times to reduce or overcome such facticity by appealing to the irreducible (idealistic and abstract) freedom of the for-itself in its transcendence, Heidegger shows the constitutive role of facticity for responsibility and choice. Let us think here briefly of three figures of facticity in Heidegger's *Being and Time*: mood, birth, and (ontological) guilt.

Whenever Heidegger describes moods in *Being and Time* (that is, mostly in terms of thrownness), it is in order to emphasize the element of opacity and withdrawal that seems to break and foreclose any possibility of appropriation. Moods reveal the opacity and inappropriability of our origins. Moods are like the "enigma," he says, of Dasein's pure "that-it-is," that is, Dasein's facticity. In the course entitled *Introduction to Philosophy*, Heidegger claims that the fact "that by its own decision Dasein has nothing to search for in the direction of its origin, gives an essential prod to Dasein from the darkness of its origin into the relative brightness of its potentiality-for-Being. Dasein exists always in an essential exposure to the darkness and impotence of its origin, even if only in the prevailing form of a habitual deep forgetting in the face of this essential determination of its facticity."[11]

Birth, our very coming into being, seems to evade any appropriative engagement as an origin from which we are excluded. Despite what some commentators claim, namely, that Heidegger privileged death over birth, mortality over natality (on natality as a resource for phenomenology, in particular in Husserl, the reader will consult

Anthony Steinbock's essay in this volume, "From Phenomenological Immortality to Natality"), Dasein is said to exist *between* birth and death. Yet Dasein does not occupy an actual place between two external limits. Dasein exists as stretching itself between birth and death such that it *is* the between of birth and death. Being that between, Dasein exists toward each of them. Dasein exists toward death, *and Dasein exists toward birth.* This is why Heidegger speaks of a "Being-toward-the-beginning" (*Sein zum Anfang*).[12]

We exist both in a "natal" way, and in a "mortal" way, in the sense that we relate to both ends, "our" ends. But are they really "ours"? In fact, they remain for Heidegger inappropriable: I can no more go back behind my coming into being than I can appropriate death by making it somehow actual. Facticity, understood as thrownness, reveals that Dasein can never go back beyond this "throw" to recapture its being from the ground up. Dasein in no way masters and appropriates its own ground and origins. As Heidegger put it: " 'Being-a-basis' means never to have power over one's ownmost Being from the ground up" (SZ, 284). I am thrown into existence on the basis of a completely opaque (non)-ground that withdraws from all attempts at appropriation. It would seem that I am expropriated from my own being, thereby rendering any meaningful sense of responsibility impossible.

Yet we should not be too quick to conclude that facticity marks the impossibility of ethics, unless it were to say, following Derrida, that the impossibility of ethics and its aporias constitute its very site and possibility. Derrida insists that the aporias and limits of ethics, what he also calls the "an-ethical" origins of ethics, do not point to the simple impossibility of ethics. On the contrary, they reveal the aporia *as* possibility of ethics. As he puts it, it is a matter of making the impossible possible, as impossible . . . This indeed is what the reader can see in Heidegger's analysis. For the inappropriability of moods, birth, and death, although it indicates the *impossibility* and radical expropriation of the human being, also and at the same time proves to be the secret resource of appropriation. It is the secret resource of responsibility, a paradoxical phenomenon that Derrida approaches with the neologism of "ex-appropriation." In *Introduction to Philosophy*, Heidegger explains that precisely that over which Dasein is not master must be "worked through" and "survived." He writes: "Also that which does not arise of one's own express decision, *as most things for Dasein*, must be in such or such a way retrievingly appropriated, even if only in the modes of putting up with or shirking something; that which for us is entirely not under the control of freedom in the narrow sense . . . is something that is in such or such a manner taken up or rejected in the How of Dasein" (GA 27, 337, emphasis added). The inappropriable in existence, as we saw in the phenomena of moods, is primarily felt as a *weight* or a *burden*. What weighs is the inappropriable. The being of the there, Heidegger writes, "become[s] manifest as a burden" (SZ, 134). Of course, the very notions of weight and burden make manifest the problematic of ethical responsibility. In a marginal note, later added to this passage, Heidegger clarified: "Burden: what one has to carry; man is charged with the responsibility (*überantwortet*) of Dasein, delivered over to it (*übereignet*)." It is this withdrawal itself that calls Dasein, which summons it to be this being-thrown as its own and be responsible for it. It is the withdrawal that calls, to be and to think, and to be "responsible" for it. What I have to make my own is thus what can never belong to me, what evades me, what will always have escaped me. Heidegger underscored this incommensurability when he claimed that: "The self, which as such has to lay the basis for itself, can never get that basis into its power; *and yet, as existing, it must take over being-a-basis*" (SZ, 284, emphasis added).

It is ultimately the inappropriable itself that is to be appropriated, precisely as inappropriable. I am not responsible, as Kant argued, because I am a subject who is the absolute and spontaneous origin of a series and therefore a subject to whom actions can be assigned. I am responsible because I am thrown in an existence that I do not originate yet which I have to answer for. To be thrown (facticity) means to be called (responsibility), they are one and the same phenomenon, such that Heidegger could speak of the "Facticity of Responsibility" (SZ, 135). Ethical responsibility is brought back to facticity as its most essential resource.

Revisited in contemporary thought, facticity would subsequently allow us to problematize regions that have been "reduced" in traditional metaphysical and onto-theological thinking. There is in facticity a dimension in our being that resists appropriation and reduction, whether practical or theoretical. These regions, not constituted by and challenging transcendental subjectivity, testify to the alterity and the passivity (i.e., finitude) of our experience, and call us to rethink the very notion of experience. What thoughts of experience, of subjectivity, of finitude, of nature, of the body, of racial and sexual difference does it mobilize? What thinking of language, of history, of birth and death, of our ethical being-in-the-world? These are some of the questions that the contributors of this volume address and explore.

CONTRIBUTIONS TOWARD RETHINKING FACTICITY

The first section of this collection reassesses the history of facticity from German Idealism, especially Fichte, to the phenomenology of Edmund Husserl and the young Martin Heidegger. Anthony J. Steinbock's contribution explores the role of facticity in Husserl's genetic and generative phenomenologies from the perspective of issues of immortality, mortality, and natality. Given that transcendental subjectivity is neither born nor dies from the perspective of genetic phenomenology, which considers the facticity of the concrete transcendental self-temporalizing subject or monad, Steinbock examines how birth and death can become significant for the constitution of meaning. Tracing Husserl's transition from genetic to generative phenomenology, Steinbock contends that Husserl's thinking of phenomenological immortality should be situated within natality rather than mortality, birth instead of death. Due to the constitutive asymmetry between being born and dying, and the apodeictic character of the past that the future lacks, phenomenology opens itself to mystery, vocation, and hope—and consequently the religious—not from the mere assertion of immortality but rather from this dimension of natality. He concludes this powerful reflection by arguing that natality should be "the new guiding feature for phenomenology" since, "[o]nly phenomenological natality can respond to or convert a phenomenological immortality such that immortality is integrated into and situated by natality."

Theodore Kisiel's historically rich and systematically complex analysis of the emergence of facticity and its synonyms in Heidegger's early works corrects the often repeated yet mistaken opinion that "facticity" only emerged as an important issue in the works of the early Heidegger. By understanding the contexts and intersection of tendencies that informed Heidegger's emphatic posing of the question of facticity, we begin to more fully appreciate how radically Heidegger reworked the notion of facticity in contrast with its earlier uses. Kisiel considers Heidegger's post–World War I project of articulating philosophy in relation to life by investigating how Heidegger's methodological reflections on the formal indication of facticity can be situated in relation to attempts to conceptualize facticity from Fichte's Idealism—for whom the self posits and throws the world rather than feels its thrownness—to Emil Lask's inquiry into transcendental logic and the doctrines of categories and judgment that helped inspire and shape Heidegger's early methodology of a formal indication of factical life. Drawing on Heidegger's sources as well as the earliest reception of Heidegger, Kisiel traces how

Heidegger, as part of his early concern with transforming transcendental philosophy and logic, resituates and transforms facticity in response to its employment and questionability in German Idealism, Neo-Kantianism, life-philosophy, and phenomenology.

François Raffoul approaches the early Heidegger in relation to questions of life in the context of the German philosopher's early response to life-philosophy and Neo-Kantianism. Raffoul attempts to measure the impact that the problem of facticity has had on the very definition of philosophy and thought. He first reconstitutes how in the early 1920s Heidegger reorients philosophy from the problematic of consciousness and the transcendental self to the question of the immanent movement of finite and factical life interpretively explicating itself. Stressing how life displays a singular immanence, to the point of being tautological, Raffoul also underlines the radical immanence of philosophy to life: facticity calls forth philosophy as its self-articulation and philosophy is to be understood in terms of the facticity that it itself unavoidably always is. Raffoul argues that for Heidegger, thought cannot be the reflexive grasp of an objectivity and can never be an external gaze *upon* life, from a position outside of life. Thus, "[o]ne should not fear facticity, one should not fear so-called relativism by appealing to an illusory 'freedom from stand-points,' for in fact the issue in relativism is not the relativity of perspectives with respect to (a nonexistent) universality, but *the very facticity and finitude of experience.*" Rejecting the understanding of thinking as a theoretical overview detached from what it sees, Heidegger conceives of thought as entirely grounded in life, and enjoying no independence with respect to its life. Reflection will be understood by Heidegger as a motion proper to life itself, life reflecting on itself. "Reflection thus means: Life coming *back* to itself. Thinking is to reflect in the sense of *repeating.*" Such repetition and reflection are in fact required by life: life is "compelled" to reflection in the sense of repetition. Life *needs* to repeat itself as "interpretation can only arise out of an 'existentiell concern.' " Philosophy thus arises out of need, which Raffoul explores in the last part of his chapter. It appears that such a need expresses a tear within life itself, which Heidegger designates as "ruinance," a motion of expropriation that calls for philosophizing as homecoming. Heidegger thus speaks of the countermotion of thought, going against life's "own" tendency to move away from itself and fall into expropriation. Ultimately, it is not a matter of philosophy attempting to overcome the ex-appropriative event of facticity but rather of giving thought to it and being responsible for it.

In the second section, attention is given to questions of how Heidegger's hermeneutics of facticity informs the development of his thought in the 1920s, particularly how the complexity of the issue of facticity sheds light on the structure and significance of *Being and Time*. Giorgio Agamben unfolds facticity as fallenness, finitude, and thrownness from Heidegger's early confrontation with issues of love, passion, and religion. Whereas the tradition stemming from Augustine judges facticity, fallenness, and finitude negatively as distance from the transcendent, Heidegger radically reworks religious concepts by exhibiting the profoundly "positive" character of these phenomena condemned by traditional theology. Facticity, fallenness, and finitude are not accidents or negative categories of human existence but constitutive. They are not merely sinful imperfections but, as they express existence's radical expropriation and "improper" structure, are the very passion and sense of human life. To articulate these claims, Agamben analyzes facticity in Heidegger's *Being and Time,* beginning with its paradoxical affinity with disclosure and openness: "How is it possible for Dasein to open itself to something without thereby making it into the objective correlate of a knowing subject? . . . It is in this context that Heidegger introduces his notion of "facticity" (*Faktizität*)." Agamben traces Heidegger's account of facticity to his reading of Augustine, who contrasted *facticius*—that which is unnatural, artificial, and made by humans—with *nativus* as that which is natural and created by God. This indicates that the term *factical* can be situated in "the semantic sphere of non-originarity and making." For Agamben, the "originary facticity" of Dasein signifies that Dasein's opening is marked by an original impropriety. He concludes that "for Heidegger, this experience of facticity, of a constitutive non-originarity, is precisely the original experience of philosophy, the only legitimate point of departure for thinking." Love is the passion of such a facticity, a passion "in which man bears this nonbelonging and darkness."

Jean-Luc Nancy responds to the perplexity of why *Mitsein* (being-with) and *Mitdasein* are deployed and presupposed throughout *Being and Time* without any extensive analysis being devoted to them: "It is therefore all the more striking that a specific interrogation of what was at stake with the terms of *Mitdasein* and Being-with-others [*Miteinandersein*] has never been attempted, given that the *with* was declared essential to the very essence of the existent (nothing in the later work allows us to believe it was forgotten or minimized: Heidegger never ceased to think in a collective or communal dimension and nothing in his work even approaches solipsism)." Nancy interrogates the factical character of the "with" of "being-with" as an unsubstantial between rather than as a common essence or identity. The issue for Nancy is to reengage the question of the "with" as it affects the very meaning of being. His question bears on the entire Western philosophical tradition, even while focusing on Heidegger as a privileged entry to these questions. As he puts it: "This question I also want to indicate straightaway did not concern Heidegger alone. Far from it. It concerns the whole of Western thought in its manner of grasping or failing to grasp in general what Heidegger first precisely revealed: the essential character of the existential *with* (that is to say, of the *with* as a condition of the possibility of factical existence—if not the very existence of all beings . . .)." Nancy invites us to think the "enigma of being-with" in several provocative steps, speaking of a "with" happening "between the proper and the improper," in a peculiar intertwining: "The intertwining of the limit and of the continuity between the several *theres* must determine proximity not as pure juxtaposition but as *composition* in a precise sense, which must rest on a rigorous construction of the *com*-." Since such an intertwining affects being and being-there, and thus must affect being-toward-death, Nancy evokes the question of a "sharing of death." "For, if it is exactly at the site of the *with* that both the opportunity and risk of existence are manifest, then one must also accept—still in accordance with the Heideggerian paradox—that this site is the site of death." Wondering how one can conceive such a sharing of death, between the solitary death of dying and the sacrificial death in the struggle for the cause of the people, Nancy asks: "How can we give thought to death between us, indeed, to death as the very co-opening of the *there*?"

The next two contributions consider the possibility and impossibility of the ethical in light of Heidegger's thinking of finitude and facticity and in response to Levinas's critique of Heidegger in the name of an ethics of transcendence and humanism of the other. Eric Sean Nelson raises the question of the continuity and difference between different senses of facticity at work in Heidegger's thinking of the 1920s, exploring them in relation to the possibility of an ethics of facticity. He contrasts the tranquilizing facticity of average everyday being-with, which is indifferent to its own possibilities, with the interruptive facticity of the uncanniness that potentially disturbs common life allowing a more radical individuation to occur. Arguing for the responsibility of individuation and promoting the individuation of the other, he rejects the standard view that Heidegger's thinking has no ethical import. Although Heidegger rejected ethics as theoretical doctrine and arbitrary assertion of value, practical questions of responsibility and individuation are crucial to the structure and argument of *Being and Time* and related works. Yet given the inescapability of everydayness, tradition, and the sociality of being-with, authenticity or responsibility can never fulfill or fully claim itself. Authenticity can only be in each case a reclamation and a modification of inauthenticity, a "proper" inevitably defined by the improper, or an interpretive individuation that responds or does not respond to its own finitude and facticity. An "ethics of facticity" accordingly occurs as responsiveness to the immanent alterity and conformity of factical life rather than as its transcendence.

Rudi Visker also addresses Heidegger's thinking of facticity in the context of contemporary discussions of alterity and ethics, but takes this issue in a different direction. He begins his chapter with a critical analysis of the problematic presuppositions underlying current discourses—which stem primarily from the work of Levinas and involve a questionable interpretation of Heidegger's thinking—of alterity and the other. Broaching the question of the untranslatability of Dasein, and how it and its characteristic of being "my own" defy common interpretations and criticisms, Visker carefully investigates Heidegger's uses of this term. Visker provocatively contends that what currently seems unfashionable in Heidegger's thought, his lack of attention to alterity, the other, and ethics, is in point of fact his strength. Heidegger is defenseless before this criticism and yet not in need of a defense. According to Visker, the intransitive character of facticity in Heidegger challenges the transitivity of self and other. Visker illustrates this point by delving into the possibility of liberation via the world rather than in its denial as well as in the phenomena of radical boredom and the "there is." Yet Visker does not only interrogate the ethical in response to Levinas's critique of Heidegger, he also finds unexpected agreement between them.

The contributors to the third section approach the topic of facticity in relation to questions of race and racism, fact and essence, the body, sensibility, and the unconscious in postwar French and French-influenced thought. In view of the idea that race is a socially constructed object and the resulting belief that racism can be easily surmounted by constructing the idea of race differently one individual at a time, Robert Bernasconi assesses whether such a conception of race has achieved its critical liberatory aspiration. Maintaining that "social constructionism, far from empowering a marginalized group that has historically been seen as a race, leaves that group deprived of agency and the specific kind of identity that it needs in order to combat racism," Bernasconi turns to the question of whether race should be thought of as involving a kind of facticity. On the basis of Jean-Paul Sartre's thinking of facticity, and its tension with his own interpretation of race as a construct imposed by the racist in works such as *Anti-*

Semite and Jew, and Frantz Fanon's varying articulation of the experiential facticity of race, in which race is seen in terms of practices and institutions rather than ideas and beliefs, Bernasconi argues that a richer, thicker, less individualist and more sociopolitical approach to race as facticity is called for. Responding to critics of Sartre, he suggests that Sartre's multilayered approach to facticity is more useful in approaching social-political issues than that of Heidegger. While continuing to challenge the reduction of race to a brute identity or a fixed unchanging essence, questioning the facticity of race would more profoundly address issues of how race actually functions at multiple levels in society and how it is lived, experienced, and actively interpreted and reinterpreted. Such an approach to the facticity of race would help to existentially articulate experiences of race and thus better identify and combat the intransigence of racism.

The following two chapters illustrate the importance of facticity in Maurice Merleau-Ponty's phenomenology and ethics as well as how vital these domains remain for the contemporary encounter with facticity. Bernard Flynn argues that Merleau-Ponty deconstructs the opposition between fact and essence, the personal and the impersonal, and the proper and improper via the fissure and the chiasm. He argues that for Merleau-Ponty, more radically than Nietzsche, "there are neither facts nor interpretations, which is to say, neither independently given facts nor interpretations, but rather a fundamental *écart,* or fissure, where Being gives itself in the register neither of the factual nor of the intelligible." Flynn shows how Merleau-Ponty deconstructs the opposition between being and consciousness. Merleau-Ponty, through flesh and facticity, rejects the "frontal confrontation with Being" that still informs Sartre's existential phenomenology. Contrary to this frontal encounter with Being—the model of modern subjectivity—Flynn cites *The Visible and the Invisible,* "Being no longer being *before me,* but surrounding me and in a sense traversing me, and my vision of Being not forming itself from elsewhere, but from the midst of Being." Merleau-Ponty thus complicates the relationship between fact and essence, moving it away from an opposition, insofar as vision is a relation to Being formed within Being: "Vision is engendered by a fold of the visible on itself." Flynn proposes that Being, what there is, is neither fact nor essence but "a certain style." He writes: "Merleau-Ponty displaces the problematic of fact and essence by the notion of *style*. Every style, unlike the traditional concept of essence, is encrusted with the thickness of Being." Flynn shows how the very concept of essence, of the pure epistemic subject, was constructed to cover over such a thickness. Arguing that the "there is," the *il y a*, does not have the nefarious quality that it has for Levinas, he concludes that nature, the body, and immanence are conditions for rather than threats to ethics.

In a rich and complex essay, Jacob Rogozinski reflects on the facticity and aporia of touch touching itself and the tactile chiasm in Merleau-Ponty. Rogozinski claims that the question of touch or of the tactile chiasm imposes itself today as a fundamental stake in French philosophy. After being eclipsed in the sixties, under the predominance of structuralism, questions pertaining to the body, the flesh, have returned to the center of French philosophical reflection. Rogozinski focuses on the phenomenon of tactile auto-affection, on the singular experience of *touch touching itself*. "When one of my hands touches the other, it perceives it at first as a physical thing; but this hand-thing also senses itself being touched. Tactile impressions awaken in it, and 'it becomes flesh' [*Es wird Leib*], a hand of living flesh that also touches the hand that touches it." The flesh is thus originarily constituted in a double mode, both flesh and material thing. Merleau-Ponty described this experience as an "intertwining" or a "chiasm." Rogozinski endeavors to problematize this enigma of what he calls "originary flesh," and challenge its supposed obviousness: "[W]e must suspend the naive certainty of being in the world and having a body; and confront both the strangeness of a primordial flesh that does not yet have eyes and hands, but only carnal poles, and the strangeness of an ego that is not yet a subject or an individual human, but that is rather dispersed into innumerable splinters of one or more selves." From this perspective, Rogozinski radicalizes the chiasm by showing both its irreducible character and by recognizing its universal scope. The chiasm not only encroaches upon the difference between myself and the other, but also the divergences between myself and things and between myself and the world. Recognizing this universal chiasm, Rogozinski nevertheless identifies an aporia in the chiasm, an impossible, which Merleau-Ponty designated as "the untouchable of touching, the invisible of vision, the unconscious of consciousness." Rogozinski wonders how one can assure the juncture or the knotting of this impossible chiasm and addresses this aporia by appealing to Derrida's claims that one needs to recognize in the chiasm and in touch that the "I touches itself by spacing itself, by losing contact with itself," that is, that it is *touched without touching itself*. Indeed, Rogozinski states that every event as event can be defined as *the possibility of the impossible*, "and this is also true for the inaugural event that is the chiasm." Touch, the flesh, its chiasm, reveal the impossible as condition of their happening.

It is often said that Lacanian psychoanalysis privileges the symbolic order of signifiers over the materiality of the body and the immanence of affects. David Pettigrew explores the extent to which Lacanian psychoanalysis offers unique access to the body and its facticity, arguing that with Lacan and Nasio the signifier is the carrier of the materiality or facticity of the body and that the signifier permeates the body-unconscious. Addressing the work of contemporary French Lacanian psychoanalyst J.-D. Nasio, Pettigrew responds to criticisms that psychoanalysis has neglected the body by reducing it to little but fragmented and repressed modes of representation. Confronting this critique, Pettigrew catalogues the dimensions of the fragmentation, the disembodiment of the body in the alienation of the mirror stage, symptomatic eruptions that accompany the psychical memory of trauma, the constitutive instability introduced by the phallus, *objet a*, and partial *jouissance*. Pettigrew asserts that through its psychoanalytic disembodiment, the body is cast out into the exile of a "body-less hole" and suggests that through psychoanalysis the body is rendered "impossible." In the second part, Pettigrew shows that a meaningful encounter with the facticity of the body must engage this impossible body—a body that does not ever cohere but only persists in excess of itself, a body without coherence, its being everywhere at once, and without subjective agency. To this end, Pettigrew interprets Nasio's more innovative formulations concerning the body, including the unconscious body "to come" that inhabits an ecstatic field, and the *semblant*, situated in the analyst as *objet a* who activates the transference, further extending the ecstatic nature of the unconscious body, and the intercorporeality of the bodies in the ecstatic experience of transference in psychoanalysis. Pettigrew identifies the need for a conceptual reorientation that gives proper consideration to the facticity of such an ecstatic experience of bodily being by turning to Heidegger. Pettigrew finds convergence between the psychoanalytic account of a desubstantialized and ecstatic body and Heidegger's thinking with respect to "bodying forth" and the ecstatic experience of being.

The chapters gathered in the final section unfold contemporary perspectives and reflections on facticity. Ed Casey reminds us that when we rely on our usual modes of classification, starting with those that belong to what we call aesthetics, "by the time we designate something as 'art,' " it has lost its disruptive presence, its radical novelty, its challenge. . . . More specifically, there is a danger in the institutionalization of aesthetics that art *as art* would have "lost its edge." Reflecting phenomenologically on the motif of the "edge," Casey shows that edges are sites of openings insofar as they disestablish and upset those structures that by their very nature obstruct "what is coming and to come," that is, the sudden, the surprising, the new. In this sense, facticity, that is, the way something happens, is precisely happening as an edge, a "cutting-edge." The work of art is exemplary in such cutting-edge opening; it is a work, Casey tells us, that "creates its own edge," recalling what is called "avant-garde art," or art "on the edge of our usual expectations that we cannot anticipate its inception or control its course once it has emerged." Casey develops a phenomenology of the edge—structure of the event, edges or limits/openings of the world—through the work of art and the motifs of frame, delineation, and representation exemplified in the works of such artists or architects as Marin, Monet, Cage, Cézanne, and Wright. According to Casey, the role of edges in art, "is not that their presence guarantees artistic creativity, nor even that it is necessary to such creativity. Instead, I am pointing to the pervasive ingredience of edge in many artworks and many kinds of such works—an ingredience that is not often assessed as such. But I am also contending that attention to edges fosters and enhances the production (and eventually the appreciation) of art." Since every site or place comes edged, and "there is no edgeless place," Casey contends that art itself must be seen as an edge and the ultimate edge-work. The edge is the place for the happening of openness. Not only since art "edges us out of habitual patterns of experience," allowing access to the unexpected and the disruptive, but also because the work of art as edge-work opens a new world, or the world as each time new. "We need to come to the edge of the work—to the work of its edges—to have such an experience, as intensive as it is ecstatic, as incoming as it is outgoing, as invasive as it is exhilarating." Recalling Merleau-Ponty's remark that artworks "have almost their entire lives [still] before them," Casey ends with the notion that edges are the future or the very form of the future.

Namita Goswami and Patricia Huntington return to the problem of facticity in Heidegger, and some of the issues raised earlier by Bernasconi such as the critical and liberatory potential of engaging facticity, in a new context of questioning. Goswami and Huntington critically explore Heidegger's thinking of facticity in light of contemporary questions of gender, race, and the postcolonial (the facticity of the lingering traces of colonialism) as well as of childhood, the family, maternity, and woman. Namita Goswami tracks the issue of facticity in Heidegger in reference to contemporary social-political discourses such as critical social theory, feminism, and postcolonialism. She provocatively demonstrates in this important and multifaceted essay that, far from reifying power and identity, facticity can be used to critically engage them and the logic of identity that they presuppose. The facticity of existence is not the assertion of a common essence or reified identity, but is something that we simultaneously belong to and transgress, are at home with and foreign to, that is, it is both proper and uncannily improper. Goswami consequently examines Heidegger's thought from the perspective of his project of a hermeneutics of facticity and in relation to the critique of identitarian thought expounded in Adorno's critical theory, the transformative facticity and reversals of Hegel's master/slave dialectic, and in response to the postcolonial feminism of Spivak in order to articulate the facticity of and possibilities for hearing the subaltern. The issue of whether the subaltern can speak, whether it is a mere construct of power or has its own resistance and facticity, leads Goswami to consider Adorno's criticisms of Heidegger in light of the project of a critique of ideology. She contrasts this with the critical and uncritical aspects of Heidegger's confrontation with "world-views" and "value-thinking." Goswami additionally confronts issues of the home, "Europe," and "the West," in light of issues of masculinity and mastery so as to place the subject of postcolonial reason in question. Her analysis suggests that thinking facticity can help problematize the very facticity of authoritarianism and the compulsion of identity.

The following richly descriptive essay might be described as a hermeneutics of the facticity of ethical life, addressing basic familial relations between woman and man, parent and child. In this insightful contribution to "rethinking facticity," Patricia Huntington considers the contemporary import of Heidegger's thinking of the primordial attunement and bearing of Dasein in relation to "bearing with" others and the phenomenon of hardening in order to interrogate the facticity of the "being-with" (*Mitsein*) of childhood, family, and woman. Beginning with the claim that "learning to bear one's life journey well is a lived precondition of bearing-with others well," Huntington addresses facticity as a profoundly ethical challenge and task with the purpose of exploring our willingness to bear life as attunement, comportment, and exposure. In light of Heidegger's discussion of attunement and fundamental moods, Huntington examines the thrownness of being in the family, of being with child and with youth, and being woman. This leads to a series of reflections on the decried hardening of woman, of her so-called fickleness vis-à-vis the facticity of maternity, the "domestic" realm, and the child-parent relation. Huntington explicates both the implicit strength of Heidegger's thinking of being-with as well as revealing its limits and possibilities for redeploying it. She accordingly shows the deeply social and ethical dimensions of Heidegger's thinking of attunement and moods and their implications for gendered social relations.

In conclusion, Gregory Schufreider asks us to consider the very facticity of this book and any attempt to "re: think" facticity: "Can we be confronted with facticity in a text or must we be struck (perhaps, dumb) by the brute fact of the book itself, as if it (and not the text) might hit us over the head and strike us senseless?" In order to face the facticity of the book itself, "Re: Thinking Facticity" engages the reader in an act of thinking at the end of the text. Schufreider wonders about the necessity of moving from a hermeneutics of facticity to a facticity of hermeneutics, that is, the return to a facticity that would not be neutralized or idealized in the hermeneutic work of making sense. Schufreider questions the fact that as a book, *Sein und Zeit* is bound to "theorize" death: "to make (a certain) sense of it by turning the brute fact into a 'being-towards-death' that we can live with." It is striking that Heidegger speaks of the end of our being, namely, death, as possibility, never to be taken as sheer actuality. Further, once derealized or virtualized as a possibility, Heidegger posits death as our ownmost possibility, as each time mine and the horizon for an authentic selfhood. Death becomes the site of appropriation and possibility of sense when perhaps its facticity would indicate the very opposite: the end of sense, the end of possibility, and the end of "me." Regarding this virtualizing of death, Schufreider argues that the "script of selfhood effectively neutralizes the brutality of death, fictionalizing the fact by turning it into a histrionic act." Schufreider wonders whether the thinker of the irreducible mortality of Dasein did not "take death seriously (enough)"; for "the ultimate (in) facticity is the end of Dasein, which brings facticity itself to an end. To resolve this double bind, the text must project a fictional end in which Dasein stands alone, "before" death. In the end, it is an issue of rethinking facticity in the following way: "[W]e would have to think, not just in terms of the hermeneutics of facticity but of the facticity of hermeneutics, and of the ergonomics of an understanding that turns the opening of the book into a historical breach: a concrete opening to freedom that is created through a new apparatus of thinking." Such a freedom would give us this sense of facticity: "This is to insist that freedom is not free to act before it does, since it does not exist as a fact until it acts; not as an initial freedom that initiates itself through action. Only in the act does freedom become a fact; in which case, we might say that the free act takes place after the fact, *ex post facto*, as if the "law" of freedom. By organizing the discussion around the × that is marked over the word "being" in Heidegger's *Zur Seinsfrage*, Schufreider argues that we are put in a position to raise the question: What becomes of Dasein when "Sein" is crossed off the page? Through a type of etymological back-formation, Schufreider reads the × back into "Dasein," as a graphic indication of the f/acticity of the

"Da" in *Being and Time*. The × functions not only as a sign of death but as a signature mark: a common proper name that may be seen to operate as a sign of the facticity of writing in the free hand of Dasein. In a final act of signing, that not only faces death in the text but acts in the face of the page, the book comes to an end by tracing an opening in the name of Dasein× that the reader is free to create.

This volume has gathered an international group of philosophers who address questions and consider the sources—some of which have only recently become available—of facticity in the works of Husserl, Heidegger, Merleau-Ponty, Sartre, and Fanon among others in order to explore facticity from life-philosophy to contemporary European thought. This inquiry from multiple directions will, hopefully, evoke further philosophical engagement with the question and questionability of facticity. It is our hope that this work would contribute in drawing this new geography of thought, when its facticity becomes what is—indeed, what remains—to be thought.

NOTES

1. Martin Heidegger, *Phenomenological Interpretations of Aristotle*, trans. Richard Rojcewicz (Bloomington: Indiana University Press, 2001), 74.

2. *Kritik der Praktischen Vernunft / Critique of Practical Reason*, trans. L. W. Beck (New York: Macmillan, 1993), 5:31.

3. Jean-Luc Nancy, *The Gravity of Thought*, trans. François Raffoul and Gregory Recco (Atlantic Highlands: Humanities Press, 1997), 60.

4. For a closer examination of the issue of facticity in Dilthey, see Eric Sean Nelson, "Begründbarkeit und Unergründlichkeit bei Wilhelm Dilthey," *Existentia*, 12, no. 1–2 (2002): 1–10; and "Empiricism, Facticity, and the Immanence of Life in Dilthey," *PLI* 18 2007, 108–128.

5. Edmund Husserl, "Philosophie als strenge Wissenschaft," *Logos* 1 (1911): 280–341.

6. Maurice Merleau-Ponty, *Phenomenology of Perception*, trans. Colin Smith (London: Routledge and Kegan Paul, 1962), vii.

7. As Jean-Luc Nancy explains in *The Sense of the World*, " 'matter' is not first the thick immanence absolutely enclosed within itself, but first, and quite to the contrary, the very difference by which some *thing* is possible, as a *thing* and as a *some*." *Le sens du monde* (Paris: Galilée, 1993), 95.

8. Jürgen Habermas, *Between Facts and Norms: Contributions to a Discourse Theory of Law and Democracy*, trans. William Rehg (Cambridge: MIT Press, 1996).

9. Jean-Luc Nancy, *The Creation of the World* or *Globalization*, trans. François Raffoul and David Pettigrew (Albany,: State University of New York Press, 2007). Hereafter cited as CW.

10. In the chapter entitled "Of Creation," Nancy would analyze the expression "to come to the world" as follows: "That 'to come to the world' means birth and death, emerging from nothing and going to nothing" (CW, 74).

11. GA 27: *Einleitung in die Philosophie* (1928–29), (Frankfurt am Main: Vittorio Klostermann, 1996), 340. *Introduction to Philosophy*, trans. Eric Sean Nelson and Virginia Lyle Jennings (Bloomington: Indiana University Press, forthcoming).

12. Martin Heidegger, *Sein und Zeit* (Tübingen: Niemeyer, 1927, 1953), 373. Hereafter SZ.

Part I

Phenomenology and Facticity

1

From Phenomenological Immortality to Natality

ANTHONY J. STEINBOCK

In this chapter, I treat the issue of "phenomenological immortality," the insight that arises within a genetic phenomenology that transcendental subjectivity is neither born nor dies. I connect it to "phenomenological natality," an essentially related matter that emerges within a generative phenomenology, namely, that birth and death become phenomenologically significant for meaning-constitution. The former theme arises in what is to my mind one of the most interesting appendices in the *Analyses Concerning Passive and Active Synthesis*, namely, Appendix 8: "The Apodicticity of Remembering."[1] Husserl brushes up against this problem of phenomenological immortality almost a decade later in a working note, now within the context of a deepened insight into generative origins. My attempt in this chapter is fourfold: first, to explain the meaning and import of phenomenological immortality, second, to illustrate how natality becomes a phenomenologically significant matter, third, to suggest how phenomenology opens itself to dimensions of mystery and hope from natality, and finally, to conclude that phenomenological immortality must be situated within phenomenological natality, and not, for example, mortality.

IMMORTALITY AND GENESIS

Why and how phenomenological immortality at all becomes an issue for Husserl must first be situated in the project of the *Analyses* and within the context of the passive genesis of meaning. Let me follow

Husserl's curt exposition of immortality, and then expound upon it more freely.

Husserl's reflections on the phenomenon of immortality come to light within what he terms a transcendental aesthetic. The project of a transcendental aesthetic emerges from an immanent critique of logic. By examining the sciences, and logic in particular, Husserl discerns an animating teleological orientation, a sense that has either been abandoned or forgotten in the very practices of those sciences. Though forgotten, it nevertheless persists as a vocation, the vocation of the critical self-justification of reason (*Analyses*, 1, 8, 387).

A transcendental aesthetic accomplishes tremendous transcendental-phenomenological preliminary work insofar as it prepares and reformulates the bases of a transcendental logic (*Analyses*, 7). For this reason, a critique of the ideal structures of logical reason, which takes as its point of departure the investigations into a formal and transcendental logic, demands a transcendental aesthetic as an investigation of the origins of truth. Such preliminary work entails, in part, tracing the achievements of thinking back to their genetic origins in *passive*, pre-cognitive syntheses. In moving from the dimension of the constituted to the constituting, Husserl incorporates a regressive, archeological movement from the *active* cognitive dimensions to the *passive* kinesthetic ones.

Focusing on the objects of possible perception that have the sense-form of time and the sense-shape of spatiality, a transcendental aesthetic investigates how sense unities are constituted through associative syntheses as the content of time-consciousness. The syntheses are called "passive syntheses" because (contra Kant) the kinesthetic sphere of experience already yields evidence and is not without epistemic import (just as intuition is not foreign to judgment).

Once we have reached back to the origins of the great world of constituting life, we describe this life, explains Husserl, "by beginning from below and ascending upward, to show how genuine thinking in all its levels emerges here, how it is motivated and is built-up in its founded accomplishment" (*Analyses*, 32). Following the passive propagation of sense through the modulations of the affective force of things exerting their allures, Husserl examines how sense comes on the scene as a "pre-constituted" or "pregiven" affective unity that elicits the attentive regard in order to be constituted as such, that is, egoically. Through many layers of passive association, through the activity of remembering and expectation, I gain the object as a "true being," as an in-itself-for-me. In this way, a transcendental-phenomenological aesthetic works toward founding a transcendental-phenomenological logic.

Having situated the sphere of engagement where Husserl arrives at the insight into phenomenological immortality, let me now examine the question of immortality more explicitly. While the issue of immortality first arises with respect to evidence in perceptual consciousness as passive experience, it will be with respect to remembering as a temporal egoic act that immortality becomes an issue for the subject as such.

In external perception an object is given in evidence. In terms of the form of time, the present is necessarily fulfilled. Whatever was intended, however it was intended, even if my protentions or expectations were disappointed or in doubt, something arises in the present. Perception, of course, always promises more than what it can deliver, namely, the complete object in-itself, because the perceptual presentation of the object is always accompanied by empty horizons. This means there is room for something else to appear otherwise than expected. But even if this does happen, even if I am disappointed by the new appearance, something emerges in the present to "throw its opponent from the saddle," writes Husserl suggestively, and we are again conscious of something (new) in the present, in evidence, even if without apodictic certainty (*Analyses*, 68). This is another way of saying that even if the presently enduring object or occurrence, like a tone, ceases the process of the enduring itself cannot cease; the enduring is "immortal."

Something can usurp something else as the new enduring thing, even if for a moment, because the cessation itself, as the cessation of the object, presupposes a non-cessation, which is to say, it presupposes consciousness to which the cessation is given (*Analyses*, 466–67). Husserl writes: "Just as the cessation is conceivable only insofar as it is in process, though the cessation of the process itself is inconceivable, so too is the beginning only conceivable in process, though not conceivable as the beginning of the process" (*Analyses*, 468).

Following Husserl, we can say that consciousness of the present is immortal. But this, we soon find, is too narrow of a scope, because this immortality shows itself up paradoxically as "only momentary." Even if we just consider immanent perceptual consciousness of the present, which is apodictic for that instant, Husserl still asks the leading question: "But what good is it, since its validity is only momentary?" (*Analyses*, 155). This is the motivation for introducing another temporal act that deepens and broadens the problematic, this time an egoic one, namely, remembering.

The present perceiver is oriented toward something that emerges affectively in the perceptual field such that the phenomena organize themselves according to primordial laws of association. In these cases, what we have are precisely the affective formation of sense-unities. There are many ways that such affective formations can emerge, among them, the propagation of sense through affective transference in the *living present* (similarity, uniformity), some that are *retroactive* in the retentional field, and some that are more explicitly *protentional* accomplishments. This orientation can yield, moreover, to a passive discernment of the phenomena by exhibiting a slightly higher awareness of affective force, which is more than being oriented toward or being oriented by; it is a distinctive discernment of and within the phenomenal field. Further, I can be receptive to the affective force by attentively turning toward the object. This turning toward is regarded by Husserl as the transition from passivity to activity. While Husserl regards turning-toward as a kind of proto-activity, the status of activity must be qualified. It must be qualified because intrinsic to the awakening is a submission that lies at the basis of an initiating egoic movement of turning-toward. Presupposed for this active turning-toward is not only the sphere of passively preconstituted objectlike structures, but the submission of the ego to the affective field. Now, when a reproductive act of remembering is motivated (e.g., by something prominent in the present linking up spontaneously with something retended), the egoic dimension of activity is "awakened" and the sphere of present consciousness and mere objectlike formations are transcended by a more encompassing, deep, temporal life and by the emergence of objects per se.

Husserl's appeal to remembering is an appeal to an egoic identifying activity that can repeatedly come back to the same presentation beyond the living present and to an identical self of the object as its in-itself or true being (*Analyses*, 155, 297–98). This is also initially the significance of entertaining the apodicticity of remembering, since it goes beyond the putative immortality of momentary consciousness. Accordingly, although affective awakenings or affective interconnections, which are understood by Husserl as "associations" and include passive syntheses that accomplish unity and diversity (through pairing, similarity, uniformity, heterogeneity, fusion and contrast, etc.)—although this is the case, Husserl tends to favor the affective awakening that is a specifically iterative *reproductive* temporal act, since it confers a selfhood on the object over time.

Remembering is favored because it is the reproductive act that reaches back to the intentional horizon belonging to the beginning of the remembered enduring object—a horizon that was retended and that can be awakened through an affective prominence and turned toward in a temporal memorial act. Through iterative remembering, we arrive at an identical unending time in the mode of unending past. This unending past necessarily varies, since all past times necessarily vary with respect to the present with which it is affiliated. "But," continues Husserl, "with the change of these modes, there is the one unending time to the extent that it is already past, and every position, every expanse of this time, is absolutely fixed and identical, namely, identifiable again and again with complete certainty as the same" (*Analyses*, 468–69). From this Husserl concludes that the whole of transcendental life and the transcendental ego—and not just transcendental consciousness limited to the momentary or lived present—cannot be born, cannot die, is eternal. Accordingly, belonging to this Now that I am is a past horizon that can be unfurled to infinity; and this means, with respect to the past, that the transcendental ego was eternal (*Analyses*, 469).

Similarly, every Now also has a future horizon constituted through expectation that anticipates a new Now. I not only expect a Now to arrive, but I expect a whole flux and its streaming-off into retended pasts that can be remembered. This directedness of the future, Husserl observes, fashions the futural bent of subjectively oriented time, oriented, that is, toward the mobile zero-point of the Now in relation to which I stand as the perceiving ego. The futural "what will be" is something identical that can be initially identified in repeated egoic anticipations of perceptions. These anticipations can only be fulfilled through the occurrence of presents and through the identifying processes of remembering after the perceptions have elapsed. "Thus, what will be must become present and past, must become identifiable time" (*Analyses*, 469).

Something will occur; this is my expectant conviction, even if my expectation of this Now gets disappointed. What never gets disappointed, however, is the form of an expected present; I experience not only possibilities but the necessity of fulfillment. While what is expected can never be apodictic, with respect to its form, expectation is apodictic. The structure of the constitution of new presents and of progressing time consciousness is an experienced necessity. The ego lives on and necessarily has its transcendental future before it, concludes Husserl, and therefore it is inconceivable that the transcendental ego would cease (*Analyses*, 467, 470). Transcendental life necessarily experiences unending futural time, which is to say, the transcendental ego will be eternal.

Husserl is quick to add on more than one occasion that to say transcendental life is immortal is not to say that the human being is immortal. On the contrary, only the human being in the world can be born and can die. Birth and death, the emergence of human beings in the world, their disappearance from nature through creation and destruction, all of this is entirely compatible with the transcendental immortality. The transcendental subject, however, "does not die and does not arise; it is an eternal being in the process of becoming" (cf. *Analyses*, 467, 469, 471).

After having given this exposition of Husserl's suggestive assertion that the transcendental ego is immortal, we can raise the following obvious objections: True enough, Husserl is making no assertions here as to human immortality; he even explicitly says that the soul of the body is not immortal. But hasn't he gone too far by asserting that we, as transcendental subjects, do not experience our own finitude and hence our own (phenomenological) mortality? If phenomenology is to describe the constitutive powers and limits of the human being as they are often presupposed and taken for granted, and in this way arrive at transcendental life, hasn't Husserl actually missed an essential feature of our experience?

In order to address these objections, it is first necessary to situate Husserl's observations in the context from which they arise. We must then ask how, within this framework, transcendental life is given to itself.

The first response concerning the context of Husserl's reflections is an immediate one: Husserl's reflections arise within the context of a genetic phenomenology. A genetic phenomenology extends beyond the static snapshot of the present or even of the living present with its structure primordial impression-retention-protention because it has as its scope genesis, that is, the process of becoming or self-temporalization. So, whereas a constitutive static analysis is unable to account for constitutive disruptions that occur beyond the living present, a genetic analysis can give constitutive accounts of experiences such as sleep, fainting spells, inhibitions of the lived-body, discordances in kinesthetic movements, etc., because, in part, its range is broad enough to allow these experiences to be meaningful (or unmeaningful), that is, to be experienced precisely as disruptions of overarching concordances of sense, or even as the instigation of new concordances.

This scope of genetic phenomenology to which I just alluded is monadic genesis, the self-temporalizing process that encompasses passive formal time-consciousness (impression, retention, protention), passive syntheses of association, egoic acts of remembering and expectation, the dynamic of apperceptions, lived-bodily kinestheses, the accruing of habits, the anticipation and formation of types, in short, the lived genetic density of the subject as a dynamic orientation. Within genesis, we can trace the *"motivations"* of the emergence of a mode of consciousness, how a phase of the subject arises and coexists in a unity of becoming.

Genetic phenomenology will therefore treat the concrete transcendental self-temporalizing subject or monad as "facticity" (cf., *Analyses*, 647). In fact, in a manuscript (published in the *Analyses*) Husserl describes precisely this self-temporalization of becoming as monadic genesis, "a genesis in which the unity of the monad arises, in which the monad is by becoming" (*Analyses*, 640).

This is not the place to develop Husserl's characterization of the monad. Let it suffice to say that the monad is a living unity of affections and acts integrated into a unity of becoming; as such, it is given fully in each moment in its continual temporal becoming, while not being exhausted in any moment. Accordingly, there are no constitutively *decisive* gaps in a monad; if this were the case, we would have two separate monadic streams, uniform with one another perhaps, but not one unique identical monad. "The ego," writes Husserl, "is absolutely identically the same, and belongs to each point of this time, and yet is not extended in it."[2] Finally, and related to the former point, the monad is absolute. It is absolute in two ways.

First, the monad is "absolute" by virtue of it uniqueness, that is, the uniqueness of its concrete dynamic self-temporalizing orientation. Accordingly, the principle of individuation of the monad is due not to the material structure of the subject, but to its unique, creative temporalizing orientation and sedimented history, its dynamic genetic density.[3] This unique temporalizing-temporalized orientation makes one monad irreducible to another. Each monad is absolute in the sense of being unique, where uniqueness (or absoluteness) cannot be identified with particularity or universality.

There is yet another, second sense in which the monad can be said to be absolute, or better, the absolute. If, within a static phenomenology, it is consciousness that can be said to be absolute—as Husserl claims in *Ideas I*—then by deepening phenomenology's scope, it is within a genetic phenomenology that this static "absolute" has to be undone. This is actually Husserl's claim as early as *Ideas I* (e.g., § 81), a claim that is recapitulated by the 1920s. The monad as factical becomes the ultimate source (*Urstätte*) of meaning (and not consciousness). By this I mean the following: Not only is the monad affected by objectlike formations in the world, which in their own way provoke sense from the side of the matter itself (cf. *Analyses*, 90–91), but the monad is self-affecting in being affected; there is not only a give and take or constitutive negotiation between the subject and world that we can call "givenness"; the monad includes a dimension of self-constitution that we can call "self-givenness."

The question before us now concerns the manner in which the monad or concrete transcendental ego is given to itself. The monad is given to itself as self-temporalizing in acts and affections. As self-temporalizing, it is not given as filling time. Of course, the transcendental subject can find itself in time after the fact, as it were, as past. Through the process of self-temporalization, the immanent stream of time is the primordial source for the "first transcendent," namely, the transcendent self, which in the immanence of original time is primordially instituted, and then through rememberings comes to self-givenness (*Analyses*, 256). But in the functions (perception, retention, protention) and acts (remembering, expectation, etc.) themselves, one is also given precisely as the source of time and as unable to be posited completely like an object: I am not temporalized from the outside, locatable in objective time, since I am the source of that time. To attempt to locate the self-temporalizing process in time would be to presuppose object-time as the already constituted standard, and then to apply it to ourselves as the measure of our mode of temporality, becoming forgetful of ourselves as self-temporalizing in this very process. Self-temporalization is both auto-temporalization, in the sense that it goes on without the active engagement of cognitive acts, and self-temporalizing, in the sense that "I attend" the passive and active operation of the temporalizing process implicitly, even if, at another level, there is egoic activity as the semi-agent of executing temporal acts, such as remembering or expectation.

If the monad is "absolute" in the senses outlined above, then we have to inquire into the constitutive parameters of self-temporalization. In particular, we have in mind the question concerning Husserl's claims about the immortality of transcendental subject. If the monad is absolute, then of course it cannot be constituted by anything outside of itself. Here by "outside of itself" I am thinking of time as already constituted (i.e., self-temporalizing does not fill time, is not located in time such as an object is located, writes Husserl). But this "outside" also concerns the scope of the self-temporalizing process itself. A genetic phenomenology does not somehow arbitrarily impose the limits or scope of analysis on the matters, and then merely assert: "This is all we will treat; from here on we will leave out the problem of birth and death as constitutive problems." Rather, the method takes its clues from the givenness of the matters themselves, in this case, from the self-givenness of the monad in the self-temporalizing process.

I am self-given to myself. On the one hand, this is an entirely legitimate phenomenological observation. Following out this observation, it is possible to say that, phenomenologically, I am given as absolute, I am the source of meaning and I am the meaning source of myself. To that extent, I can be considered as constitutively self-grounding. To the extent that I am self-temporalizing and self-grounding, I cannot simultaneously be constitutively before or after, that is, outside of myself—again, where the process of self-temporalizing is concerned. Thus, not only do we encounter "a genesis in which the unity of the monad arises, in which the monad is by becoming" (*Analyses*, 640), but "an *eternal* being in the process of becoming" (*Analyses*, 471).

The transcendental subject is immortal, and phenomenological birth and death cannot become constitutive problems. I only experience myself, my transcendental life only gets meaning, as self-becoming in the process of becoming. I am transcendentally independent. This is not to say that I am, transcendentally, not dependent upon other monads. Husserl recognized this clearly in his genetic phenomenological analyses with respect to the compossibility of monads as essentially, concretely interdependent (see *Analyses*, 635 ff.). Each monad is interdependent with others as each is absolute, as each is eternal, immortal, self-grounding. This does not point to an individualism, but to an essential interdependency of absolute self-grounding monads.

I mentioned above that it is legitimate to inquire into self-givenness, and on the basis of this, to describe transcendental subjectivity as absolute. The extent to which it is not legitimate, or better, the extent to which it is arbitrary, is the extent to which these phenomenological reflections stop too short. In the next section of this chapter, I follow Husserl's extension of these phenomenological reflections on phenomenological immortality to the insight into Generativity, and in the final section, into the implications it has for phenomenological natality.

NATALITY AND GENERATIVITY

Phenomenological immortality is not the final word for phenomenology, because there is something that escapes the sphere of self-temporalizing genesis, and hence the transcendental eternity of the subject. Penned in the early 1930s, also in a working note, Husserl revisits directly, if only laconically and incompletely, the issue of birth and death. This time, however, they are entertained as constitutive problems. His title of these terse reflections reads: "Problem:

Generativity—Birth and Death as Essential Occurrences for World-Constitution."[4] Husserl asserts that it must be shown that birth and death must be valid as constitutive occurrences for the very possibility of constituting a world, that is, as essential elements for a constituted world, which is to say, Generativity with birth and death (Hua 15, 171).

For birth and death to be constitutive features at all, the scope of phenomenological analysis must extend even beyond genesis, that is, the genesis of the transcendental subject as self-temporalizing. But again, if this is not to be just an arbitrary imposition of a broader context on the phenomena, there has to be something guiding the phenomenologist to discover and implement the broader scope.

Husserl's point of entry into these reflections is the problem of intersubjectivity. Implicitly returning to the concrete monad, now within a social context, he writes: "The extent to which 'alien' memory coincides with a possible memory of my own, the extent to which my memory only has the limit of forgetting, the extent to which my inability of memory is merely forgetfulness (which simultaneously leaves open the potentiality of the memory of forgetting), to this extent we do not do justice to a constitution of the world. That would indeed be as if Generativity, with birth and death, were an incidental fact of the world" (Hua 15, 171). Thus, as long as we only consider the self and the other as merely contemporaneous, each uniquely a process of self-temporalizing that cannot constitutively leap before or after the self-constituting process itself, we cannot consider birth and death as constitutive features. They are not given within the concordance of the self-temporalizing process. They remain only empirical facts of the world that are peculiar to human beings as natural subjects and not to transcendental subjects.

Given his deepened reflections on intersubjectivity, however, it would not be wrongheaded to assume that it is Husserl's analyses of the experience of the alien, and more profoundly, his analyses of the interdynamics of homeworld and alienworld that allow him to treat within a broader concordance the constitutive features of birth and death, thus transcending the sphere of self-temporalizing genesis. This would be the case because now the problem of intersubjectivity is framed not merely in terms of a synchronic community of monads, but in terms of geo-historical, social, normatively significant lifeworlds, namely, homeworlds and alienworlds—a sphere of experience initially broached as a deepened investigation into a transcendental aesthetic.[5] The smallest generative unit of a homeworld Husserl considers to be the intergenerational home of mother or parent and child. Other dimensions of home and alien would be intergenerational communities that might extend globally, spiritually (and, nonbiologically), politically, economically, and historically (e.g., the homeworld of Judaism, Christianity, Europe, etc.).

Within these generative intersubjective considerations, the self's constitutive powers are now seen to encompass the appropriation and disappropriation of pregiven acquisitions—acquisitions that always remain in the process of being acquired, be they language, traditions, ways of walking, etc. Further, I am immediately given over to a world with others, exposed before them; I become constituted through my other home-companions, for example, through stories that are told, games that are played, rituals that induct me into the homeworld; my transcendental home-companions extend to my progenitors and successors: for example, through my birth, my parents take on a new constitutive sense, namely as parents; or alternately, I as a concrete monad get constituted differently, now as father or mother through the birth or adoption of my child—something that could not be said within the scope of the "genesis of becoming." In Generativity, we share with others a "generatively communicative time." All these things and more go into the constitution of my constitutive "place" qua generative place in the homeworld (cf. for example, Hua 15, Beilage X and Text No. 14).[6]

Suggested here, then, is that by virtue of the transgenerational, historical home into which I emerge as a constitutive home-companion, my birth and death become constitutively significant. They emerge here as constitutively significant because it is the generative nexus that is itself constituted iteratively—an iterative constitution that transcends remembering peculiar to self-temporalization. As it concerns the question of apodicticity, we have a new intersubjective framework within which something is going to be able to count as an object. It is not just something that escapes a Now, not an iteration that can be appealed to through remembering merely and that yields something that counts as a genuine object *for me*. Rather, it is the possibility of an apodicticity that emerges in a geo-historically, normatively significant homeworld in its encounter with alienworlds. Only in a normatively significant, intersubjective homeworld (not a neutral lifeworld or abstract plurality of lifeworlds) can an object in its fullest sense be given as such. Only now can we raise the question concerning apodicticity; only now can the "tremendous preliminary work" of a transcendental aesthetic yield investigations concerning a transcendental logic.

THE PHENOMENOLOGICAL PRECEDENCE OF NATALITY

Let me turn back to the problem of transcendental immortality and natality that arises within this context. There is much more to be said on this issue than I have intimated by these brief remarks. As helpful as such considerations are, and as accurate as they may be, I do not believe that they can be decisive for these considerations of phenomenological immortality and phenomenological natality. For them to be decisive, we have to take a step beyond Husserl using clues he has left here and there in his writings on Generativity.

Let me begin by reposing the question: How am I given to myself? From the perspective of the insights into genesis and genetic phenomenology, we can respond by saying that the individual is given to him or herself as self-temporalizing and as self-grounding. But this phenomenological immortality, which is eternal within its own nexus of genetically formed temporalization, itself stands in relation to a *"generatively formed temporalization"* (Hua 15, 138 fn 2.). Within genesis, the self-temporalizing individual is given to itself by itself; it is self-grounding; within Generativity, the self-temporalizing individual is given to itself "from" something outside of itself, "from" or "by" Generativity. Accordingly, if monadic genesis can be described as absolute within genetic phenomenology, it is Generativity that has to be described as the newer, deeper, absolute within a phenomenology that takes its clues from the givenness of Generativity. Generativity becomes the new absolute in relation to which the absolute self-temporalization is given to itself as such. Remaining within a phenomenological perspective, we are trained on the manner of givenness. The inquiry into givenness can yield the question concerning self-givenness when birth and death are at issue. I continue to inquire after "how" I am given to myself. Here we detect a shift in response; now it concerns Generativity and not the self.

Because the self is given to itself in Generativity, birth and death have to become constitutive concerns. But if I am given to myself in such a way that birth and death are constitutive occurrences, then I cannot be the ultimate source of meaning and I cannot be self-grounding. The ultimate source of meaning is Generativity in relation to which monadic genesis gets its meaning. As self-temporalizing, I am grounded in Generativity, which gives me to myself. But this Generativity is not biological or vital, but a spiritualizing-temporalizing process (cf. Hua 15, 174–85). I am placed by Generativity in relation to Generativity. This being-placed means that I am given to myself uniquely; my vocation is a "good-in-itself-for me," and this has to be taken into account in any phenomenological analysis of individuation.[7]

Accordingly, within a genetic perspective we could say the following: *"I am* eternally given to myself as *self-giving"* or *"I give* myself to myself, eternally." Within Generativity, however, we would have to say the following: "(I am) *given to myself* by Generativity as self-giving." It is not that we lose the self (or as we might say, "transcendental subjectivity") as absolute, but the meaning of this self is transformed because it is given to itself as "absolute" from a deeper absolute, Generativity.

When we considered self-temporalization, it made sense to assert that the transcendental subject is immortal: Concerning the past, we could say with Husserl, I was eternal; concerning the future, I will be eternal. There is symmetry here with respect to past and future. Within Generativity, however, we encounter a different structure. Let me explain.

When I inquire into my self-givenness, I find myself as taking up Generativity, without any constitutive gaps, without any neutrality outside of Generativity. Here I am: My functions and actions are already the taking up of Generativity through which I am given to myself. In this way, I originate my origins without being before my origins. On the other hand, in a generative sense, I am before my origins because I am "within" Generativity from the start, and *I* take it up as it is given "before" me, or given when I already come on the scene. This is how I participate in more than myself. I am already before my origins as being given to myself by Generativity. In this sense, my own origin becomes a constitutive *problem*. I reflect on origins of the world. The world becomes a "problem"; *I* become a "problem." But I become a problem because I am already beyond myself, as given to myself. It is this problematic nature that is my individuated finitude; finitude does not arise from my empirical birth or death.

We are witness now to a different structure than what we encountered with respect to the genesis of becoming. First, "mystery" becomes constitutively significant. Here we can say phenomenologically: I am given to myself. But unlike the case within genesis, here the *"motivation"* (to use the phenomenological term mentioned above) for my emergence cannot be traced back; it is not clear and perhaps may never be clear; nevertheless, I am given to myself—this is apodictically certain, that is, it cannot be "crossed-out," it is *undurchstreichbar*. What was I given to myself? What is my purpose and the purpose of my sudden appearance? These and similar questions are dependent upon the phenomenological insight into mystery.

When we do ask such questions, we recognize that being given to ourselves already orients us toward Generativity and thereby transcends the mere psycho-physical such that our appearance is not merely arbitrary or meaningless; rather, our intrinsic directedness concerns the very movement of Generativity itself. My individual being to myself is my vocation, a "good in-itself for me." Of course, Husserl stopped just short of saying all of this, but I would push these insights farther and say that Generativity is given in a peculiar way, namely, in the mode of epiphany, precisely as Holy, as Person, allowing the Generative structure to be qualified as inter-Personal. Moreover, as given to ourselves from Generativity as meaning-giving, we would find the internal sense of this meaning-giving to be the vocation of becoming deiform, that is, co-becoming in the manner of the Holy for all persons, and the realization of the Holy in history. In this way, the futural dimension would also open up in its own way to the dimension of mystery.

Do we have apodicticity with respect to the future? For example, can we say apodictically that "I will be taken from myself?" Is a not-being-taken-from-myself *undurchstreichbar*? Let us recall that we are not speaking simply of empirical birth and death, but that we are speaking phenomenologically. To assert something about the future in this regard would amount to being able to experience this being-taken-from-myself, and we cannot too hastily claim that being-taken-from-myself is equivalent to empirical death. We cannot identify these two out of hand, first because we do have the apodictic evidence of being given to ourselves. If you like, this being-given is a phenomenological given. We are given to ourselves as absolute, as the source of meaning in relation to the world, etc. Since individuated finitude is not reducible to material nature, but is intrinsically tied to being-given, and for Husserl to the free activities of the monad in and through its self-temporalizing and spiritualizing process, empirical death cannot ipso facto be a phenomenological being-taken-from-myself. Because individuation is rooted in a being given to oneself formed through a spiritual-temporalizing process, vital death does not automatically mean that I lose this individuated uniqueness. Accordingly, empirical death cannot mean that the concrete monad is definitively stripped of its absolute character such that it would be merely relative as relative to Generativity. Of course, this is not to assert that I will not be taken from myself, either. What we can say is that in our given monadic absoluteness we are relative to Generativity as the absolute source of our experienced absoluteness. We can say nothing apodictically with respect to the future on this issue. Phenomenologically, mortality cannot be decisive.

This being said, on the basis of this individuated structure, we can say the following. Because the Generative framework is not a naturalism or a vitalism, we do have grounds *to assume* that we will not be taken from ourselves, or again, that being given as absolute ourselves and relative to the absoluteness of Generativity as the source, we will somehow endure. Given the Generative framework, this is a viable possibility; but it is essentially different from asserting, within genesis, that I will be eternally. This opens up to the constitutive dimension of hope. Hope is neither arbitrary nor a guarantee, for in neither case could this constitute the experience of hope. Rather, hope is founded precisely in being given to ourselves, and this allows us to face the impossible as possible. With the understanding that I intimated above, such a hope would have to be founded in the Person of the Holy and in the inter-Personal movement of giving us to ourselves. Working out the implications of this understanding takes us far beyond the scope of this chapter.[8]

My point here is that the dimension of the past as birth yields the constitutive dimension of mystery, that the dimension of the future is given in birth in terms of vocation (which in turn qualifies the meaning of birth), and that facing morality, it yields the constitutive dimension of hope.

Finally, let me entertain the question concerning the place of birth and death as constitutive problems. I noted above that there is a constitutive asymmetry of the past and future that corresponds neither to the symmetry with respect to transcendental genesis nor to the symmetry with respect to empirical birth and death. While we do have apodicticity where birth is concerned—I am given to myself, although I can find no motivation for it (hence the constitutive phenomenon of mystery)—there is no apodicticity concerning the future. Just as I cannot assert that I will be eternally, I cannot assert apodictically that I will be taken from myself, that my individuation will dissipate with my death. This is not to say that death is not a transcendental or constitutive feature within Generativity; it is. Rather, the evidence for death is not decisive or apodictic, as it is for birth. Consequently (and to use Heidegger's expression), being-toward-death cannot be an apodictically constitutive phenomenological feature, even if we expand our scope from genetic self-temporalization to generative considerations. Only a phenomenological mortality could have as an apodictically constitutive feature, being-toward-death. And although I do not want to equate "natality" here with Heidegger's "thrownness," at least the extent to which his understanding of thrownness entails a not being self-grounding, thrownness cannot be subordinated to being-toward-death, but just the reverse. There are no decisive experiential grounds for phenomenological mortality, and phenomenological mortality could give no decisive response to, let alone resituate a phenomenological immortality.

Rather, what becomes the new guiding feature for phenomenology is natality, the phenomenological meaning-orientation of birth. Only phenomenological natality can respond to or convert a phenomenological immortality such that immortality is integrated into and situated by natality.

NOTES

1. Edmund Husserl, *Analyses Concerning Passive and Active Synthesis: Lectures on Transcendental Logic*, trans. Anthony J. Steinbock (Dordrecht: Kluwer Academic Publishers, 2001); hereafter, *Analyses*.

2. Edmund Husserl, *Zur Phänomenologie der Intersubjektivität. Texte aus dem Nachlaß. Zweiter Teil: 1921–1928*, ed. Iso Kern. *Husserliana* Vol. 14 (The Hague: Martinus Nijhoff, 1973), 42–3; cf. 43–44.

3. Addressed, in part, in my "Individuation, Particularization, and the Scope of Eidetic Insight," in *Husserl Studies in Japan: The Exploration of New Horizons in Husserlian Phenomenology*, Vol. 1 (March 2003), 211–234.

4. See Edmund Husserl, *Zur Phänomenologie der Intersubjektivität. Texte aus dem Nachlaß. Dritter Teil: 1929–1935*, ed. Iso Kern. *Husserliana* Vol. 15 (The Hague: Martinus Nijhoff, 1973), 171–72; hereafter, Hua 15. For related passages, see 138, 209.

5. See my *Home and Beyond: Generativity after Husserl* (Evanston: Northwestern University Press, 1995). On the point concerning the problematic of homeworlds and alienworlds belonging to a transcendental aesthetic, see Hua 15, 214, 234 ff.

6. I have treated these and similar issues in a different article entitled, "Limit-Phenomena and the Liminality of Experience," *Alter: revue de phénoménologie* 6 (1998), 275–96.

One should also recall that even though Husserl's "Kaizo" ("Renewal") articles were written in the 1920s, and hence in the period of his genetic phenomenology, many of their themes are actually generative, including the leading topic of "renewal" or rebirth. See Edmund Husserl, *Aufsätze und Vorträge* (1922–1937), ed. T. Nenon und H.-R. Sepp, Hua 27 (Dordrecht: Kluwer Academic Publishers, 1989). And see chapter 12 in my *Home and Beyond*.

7. See Note 3 above.

8. I am presently working on a three-volume study entitled *Verticality and Idolatry* which works out the religious, moral, and ecological dimensions of these insights.

2

On the Genesis of Heidegger's Formally Indicative Hermeneutics of Facticity

THEODORE KISIEL

> The problems of facticity persist for me with the same intensity as they did in my Freiburg beginnings, only much more radically now, and still in the perspectives that were guiding me even in Freiburg. That I was constantly preoccupied with Duns Scotus and the middle Ages, then back to Aristotle, is by no means a matter of chance. And one cannot judge the work by what was simply said in the lecture courses or seminar exercises. I first had to go all out after the fact*ic*, taking it to its extremity, in order to come to fact*icity* itself as a problem. Formal indication, critique of the customary doctrine of the *a priori*, formalization and the like, all of that is still there [in *Being and Time*] for me even if I do not talk about them now.
>
> —Martin Heidegger to Karl Löwith,
> in a letter dated August 20, 1927[1]

Leave it to philosophy, in particular to German philosophy, to take the simple concrete "fact," a prize much sought after in the empirical practices of law, science, history, and so of the best journalism, and turn it into the abstraction "facticity." It then becomes a fit topic for detailed discussion and speculation by philosophers. According to the currently standard German dictionary of philosophical terms, *Faktizität* entered into the philosophical tradition by way of Martin Heidegger, whom Jean-Paul Sartre then followed with his stress on the *facticité de la liberté* and the utter meaninglessness and "dereliction" of the *facticité* of the human situation.[2] Such dictionary entries often begin with a list of related synonyms which together suggest a prehistory of the term, as does the entry in the *Brockhaus Enzyklopädie*:

> Facticity, factuality, unalterable and underivable givenness ("facticity of events"). Facticity became a philosophical term through Heidegger. Facticity accordingly designates the factuality [*Tatsächlichkeit*] of (human) being-there in the world, the historically fated "being-in-the-world" of the human being, the fact that he at first did not produce his own world but instead already finds himself in it ("thrownness").[3]

A similar testimony comes to us from a firsthand witness of the times of the early Heidegger, accompanied by a detailed indication of the philosophical prehistory out of which the term *facticity* may well have emerged. Ludwig Landgrebe had attended Heidegger's course of Summer 1923 on "Ontology: Hermeneutics of Facticity" and so speaks as a witness of the time when he asserts, in an illuminating book on the primal matter (*Ur-Sache*) of phenomenology entitled *Faktizität und Individuation*, that "in the tradition of philosophical usage, the abstract term 'facticity' is not to be found earlier" than Heidegger's use of it.[4] Yet Landgrebe was not unaware that his question takes us to the very heart of the tradition of modernity from Descartes to Husserl, which finds its starting point in the "regress to the fact of the I-think" (118, 110) understood as the irreducible limit of reflection "behind which one cannot go any further" (*unhintergehbare Grenze*). Among the "facts of consciousness" in the transcendental I, the early Fichte found not only the logical principle of identity but also what Kant proclaimed, early in the Second Critique, to be "the sole fact of pure reason," namely, the fact of the moral law, or of pure practical reason itself. Fact here "means for Kant a datum or given that cannot be questioned any further [*hinterfragende*] and that can no longer be accounted for by way of a reason or ground."[5] Does Heidegger find something more in "being's throw" of the facticity "that I am and have to be," of the facticity of the can-be that thus distinguishes itself from the mere factuality of the *factum brutum*, the mere "that it is"? Landgrebe's book demonstrates the need to reevaluate not only the self-understanding of the entire modern tradition but also phenomenology's understanding of its maxim of getting "back to the things themselves," each tradition now understood as a return to the "transcendental fact" or "facticity" of reason, of being, or of the reason for being.

The phenomenological reduction of the Marburg neo-Kantian starting point in the purported "fact of science" (Cohen et al.) back to a prescientific and pretheoretical domain of being and reason is but an early testimony to this radical concern. An early counter-Kantian reduction typically expressed in the synonyms of the "underivable givenness" of facticity comes to us from Dilthey, who, in his quest for a critique of historical reason, gradually renounces the elevated reason of the detached transcendental ego and calls instead for a return to the "this-side" of life, to the full "factuality" of *unhintergehbares* life itself, "behind which thought cannot go" any farther. Nevertheless, this historical life is not opaque and mute, but teeming with the meaningful structures of inherited customs and institutions, with artworks and other artifacts as well as the written documents of more literate cultures transmitted in the textured structures more properly called texts. In short, in Dilthey's pregnant phrase, *Das Leben legt sich aus*, "Life lays itself out, it articulates itself, it interprets itself," generating its own meaning and sense of direction in the combined shape and thrust of a working context and operative continuity of structure (*Wirkungszusammenhang*). The goal of a more overt hermeneutics of factic life is accordingly "to understand life from life itself," in terms of categories explicated directly from life itself that would articulate precisely how "life [already] interprets itself" into contexts and continuities of meaning.[6]

The synonyms of facticity (but not yet the term *facticity*) likewise play a prominent role in Heidegger's habilitation work at the University of Freiburg (1915–16), *The Doctrine of Categories and Meaning in Duns Scotus*, which Heidegger will later proclaim to be the work in which he first went "all out after the fact*ic* in order to make fact*icity* itself into a problem."[7] In its approach to the problem of how reality is categorized and invested with meaning, this early work by the student Heidegger brings into play a remarkable amalgam of scholasticism, neo-Kantianism, and phenomenology. The phenomenological "back to the matters themselves!" becomes "back to factualities, back to the Scotian *haecceitas* (thisness)." To the questions, How do we know that there are different domains of reality? How are such domains articulated?, the young Heidegger responds in a paragon expression of the basic phenomenological conviction in the possibility of direct description of these factualities: Such differentiations can only be "read off" (*abgelesen*) directly from the reality itself (FS 197, 257, 263, 346),[8] understood as an immediate givenness that is already *categorially* structured and accordingly amenable to explicit differentiation into *categories*. "Factualities can only be pointed out" (FS, 155), indicated, simply apprehended, and not deduced by a priori means from valid sentences, as in Kant's metaphysical deduction. When irreducible ultimates are invoked, our only recourse is to direct acquaintance, to something like Husserl's categorial intuitive seeing (*Hinsehen*), which the scholastics called *simplex apprehensio*, and Emil Lask *Hingabe*, immersive dedication to the subject matter. "To give a schoolbook definition of it will not be possible, since it is an ultimate, something which is 'last.' Its essence can only be described, pointed out (*notificari*)" (FS, 189). And what exactly is this "last" and ultimate in a scholastic context? "The initial, objectively categorial meaning of the *maxime scibile* [most knowable] shows that *ens* [being] presents a *'last* [and] *highest,'* behind which one can no longer inquire any further" (FS, 157). And in another passage that is remotely reminiscent of the later "Da-sein" experience: "The individual is an *underivable irreducible ultimate or 'last.'* . . . Everything that really exists is a 'such-now-here.' The form of individuality (*haecceitas*) is thereby called to provide a primal determination of real actuality" (FS, 195).

The underivable irreducible ultimate behind which one can no longer inquire any further is thus for scholastics such as Scotus the *ens* whose primal form is that of individuality and whose *esse* can therefore never be expressed as a genus, in reference to an *ens commune*. It was Duns Scotus who developed "a greater and more refined proximity to real life (*haecceitas*), its multiplicity and possibilities of tension, than the scholastics before him" (FS, 145). But this is only one extreme of the work of "the sharpest of all scholastics" (so Dilthey). For Scotus is especially noted for his logical acumen, demonstrating his mastery over the fine formalities of the "gray on gray" of philosophy as well as his sensitivity to the "shapes of life." These two extremes of formality and individuality come together in an inseparable unity to such a degree that we must again revise the quasi-phenomenological maxim proclaimed above to "Back to the forms of individuality." For it is from what might be called a Scotian "speculative *formal* grammar of thisness" that the early Heidegger is destined to find the first stirrings of his *"formally* indicative hermeneutics of facticity." Shortly after *Being and Time* appeared, Heidegger testifies to this intimate bond between formality and individuality in his comments on the basic impulse of the Scotus book: "I first had to go all out after the fac*tic*, taking it to its extremity, in order to make fac*ticity* itself into a problem. Formal indication, critique of the customary doctrine of the a priori, formalization, and the like, all of that is still there for me, even if I do not talk about them now." If we read the habilitation in its filigree with this guiding clue in mind, we should be able to trace the initial steps that Heidegger takes toward his own formal hermeneutics of facticity, developed by way of Scotus's speculative formal grammar of *haecceitas*.[9]

To which we must add . . . and by way of Emil Lask's "logic of philosophy." For there is more. Heidegger's stated purpose in the Scotus dissertation is to approach this medieval logic of concept and category formation (*simplex apprehensio*) through the insights and resources of modern philosophical logic, especially those of Husserl's *Logical Investigations* and the various transcendental logics developed by the neo-Kantians. It is from this neo-Kantian source that the massive influence of Emil Lask's *Logik der Philosophie* upon the dissertation derives, as his dissertation director, Heinrich Rickert, Heidegger's *Doktorvater*, observes in his final report, at once remarking, "perhaps more than [Heidegger] himself is conscious of."[10] Out of the dense jungle of the habilitation, out of this "melting pot" fusing scholasticism, neo-Kantianism, and phenomenology, it will be necessary to at least briefly specify Lask's unique fusion of these traditions into a transcendental (ontological, phenomenological) logic that enters into the interstices of Heidegger's formally indicative hermeneutics of individuated being-here.

But there is still more. A closer reading of Lask takes us (as it did Heidegger) back to his 1902 dissertation, *Fichte's Idealism and History*[11] and its abundance of citations out of the middle and later Fichte, which reveals that it was Fichte who coined the term *Facticität* for the philosophical tradition, in his middle "positivist" phase circa 1800, and continued to develop the term in his teachings and writings until his death in 1814. The posthumous publication of these lecture courses and works by his theologian son, Immanuel Hermann Fichte, could be considered the most proximate source of the diffusion of the term *Facticität* into the nineteenth-century literature of both philosophy and theology, quite often in reference to the facticity of the events of Christian "salvation history." The persistent albeit sporadic use of the term in nineteenth-century writers such as Kierkegaard, Feuerbach, and Dilthey is a matter of lexical record,[12] serving to disqualify the oft-repeated encyclopedic assertion that "facticity became a philosophical term through Heidegger." Of special interest to us is the continued use of the term in the confluence of late neo-Kantianism and early phenomenology in dialogue with one another, at the point when the graduate student Heidegger is voraciously reading the literature in his field and the young *privatdocent* Heidegger is conducting seminar exercises and giving lecture courses on "Phenomenology and Transcendental Philosophy of Value" (SS 1919). For it is at this point, with the identification of his central topic as the "historical (situated, factic) I" being subjected to "worlding" (KNS 1919) and as "factic life(-experience)" (WS 1919–20) that the abstractum *Faktizität* is interjected into the Heideggerian opus, never to depart.[13]

The revival and repeated recall of this intercalated tradition of "facticity" (with its related synonyms) from Fichte through Lask to the early Heidegger is accordingly the leading thrust of this genealogical study.

The converging tendencies of phenomenology and neo-Kantianism, which, in the first two decades of the century, in their mutual critique nevertheless held each other in high esteem, degenerated into highly charged polemic only after the appearance of *Sein und Zeit* in 1927. But one remarkable aspect of the Davos Disputation with the neo-Kantian Ernst Cassirer in early 1929 is that Heidegger, when asked what he meant by neo-Kantianism, "that scapegoat of the new philosophy," includes neither Lask nor Natorp.[14] I would guess that for Heidegger, both broke ranks with the neo-Kantians when they, each in his own penetrating way, began to explore the Fichtean problem of facticity and the purported "irrationality" of the transcendental ego, which Cassirer himself underscores in the debate as the Kantian problem of the "inconceivability of freedom."[15]

In 1930, when the supercession of neo-Kantianism by phenomenology was still in full swing, a remarkably perceptive and for our topic highly instructive reading of the "hermeneutic situation" of the "actual tendencies of German philosophy" appeared in France, authored by the Fichte scholar, Georges Gurvitch.[16] Following Lask's dissertation on *Fichte's Idealism and History*, Gurvitch takes his vantage on the emerging phenomenological literature from what the middle Fichte calls the "hiatus irrationalis" or transcendental abyss that opens between the various polar pairings of the empirical and the transcendental, the individual and the universal, intuition and concept, a posteriori and a priori, *quid facti* and *quid juris*, and finally, in Fichte's new coinage, between facticity and logicity/lawfulness. Gurvitch finds the irrational hiatus manifesting itself in Husserl's "positivism" of material essences that as separated "pure givens" are ineluctably irreducible to one another (65), in Scheler's emotional intuition of value essences (67, 144, 151), in Lask's moment of logical nudity even of logical (categorial) forms (164f), in the alogical dispersion of forms through their matter, thereby making forms themselves opaque to one another (169 = Lask II, 63).[17] All of these currents, and more, fuse in Heidegger's "hermeneutics of existence" (210), for example, in the irreducible equiprimordiality of existential categories and in the thrownness of emotive disposition, especially in the uncanniness of angst. "Anguish is the sentiment of the abyss, of the impenetrable and opaque *hiatus irrationalis* into which human existence is plunged" (215f), of the "Nothing" out of which the finitude of its radical temporality is disclosed (229). This for Gurvitch is the strongest indication of Heidegger's return to the German tradition of the later Fichte and Schelling, as mediated to him by Lask and Kierkegaard (229, 234).

The "transcendental abyss" of the "hiatus irrationalis" is, in Kant's language, precisely the domain of spatio-temporal schematization lying between the abstract universal and the sensory individual, between intellection and sensation, that now becomes the location or "home" of the transcendental (ontological, hermeneutical) logic that Lask and the youthful Heidegger seek to develop. In his Kant-book of 1929, Heidegger clearly underscores the primacy—"the third that is first"—of this "mysterious" middle realm of the schematism of the transcendental imagination that Kant discovered but from which he eventually "shrank back" in a "horror before the abyss" of irrationality posed by time.[18] In contrast, Lask calls this realm the pre-judicative "supra-oppositional panarchy of the logos," an a priori categorized realm of intentionally structured meaning (intelligibility, truth) that will eventually become the matter of judgment. We already live "in the truth," Lask liked to say, which Heidegger would reiterate in *Being and Time*,[19] referring to Dasein's intimate involvement as being-in-the-world in this realm of meaning. The young Heidegger, following Dilthey, calls it a facticity that is through and through hermeneutical (understandable, "intelligible," meaningful), soon to become his lifelong topic under the rubric of *Da-sein*. As a term then current among fin-de-siècle neo-Kantians, "facticity" *of* meaning as Lask portrays it eventually turns into allusions to the odd hybrid of a "transcendental fact" in the phenomenological school, once again recalling the Kantian middle realm of the transcendental schematism as well as the basic "principles" of Kant's pure practical reason, namely, freedom and obligation. It also recalls another historical difference in the two schools of "neo-Kantianism" at the turn of the century, namely, the neo-Fichtean tendency of the southwest German school and the more neo-Hegelian thrust of Marburg, especially with Natorp and Cassirer. Lask's "panarchy of the logos," which categorially forms and structures a multiplicity of "irrational" matter, is coined in explicit contrast to the panlogicism of the Hegelian school (Lask II, 133) and explicit rejection of Kant's metaphysical deduction of the categories from the forms of judgment. It is also the source of the recurring charge of "irrationalism" against this direction of thought by more formal-deductive minds such as Carnap.[20]

Lask himself nicely situates his panarchy of the logos in a phenomenological context in a letter to Husserl in 1911. In transmitting his work on philosophical logic to Husserl, Lask attempts to delineate their common ground in the "detachability of meaning from the acts" of consciousness:

> I believe that my decade-long preoccupation with your major book, by no means yet over, has contributed decisively toward determining all of my views on the subject-object relation and how the subject is directed toward objective meaning. . . . When I spoke of your influence upon my understanding of the subject-object relationship, I perhaps should have formulated this by indicating that I substitute the kind of intentionality that you represent for all concepts of a consciousness in general. Because of this, I am accused by my teacher Rickert of abandoning Kant and of a reactionary regression to antiquity.[21]

The "reactionary regression" to Greek philosophy is a reference to Aristotle's move away from Plato's idealism toward a hylomorphic theory that situates eidetic structures or "forms" first and foremost in "the matters themselves."

We will thus take our starting point in the mediating and catalytic role of Lask's first book, *Fichte's Idealism and History* (1902), in the development of the young Heidegger's choice of problems in his student years, and then turn our attention to Lask's second book, *Logic of Philosophy* (1911), and the dominant role that it plays in Heidegger's habilitation of 1915.

SITUATING TRANSCENDENTAL (MATERIAL) LOGIC BY DEFINING ITS TOPIC

Fichte distinguishes two extremes of facticity: on the one hand, the minimal epistemological sense of individuation that starts from the multiplicity of "bare" sense data, the positivists' starting "facts" of the natural sciences; on the other, the fuller cultural sense of the factic individual in history. Paradigms of the historically individual in its fullest manifestation of humanity include Kant's "genius," the hero, artist, scientist, saint, in short, those individuals who "have had a decisive impact on the progress of humankind" (Lask I, 17, 196, 206). Thus, the starting category of the "idiographic" historical sciences for Lask and other neo-Kantians is the rich fact of "value individuality." Its precedent is to be found in Kant's second Critique, which declares freedom and its correlative of the moral law to be "the sole *fact* of pure reason," ergo a transcendental fact. At the end of the historical series of individual manifestations of freedom and value stand the deeds of the Divine intervening in history in an "irrational" revelation, such as the Word made flesh in the person of Jesus. Such acts of God's grace constitute a "breakthrough" of absolute values and a unique "influx into history of the ever fresh and new" (Lask I, 226ff, 240f). All of these surcharged manifestations of "irrationality" mark the entry into human history of the unexplainably new, unprecedented, and creative.

The trailmarkers of the still neo-Fichtean young Heidegger's swelling interest in this higher level of facticity of "the historical in its individuality" (FS, 204) are clearly recorded, especially in his formal trial lecture on "The Concept of Time in Historical Science" (FS, 357–75) in July 1915 and the 1916 Conclusion to his habilitation, which calls for history, as the arena of value formation and worldview, to become a meaning-determining element (i.e., a form-differentiating matter) for the category problem. The most striking example out of the trial lecture may suffice here, namely, the mention of an especially significant unique Event (*Ereignis*), such as the founding of Rome, the birth of Christ, or the Islamic Hijrah, to exemplify the value-ladenness manifesting itself uniquely in qualitatively selective moments of historical time (FS, 374). It will take several years and a world war before Heidegger deconstructs these neo-Kantian progressivist assumptions of value and backtracks to the sheer "happening" of the "historical I" (the first precursor to Da-sein), which happens first by "properizing" (*Es er-eignet sich!*), thereby giving the historical I its proper name and presenting proper time with its unique situational meaning.

The facticity (matter) of the historically individual thereby becomes for Heidegger the privileged place (location, home) for his own hermeneutic logic. Ever since the student Heidegger reviewed Lask's *Logik der Philosophie* in a 1912 journal article,[22] logic for him meant philosophical logic. Called "a logic of logic" in the Scotus dissertation, it is for the neo-Kantian Lask a transcendental logic. The 1912 review already notes Lask's thorough aversion to the "bogey of psychologism"[23] in refusing to situate such a logic in the mind, subject, consciousness, or psyche. Nor, for that matter, in either one of the two worlds of entities inherited from philosophy, whether physical or metaphysical, but rather in a nonentitative Third Reich variously called validity, meaning, sense, and logos. Here we have the first appearance in Heidegger, as early as 1912 by way of Lask, not only of the theme of the ontological difference between be-ing and beings, but also of its oblivion by way of the metaphysical "in the entire course of the history of philosophy." For, as Lask notes, this difference had since Plato been repeatedly obscured by the "hypostatizing of the logical into metaphysical entities." The distinction expressed in Hermann Lotze's famous one-liner from the nineteenth century, "Es 'ist' nicht, sondern es gilt: It 'is' not, rather it holds, validates, empowers," must, insist both Lask and Heidegger, be understood non-Platonically and, more generally, nonmetaphysically. What and where is this empowering IT of *Es gilt* that holds, validates, carries weight, yields sense, which in our present context is to be the seat of logic? Is IT knowledge or is IT life, or perhaps neither, but rather some other, more impersonal realm? Out of the tradition of neo-Kantianism and the "treasure-trove [thesaurus]" of the German language, Heidegger will over a long career respond with a veritable litany of dynamic impersonal sentences after the model of *es gilt,* which attempt to name the sheer activity of being's *dunamis* in giving meaning: "Es wertet, Es weltet, Es ereignet sich, Es gibt, Es zeitigt sich, Es schickt, Es reicht," etc. etc. But never "It is" (Parmenides' *estin*), an impersonal that belongs properly to a being, and never to its being. "There it is!" tends to reify a static "brute" facticity, whereas "that I am and have to be" indicates the dynamics of possibility and destiny. The impersonal sentence formally indicates a dynamically active "facticity" and therefore is best translated in the present progressive form, such that the indicative (and *by no means* substantifying) "it" serves only to announce and give way to the verbal dynamics of a giving of meaning: "It's worlding, It's contextualizing, It's properizing, It's destining (indicating unique directions of sense and sending us on our way), It's temporalizing, It's tensing the stretch and reach of my temporal playing field, It's propriating my proper being and proper time."

The transcendental logic that Heidegger is after is thus a temporally ontological logic. Beginning in WS 1925–26, in a series of courses intermittently taught by Heidegger entitled simply "Logik," it is portrayed as an original logic (hence a "logic of origins") that precedes the formal logic of judgments and whose first function is to "produce" the fundamental concepts or categories that articulate the ground of all of reality as well as of its different domains. In Heidegger's first explicit venture into such a "productive" logic of philosophical concept formation, the fundamental concepts articulating the "ways to be" that course across the historical human situation called Da-sein, are first called *Temporalien,* tensors, before they become the *Existenzialien,* existentials, those tradition-breaking categories of *Being and Time* intended to displace both the Aristotelian and Kantian categories of traditional substance metaphysics.

This logical development is in fact first launched in the Scotus dissertation of 1915. Its topic is a medieval version of philosophical logic aiming to "produce" the transcendentals of *ens, unum, verum, et bonum* around what Scotus calls *haecceitas* (thisness), the very form of individuality that invests each individual with its own "this-here-now." Only the transcendentals of *unum* and *verum* are treated, not only in medieval terms but by and large along the lines suggested by Lask's philosophical logic. What follows is a brief structural summary of the Laskian elements applied in the habilitation that point the way toward a formally indicative hermeneutics of facticity.[24]

WHAT DID THE YOUNG HEIDEGGER FIND IN EMIL LASK?

In his *Logik der Philosophie*, Lask distinguishes between the *constitutive* categories generated by the *differentiation* of the domains of reality according to different matters, and the more formal and so "empty" *reflexive* categories oriented toward the *unification* of the comprehensive field of being. This basic distinction will serve to guide our discussion of the Laskian harbingers of a formally indicative hermeneutics of facticity in the habilitation. Two basic terminological interchanges in the translation template "Heidegger—medieval transcendentals—Lask" serve to unravel the intertwining traditions interwoven into the habilitation text:

1. facticity—*verum*—constitutive matter.
2. formal indication—*unum*—reflexive forms.

Back to Matter and the Facticity of Meaning

The all-out drive toward facticity in the still hylomorphic elements of the habilitation is evident especially in the recurring tendency to get back to the "matter" of things. This return to the matters involves the repeated application of what the young Heidegger calls the "principle of the material determination of form," which in language and content is clearly an outgrowth of Lask's "doctrine of the differentiation of meaning." "Form receives its meaning from matter" (FS, 193). The form accommodates ("tailors": Lask II, 59) itself to a particular matter such that it is itself particularized in meaning. Meaning is thus the particular fruit of the union of form and matter. Meaning is that very union, which is why the ultimate answer to the question "whence sense?" cannot simply be "matter" but rather "by way of matter," "relatedness to matter." Form "laden" with meaning thus becomes the fuller and more "specific" constitutive form, "the categorial determination called for by non-validating matter," which "lets the essence of matter shine through, as it were" (II, 172, 103). The constitutive form is accordingly an intrinsic "reflection of material determination" (II, 65). The "moment of meaning" is the "relatedness of the validlike to the outside" (Lask II, 170). Such an answer is perhaps not surprising, in view of the operative concept of intentionality that governs Lask's *Hingeltung*, "validition of . . . ," where the German particle "hin" first announces the "enclitic" character of forms, the intrinsic need of valid forms for *fulfillment* in a matter. From the standpoint of "pure" form and its intrinsic validity, meaning is an "excess" arising from its reference "to a something lying outside of it," to its individuating matter.

By way of this intentional relation of form to its matter, Lask's hylomorphic theory of meaning at once involves the shift in the locus of truth in the prejudgmental direction of the transcendental *verum*, being as knowable or intelligible. This is not the formal truth of judgment, truth as validity, but the prior material truth of simple apprehension, scholasticism's first "act of the mind," truth as meaning, that of the simple encounter at the interface of the orders of knowing and being, "the essential union of the object of knowledge and the knowledge of the object" (FS, 344, 208), intentionality at its most direct. It is the truth of simply having an object as "a meaning independent of judicative characterizing. . . . The truth is consummated in givenness and does not extend beyond it" (FS, 210). Material givenness, and not judicative forming, plays the major role at this rudimentary level of truth, where the categorial forms of thought are dependent on the matter of being for their meaning. Not an ideal and theoretical realm of validity, but still a "transcendental" realm of pretheoretical meaning flowing from and through life itself (I.A of the KNS-Schema below) as the original setting of the human being. Lask calls it a "supra-oppositional panarchy of the logos" (Lask II, 133) in which I already "live in truth" (i.e., intelligibility, meaning). This theme of already "living in the truth" taken from Lask's aletheiology will be repeated in *Being and Time* (SZ, 221f, 226f, 229f) for the even more encompassing sense of truth that Heidegger finds in the disclosedness the total human situation.

Even Heidegger's discovery in KNS 1919 of a preobjective, pretheoretical world (I.B of the KNS-Schema below) as the meaningful context for the truth of the things within it seems in part to have been suggested by Lask's hylomorphic way of describing the intentional relation. Since we live immediately in the form in order to know the matter mediately, we, as it were, live in categories as in contexts through which we experience the things included within them. The relation of form to its matter is thus one of "environment" (*Umgebung*). Matter is encompassed, embraced (*umgriffen*), surrounded or environed (*umgeben*), horizoned or bordered (*verbrämt*) by the form; it is enveloped (*umhüllt*), enclosed (*umschlossen*) in the form (Lask II, 75f). Lask's exploratory metaphors here may have been one of the lines of suggestion that prompted the early Heidegger to make the leap from regional category to world, more specifically to the environing world (*Umwelt*) as signifying element, a central thrust of his hermeneutic breakthrough in KNS 1919. One indication of such a neo-Kantian "world" connection: Heidegger at this time manifests a peculiar penchant to use the Husserlian term *lifeworld* in the plural, typically in reference to the scientific, ethical, aesthetic, and religious lifeworlds, matching the fourfold division of normative forms into the true, good, beautiful, and the Holy that he learned from his teachers in the Southwest German school of neo-Kantianism. Another indication that Lask's panarchy of the logos is ultimately experienced as a world-context comes to us from Heidegger's own admission in the opening hour of Heidegger's survey of neo-Kantianism in SS 1919: "Lask discovered in the ought and in value, as in an experienced ultimate, *the world*, which was non-thinglike, non-sensorily metaphysical, as well as not unthinglike, not extravagantly speculative, but rather was factic" (ZBP, 122).[25]

Formal Indication of the One and Other

The simply apprehended truth of meaning and the hermeneutically meaningful context of the world are the first forms of facticity ("experienced ultimate") that Heidegger found in his effort "to go all out after the fact*ic* in order to make fact*icity* itself into a problem" by way of the transcendental *verum*. On the other hand, the first stirrings of the method of "formal indication," central to Heidegger's hermeneutical method, occur in the discussion of the transcendental *unum* (the one), at the point where Lask's reflexive category is related to the medieval doctrine of the analogy of being and its extremities of univocity and equivocity. Lask not only contributes to a new sense of facticity, but also to the question of how to express this precognitive realm of lived meaning in the special language that Heidegger will soon call "formal indication." In this vein, Lask's treatment of the reflexive category appears in the habilitation text expressly in the section on the medieval doctrine of speech significations. But it had already appeared unannounced in the earlier section on the transcendental *unum*. While the constitutive category plays a central role in the differentiation of the domains of reality, their regionalization into various material logics, the role of the reflexive category is that of their unification, in a logic tending toward the most general and formal of considerations. Its utter generality suggests that it is the emptiest and most *abstract* of categories. But Lask's account of its genesis at the very outskirts between knowing and being, in the very first stirrings of taking thought and reflecting upon an initially amorphous absorption (*Hingabe*) in a homogeneous experience, suggests instead a proximity to the *concrete whole* of being itself (Lask II, 129f). Thus, Heidegger in KNS 1919 can say that the formal objective "anything whatsoever" (*Etwas überhaupt*: II.A) of the reflexive category is "motivated" in the undifferentiation of the primal something of the pretheoretical "life in and for itself" (I.A), the most basic isomorphism (A-A) of the KNS-Schema below:[26]

KNS-Schema

I. The *pretheoretical* something:

A. *The preworldly something*	B. *World-like something*
(basic moment of life as such)	(basic moment of particular spheres of life)
The primal something	Genuine lifeworld

II. The *theoretical* something:

A. *Formal-logical objective something*	B. *Object-kind something*
(motivated in primal something)	(motivated in a genuine lifeworld)
[anything whatsoever]	[kinds of objects]
[A = reflexive categories]	[B = constitutive categories]

The medieval discussion of the categories expresses this primal indifference in the concept of *ens commune*, about which one can indifferently say, "it is." "Aliquid indifferens concipimus" (FS, 156), "we first conceive the something indifferently." If this indifference is thought to its extremity, "the 'general' here loses all meaning" (FS, 159), and *ens commune* can no longer be made subject to predicative subsumption according to the hierarchy of kinds, that is, of genera and species (II.B) that constitutive categories yield. Because it is beyond such hierarchical generalization and has its own unique universality, being is called a "transcendental." In the language of neo-Kantianism, something in general, "anything whatsoever," the object pure and simple, is not an object at all but rather a homogeneous continuum. This "indifference of the on-hand [*Vorhandenheit*]" surfaces in a surprising number of places in *Being and Time*, along with a parallel limit-experience, that of the indifference of everyday absorption in the environing world.

The reflexive category first arises at the utter limit between the indifference and difference of being. For the starting stuff of the reflexive category is this "some-thing in general" (II.A), and its initial form is the "there is" (*es gibt*), as in the indicative assertion, "There is something." Put otherwise, the very first reflexive category is "persistent being" (*Bestand*), sheer presence. This indifferent identity then gives rise to the categorial pair of identity *and* difference, which belong together in the relation of heterothesis (Rickert's term for it) or the transcendental *unum*. It is only at this point that an object clearly becomes an object. "There is (*es gibt*) no object, no object is given, when the One *and* the Other are not given" (FS, 173, citing Rickert).[27] "Why is the something a something, one something? Because it is not an other. It is a something and in being-something it is not-the-other" (FS, 160). Being an object at all means being identical with itself *and* being different from anything else. These two elements are "equally primordial" (*gleich ursprünglich*: FS, 172, 323; also 158, 166: a key structural term in BT that can also be traced through Lask back to Fichte). It is the very first use of this important Fichtean term in Heidegger's thought, here associated with the "convertibility" of the transcendentals *ens* and *unum* (FS, 160), being and one. In proximity to the primal indifference, basic terms tend to converge. What this basic convergence yields is the most minimal order (form, determination) necessary to apprehend an object at all; Rickert would add, necessary for anything whatsoever to be thought at all: For a pure monism without opposites cannot even be thought. The apparent tautology *ens est* necessarily already involves a heterology. In an account of the difference in function of the noun *ens* versus the verb *esse* in this sentence, which already calls to mind his later reflection on the ontological difference between being and beings, the young Heidegger writes: "Equally primordial as the object in general is the object's state of affairs; with every object there is an 'intentional nexus' [*Bewandtnis*], even if it be merely that it is identical with itself and different from another" (FS, 323). Thus, in *Being and Time* (SZ, 114), the crucial term *equiprimordial* first appears in conjunction with the formal indication of the self-other relation in Dasein.

The ordinary-language examples from the young Heidegger's account of a speculative grammar (Scotus) or a priori logical grammar (Husserl) illustrate what the reflexive order of categories promises for him: logical insight into the structural resources of a living language that would abet especially the "logic of philosophy." In today's jargon, one might even call it a "gramma(on)tology." Lask too alludes to this connection between logic and language. At one point in his defense of the seemingly ethereal and remote reflexive categories (persistent being, identity and difference, unity, multiplicity, plurality, etc.), he poses the rhetorical question: What would we do with a language without words such as "and," "or," "one," "other," "not" (Lask II, 164)? Accordingly, such hyperreflective categorial artifices, which buy transparency at the price of depleting the constitutive categorial forms upon which they are parasitical (Lask II, 158, 163, 68), still have their concretion. For the reflexive categories draw their moment of meaning-differentiation from the subject-object duplicity rather than from the form-matter relation (Lask II, 137). In its own way, therefore, the reflexive category constitutes a formal skeletal structure of the *intentional* structure of life itself. Lask thus describes his panarchy of the logos as a "bundle of rays of relations" (II, 372), which Heidegger would latter call a "world." The reflexive object is the pure ob-ject as such; in relation to subjectivity, it is a "standing over against" (*Entgegenstehendes*: II, 72f). Its being "is stripped down to the bare reflexive being of the shadowy anything whatsoever, to the naked something in general of the 'there it is.' " (II, 229).

> A something stands as logically naked and preobjective only before the "immediate," unreflected and theoretically untouched dedication and surrender [*Hingabe*: I.A. in the KNS-Schema]. By contrast, it always confronts reflection as an object, standing over against us. . . . Of course, only a minimum of objectivity need be involved in such reflecting [II.A]. In such a case, the matter needs to be legitimized theoretically merely as a "something" which "is given" or "is there" ["*es gibt*"]. It remains to be seen what the precise intentional nexus [*Bewandtnis*] of this bare "reflexive" category of the mere "there it is" ["*Es-Geben*"] may be. (Lask II, 129f)

The young Heidegger sees the need to supplement Lask's terms here and finds that the medieval theory of speech acts and their contents already "manifests a sensitive and sure disposition of attunement to the immediate life of the subjectivity and its immanent contexts of meaning" (FS, 343), especially in sorting out the signifying functions of univocity, equivocity, and analogy, "which originate in the use of expressions in living thinking and knowing" (FS, 277). In the same vein, Heidegger tantalizingly suggests that the variety of domains in any category system, even though they are differentiated primarily in objective accordance with the actual domains themselves, at least to some extent receive their identity-difference relations from the "subjective side," which finds expression in the reflexive categories (FS, 346). This side is at least partly met by the concerns of medieval speech theory for privations, fictions and other nonentities or "beings of reason" (FS, 254f). In coping with such articulations, linguistic forms, in contrast to empirically oriented constitutive categories and much like the reflexive categories, develop a peculiar dilution and indeterminateness that make them amenable to "anything whatsoever" (II.A), the very matter of reflexive categories (FS, 256f).

It is precisely these resources of a living language that philosophical discourse must draw upon in order to perform its comprehensive tasks; in short, not so much upon empirical metaphors but more upon structural considerations already latent in the comprehension of being by language. Heidegger's lifelong penchant toward the impersonal sentence (*es gibt*), double genitive (hermeneutics *of* facticity), middle-voiced infinitives, reflexive verbs and pronouns, perfectly tensed verbs, etc. exemplifies this quasi-structuralist grammatical sense of language. The perennial embarrassment of philosophical language to attain its goals might well be lessened by a fuller explication of the formal-reflexive schematization of intentionality already operative in our extant language. This accounts for the importance of Lask's distinction between the reflexive and the constitutive category. It coincides with the medieval distinction between the unique universality of being (II.A) and the stepwise hierarchical generality of beings (II.B: cf. SZ, 2), Husserl's distinction (*Ideen I*, §13) between formalization and generalization, and the one in the KNS-Schema between two kinds of the "theoretical something." In KNS 1919, in the face of phenomenology's embarrassment to express the primal something of life as such, this distinction yields the method of "formal indication" as a way of approaching a subject matter that traditionally borders on ineffability: "individuum est ineffabile." The expanse opened up by the reflexive category between the extremes of homogeneity and heterogeneity, indifference and difference, serve as Heidegger's initial space of articulation of that purportedly ineffable domain of immediacy.

BEYOND KNS 1919

KNS 1919 constitutes Heidegger's *hermeneutic* breakthrough to his lifetime topic, even though it is only in subsequent semesters that the terms *formal indication* (WS 1919–20), *phenomenological hermeneutics* (SS 1919), and *facticity* (SS 1920) are first expressly used. KNS 1919 also for the first time names three recurring impersonal expressions that formally indicate the dynamics of the "active" facticity of *be-ing*: "It's giving, it's worlding, it's properizing/propriating [*es er-eignet sich*]."

And phenomenology is defined as the "pretheoretical primal science of original experience." Phenomenology must therefore "pregrasp" (*vor-greifen*) the differentiation of life experience at its vital *pre*objective incipience, before it "stills the stream-of-life" (ZBP, 101) and becomes an ob-ject standing over against a subject, the latter being the ultimate intentional structure of logical formality and its formal ontology (à la Leibniz). Logical formality is theoretical, while phenomenological formality seeks to remain pretheoretical. How is phenomenology to avoid every vestige of the theoretical infringement already embodied in categories such as "object" and even "givenness"? Once again, the guiding clue of intentionality, itself understood as a formal schematism or "prestructuration," provides the answer. The undifferentiated primal something of life, which is not yet differentiated and not yet worldly (I.A), nevertheless, in that very "not yet," contains within itself the "index [indication!] for the highest potentiality of life" (ZBP, 115). This potentiality is the basic trait or "pull" (*Zug*) of life to live "out toward" something, in the KNS-Schema to "world out" (*auszuwelten*) into particular lifeworlds (I.B). And this *Es weltet* is "the basic moment of life as such" (so under I.A). The schema serves to divide the event of world-ing into its two pretheoretical divisions, giving primacy to the active suffix, to the structuring, articulating, thus meaning-giving dynamism of life in and for itself. The primal something, thus singled out as a dynamic center, may be a "not yet," but this undifferentiated "not" contains within itself the power to differentiate worlds. It is a differentiating indifference or, in more Kantian language, a determinable indetermination. The indifference can do something. And this potency is the primal something. How to conceptualize and define this "deed" (re-placing Fichte's *Tathandlung*!) in its incipient upsurge? For the Kantians, all concepts have the function of determining. According to our already established precautions, this is to be a purely formal determination rather than the hierarchical determination of genera and species. Heidegger finds such a formal determination in the schematism of intentionality itself. Within the undifferentiated dynamism of the primal something, in its undiminished "vital impetus," there is the bare intentional moment of "out toward," "in the direction of," "into a (determinate) world" (ZBP, 115), the tendency to "world out" (*auszuwelten*) into particular lifeworlds.

Put in another way, this *dunamis* of being toward something is "life in its motivated tendency and tending motivation" (ZBP, 117). The primal something may be undifferentiated and unformed, but it is not the "amorphous irrational X" (Rickert) of brute facticity. For it contains within itself the tendency toward differentiation and determination and so has an intrinsic directional sense.

With this positive development of the undifferentiation of life, we can see how Heidegger answers the final objection against a "pretheoretical science" (which borders on being a "square circle"), namely, the objection that an objectifying diremption between knowledge and its object always remains, since every intuitive comportment is inescapably a comportive "relation to *something*" (ZBP, 112). The answer of Heidegger's phenomenology is ingeniously simple: When it comes to the original something, the *Ur-etwas*, the "something" is the comporting relation (*Verhalten*) itself, without any prior determination as to who or what is doing the comporting or is being comported. It is not an ob-ject at all but instead the sheer intentional movement of "out toward," what Heidegger two semesters later will structurally distinguish as the relational sense (*Bezugssinn*) of intentionality. All formally indicative concepts aim, strictly speaking, to express only the pure "out toward" without specifying any content or ontic fulfillment. From the relational sense of "out toward," accordingly, the formal indication of "object in general" becomes the pure "toward which" (*das Worauf*), in opposition to Lask's more *reflexive* formulation of "standing over against" (*Entgegenstehendes*: Lask II, 72f), which takes the ob-ject more from the side of its content sense, and so is still too objectively formulated. And *das Worauf* in KNS 1919 is clearly the conceptual predecessor of "das Woraufhin des primären Entwurfs" (SZ, 324, 152), "the toward-which according-to-which of the primary project" of Dasein that in *Being and Time* is formally defined as the "circular" movement of its "sense" (*Sinn*), which in turn is transformed into the very temporality of Dasein.

Thus, formal *object*ification, even though "motivated" in the primal something, is still not near enough to life's origin, to its "primal leap" (*Ur-sprung*, Natorp's favorite play on the word *origin*) and incipient upsurge, for Heidegger's formally indicative concepts. In the end, formal objectification is still an un-living that "stills the stream-of-life" into the rigid duality of subject over against object, which must be dismantled and revivified by the more unified relation of motive to tendency, which is at the "heart" of the intentional movement here. The conceptual pair of motivated tendency, destined to be replaced by the pair passionate action in 1924 and by thrown projection in BT, in each case to be understood as a single movement in its paired equi-primordiality, is therefore not a duality, but rather the "motivated tendency or tending motivation" (ZBP, 117) in which "outworlding" life expresses itself. Expression, articulation, differentiation arises out of a matrix of undifferentiation focused in a single thrust of intentionality, no longer to be understood in terms of subject-object, form-matter, or any other duality. What remains of the old objectification is the indifferent continuum of the toward-which on the noematic end, and the tending motivation on the noetic.

In the next decade, Heidegger will rename his formal schematism or "prestructuration" of intentionality in different ways in order to "logically" guide him to generate new and different conceptual schemes incorporating new intentional nuances, one after another in close succession. But every one of these supplemental formal indications always bears the mark of intentionality as the middle-voiced "sich richten nach," being directed toward//directing itself toward, at the core of human experience: a triple-vectored "prestructuration" of intentionality according to its sense (*Sinn*) of relation, content, and fulfillment (1920) that integrate into a comprehensive temporal sense (1922), Dasein (1923), being-in-the-world (1924), (having)-to-be (*Zu-sein*: 1925), ex-sistence (1926), transcendence (1927–29). The best known of these transcendental-logical exercises in philosophical concept formation is *Being and Time*, guided by the formal indication of ex-sistence to generate the cluster of existential categories that permits the articulation of an ex-static temporality, in contrast to a static temporality of constant presence. One striking feature of this concept-forming method of formal indication is its schematizing power, its power to prefigure the structures that underlie an original life-phenomenon, exposing its vectorial web that weaves the fabric of time. Thus, blackboard diagrams of the conceptual schemes of one or another philosopher, as well as his own, abound in Heidegger's early lecture courses. Especially noteworthy are the two intentional schematisms on "becoming a Christian" according to Paul's letters (WS 1920–21) and according to Augustine's *Confessions* (SS 1921).[28]

After the phenomenological decade outlined above and with his entry into the "turn" of emphasis from Da-sein to its ever more archaic be-ing (*Seyn*), Heidegger in fact continues to supplement the above series of formal indications of an ever more factically embedded "intentionality" between Da-sein and be-ing, first by the displacement of ex-static ex-sistence into its "in-stanciation" (*Inständigkeit*: first in 1931) in the truth of be-ing, followed shortly by the "usage" (*Brauch*: 1936–38) of the tradition of be-ing (called the *ethos* in 1948), the hold of a relational bearing (*Ver-hältnis*: 1946) of be-ing, be-longing (*Zu-gehörigkeit*: 1952), the tractional draw (*Be-zug*: 1954) of be-ing's withdrawal, etc. But in each instantiation, what continues to be formally indicated is the abyssal facticity of the unique time of the propriative event of be-ing, whether the instantiation be that of the one-time-only time of Da-sein proper, of a unique historical people thrown into its heritage rooted in a native language, or of the epochal age in which we now find ourselves. For what in factic life itself could be more formal than time? And with respect to its indicative indexical function, what in factic life could be more concrete and immediate, nearer to us than time, my time, our time? Time is the ultimate formality and at once the most immediate proximity of be-ing, the original thrust (*Urwurf*) of its facticity.

GENEALOGICAL ADDENDUM: FICHTE ON FACTICITY

Heidegger's courses on German idealism in the thirties bear witness to his fascination with the sense of the "transcendental fact" of this tradition that precedents his own sense of facticity. The course in Summer 1930 returns again and again to the single Kantian fact of practical freedom and the moral law,[29] and the course on Schelling in 1936 to the facticity of the "feeling" of freedom. But in 1941, Heidegger, in situating his own initiative within an epochal "history of being," will seek to distance himself from such comparisons with German idealism. "[T]he thought in *Being and Time* is not just 'realistic' in contrast to the unconditioned 'egoistic' idealism of Fichte. . . . According to Fichte it is the ego that throws the world. But according to *Being and Time*, the ego does not first throw the world, it is rather the Da-sein, essentially presencing before all humanity, that is thrown."[30] Nevertheless, the comparison between the two, between the Fichtean I understood in its "irrational facticity" (Lask I, 238) and "brutality of its reality" (so Lask: I, 172f, 284), and the thrown Da-sein in the "facticity of its being delivered over," in finding itself always displaced into its "that it is and has to be" (SZ, 135), is inevitable, even fruitful in illuminating a fateful vein of the German philosophical tradition of the last two hundred years. For it was Fichte in his middle "positivistic" phase who first interjected the term *facticity* into the philosophical tradition.

The first clear signs of a "transcendental empiricism" of a "positivistic" Fichte occur around 1797. But Lask finds hints of it in the idealistic *Wissenschaftslehre* of 1794, even an initial acknowledgment of an irrational cleft between the I and non-I, in the theoretical incomprehensibility of the empirical "collision" (*Anstoss*) which speculation can override only in the practical realm. A complete and full conceivability is thus seen as a task, an infinite idea that is approximated by the heroes of human history. By way of this admission of irrationality, the absolute I or the totality of knowledge is grasped no longer as a principle but as an idea (I, 92f).

Indeed, in the "Second Introduction to the *Wissenschaftslehre*" of 1797, Fichte himself accuses his first readers of "the remarkable confusion of the I of intellectual intuition, from which the *Wissenschaftslehre* starts, with the I as idea, where it concludes" (SW I, 515). The I as intellectual intuition is merely the form of I-hood and self-reverting action, the form that is only for the philosophers. The I as idea is instead present for the I itself, which the philosopher then beholds. The I as idea holds the actual material of the I, which itself can be thought only by thinking of a historical world (SW I, 516). This opposition of form and matter is itself a sign of human limits. The idea of idealism, as an unattainable reality and the overcoming of limits in infinity, is a rejection of absolute rationalism and assumption of a "critical anti-rationalism" (Lask I, 103). Philosophy becomes an infinite series of acts of conceiving the inconceivable.

> The fact of the hiatus is the constant reference to an infinite progress of knowledge which cannot be actualized except in a never finished "system of becoming." Hegel's "polemic against infinite progress" and "bad infinity" thus again clearly manifests the great divide between panlogicism and the *Wissenschaftslehre*. (Lask I, 177)

In this regard, the concrete realization of knowledge displays an "infinite facticity of individual knowing" (SW II, 55: a first use of *Facticität* in Fichte), the individual displays an infinite in its particulars, an "infinite manifold" or "into an infinite manifold" (Lask I, 178f).

The fact of the *hiatus irrationalis*, of the abyss, itself assumes a manifold of polar forms: finite knowing and infinite progress, the universal I and the individual I-concentration, the conceiving of form and the inconceivability of matter, the metaphysical and the empirical, philosophy and life, *quid juris* and *quid facti*, etc. etc. The inability to fill the factic cleft is the encounter with incalculable facticity, accident, the "brutality of reality" (Lask I, 172).

Brutality is the "law" of reality, the sole and absolute law. Brutality has the further consequence that reality can only be anticipated and accepted, must always be "new" and surprising. This sudden breaking of all threads of speculation in the fact of brutal reality is what Fichte calls the absolute hiatus, which cannot be filled by any reflection but which itself constitutes the *ultimate that is unattainable* by knowledge. . . . Absolute "facticity" is itself the highest and sole law, that is, it is the violent breaking of all laws. Facticity as brutality of reality is pure and simple lawlessness itself (Lask I, 172f).

Underivable facticity is the "principle of infinity, of eternal coming to be and passing away" (NW III, 384).[31] It is the material principle of the absolute I over against the formal principle of the absolute I in its formal identity, the I as intellectual intuition. Taken together, they constitute the ultimate doubling that grounds the overall process of knowledge and life (Lask I, 188, 116).

A doctrine of life first emerges with the positivistic Fichte. Fichte the *Wissenschaftslehrer* now becomes Fichte the philosopher of culture and history. Here we have the first appearance of the theoretically unfathomable value-individuality, of the I-concentration in a historical context of value. "Instead of cold reflection, immediate feeling, beholding, experiencing, and being moved is now demanded of philosophy" (I, 198). This return to life is most clearly expressed in the "Lucid Report Clear as Day" (1801: cf. Lask I, 148). The really real is "the true fact of your present experiencing and living, what you really live and experience" (SW II, 335), the "actually real occurrence of your life" (336), "the truly factic, the flowing moments filling your life" (339), forgetting yourself and being immersed, given over to the devout abandon (*Hingabe*) of sheer beholding. This is life at ground level with its ground determinations, life at the first power (*Potenz*: 344), "the immersing of your consciousness in its lowest power" (400). This lowest power yields an impenetrable mass, which is "the actual footing and rooting of all other life" (345). "We also call what resides in this sphere the privileged first reality, *fact* of consciousness. We also call it experience" (345). Not at all a "sphere of things in and for themselves," these facts are given to consciousness. "We only have to give ourselves over and surrender to them . . . and let yourself be gripped by them, in order to appropriate them to yourself and make them into your real life" (SW II, 344). Thus is life itself given to us. The realism of the "life *of consciousness*" here is still tied to the consistent standpoint of idealistic immanence (Lask I, 149).

But in the *Wissenschaftslehre* of 1804, Fichte suggests—I am now going beyond Lask's account—that the consciousness itself is a fact, that is, that the expression "fact *of* consciousness" is in fact a double genitive. "In such an idealistic system, if the consciousness were itself a fact, and the consciousness is the absolute, then the absolute would be a fact" (NW II, 194). "The primal fact and the source of everything factic is the consciousness" (NW II, 195). But the absolute in the

Wissenschaftslehre is a "deed-action" (*Tathandlung*), which Fichte in this lecture course of 1804 had already called "genesis."

> Accordingly, facticity and genesis here completely collapse into one another. The immediate facticity of knowing is absolute genesis. And the absolute genesis *is*—it exists as a sheer fact—without any further possible ground outside of itself. . . . Fact is genesis and genesis fact. (NW II, 268; 308)

But such a synthesis is possible only for the *transcendental* fact, as the fact *of* consciousness, like the fact of the "I think" and of the moral law that Kant regarded as "the sole fact of pure reason." It is a "lawgiving" fact, a *factum fiens* and not a *factum brutum*, the empirical fact (NW I, 538: "Tatsachen des Bewußtseins," 1813).

It seems that the Heidegger of 1941 is right, and not the Lask of 1902. The self-positing absolute I of Fichte still does not feel its thrownness, it rather posits and "throws the world." The absolute I is a pure *factum fiens* without the brutality of the world, the world that was fated to blow Lask to smithereens on the Eastern front.

NOTES

1. The German text of this letter, edited by Hartmut Tietjen, is to be found in *Zur philosophischen Aktualität Heideggers*, ed. D. Papenfuss and O. Pöggeler, Vol. 2, *Im Gespräch der Zeit* (Frankfurt: Klostermann, 1990), 33–38. An English rendition is to be found in Karl Löwith, *Martin Heidegger and European Nihilism*, ed. Richard Wolin (New York: Columbia University Press, 1995), 239–43.

2. *Historisches Wörterbuch der Philosophie*, Joachim Ritter, editor-in-chief (Darmstadt: Wissenschaftliche Buchgesellschaft, 1972), Vol. 2, 886. The article on *Faktizität* was written by H. Fahrenbach.

3. *Brockhaus-Enzyklopädie*, 17th ed., Vol. 6, 28. An early essay of pertinence to this tradition of dictionaries and a history of "facticity" from Fichte to Natorp and Heidegger is Theodore Kisiel, "Das Entstehen des Begriffsfeldes 'Faktizität' im Frühwerk Heideggers," *Dilthey-Jahrbuch* 4 (1986–87): 91–120.

4. Ludwig Landgrebe, *Faktizität und Individuation. Studien zu den Grundfragen der Phänomenologie* (Hamburg: Meiner, 1982), 109, 117.

5. Ludwig Siep, "Methodische und systematische Probleme in Fichtes 'Grundlage des Naturrechts,' " in *Der transzendentale Gedanke. Die gegenwärtige Darstellung der Philosophie Fichtes*, ed. Klaus Hammacher (Hamburg: Meiner, 1981), 292.

6. A succinct summary of the categories of Wilhelm Dilthey's hermeneutics of life can be found in my article, "Heidegger (1907–27): The Transfor-

mation of the Categorial," now in Theodore Kisiel, *Heidegger's Way of Thought: Critical and Interpretative Signposts*, ed. Alfred Denker and Marion Heinz (London/New York: Continuum, 2002), 84–101, esp. 91–93.

7. See the epigraph to this chapter and Note 1 above.

8. Martin Heidegger, *Die Kategorien- und Bedeutungslehre des Duns Scotus* (1915–1916), cited from the first edition of Heidegger's *Frühe Schriften* (Frankfurt: Klostermann, 1972), 133–353. Hereafter FS in this pagination.

9. For a detailed analysis of the habilitation in its intertwining of the Scotian and Laskian threads of a formal indication of facticity, see Theodore Kisiel, "Why Students of Heidegger will have to Read Emil Lask," *Man and World* 28 (1995): 197–240. This essay is now reprinted in Theodore Kisiel, *Heidegger's Way of Thought*, op. cit., 101–36, 206–13. The phrase "formally indicative hermeneutics" comes to us from Otto Pöggeler and not Heidegger. See Theodore Kisiel, "Gibt es eine formal anzeigende Hermeneutik nach der Kehre?" in *Kultur—Kunst—Öffentlichkeit: Philosophische Perspektiven auf praktische Probleme. Festschrift für Otto Pöggeler zum 70. Geburtstag*, ed. Annemarie Gethman-Siefert and Elisabeth Weisser-Lohmann (Munich: Wilhelm Fink, 2001), 173–79.

10. Heinrich Rickert, "Gutachten über die Habilitationsschrift des Herrn Dr. Heidegger" (July 19, 1915), is to be found in Appendix IV of Thomas Sheehan, "Heidegger's Lehrjahre," ed. J. C. Sallis, G. Moneta, and J. Taminiaux, *The Collegium Phaenomenologicum: The First Ten Years*, Phaenomenologica Vol. 105 (Dordrecht/Boston: Kluwer, 1994), 118.

11. Emil Lask, *Gesammelte Schriften*, Volume I, ed. Eugen Herrigel (Tübingen: Mohr, 1923). Lask's dissertation, *Fichtes Idealismus und die Geschichte* (1902), is on pp. 1–274. It shall be cited internally according to the posthumous Herrigel edition as "Lask I" followed by the page number.

The earliest instances of the term *Facticität* in Fichte that I am aware of occur in his "Darstellung der Wissenschaftslehre" of 1801. See Johann Gottlieb Fichte, *Sämmtliche Werke*, ed. Immanuel Hermann Fichte (Berlin: Viet und Comp, 1845), Vol II, 47, 55, 132, 162. Hereafter cited as SW.

12. For detailed examples, see Kisiel, "Das Entstehen des Begriffsfeldes 'Faktizität' . . . ," Note 3 above.

13. From the record of student transcripts, I had early gathered that the abstractum *facticity* first appeared in Heidegger's lecture course in SS 1920, at first in its neo-Kantian usages by Rickert and Natorp and eventually in Heidegger's unique hermeneutic sense of a finite historical life encountering the limits and thereby the possibilities of that sense. Theodore Kisiel, *The Genesis of Heidegger's BEING AND TIME* (Berkeley/Los Angeles/London: University of California Press, 1993), 136, 496f. See also "Das Enstehen des Begriffsfeldes 'Faktizität' . . . ," 106–108. The sporadic occurrence of "facticity" in the recently published edition of the course of WS 1919–20 does not compel me to modify this conclusion, since the only statement of Heidegger's unique sense of facticity occurs in a note *supplementing* the lecture manuscript: "Factic life in its facticity, its realm of relations, is for us the nearest: we ourselves are it. . . . [Any standpoint that I take upon my facticity] can be tested only when

I am the factic in a wholly factic way and find possible ways *out* of it already prefigured *in* it." Martin Heidegger, *Grundprobleme der Phänomenologie* (1919/20), GA-Volume 58. Ed. Hans-Helmuth Gander (Frankfurt: Klostermann, 1993), 173; see also 86, 107.

14. Martin Heidegger, *Kant und das Problem der Metaphysik* (Frankfurt: Klostermann, 1929, 1973), 246.

15. Ibid., 248, 257.

16. Georges Gurvitch, *Les Tendances actuelles de la philosophie allemande: E. Husserl—M. Scheler—E. Lask—M. Heidegger* (Paris: Vrin, 1930, 1949). Cited pagination is from the 1949 edition.

17. Emil Lask, *Gesammelte Schriften*, Volume II, ibid. Lask's major work, *Die Logik der Philosophie und die Kategorienlehre* (1911), is on pp. 1–282. Cited as Lask II.

18. *Kant und das Problem der Metaphysik*, Section 3. B, § 31, 146–56.

19. Note, however, that Heidegger immediately adds the hermeneutic qualifier that "Dasein is equiprimordially in the untruth." Martin Heidegger, *Sein und Zeit* (Tübingen: Niemeyer, 1927, 1953), 221f, 226f, 229, 256f. Hereafter SZ.

20. Michael Friedman, "Overcoming Metaphysics: Carnap and Heidegger," *Origins of Logical Empiricism*, ed. R. Giere and A. Richardson, Minnesota Studies in the Philosophy of Science, Vol. XVI (Minneapolis: University of Minnesota Press, 1996), 45–79.

21. Lask's letter to Husserl on December 24, 1911. Edmund Husserl, *Briefwechsel*, Vol. 5: *Die Neukantianer*, ed. Karl Schuhmann in conjunction with Elisabeth Schuhmann (Dordrecht: Kluwer, 1994), 33f.

22. "Neuere Forschungen über Logik (1912)," in Martin Heidegger, *Frühe Schriften (1912–1916)*, Gesamtausgabe Vol. 1, ed. F.-W. von Herrmann (Frankfurt: Klostermann, 1978), 17–43.

23. Lask's theme of a "home" for both formal and transcendental logic is pursued especially in Steven Galt Crowell, "Lask, Heidegger, and the Homelessness of Logic," *Journal of the British Society for Phenomenology* 23, no. 3 (October 1992): 222–39. See also Crowell's dissertation, *Truth and Reflection: The Development of Transcendental Logic in Lask, Husserl, and Heidegger* (Ann Arbor: University Microfilms International, 1981). Also Steven Galt Crowell, "Husserl, Lask, and the Idea of Transcendental Logic," in *Edmund Husserl and the Phenomenological Tradition: Essays in Phenomenology*, ed. Robert Sokolowski (Washington, DC: Catholic University Press, 1988), 63–85.

24. A more complete and detailed account of what follows is to be found in Theodore Kisiel, "Why Students of Heidegger Will Have to Read Emil Lask," op. cit. in Note 9 above; *Genesis*, Chapter 1; "Heidegger—Lask—Fichte," in *Heidegger, German Idealism, and Neo-Kantianism*, ed. Tom Rockmore (Amherst: Prometheus/Humanity Books, 2000), 239–70; "Heideggers Dankesschuld an Emil Lask. Sein Weg vom Neufichteanismus zu einer Hermeneutik der Faktizität," *Studia Phaenomenologica* I, no. 3–4 (2001): 221–47.

25. ZBP = Martin Heidegger, *Zur Bestimmung der Philosophie*, GA 56/57, three lecture courses of 1919, ed. Bernd Heimbüchel (Frankfurt: Klostermann,

1987), 122. The first is the postwar course of *Kriegsnotsemester* (KNS) 1919, the other two are of Summer 1919. GA 56/57 has recently been translated by Ted Sadler as *Towards the Definition of Philosophy* (London: Athlone/Continuum, 2000).

26. The "KNS-Schema" (my nomenclature) is a four-column conceptual schematism that Heidegger diagrammed on the blackboard in the last hour of his course of KNS 1919, "The Idea of Philosophy and the Problem of Worldviews." This diagram is to be found in all of the student transcripts but fails to appear in the first "edition of the last hand" of this course in GA 56/57 (1987), 1–117 (see Note 25 above). It first appeared in print in my article, "Das Kriegsnotsemester 1919: Heideggers Durchbruch zur hermeneutischen Phänomenologie," *Philosophisches Jahrbuch* 99 (1992/1): 105–22. The modified double-column version that appears here, along with a few clarifying insertions in brackets to suit the present occasion, was first published in my "*Kriegsnotsemester* 1919: Heidegger's Hermeneutic Breakthrough," in *The Question of Hermeneutics: Essays in Honor of Joseph J. Kockelmans*, ed. T. J. Stapleton (Dordrecht: Kluwer, 1994), 155–208, esp. 161. The four-column schema was finally incorporated into the second "enlarged" edition of GA 56/57 (1999), 219, so that it is now to be found in a somewhat defective form in the new English translation, p. 186.

27. Heinrich Rickert, "Das Eine, die Einheit und die Eins," *Logos* 1 (1911).

28. Theodore Kisiel, "Heidegger (1920–21) on Becoming a Christian: A Conceptual Picture Show," in *Reading Heidegger from the Start*, ed. T. Kisiel and J. van Buren (Albany: State University of New York Press, 1994), 175–92; "Die formale Anzeige: Die methodische Geheimwaffe des frühen Heideggers. Heidegger als Lehrer: Begriffsskizzen auf der Wandtafel," in *Heidegger—neu gelesen*, ed. Markus Happel (Würzburg: Königshausen and Neumann, 1997), 22–40.

29. The course of Summer 1930 is published as Heidegger *Gesamtausgabe* Volume 31, *Von Wesen der menschlichen Freiheit. Einleitung in die Philosophie*, ed. Hartmut Tietjen (Frankfurt: Klostermann, 1982, 1994). English translation by Ted Sadler, *The Essence of Human Freedom: An Introduction to Philosophy* (London: Continuum Books, 2002). The discussion of the facticity of practical freedom and its correlative moral law occurs primarily in §§ 27–28, 265–97/182–201.

30. Martin Heidegger, *Schellings Abhandlung über das Wesen der menschlichen Freiheit (1809)*, ed. Hildegard Feick (Tübingen: Niemeyer, 1971), 227f. English translation by Joan Stambaugh, *Schelling's Treatise on the Essence of Human Freedom* (Athens, Ohio: Ohio University Press, 1985), 187f. Citation is from the Appendix of notes for a Schelling seminar in Summer 1941. References to the facticity (*Tatsächlichkeit*) of the feeling of freedom in Summer 1936 are to be found on English pages 15, 20, 38, 82–85, *et passim*. The text of the course of Summer 1936 upon which this book of 1971 is based is now published as *Gesamtausgabe* Volume 42, edited by Ingrid Schüssler under the title *Schelling: Vom Wesen der menschlichen Freiheit (1809)* (Frankfurt: Klostermann, 1988).

31. Johann Gottlieb Fichte, *Nachgelassene Werke*, ed. Immanuel Hermann Fichte (Bonn: bei Adolph Marcus, 1834). Hereafter NW.

3

Factical Life and the Need for Philosophy

François Raffoul

INTRODUCTION

We know the crucial place that the motif of facticity occupies in the early work of Martin Heidegger. Recent scholarly studies have reconstructed the central presence of facticity—factical life, hermeneutics of facticity, etc.—in the early courses of the German thinker. Further, Heidegger has stressed that facticity is an *irreducible* phenomenon for philosophy. For instance, in the 1921–22 Winter Semester course, he writes that the determinations of factical life "are not merely trivial and arbitrary observations, such as the statement that 'the thing there is red.' Furthermore, it must be understood that they are alive *in facticity*; i.e., they include factical possibilities, from which they are (thank God) never to be freed. Therefore a philosophical interpretation which has seen the main issue in philosophy, namely, facticity, is (insofar as it is genuine) factical and specifically philosophical-factical."[1] The very element of philosophizing, then, is facticity, and the theme of philosophy, in turn, is facticity. I would like in these pages to explore further this circle, by way of an interrogation on the nature of thought in light of Heidegger's hermeneutics of facticity and on the relation between what Heidegger calls "factical life" and philosophizing.

Commentators often stress that Heidegger has excluded life from his ontological inquiries, reducing it instead to an ontic domain, aligning it with animality—which is said to be foreign to the "essence of the human"—and generally treating it with great skepticism. Life philosophies are identified with metaphysical problematics, in the various guises of vitalism, biologism, Darwinism, etc. One recalls paragraph 10 of *Being and Time* where the analytic of Dasein is clearly distinguished from any biology, or life philosophy in general. The existential analytic of Dasein has a methodological priority over such ontic investigations, Heidegger going so far as to write: "The existential analytic of Dasein is *prior* to any psychology, anthropology, *and especially biology*."[2] This ontological precedence or priority indicates that these disciplines are not mastering their own fundamental-ontological basis: they leave such a basis unclarified, they do not undertake an ontological clarification of the very domain and subject matter that they propose to investigate scientifically. It is thus the very sense of the being of life that requires further explication and unfolding and, according to Heidegger, biology simply assumes and presupposes such a sense of being and all the while neglects it. Because of such a neglect, those disciplines, he continues, have become "completely questionable," and are "in need" of "new impulses which must arise from the ontological problematic" (BT, 45). The very expression "philosophy of life" is said to "say as much as the 'botany of plants' " (BT, 46), that is, very little: it is completely underdetermined in its sense. Further, Heidegger would insist that life itself could not be that through which we, in our most proper selves and being, can be defined. "Dasein should never be defined ontologically by regarding it as life (ontologically undetermined) and then as something else on top of that" (BT, 50) (that something else is "personhood," for instance, but principally reason or Logos as in the definition of man as rational animal). What is important in this sentence is what is in the parentheses: life as "ontologically undetermined." In biologism in all of its forms, the question: "What is the *being* of life?" is simply not asked. Such an omission is what Heidegger takes issue with. He writes very clearly on this point: "What strikes us first of all in such a philosophy (and this is its fundamental lack) is that life itself as a kind of being does not become a problem ontologically" (BT, 46).

This indicates straightaway that in his critiques Heidegger only takes aim at the metaphysical accounts of life: he does not so much reject the motif of life as such but rather the problematics that presuppose and ignore the sense of being of their very theme, namely, life. And it is a fact, now made manifest by the recent publications of his early courses, that he in fact first undertook a *positive* investigation of life, in contrast to his later rejection. Heidegger was in these early writings so concerned with a philosophy of life that he defined his own thought as a "hermeneutics of factical life," against the various metaphysical objectivisms, idealist philosophies, and scientist prejudices (but also against the objective metaphysics of Life, à la Bergson, for instance). Therefore, although Heidegger is often portrayed as having excluded or omitted life from his questioning, one can see that in his early work he undertook an ontological clarification of life, calling for an authentic return to (factical) life as the very ground of experience and thought. His eventual rejection of life, then, can only be approached and understood in light of his first *embracing* of life, however paradoxical that may seem.

LIFE AS FUNDAMENTAL FACT

The issue, then, for the young Heidegger, was to undertake an *ontological clarification* of life. But first—and this is most striking—Heidegger identifies life as *the* fundamental Fact, the central concern of his thought, the *Sache selbst* of phenomenology. Phenomenology, for Heidegger at that time, is a phenomenology of life itself. In *Phenomenological Interpretations of Aristotle*, Heidegger states from the outset: " 'Factical life': 'life' expresses a basic phenomenological category; it signifies a basic phenomenon" (PIA, 61). Far from reducing it to an ontic, regional domain, subordinated to a prior, more originary, ontological level, Heidegger on the contrary approaches life as the fundamental fact—indeed as "something ultimate" (PIA, 62)—to which all thought must return as to its ground. He also places himself explicitly within the tradition of life-philosophy in its various forms, which are for him like the foreshadowing of a genuine phenomenology of what he terms "factical life." He recognizes, for instance, that some of his analyses "came forth already in modern life-philosophy," a philosophical movement that he praises in these terms: "I understand [life-philosophy] to be no mere fashionable philosophy but, for its time, an actual attempt to come to philosophy rather than babble idly over academic frivolities." He then puts forward two names, placing himself under their authority: "Dilthey, Bergson" (PIA, 61). Against the Neo-Kantians, and in particular Rickert, he also suggests: "Instead, we need to read Nietzsche, Bergson, and Dilthey . . ." (PIA, 62). However, what he calls the "coming forth" initiated in modern life-philosophy "was in itself unclear" (PIA, 61), and encouraged the unhelpful "gushing" of "litterateurs," "those who would rather gush with enthusiasm than think" (ibid.). Against these "decadent productions," it would be a matter for Heidegger of "explicating life" (and we will see, a crucial point, that this will be tantamount to saying: "life explicating itself"). For, on the one hand, the term *life* is vague, unclarified, used in a variety of contexts; and on the other hand, it has been "captured," as it were, by biology, or biological thinking, that is to say, by a scientific thinking oblivious of its ontological basis, to wit, the sense of being of its very subject matter. Here lies the first decisive step in Heidegger's analysis: one needs to separate life from biology. He writes in no uncertain terms: "Biological concepts of life are to be set aside from the very outset"; they are, he continues, "unnecessary burdens" and subordinated to "an understanding of life which is essentially older than that of modern biology" (PIA, 62). To be more precise, then, we should say the issue is to explicate—to unfold—such an "older" understanding of life, that is, an ontological explication of life.

It is not the ambition or purpose of this chapter to undertake a detailed account of the fundamental characteristics of life as Heidegger phenomenologically retrieves them in this lecture course. These basic categories of life will of course be further elaborated a few years later as the very existentials of Dasein in *Being and Time*. To briefly reconstruct such characteristics: Life is said to be worldly, that is, not a self-enclosed phenomenon (as Michel Henry would have it), but essentially ek-static: *Life is an openness*. It is said to be essentially relational, that is, constituted by a series of intentional involvements. It is said to be a fundamental caring, marked by the difficult weightiness of a task, and an irreducible problematicity or questionableness (here we can already anticipate that thought will be said to be rooted in such problematicity of Life, and not in some external sphere). Life is said to have a specific motility or movedness (*Bewegtheit*), specified as both "Relucence" and "Prestruction," and further qualified by the so-called ruinance, etc. In fact, one needs to approach life essentially as a motion, a specific movement. Heidegger writes: "In our rough characterization of life, we have often spoken of actualization, nexus of actualization. Elsewhere, people speak of process, stream, the flowing character of life. This latter way of speaking is motivated by and follows a fundamental aspect in which we encounter life, and we take it as a directive toward the ensemble of the basic structures of life as *movement*, motility" (PIA, 85). Also: "The movedness [*Bewegtheit*] of factical life can be provisionally interpreted and described as *unrest*. The 'how' of this unrest, in its fullness as a phenomenon, determines facticity" (PIA, 70). This is a very complex development on Heidegger's part, which is beyond the scope of this chapter to address with justice. Rather, I am concerned here with the relation between life and philosophy. Why? Because in this course Heidegger tells us that Life, in its very ontological constitution, calls for philosophy, that is, is self-interpretative, and that philosophy or thought is radically dependent on Life, or if you will, that thought is radically immanent to Life: The origin of philosophy, Heidegger states, is "factical life as a fact."[3] This is why, Heidegger continues, the phenomenologist only deals with phenomena of life as they are lived, and therefore nothing extravagant, extraordinary, or mystical: Let us not be afraid, he exclaims, of "trivialities"! (GA, 58, 103), for in a sense this is what philosophy is about! Thought is assigned to the fact of life, and to life as fact. All life or existence, as Nietzsche insisted, is an *interpreting* existence. This fundamental hermeneutical character of life is grounded on the fact that life is at issue for itself, that it is "anxiously concerned" with itself. And philosophy or thought then becomes a phenomenon of life, radically immanent to it. It remains for us to clarify this relationship.

THE RADICAL IMMANENCE OF PHILOSOPHY TO LIFE

The first target in Heidegger's reevaluation of the relation between Life and Philosophy is the reliance on the notion of objectivity, along with the corresponding "reflexive attitude," or philosophies of reflection engaging in abstract theorizing, ruled by the demands of universal validity. Reading those passages from Heidegger on the structure of thought, one is indeed struck by his violent attacks on "objectivity," the scientific and reflexive ideal of objectivity. He takes issue with the positioning of objectivity—and nature—as the standard model for being. He articulates such a critique in the following way: "It is not the case that objects are first present as bare realities, as objects in some sort of natural state, and that they then in the course of our experience receive the garb of a value-character, so they do not have to run around naked. This is the case neither in the direction of the experience of the surrounding world nor in the direction of the approach and the sequence of interpretation, as if the constitution of nature could, even to the smallest extent, supply the foundation for higher types of objects. *On the contrary, the objectivity, 'nature,' first arises out of the basic sense of the Being of objects of the lived, experienced, encountered world*" (PIA, 69, my emphasis). Objectivity, nature, are here derived from a more primordial sense of Being, namely, facticity. Such a derivation will of course be repeated in *Being and Time* in the derivation of the mode of presence at hand from readiness to hand, *Vorhandenheit* from *Zuhandenheit*.[4] Thought, Heidegger insists, does not make one accede to any objective realm, that is, a realm that somehow would lie beyond or be distinct from life as factically lived. Heidegger thus speaks disparagingly of "so-called Objective life," one that would be "totally lived in the world of objects," which would be, as it were, "self-sufficient," "full of possessions," "self-sure," etc., in short, all characteristics that are foreign—indeed contrary—to life itself! One thinks here of the implicit contrast that Heidegger draws with respect to the ancient meaning of being as *ousia*, and its original sense as a "having," a "possession." Here on the contrary factical life is marked by privation, lack, and need. Heidegger would go so far as to claim that "privation (*privatio, carentia*) is both the relational and the intrinsic basic mode and sense of the Being of life" (PIA, 68).

Having been disguised and misrepresented as its contrary, life is then forced to submit to the inappropriate categories of theory. The categories of objective reflection are for Heidegger "something forced upon [factical life] capriciously," "an unwarranted forcing, with the violence and arbitrariness of a rootless, foreign, and ordering systematization, typologization, or the like" (PIA, 66). To "brood upon . . . universal validity," he continues, would be to completely misconstrue the basic meaning of life, and in fact of thought as well. Both life and thought are misconstrued respectively as Objectivity and as abstract reflection when they are neither.[5]

Consequently, one should not fear facticity, one should not fear so-called relativism by appealing to an illusory "freedom from standpoints," for in fact the issue in relativism is not the relativity of perspectives with respect to (a nonexistent) universality, but *the very facticity and finitude of experience*. Heidegger thus rejects the dogmatic tendencies that claim to espouse an absolute principle, that absolutize claims: "[B]asically the ideal possibility of absolute knowledge is but a dream. As historiological knowledge, philosophy not only *can* not, but also *must* not, entertain any such a dream" (PIA, 123). And he also rejects the accompanying charge of relativism and skepticism: for if "absolute truth thus has no claim to be taken as the norm and the goal," then its contraries, relativism and skepticism, "cannot be considered valid labels" (PIA, 124). Fear in the face of facticity is also fear in the face of philosophy. The calls for Objectivity are nothing but "the masked cries of anxiety before Philosophy," Heidegger writes. "Self-sure Objectivity is insecure flight from facticity, and this Objectivity mistakes itself precisely in believing that this flight increases Objectivity, whereas it is precisely in facticity that Objectivity is most radically appropriated" (PIA, 68). Facticity is thus the basis for any sense of objectivity that could be phenomenologically attested.

In the 1923 summer semester course, *Ontology. The Hermeneutics of Facticity*, Heidegger would clarify that the relationship between interpretation (hermeneutics) and life (facticity) "is not a relationship between the grasping of an object and the object grasped."[6] Scientific ideals as well as Husserl's phenomenology are targeted here. A few pages later, he will continue his attacks on objectivity by stating that existence would be "ruined" if measured against the ideal of objectivity, and he concludes: "Existence is never an 'object' "; existence is "rather being—it is *there* only insofar as in each case a living 'is' it" (HF, 15). We could say: *there is* life (objectivity) only when it is lived (facticity). Therefore, thought cannot be the theoretical grasp of an objectivity, under the vain pursuit of universality, but instead the phenomenological and hermeneutic seizing of life itself. Heidegger states firmly: "The question in philosophy is not whether its propositions can be shown to have universal validity, or whether the approval of very many or even all people can be exacted, as if these matters determined in the least the sense and sense-intention of a philosophical explication. What is in question is not the Objective demonstrability to the whole world but whether the intended binding force of the interpretation is a *living* one" (PIA, 125). Such living, however, remains to be determined in its sense of being, and not simply presupposed as some kind of "lived experience" of transcendental consciousness. It will indeed also be a matter for Heidegger of breaking with the Cartesian horizon still prevalent in Husserl's phenomenology when attempting to think Life phenomenologically, breaking with the understanding of Life as a feature of consciousness or of the subject. *Life will not be the life of a subject.*

LIFE COMING BACK TO ITSELF: REFLECTION

Correspondingly, as we suggested, thought cannot be the reflexive grasp of such objectivity. In fact, if all there is is life, thought can never be an external gaze *upon* life, from a position outside of life. This is why Heidegger rejects such understanding of thinking as an overview detached from what it sees. Thinking will be conceived instead as entirely grounded in life, and enjoying no independence whatever with respect to life. As we will see, reflection will be understood by Heidegger as a motion proper to life itself, life reflecting on itself. Philosophizing "about" (an inappropriate formulation) life is thus a phenomenon that belongs to life itself. Heidegger writes that, "Philosophy is a basic mode of life itself" (PIA, 62). Interpretation is also a phenomenon of life: "Hermeneutics is not an artificially devised mode of analysis which is imposed on Dasein and pursued out of curiosity. What needs to be brought into relief from out of facticity itself is in what way and when it calls for the kind of interpretation put forth." (HF, 12). We see already here the emergence of the motif of a call, out of factical life itself, calling for an interpretation, a call that will be specified further as a need . . . But what is certain at this stage is that for Heidegger, "Interpreting is a being which belongs to the being of factical life itself" (ibid.).

To that extent, the categories of thought (a category is that which interprets a phenomenon in the direction of sense) will not need, as in Kant, a transcendental deduction to ensure that they indeed correspond to what they are the categories of. Categories are not "logical schemata," not "inventions," they are not "foreign to life itself," "as if they pounced down upon life from the outside" (PIA, 66). Quite the reverse: "[I]t is in these categories that life itself *comes to itself*" (PIA, tr. modified). They represent instead life's own self-understanding, if one understands that life is not some brute biological datum prior to sense, but a hermeneutic movement through and through. There is therefore no opposition here between meaning and fact, life and sense, as if meaning were added to an otherwise senseless or irrational life. As Heidegger writes playfully, meaning "does not fall from the heavens"! (especially if the "problem of facticity—most radical phenomenology . . . begins 'from below' in the genuine sense" (PIA, 146).[7] Rather, "reflection is a way within movedness," he notes suggestively (PIA, 119).

More concretely, Heidegger explains that the categories of thought are grounded in language itself, defined as the "immanent speaking *of* life itself" (a sort of self-speaking). The genitive here is clearly subjective: it is life that speaks itself in language, sense, and thought, and the categories of grammar, insists Heidegger, "in fact originate in those of living speech, in those of the immanent speaking of life itself" (PIA, 63), an immanent self-speaking that is historical through and through.[8] Understanding is life's self-interpretation, out of an anxious concern for itself. This refers to a basic hermeneutic "capability" of life, always already explicating itself, getting a sense of itself: thinking itself. Heidegger clarifies that philosophy is not a reflection upon life, but springs out of life itself: "The object of philosophical research is human Dasein insofar as it is interrogated with respect to the character of its being. This basic direction of philosophical questioning is not externally added and attached to the interrogated object, factical life. Rather, it needs to be understood as an explicit taking up of a basic movement of life."[9] Thus, if there is any sense of reflection, it would only be a reflection, not *on* life, but *of* life and *from* life.

Reflection, which has defined thinking since Descartes all the way to Husserl, should be renamed in light of this new conception of the radical immanence of thought to life. This new name is: *repetition* as in "Relucence" (*Reluzenz*) from the Latin *reluceo*, "reflect a gleam." How is this term to be understood? We have already stressed that it can only be a movement proper to life itself. Now life is characterized by a fundamental caring, a caring that is inclined toward the world with which it is inextricably related. What life encounters in its inclined caring, says Heidegger, "is life itself" (PIA, 88). Therefore, inclination is by itself reflexive in that sense: life encounters itself from its inclined caring in the world. This is how Heidegger describes such "relucence": "Self-dispersed life encounters its world as 'dispersion,' as dispersing, manifold, absorbing, engaging, unfulfilling, boring. This means that inclination shows itself as something that moves itself toward itself. Life, caring for itself in this relationality, reflects light back on itself, which produces a clarification of the surroundings of the currently immediate nexus of care. As so characterized, *the movement of life toward itself within every encounter* is what we call *relucence*" (PIA, 88–89).

Reflection thus means: Life coming *back* to itself. Thinking is to reflect in the sense of *repeating*. " 'Repetition': everything depends on its sense. Philosophy is a mode of life itself, in such a way that it authentically 'brings back,' i.e., brings life back from its downward fall into decadence, and this 'bringing back' [or re-petition, 're-seeking'], as radical re-search, is life itself" (PIA, 62). The understanding of cognition as "concept," for instance in Rickert, is "a phantasm" (PIA, 62). Philosophy is not the cognition of ideal supra-temporal principles but, instead, the actualization of such a return of life to itself. This return is *needed*: cognitive categories "can be understood only insofar as factical life itself is *compelled* to interpretation." (PIA, 66, my emphasis), for an interpretation can only arise out of an "existentiell concern." We see here appear for the first time the problematic of a "need" for interpretation and thinking. Thinking is *needed* by Life in the sense that Life *needs to repeat itself* in the attempt to appropriate itself, in the form of the interpretive categories that guide reflection. Here philosophy loses all pretense of a detached, self-sure knowledge of an Objective, absolute and universal order: philosophy is instead in a constant state of neediness, the neediness of finite factical life.

THE NEED FOR PHILOSOPHY: RUINANCE

Life is thus "compelled" to reflection in the sense of repetition. Life *needs* to repeat itself. What is at stake is clearly stated: it is a matter for Heidegger of a "derivation of the phenomenological interpretation out of the facticity of life itself" (PIA, 66), that is, out of the compulsion to philosophize. Philosophy (that is first and foremost a philosophizing) arises out of the need for philosophy. This compulsion, Heidegger specifies, is not an "unwarranted forcing," "capriciously or for the sake of acquiring a novel sphere of knowledge," nor the "violence and arbitrariness of a rootless, foreign, or ordering systematization"; nor is it based on some "brooding" on universal validity. No: the compulsion or *need* for philosophy "is demanded by factical life itself, still in privation" (PIA, 66). What privation? What lack? What need? How does need, and here the need for philosophy, manifest what Heidegger calls "ruinance" and privation?

Heidegger clarifies that to live essentially means "to care": "In unrestrained rapture, in indifference, in stagnation—here, as everywhere, 'to live' means to care" (PIA, 68). Caring is for and about something, living from something and caring for it. In its broadest sense, to care is to care for one's daily bread. Heidegger names this phenomenon "privation," defining it as being both the relational and intrinsic basic mode and sense of the being of life. This reveals that life includes a radical lack and deficiency, that indeed neediness is the fundamental character of life. This lack is not a temporary situation, and even less an accident, but rather the most proper movement of life. Lack is *the* state of factical life, its essential movement, which explains why it cannot even be identified in any determinable way: "In ruinance, as a basic movedness of caring, what becomes validated is the fact that somehow or other something is constantly lacking in factical life itself and indeed in such a way that at the same time there is also lacking a determination of that which properly is lacking" (PIA, 115). In a sense, such poverty is life's own motion and possibility. Life's movedness (which Heidegger calls "collapse," *der Sturtz*), is a movement which "by itself forms itself—and yet not by itself but by the emptiness in which it moves; its emptiness is its possibility of movement" (PIA, 98). *Life comes out of a "not,"* if it is the case that "this 'not' resides in the very structure of facticity" (PIA, 120). He proposes to call this phenomenon "ruinance (*ruina*—collapse)" (PIA, 98). Further, he explains that ruinance can be characterized as thus: "the movedness of factical life which 'actualizes itself' and 'is' factical life *in* itself, *as* itself, *for* itself, *out* of itself, and, in all this, *against* itself" (PIA, 98).

This "going against itself" reveals why Heidegger does not, and cannot, equate life and its caring with the struggle for existence, as some commentators imprudently assert. He actually says so explicitly in the 1921–22 course, emphasizing that "[c]aring is not a factually occurring *struggle for existence*" (PIA, 100). This is the case because, if life is indeed a struggle, it is fundamentally a struggle *with and against itself*, a movement that goes against itself! Let us simply think here of Heidegger's understanding of the meaning of being as "at issue" in Dasein: it is at issue, that is, is in contention, a site of struggle and war, as Heidegger would specify in *Introduction to Metaphysics*. No social Darwinism here; rather, life is at war *with itself*, an essential *polemos* that also constitutes the life of thought. One sees this phenomenon in the notion of a difficulty of life. With respect to such difficulty, Heidegger stresses the following: "A characteristic of the being of factical life is that it finds itself hard to bear. The most unmistakable manifestation of this is the fact that factical life has the tendency to make itself easy for itself. In finding itself hard to bear, life *is* difficult in accord with the basic sense of its being, not in the sense of a contingent feature. If it is the case that factical life authentically is what it is in this being-hard and being-difficult, then the genuinely fitting way of gaining access to it and truly safekeeping it can only consist in making itself hard for itself" (*Supplements*, 113). In this hardness and difficulty, life is marked by an essential inner struggle, to such an extent that Heidegger states that life *is* such a struggle, unfolds as such a struggle, comes to itself in such a struggle, and *is* a struggle, then, for and with itself. The struggle defines life from within, and life can only gain access to itself from this struggle: this is why life is polemical by essence, it is at war and it is at war with itself.

Such a war begins in life's expropriation from itself. Life is indeed characterized by a constant moving away from itself (*Abfallen*), a constant fleeing from itself. Here is the way in which Heidegger presents this fleeing in the essay "Phenomenological Interpretations in connection with Aristotle": he begins by stating that what lives within the movement of caring is its "inclination" toward the world (*Supplements*, 117). This inclination takes the form, he continues, of a "propensity" to becoming absorbed in the world, and be taken along by it; a movement that is a falling away. "This propensity of the anxious concern of life is the expression of a basic factical tendency in life toward *falling away* from itself and, as included in this, *falling into* the world and itself *falling into ruin*" (*Supplements*, 117). Further, he clarifies that such a propensity "is the most profound fate that life factically has to endure within itself" (*Supplements*, 117). Heidegger speaks indeed of this falling away as "the ownmost character of movement belonging to life," and the expropriation of ruinance is thus the most "proper" movement of life (ex-appropriation, as Derrida would write). Ruinance is life going to its ruin, always going "against itself," an event of a "non-occurrence," a sort of "uneventing." Heidegger speaks of this negativity (which nonetheless happens) in this way: "the nothingness of factical life's own proper *non-occurrence of itself in ruinant existence,* a non-occurrence brought to maturation by and for factical life itself" (PIA, 110). There is therefore in this movement of falling away into ruin a tear or wound within life that tears life away from itself. In this tearing away, a sort of ecstatic happening, life is opened to its possibility and becomes an issue for itself in an originary strife with itself. That strife is the origin of what Heidegger would call the countermotion of thought, going against life's "own" tendency to fall into expropriation.

Indeed, even when life attempts to flee from itself, "even when it goes out of its way to avoid itself," it nevertheless and constantly "is anxiously concerned about its being" (*Supplements,* 113). This concern for itself, which always takes the form of a going-against itself, is the very life of thought. Thinking originates from the inner movement of life as anxious concern for itself. More precisely, it originates from a *need,* Heidegger tells us: the need for philosophy, the need to go counter to life's tendency to move away from itself. In his *Ontology; Hermeneutics of Facticity* (HF, 11), he explains that hermeneutics shows that the "object" of hermeneutics is "in need of interpretation." Life needs, he says, to be "encountered, seen, grasped, and expressed in concepts" (HF, 11). It *needs* to be made "accessible" to itself; it "needs to be made transparent" (PIA, 25), explicated, etc. And then he adds: "communicating Dasein to itself, hunting down the alienation from itself with which it is smitten" (HF, 11). We remember that Heidegger speaks of the need to bring life back from a so-called "downward fall," from the tendency to fall into decline. That tendency, he calls "ruinance," and it is therefore in this phenomenon that we are to look for the origins of philosophy. Not in wonder, as we are told in the *Theaetetus,* but in *ruinance.* Ruinance designates that movement of the expropriation that tears life apart from itself. We recall in this respect how in the 1929–30 lecture course, Heidegger defined philosophy as homesickness, exiled as it is in the "not-at-home" of expropriated existence. *Homelessness* is therefore the origin of philosophy. Thinking is brought to itself from these ruins: it runs counter to the countermovement of ruinance, thought is "a motion running counter to the falling of its care" (*Supplements,* 118). Also, in the 1921–22 winter semester course, he wrote of "the constant *struggle* of factical, philosophical interpretation *against its own factical ruinance,* a struggle that accompanies the process of the actualization of philosophizing" (PIA, 114). This is tantamount to an anxious concern of life for itself, in the sense that "when in factical life one worries about existence in this way, this is not a matter of brooding over oneself in egocentric reflection. Rather, such a worry is what it is only as a motion running counter to the tendency of life toward falling" (ibid). Life: a movement fleeing itself and falling into ruins. Thought: a movement going against life's ruinance. Thought is counter-ruinance.

Reflection, far from being some theoretical objectification, can now be further determined as re-flexion, and not simply as a repetition or as a return *to*, but rather a return *against* that very going-against-itself of life, a "counter-movement": "Phenomenological interpretation . . . manifests by its very essence a 'counter-movedness' " (PIA, 99). It is a countermovedness to the prior going against itself or "not" of life as ruinance, a counter-not responding to the first "not" of life's expropriation. There is a counterviolence of thought to the originary violence of the ruinance and self-estrangement of life, indicating the essential *polemos* of philosophy, a *polemos* that is certainly apparent in philosophical life! The violence of interpretation responds to the violence of the self-estrangement of life and goes against it. This is how Heidegger conceives of life's relation to thought and to philosophy. We could call this a logic of negation: "Here the *'counter to'* as a *'not'* attests to a primordial achievement that is constitutive on the level of being. In view of its constitutive sense, negation has an original primacy over any position-taking" (*Supplements*, 120).

CONCLUSION: THE TEAR OF LIFE

Are we to conclude that the task of philosophy is to overcome such estrangement and expropriation, that its task would be to appropriate life by reducing life's distance from itself and thereby overcome what one could call here its "tearing"? We are authorized to doubt this since ruinance is not a fall from a pure origin, and since life itself *is* in its very movement and coming forth *in ruins*. The fall of existence is its advent. *It happens as it falls. Its fall is its movement.* Heidegger is very clear on this point: the collapse of life does not "arrive" anywhere; it does not come to rest "in anything whose objective or ontological character would be different from its own" (PIA, 108). After asking: Upon what does the collapse of life crash down? He answers: it falls on itself, its fall is its advent and maturation, it is *"the nothingness of factical life"* (PIA, 108). By thinking ruinance, philosophical interpretation in fact accompanies this fall, perhaps accomplishes it as one accomplishes a negation. The going against the going against-itself of life—thinking—does not overcome ruinance but reveals it as such.

This helps us understand Heidegger's enigmatic statement in *Being and Time* that authenticity is the grasp of inauthenticity as such.

Let us open here a digression and think of Hegel and how Heidegger reads him on the "tear" and on the "need for philosophy" in *Four Seminars,* Heidegger's last seminars held in France and Germany in the late sixties and early seventies. Heidegger undertakes in the 1968 Thor seminar a close reading—line-by-line analysis—of some passages from Hegel's *Differenzschrift,* focusing on the nature of separation, division, and difference within Hegelian thought.[10] Heidegger begins by pondering this claim from Hegel that "a torn sock is better than a mended one" (FS, 11). Why is this the case, asks Heidegger, while noting the paradoxical nature of this claim, its reversal of common sense. Heidegger thus proceeds to give a phenomenological account of Hegel's notion of tear, tearing, tearing apart (*zer-reissen*).

Calling us to an exercise in "phenomenological kindergarten" (FS, 11), Heidegger analyzes: "To tear apart means: to tear into two parts, to separate: to make two out of one. If a sock is torn, then the sock is no longer present-at-hand—but note: precisely not *as* a sock. Indeed, the sock 'in a good state'; if I have it on my foot, I precisely do not grasp it *as* sock. On the contrary, if it is torn, then THE sock appears with more force through the 'sock torn into pieces.' In other words, what is lacking in the torn sock is the UNITY of the sock" (FS, 11). It then appears that the torn sock is what allows the sock to come forth as sock, in its unity of a sock, so that the tear is not the destruction of the unity, but its condition. This is why Heidegger specifies: "However, this lack is paradoxically the most positive, for this Unity in the tear is *present* [gegenwärtig] as a *lost* unity" (FS, 11). Heidegger stresses that for Hegel the tear or dichotomy" (*Entzweiung*) is the source of the *need for philosophy*. The tear remains in the work of unification—conjoining—of philosophy. "In the conjoining—insofar as it is the work of the Absolute—*the oppositions do not disappear*" (FS, 12). It is even asked whether, since "philosophy is not a piecing-together and if the tearing is necessary, *then can one speak of a unity before the tearing*?" (FS, 13).

Heidegger explains that the expression "need of philosophy" is to be taken in both senses of the genitive, as *genitivus objectivus* and *genitivus subjectivus,* with the *gentivus subjectivus* predominant. For the human being, we are told, is used/needed by being, as indicated in the verb (*Brauchen*). The human being is used in the sense that one has need of that which one uses. One could not emphasize enough the importance of such a neediness for Heidegger, which will be made to reformulate his understanding of the human being (as needed by the event of being) but also of the essence of being itself: Heidegger would go so far in the *Contributions to Philosophy* as to state that needing (*Brauchen*) constitutes what is ownmost to be-ing. Needing as essence of be-ing reveals the co-belonging between man and be-ing, and human beings stand in the open as needed: for its opening, being needs man as the there of its manifestation. Being needs humans because of a finitude of being that prevents a self-sufficiency of being: being is not without its relation to us. We are needed in this sense. But this means that the tear from which the need arises is maintained throughout, a tear or *Zug* that appropriates being and human beings. Hegel's quote, "A torn sock is better than a mended one" is an expression that Heidegger cites at different occasions[11] and that he appropriates in terms of the finitude of being and of the tear of the play between appropriation and expropriation. What is alive in life is thus the tear, the ecstatic, and philosophy is what preserves life alive in its proper unity, by keeping the tear open because the tear *is* the opening of life. This is why Heidegger concludes, "All the attempts to suppress the 'tearing' [*Zerrissenheit]* must be abandoned—insofar as the 'tearing' is what remains and must remain at the basis. Why? Answer: it is only in the tearing that the Unity, as absent, can appear." "In the tearing," Heidegger continues, "the unity, or necessary conjoining, always reigns, that is, the *living* unity" (FS, 11).

Authentic philosophizing is the grasp and explication of the inauthentic or improper movement of life, an impropriety or ruinance that is life's very movement. In that sense, we could say that thinking accomplishes the estrangement. What the self-explication of life reveals is the need for such self-explication—that is, ruinance—and nothing beyond that. Thought simply reveals the ruinance that calls for thinking. It is called by it in order to preserve it. Thought is then remembering the ruinance and tear of life, of life as tear. We are then allowed to conclude on this point: what is alive in life is the tear, and philosophy is what preserves life alive in its proper questionableness, by keeping the tear open.

NOTES

1. Martin Heidegger, *Phenomenological Interpretations of Aristotle* (Bloomington: Indiana University Press, 2001), 74. Hereafter cited as PIA, followed by pagination of the translation.

2. *Being and Time* (New York: Harper and Row, 1962), 45, my emphasis. Cited as BT, following German pagination of seventh edition in margins.

3. *Grundprobleme der Phänomenologie* (*Wintersemester* 1919/1920) (Frankfurt-am-Main: Klostermann, 1992), 162. Hereafter cited as GA 58 (volume 58 of Heidegger's *Gesamtausgabe*), followed by pagination of the translation.

4. On this question, see my chapter "The Destruction of *Vorhandenheit*," in *Heidegger and the Subject* (Amherst, NY: Humanity Books, Prometheus, 1999), 166–81.

5. One thinks here of Merleau-Ponty, on how he stresses that the lived body, the perceptual world, is the origin of thought, and how this engaged him to recognize that if the lived body is indeed the origin of thought, then the task of philosophy can only be to reflect such original perception, that is, to bring into language the mute experience of the perceptual world, to make the implicit explicit. There is therefore no independence of philosophical reflection whatsoever, no proper realm of thought either, because of this veritable chiasm between perception and philosophical reflection, each engaging the other, each encroaching over the other. Once brought back to its factical soil from which it springs, reflection loses any pretense to independence or autonomy, any pretense to an access to some idealized objective realm. We are here invited to recognize the birthplace of philosophy in facticity, in a radically nonintellectual origin. Philosophy loses, for both Heidegger and Merleau-Ponty, the illusion of being some overview of the world and of life.

6. Martin Heidegger, *Ontology. The Hermeneutics of Facticity* (Bloomington: Indiana University Press, 1999), 12. Hereafter cited as HF, followed by pagination.

7. Heidegger clearly has Husserl in mind in this critique, as when he writes: "What has always disturbed me: did intentionality come down from heaven? If it is something ultimate, in which ultimacy is it to be taken? Indeed, not secured as discoverable and experienceable in a determinate theoretical way. That I must live and 'exist' intentionally—'explain'!" PIA, 98.

8. "The grammatical categories originate, in great part, historiologically, which explains how the explication of life itself fell very early on into the hands of a determinate theoretical explication and articulation of life; cf. the development of grammar by the Greeks." PIA, 63.

9. "Phenomenological Interpretations in Connection with Aristotle," in *Supplements*, (Albany: State University of New York Press, 2002), 113.

10. *Four Seminars*, trans. Andrew Mitchell and François Raffoul (Bloomington: Indiana University Press, 2004). Hereafter cited as FS, followed by page number. Heidegger's analysis focuses on the closing paragraphs of the section entitled "The Need of Philosophy" and the opening paragraphs of the following section, "Reflection as Instrument of Philosophizing." These paragraphs read: "In the struggle of the understanding with Reason the understanding has strength only to the degree that Reason foresakes itself. Its success in the struggle therefore depends upon Reason itself, and upon the authenticity of the need for the reconstitution of the totality, the need from which Reason emerges. The need of philosophy can be called the *presupposition* of philosophy if philosophy, which begins with itself, has to be furnished with some sort of vestibule; and there has been much talk nowadays about an

absolute presupposition. What is called the presupposition of philosophy is nothing else but the need that has come to utterance. Once uttered, the need is posited for reflection, so that [because of the very nature of reflection] there must be two presuppositions.

"One is the Absolute itself. It is the goal that is being sought; but it is already present [*vorhanden*], or how otherwise could it be sought? Reason produces it, merely by freeing consciousness from its limitations. This sublation of the limitations is conditioned by the presupposed unlimitedness. The other presupposition may be taken to be that consciousness has stepped out of the totality, that is, it may be taken to be the *split* into being and not-being, concept and being, finitude and infinity. From the standpoint of the dichotomy, the absolute synthesis is a beyond, it is the undetermined and the shapeless as opposed to the determinacies of the dichotomy. The Absolute is the night, and the light is younger than it; and the distinction between them, like the emergence of the light out of the night, is an absolute difference—the nothing is the first out of which all being, all the manifoldness of the finite has emerged. The task of philosophy, however, consists in uniting these presuppositions: to posit being in non-being, as becoming; to posit dichotomy in the Absolute, as its appearance; to posit the finite in the infinite, as life. It is clumsy, however, to express the need of philosophy as a presupposition of philosophy, for the need acquires in this way a reflective form." Cited in FS (following English translation, *The Difference between Fichte's and Schelling's System of Philosophy*, State University of New York Press, 1977), 105–106, Note 49. The key here is that philosophy is based on the need for philosophy, and that in a sense it is entirely contained in such a need.

11. For instance in *What Is Called Thinking?*, trans. J. Glenn Gray (New York: Harper and Row, 1968), 89. Also: *Hegel's Concept of Experience*, (San Francisco: Harper and Row, 1970), 44.

Part II

Heidegger and the Hermeneutics of Facticity

4

The Passion of Facticity

GIORGIO AGAMBEN

THE ABSENT "MOOD" (*STIMMUNG*)

It has often been observed that the problem of love is absent from Heidegger's thought. In *Being and Time*, which contains ample treatments of fear, anxiety, and *Stimmungen* in general, love is mentioned only once, in a note referring to Pascal and Augustine. Thus W. Koepps[1] in 1928, and Ludwig Binswanger,[2] in 1942, reproached Heidegger for not having included love in his analytic of Dasein, which is founded solely on "care" (*Sorge*); and in a *Notiz* that is undoubtedly hostile, Karl Jaspers wrote that Heidegger's philosophy is "without love, hence also unworthy of love in its style."[3]

Such critiques, as Karl Löwith has remarked,[4] remain fruitless as long as they do not succeed in replacing Heidegger's analytic with an analytic centered on love. Nevertheless, Heidegger's silence—or apparent silence—on love remains problematic. We know that between 1923 and 1926, while Heidegger was preparing his greatest work, he was involved in a passionate relationship with Hannah Arendt, who was at this time his student in Marburg. Even if the letters and poems in the *Deutsches Literaturarchiv* in Marbach that bear witness to this relationship are not yet accessible, we know from Hannah Arendt, herself that, twenty years after the end of their relationship, Heidegger stated that it had been "the passion of his life" (*dies nun einmal die Passion des Lebens gewesen sei*) and that *Being and Time* had thus been composed under the sign of love.[5]

How, then, is it possible to explain the absence of love from the analytic of Dasein? It is all the more perplexing if one considers that on Hannah Arendt's part, the relationship produced precisely a book on love. I am referring to her *Doktordissertation* (published in 1929), *The Concept of Love in St. Augustine*, in which it is not difficult to discern

Heidegger's influence. Why does *Being and Time* remain so obstinately silent on the subject of love?

Let us closely examine: the note on love in *Being and Time*. It is to be found in §29, which is dedicated to the analysis of "state-of-mind" (*Befindlichkeit*) and "moods" (*Stimmungen*). The note does not contain even one word by Heidegger; it is composed solely of two citations. The first is from Pascal: "And thence it comes about that in the case where we are speaking of human things, it is said to be necessary to know them before we love them, and this has become a proverb; but the saints, on the contrary, when they speak of divine things, say that we must love them before we know them, and that we enter into truth only by charity; they have made of this one of their most useful maxims." The second is from Augustine: "One does not enter into truth except though charity" (*Non intramur in veritatem, nisi per charitatem*).[6] The two citations suggest a kind of ontological primacy of love as access to truth.

Thanks to the publication of Heidegger's last Marburg lectures from the summer semester of 1928, we know that the reference to this fundamental role of love originated in conversations with Max Scheler on the problem of intentionality. "Scheler first made it clear," Heidegger writes, "especially in the essay '*Liebe und Erkenntnis*,' that intentional relations are quite diverse, and that even, for example, love and hatred ground knowing [*Lieben und Haß das Erkennen fundieren*]. Here Scheler picks up a theme of Pascal and Augustine."[7] In both the essay cited by Heidegger and a text of the same time published posthumously under the title *Ordo amoris*, Scheler repeatedly insists on the preeminent status of love. "Before he is an *ens cogitans* or an *ens volans*," we read in *Ordo amoris* "man is an *ens amans*." Heidegger was thus perfectly conscious of the fundamental importance of love, in the sense that it conditions precisely the possibility of knowledge and the access to truth.

On the other hand, in the lectures of the 1928 summer course, love is referred to in the context of a discussion of the problem of intentionality in which Heidegger criticizes the established notion of intentionality as a cognitive relation between a subject and object. This text is precious since it demonstrates how Heidegger, through a critique that does not spare his teacher, Husserl, overcame the notion of intentionality and arrived at the structure of transcendence that *Being and Time* calls Being-in-the-world.

For Heidegger, what remains unexplained in the conception of intentionality as a relation between a subject and an object is precisely what is in need of explanation, that is, the relation itself:

> The vagueness of the relation falls back on the vagueness of that which stands in relation. . . . The most recent attempts conceive the subject-object relation as a "being relation," [*Seinsbeziehung*]. . . . Nothing is gained by the phrase "being relation," as long as it is not stated what sort of being is meant, and as long as there is vagueness about the sort of being [*Seinsart*] of the beings between which this relation is supposed to obtain. . . . Being, even with Nicolai Hartmann and Max Scheler, is taken to mean being-on-hand [*Vorhandensein*]. This relation is not nothing, but it is still not being as something on hand. . . . One of the main preparatory tasks of *Being and Time* is to bring this "relation" radically to light in its primordial essence and to do so with full intent.[8]

For Heidegger, the subject-object relation is less original than the self-transcendence of Being-in-the-world by which Dasein opens itself to the world before all knowledge and subjectivity. Before the constitution of anything like a subject or an object, Dasein—according to one of the central theses of *Being and Time*—is already open to the world: "[K]nowing is grounded beforehand in a Being-already-alongside-the-world [*Schon-Sein-bei-der-Welt*]."[9] And only on the basis of this original transcendence can something like intentionality be understood in its own mode of Being.

If Heidegger therefore does not thematically treat the problem of love, although recognizing its fundamental status, it is precisely because the mode of Being of an opening that is more original than all, knowledge (and that takes place, according to Scheler and Augustine, in love) is, in a certain sense, the central problem of *Being and Time*. On the other hand, if it is to be understood on the basis of this opening, love can no longer be conceived as it is commonly represented, that is, as a relation between a subject and an object or as a relation between two subjects. It must, instead, find its place and proper articulation in the Being-already-in-the-world that characterizes Dasein's transcendence.

But what is the mode of Being of this Being-already-in-the-world? In what sense is Dasein always already in the world and surrounded by things before even knowing them? How is it possible for Dasein to open itself to something without thereby making it into the objective correlate of a knowing subject? And how can the intentional relation itself be brought to light in its specific mode of Being and its primacy with respect to subject and object? It is in this context that Heidegger introduces his notion of "facticity" (*Faktizität*).

FACTICITY AND DASEIN

The most important contribution made by the publication, which has barely begun, of Heidegger's lecture courses from the early 1920s consists in decisively showing the centrality of the notions of facticity and factical life (*faktisches Leben*) in the development of Heidegger's thought. The abandonment of the notion of intentionality (and of the concept of subject that was its correlate) was made possible by the establishment of this category. The path taken here was the following: intentionality-facticity-Dasein. One of the future tasks of Heideggerian philology will no doubt be to make this passage explicit and to determine its genealogy (as well as to explain the progressive eclipse of the concept of facticity in Heidegger's later thought). The observations that follow are only a first contribution in this direction.

First of all, it must be said that Heidegger's first students and friends long ago emphasized the importance of the concept of facticity in the formation of Heidegger's thought. As early as 1927, in a work that appeared as the second half of the *Jahrbuch für Philosophie und Phänomenologische Forschung* in which the first edition of *Being and Time* was published, the mathematician and philosopher Oskar Becker wrote, "Heidegger gives the name of ontology to the hermeneutics of facticity, that is, the interpretation of human Dasein."[10] Becker is referring here to the title of Heidegger's 1923 summer semester course held in Freiburg, "Ontology, or Hermeneutics of Facticity."[11] What does this title mean? In what sense is ontology, the doctrine of Being, a doctrine of facticity?

The references to Husserl and Sartre that one finds in philosophical dictionaries under the heading "Facticity" are misleading here, for Heidegger's use of the term is fundamentally different from theirs. Heidegger distinguishes Dasein's *Faktizität* from *Tatsächlichkeit*, the simple factuality of intraworldly beings. At the start of his *Ideas*, Husserl defines the *Tatsächlichkeit* of the objects of experience. These objects, Husserl writes, appear as things found at determinate points in space and time that possess a certain content of reality but that, considered in their essence, could also be elsewhere and otherwise. Husserl thus insists on contingency (*Zufälligkeit*) as an essential characteristic of factuality. For Heidegger, by contrast, the proper trait of facticity is not *Zufälligkeit* but *Verfallenheit*. Everything is complicated, in Heidegger, by the fact that Dasein is not simply, as in Sartre, thrown into the "there" of a given contingency; instead, Dasein must rather itself be its "there," be the "there" (*Da*) of Being. Once again, the difference in modes of Being is decisive here.

The origin of the Heideggerian use of the term *facticity* is most likely to be found not in Husserl but in Augustine, who writes that *facticia est anima,*[12] "the human soul is *facticia,*" in the sense that it was "made" by God. In Latin, *facticius* is opposed to *nativus*; it means *qui non sponte fit,* what is not natural, what did not come into Being by itself ("what is made by hand and not by nature," as one finds in the dictionaries). The term must be understood in all its force, for it is the same adjective that Augustine uses to designate pagan idols, in a sense that seems to correspond perfectly to our term *fetish*: *genus facticiorum deorum,* the nature of "factical" gods.

If one wants to understand the development of the concept of facticity in Heidegger's thought, one should not forget this origin of the word, which ties it to the semantic sphere of non-originarity and making. What is important here is that for Heidegger, this experience of facticity, of a constitutive non-originarity, is precisely the original experience of philosophy, the only legitimate point of departure for thinking.

One of the first appearances of this meaning of the term *faktisch* is to be found (as far as one can judge from the present state of Heidegger's *Gesamtausgabe*) in the 1921 summer course on Augustine and Neoplatonism, which Otto Pöggeler and Oskar Becker have summarized.[13] Here Heidegger seeks to show that primitive Christian faith (as opposed to Neoplatonic metaphysics, which conceives of Being as a *stets Vorhandenes* and considers *fruitio dei,*[14] consequently, to be the rapture of an eternal presence) was an experience of life in its facticity and essential restlessness (*Unruhe*). As an example of this "factical experience of life" (*faktische Lebenserfahrung*), Heidegger analyzes a passage from chapter 23 of Book 10 of the *Confessions,* where Augustine questions man's relation to truth:

> I have known many men who wished to deceive, but none who wished to be deceived. . . . Because they hate to be deceived themselves, but are glad if they can deceive others, they love the truth when it reveals itself but hate it when it reveals them [*cum se ipsa indicat . . . cum eos ipsos indicat*]. They reap their just reward, for those who do not wish to stand condemned by the truth find themselves unmasked against their will and also find that truth is veiled for them. This is precisely the behaviour of the human heart. In its blind inertia, in its abject shame, it loves to lie concealed, yet it wishes that nothing should be concealed from it [*latere vult se autem ut lateat aliquid non vult*]. Its reward is just the opposite of its desire, for it cannot conceal itself from the truth, but truth remains hidden in it [*ipse non lateat veritatem, ipsum autem veritas lateat*].[15]

What interests Heidegger here as a mark of factical experience is this dialectic of concealment and unconcealment, this double movement by which whoever wants to know everything while remaining concealed in knowledge is known by a knowledge that is concealed from him. Facticity is the condition of what remains concealed in its opening, of what is exposed by its very retreat. From the beginning, facticity is thus characterized by the same co-belonging of concealment and unconcealment that, for Heidegger, marks the experience of the truth of Being.

The same movement, the same restlessness of facticity was at the center of Heidegger's lectures for the Freiburg winter course of 1921–22, which bore the title "Phenomenological Interpretations of Aristotle." This course was to a large degree dedicated to the analysis of what Heidegger later called "factical life" (*das faktische Leben*), which still later would become Dasein. In the lectures Heidegger begins by describing the original and irreducible character of facticity for thought:

> [The determinations of factical life] are not indifferent qualities that can be harmlessly established, as when I say, "this thing is red." They are alive in facticity, that is, they enclose factical possibilities of which they can never be freed—never, thank God [*God sei Dank nie*]. As a consequence, to the degree that it is authentic, a philosophical interpretation directed toward what is most important [*die Hauptsache*] in philosophy, facticity, is itself factical; and it is factical in such a way that, as philosophico-factical, it radically gives itself possibilities of decision and thus itself. But it can do so only if it exists, in the guise of its Dasein [*wenn sie da ist—in der Weise ihres Daseins*].[16]

Far from signifying the immobility of a factual situation (as in Sartre or Husserl), facticity designates the "character of Being" (*Seinscharakter*) and "e-motion" (*Bewegtheit*) proper to life. The analysis Heidegger sketches here constitutes a kind of prehistory of the analytic of Dasein[17] and the self-transcendence of Being-in-the-world, whose fundamental determinations are all to be found here under different names. For factical life is never in the world as a simple object: "[T]he e-motion [of factical life] is such that, as movement, it gives itself, in itself, to itself; it is the e-motion of factical life that constitutes factical life, such that factical life, insofar as it lives in the world, does not properly speaking produce its movement but, rather, lives in the world as the in-which [*worin*], the of-which [*worauf*] and the for-which [*wofür*] of life."[18]

Heidegger calls the "fundamental movement" (*Grundbewegung*) of facticity *Ruinanz* (from the Latin *ruina*, "tumbling," "fall"). This is the first appearance of the concept that will become *die Verfallenheit*, "falling," in *Being and Time*. *Ruinanz* presents the same intertwining of the proper and the improper, the *spontaneous* and the *facticious*, as the "thrownness" (*Geworfenheit*) of Dasein: "a movement that produces itself and that, nevertheless, does not produce itself, producing the emptiness in which it moves; for its emptiness is the possibility of movement."[19] And Heidegger likens facticity, insofar as it expresses the fundamental structure of life, to Aristotle's concept of *kinēsis*.[20]

What had not yet found definite expression in the courses at the start of the 1920s takes on, in *Being and Time*, the theoretical form that has become familiar to us today. Heidegger introduces the concept of facticity as early as §12, when he defines the "basic constitution" (*Grundverfassrung*) of Dasein. To situate this concept correctly, one must, above all, place it in the context of a distinction between modes of Being. Being-in-the-world, Heidegger says, is not the property of a "present-at-hand" being (*ein Vorhandenes*) such as, for example, a corporeal thing (*Körperding*) that is in another thing of the same mode, like water in a glass or clothes in a wardrobe. Instead, Being-in-the-world expresses the very structure of Dasein; it concerns an "existential" and not a "categorial." Two worldless (*weltlose*) beings can certainly be beside each other (one thus says, for example, that the chair is near the wall), and we can even say that one touches the other. But to speak of touching in the proper sense of the word, for the chair, to be truly near the wall (in the sense of Being-already-alongside-the-world), the chair would have to be able to encounter the wall.

How do matters stand with Dasein, who is not "worldless"? It is important to grasp the conceptual difficulty at issue here. It goes without saying that if Dasein were simply an intraworldly being, it could encounter neither the being it is nor other beings. On the other hand, however, if Dasein were deprived of all factuality, how could it encounter anything? To be near beings, to have a world, Dasein must so to speak be a "fact" (*Faktum*) without being factual (*Vorhandenes*); it must both be a "fact" (*Faktum*) and have a world. It is here that Heidegger introduces the notion of facticity:

> Dasein itself . . . [is] present-at-hand "in" the world, or, more exactly, *can* with some right and within certain limits be *taken* as merely present-at-hand. To do this, one must completely disregard or just not see the existential state of Being-in [*In-Sein*]. This latter kind of presence-at-hand becomes accessible not by disregarding Dasein's

> specific structures but only by understanding them in advance. Dasein understands its ownmost Being in the sense of a certain "factual Being-present-at-hand" [*tatsächlichen Vorhandenseins*]. And yet the factuality [*Tatsächlichkeit*] of the fact [*Tatsache*] of one's own Dasein is at bottom quite different ontologically from the factual occurrence of some kind of mineral, for example. Whenever Dasein is, it is as a Fact; and the factuality of such a Fact is what we shall call Dasein's *facticity*. This is a definite way of Being [*Seinsbestimmtheit*], and it has a complicated structure which cannot even be grasped *as a problem* until Dasein's basic existential states have been worked out. The concept of "facticity" implies that an entity "within-the-world" has Being-in-the-world in such a way that it can understand itself as bound up in its "destiny" with the Being of those entities which it encounters within its own world.[21]

As far as form is concerned, facticity presents us with the paradox of an existential that is also a categorial and a "fact" (*Faktum*) that is not factual. Neither "present-at-hand" (*vorhanden*) nor "ready-to-hand" (*zuhanden*), neither pure presence nor object of use, facticity is a specific mode of Being, one whose conceptualization marks Heidegger's reformulation of the question of Being in an essential manner. It should not be forgotten that this reformulation is above all a new articulation of the modes of Being.

The clearest presentation of the characteristics of facticity is to be found in §29 of *Being and Time*, which is devoted to the analysis of "state-of-mind" (*Befindlichkeit*) and "moods" (*Stimmungen*). An opening that precedes all knowledge and all lived experience (*Erlebnis*) takes place in the "state-of-mind" *die primäre Entdeckung der Welt*; "the original disclosure of the world." But what characterizes this disclosure is not the full light of the origin but precisely irreducible facticity and opacity. Through its "moods," Dasein is brought before other beings and, above all, before what it itself is; but since it does not bring itself there by itself, it is irremediably delivered over to what already confronts it and gazes upon it as an inexorable enigma:

> In having a mood, Dasein is always disclosed moodwise as that entity to which it has been delivered over, in its Being; and in this way it has been delivered over to the Being which, in existing, it has to be. "To be disclosed" does not mean "to be known as this sort of thing." . . . The pure "that it is" shows itself, but the "whence" and the "whither" remain is darkness. . . . This characteristic of Dasein's Being—this "that it is"—is veiled in its "whence" and "whither," yet disclosed in itself all the more unveiledly; we

> call it the "thrownness" of this entity into its "there." The expression "thrownness" is meant to suggest the *facticity of its being delivered over. . . . Facticity is not the factuality of the* factum brutum *of something present-at-hand, but a characteristic of Dasein's Being—one which has been taken up into existence, even if proximally it has been thrust aside [abgedrängt].*[22]

Let us pause to consider the traits of this facticity, this factical being-thrown (we have seen that Heidegger leads "thrownness" back to facticity). Its origin and characteristic structure as a category organizing the analytic of Dasein have rarely been considered.

The first trait of facticity is *die ausweichende Abkehr*, "evasive turningaway." Dasein's openness delivers it over to something that it cannot escape but that nevertheless eludes it and remains inaccessible to it in its constant distraction: "[T]he first essential characteristic of states-of-mind [is] that *they disclose Dasein in its thrownness, and—proximally and for the most part—in the manner of an evasive turning-away.*"[23]

A kind of original-repression thus belongs to this character of Dasein's Being. The term Heidegger uses, "repressed" (*abgedrängt*), designates something that has been displaced, pushed back, but not completely effaced, something that remains present in the form of its retreat, as in Freudian "repression" (*Verdrängung*).[24] But Heidegger expresses the most essential trait of facticity, the trait from which all others derive, in a form that has many variations, even though it remains constant in its conceptual core: "Dasein is delivered over to the being that it is and must be," "Dasein is and must be its own 'there,' " "Dasein is each time its possibility," "Dasein is the being whose Being is at issue for it in its very Being." What do these formulas mean as expressions of facticity?

Heidegger's 1928 Marburg summer semester lectures (which often contain invaluable commentaries on certain crucial passages in *Being and Time*) explain the matter in absolutely unambiguous terms: "By it [the term *Dasein*] we designate the being for which its own proper mode of Being in a definite sense is not indifferent" [*Dasein*] *bedeutet das Seiende, dem seine eigene Weise zu sein in einem bestimmten Sinne ungleichgültig ist.*)[25]

Dasein must be its way of Being, its manner, its "guise," we could say, using a word that corresponds etymologically and semantically to the German *Weise*.[26] We must reflect on this paradoxical formulation, which for Heidegger marks the original experience of Being, without which both the repetition of the "question of Being" (*Seinsfrage*) and the relation between essence and existence sketched in §9 of *Being and Time* remain absolutely unintelligible. Here the two fundamental determinations of classical ontology—*existentia* and *essentia, quod est* and *quid est, Daßsein* and *Wassein*—are abbreviated into a constellation charged with tension. For Dasein (insofar as it is and must be its own "there"), existence and essence, "Being" and "Being such," *on* and *poion* are as inseparable as they are for the soul in Plato's Seventh Letter (343 b–c).

> *The "essence" of Dasein lies in its existence.* The characteristics that can be exhibited in this entity are not, therefore, present-at-hand "properties" of some present-at-hand entity with particular properties; they are in each case possible ways for it, to be, and no more than that. All the Being-as-it-is [*So-sein*] which this entity possesses is primarily Being.[27]

"All the Being-as-it-is [*So-sein*] which this entity possesses is primarily Being": one must think here not so much of the definition of the ontological status of God (*Deus est suum esse,* "God is his Being")[28] as of Schelling's positive philosophy and his concept of *das Seyende-Sein,* "being Being," where the verb *to be* also has a transitive sense; Dasein must be its being-such, it must "existentiate" its essence and "essentialize" its existence.[29]

As a "character of Being" (*Seinscharakter*), facticity thus expresses Dasein's original ontological character. If Heidegger can simultaneously pose the question of the meaning of Being anew and distance himself from ontology, it is because the Being at issue in *Being and Time* has the character of facticity from the beginning. This is why for Dasein, quality, *Sosein,* is not a "property" but solely a "possible guise" (*mögliche Weise*) to be (a formula that must be heard in accordance with the same ontological contraction that is expressed in Nicholas of Cusa's *possest*). Original opening is produced in this factical movement, in which Dasein must be its *Weise,* its fashion of Being, and in which Being and its guise are both distinguishable and the same. The term *fashion* must he heard here in its etymological sense (from *factio, facere*) and in the sense that the word has in Old French: "face," like the English "face." Dasein is factical, since it must be its face, its fashion, its manner—at once what reveals it and that into which it is irreparably thrown.

It is here that one must see the root of *ausweichende Abkehr,* "evasive turning-away," and of the impropriety constitutive of Dasein. It is because it must be its guise that Dasein remains disguised—hidden away in what opens it, concealed in what exposes it, and darkened by its own light. Such is the factical dimension of this "lighting" (*Lichtung*), which is truly something like a *lucus a non lucendo*.[30]

Here it is possible to see the full sense in which Heidegger's ontology is a hermeneutics of facticity. Facticity is not added to Dasein; it is inscribed in its very structure of Being. Here we are in the presence of something that could be defined, with an oxymoron, as "original facticity" or *Urfaktizität*. And it is precisely such an "original facticity" that the 1928 summer lectures call *transzendentale Zerstreuung*, "transcendental distraction, dispersion, or dissemination," or *ursprüngliche Streuung*, "original dispersion." I do not want to dwell on these passages, which have already been analyzed by Jacques Derrida.[31] It suffices to recall that here Heidegger sketches the figure of an original facticity that constitutes *die innere Möglichkeit für die faktische Zerstreuung in die Leiblichkeit und damit in die Geschlechtlichkeit* ("the intrinsic possibility for being factically, dispersed into bodiliness and thus into sexuality").[32]

FACTICITY AND FETISHISM

How are we to understand this original facticity? Is *Weise* something like a mask that Dasein must assume? Is it here that a Heideggerian ethics finds its proper place?

Here the terms *factical* and *facticity* show their pertinence. The German adjective *faktisch*, like the French *factice*, appeared relatively late in the European lexicon: the German in the second half of the eighteenth century, the French a little earlier. But both terms are, in fact, erudite forms, based on the Latin, which hark back to ancient linguistic history. Thirteenth-century French, in accordance with its phonological laws, thus formed a number of terms on the basis of the Latin *faticius*, such as the adjective *faitis* (or *faitiche*, *fetiz*) and the noun *faitisseté*. At the same time, German, perhaps by borrowing the French term, formed the adjective *feit*. *Faitis*, like its German counterpart, *feit*, simply means "beautiful, pretty." In particular, it is used in conformity with its etymological origin to designate that which, in a human body, seems made by design, fashioned with skill, made-for, and which thereby attracts desire and love.[33] It is as if the Being-such of a being, its guise or manner, were separated from it in a kind of paradoxical self-transcendence. It is in the context of this semantic history that one must situate the appearance of the term *fetish* (in German, *Fetisch*). Dictionaries inform us that the term entered into European languages in the late seventeenth century by means of the Portuguese *feitiçio*. But the word is in fact morphologically identical to the French *faitis*, which, through the borrowing from the Portuguese, is thus in some way resurrected.

An analysis of the term's meaning in its Freudian and Marxian senses is particularly instructive from this point of view. Let us recall that for Marx, the fetish character of the commodity, what makes it inappropriable, consists not in its artificial character but rather in the fact that in it a product of human labor is given both a use value and an exchange value. In the same way, for Freud, the fetish is not an inauthentic object. Instead, it is both the presence of something and the sign of its absence; it is and is not an object. And it is as such that it irresistibly attracts desire without ever being able to satisfy it.

One could say that in this sense the structure of Dasein is marked by a kind of original fetishism, *Urfetischismus*[34] or *Urfaktizität*, on account of which Dasein cannot ever appropriate the being it is, the being to which it is irreparably consigned. Neither something "present-at-hand" (*Vorhandenes*) nor something "ready-to-hand" (*Zuhandenes*), neither exchange value nor use value, Being—which must be its manners of Being—exists in facticity. But for this very reason, its "guises" (*Weisen*) are not simulacra that it could, as a free subject, assume or not assume. From the beginning, they belong to its existence and originally constitute its *ēthos*.[35]

THE PROPER AND THE IMPROPER

This is the perspective from which we must read the unresolved dialectic of *eigentlich* and *uneigentlich*, the proper and the improper, to which Heidegger devotes some of the most beautiful pages of *Being and Time*. We know that Heidegger always specified that the words *eigentlich* and *uneigentlich* are to be heard in the etymological sense of "proper" and "improper." On account of its facticity, Dasein's opening is marked by an original impropriety; it is constitutively divided into "propriety" (*Eigentlichkeit*) and "impropriety" (*Uneigentlichkeit*). Heidegger often emphasizes that the dimension of impropriety and everydayness of the "They" (*das Man*) is not something derivative into which Dasein would fall by accident; on the contrary, impropriety is as originary as propriety. Heidegger obstinately reaffirms the original character of this cobelonging: "*Because Dasein is essentially falling, its state of Being is such that it is in 'un-truth.'*"[36]

At times, Heidegger seems to retreat from the radicality of this thesis, fighting against himself to maintain a primacy of the proper and the true. But an attentive analysis shows not only that the co-originarity of the proper and the improper is never disavowed, but even that several passages could be said to imply a primacy of the improper. Whenever *Being and Time* seeks to seize hold of the experience of the proper (as, for example, in proper Being-toward-death), it does so solely by means of an analysis of impropriety (for example, factical Being-toward-death). The factical link between these two dimensions of Dasein is so intimate and original that Heidegger writes, "*[A]uthentic* existence is not something which floats above falling everydayness; existentially, it is only a modified way in which such everydayness is seized upon."[37] And on the subject of proper decision, he states, "[R]esoluteness appropriates untruth authentically."[38]

Authentic existence has no content other than inauthentic existence; the proper is nothing other than the apprehension of the improper. We must reflect on the inevitable character of the improper that is implied in these formulations. Even in proper Being-toward-death and proper decision, Dasein seizes hold of its impropriety alone, mastering an alienation and becoming attentive to a distraction. Such is the originary status of facticity. But what does it mean to seize hold of impropriety? How is it possible to appropriate untruth properly? If one does not reflect on these questions and merely attributes to Heidegger a simple primacy of the proper, one will not only fail to understand the deepest intention of the analytic of Dasein; one will equally bar access to the thought of the *Ereignis*, which constitutes the key word of Heidegger's later thought and which has its "original history" (*Urgeschichte*), in Benjamin's sense of the term, in the dialectic of the proper and the improper.

THEORY OF PASSIONS

Let us now return, after this long detour, to the problem of love that was our point of departure. An attentive analysis shows that the statement that Heidegger's thought is "without love" (*ohne Liebe*) is not only inexact from a philosophical point of view but also imprecise on the philological level. Several texts could be invoked here. I would like to pause to consider the two, that strike me as the most important.

Almost ten years after the end of his relationship with Hannah Arendt, in the 1936 lecture course on Nietzsche entitled "The Will to Power as Art," Heidegger thematically treated the problem of love in several very dense pages in which he sketched an altogether singular theory of the passions. He begins by withdrawing passions from the domain of psychology by defining them as "the basic modes that constitute Dasein . . . the ways man confronts the *Da*, the openness and concealment of beings, in which he stands."[39] Immediately afterward, he clearly distinguishes love and hate from other feelings, positing them as passions (*Leidenschaften*) as opposed to simple affects (*Affekte*). While affects such as anger and joy are born and die away in us spontaneously, love and hate, as passions, are always already present and traverse our Being from the beginning. This is why we speak of "nurturing hatred" but not of "nurturing anger" (*ein Zorn wird genährt*).[40] We must cite at least the decisive passage on passion:

> Because hate traverses [*durchzieht*] our Being more originally, it has a cohesive power; like love, hate brings an original closure [*eine ursprüngliche Geschlossenheit*] and perdurance to our essential Being. . . . But the persistent closure that comes to Dasein through hate does not close it off and bind it. Rather, it grants vision and premeditation. The angry man loses the power of reflection. He who hates intensifies reflection and rumination to the point of "hardboiled" malice. Hate is never blind; it is perspicacious. Only anger is blind. Love is never blind: it is perspicacious. Only infatuation [*Verliebtheit*] is blind, fickle, and susceptible—an affect; not a passion [*ein Affekt, keine Leidenschaft*]. To passion belongs a reaching out and opening up of oneself [*das weit Ausgreifende, sich Öffnende*]. Such reaching out occurs even in hate, since the hated one is pursued everywhere relentlessly. But such reaching out [*Ausgriff*] in passion does not simply lift us up and away beyond ourselves. It gathers our essential Being to its proper ground [*auf seinem eigentlichen Grund*], it exposes our ground for the first time in so gathering, so that the passion is that through which and in which we take hold of ourselves [*in uns selbst Fuß fassen*] and achieve lucid mastery of the beings around us and within us [*hellsichtig des Seiende um uns und in uns mächtig werden*].[41]

Hatred and love are thus the two *Grundweisen*, the two fundamental guises or manners, through which Dasein experiences the *Da*, the opening and retreat of the being that it is and must be. In love and hate, as opposed to affects (which are blind to the very thing they reveal and which, like *Stimmungen*, are only uncovered in distraction), man establishes himself more deeply in that into which he is thrown, appropriating his very facticity and thus gathering together and opening his own ground. It is therefore not an accident that hatred, with its "original closure," is given a primordial rank alongside love (like evil in Heidegger's course on Schelling and fury [*das Grimmige*] in his "Letter on Humanism"): the dimension at issue here is the original opening of Dasein, in which "there come[s] from Being itself the assignment [*Zuweisung*] of those directions [*Weisungen*] that must become law and rule for man."[42]

POTENTIA PASSIVA

This original status of love (more precisely, of passion) is reaffirmed in a passage in the "Letter on Humanism" whose importance here cannot be overestimated. In this text, "to love" (*lieben*) is likened to *mögen* (which means both "to want" and "to be able"), and *mögen* is identified with Being in a context in which the category of potentiality-possibility is considered in an entirely new fashion:

> To embrace a "thing" or a "person" in its essence means to love it [*sie lieben*], to favor it [*sie mögen*]. Thought in a more originary way, such favoring [*mögen*] means to bestow essence as a gift. Such favoring is the proper essence of enabling [*Vermögen*], which not only can achieve this or that but also can let something essentially unfold [*wesen*] in its provenance, that is, let it be. It is on the "strength" [*kraft*] of such enabling by favoring that something is properly able to be. This enabling is what is properly "possible" [*das eigentlich "Mögliche"*], that whose essence resides in favoring. . . . Being is the enabling-favoring, the "may be." As the element, Being is the "quiet power" of the favoring-enabling, that is, of the possible. Of course, our words *möglich* and *Möglichkeit*, under the dominance of "logic" and "metaphysics," are thought solely in contrast to "actuality"; that is, they are thought on the basis of a definite—the metaphysical—interpretation of Being as *actus* and *potentia*, a distinction identified with the one between *existentia* and *potentia*. When I speak of the "quiet power of the possible" I do not mean the *possibile* of a merely represented *possibilitas*, nor *potentia* as the *essentia* of an *actus* of *existentia*; rather, I mean Being itself.[43]

To understand the thematic unity evoked here, it must be considered with respect to the problem of freedom as it is presented in the last pages of "On the Essence of Reasons." Once again, the dimension of facticity (better: of original or transcendental facticity) is essential: "For Dasein, to exist means to behave toward being [*Seiendes*] while situated in the midst of being [*Seiendes*]. It means to behave toward being that is not like Dasein, toward itself and toward being like itself, so that what is at issue in its situated behaving is the capacity to be

[*Seinskönnen*] of Dasein itself. The project of world outstrips the possible; the Why arises in this outstripping."[44]

Freedom thus reveals Dasein in its essence to be "capable of being, with possibilities that gape open before its finite choice, that is, in its destiny."[45] Insofar as it exists factically (that is, insofar as it must be its manners of Being), Dasein always exists in the mode of the possible: in the excess of possibilities with respect to beings and, at the same time, in a lack of possibilities with respect to them, since its possibilities appear as radical incapacities in the face of the very being to which it is always already consigned.

This co-belonging of capacity and incapacity is analyzed in a passage in the 1928 summer lecture course, which anticipates the themes of "On the Essence of Reasons" in urging the superiority of the category of the possible over the category of the real:

> Insofar . . . as freedom (taken transcendentally) constitutes the essence of Dasein, Dasein, as existing, is always, in essence, necessarily "further" than any given factical being. On the basis of this upswing, Dasein is, in each case, beyond beings, as we say, but it is beyond in such a way that it, first of all, experiences beings in their resistance, against which transcending Dasein is powerless. The powerlessness is metaphysical, i.e., to be understood as essential; it cannot be removed by reference to the conquest of nature, to technology, which rages about in the "world" today like an unshackled beast; for this domination of nature is the real proof for the metaphysical powerlessness of Dasein, which can only attain freedom in its history. . . . Only because, in our factical intentional comportment toward beings of every sort, we, outstripping in advance, return to and arrive at beings from possibilities, only for this reason can we let beings themselves be what and how they are. And the converse is true. Because Dasein, as factically existing, transcending already, in each case, encounters beings and because, with transcendence and world-entry, the powerlessness, understood metaphysically, is manifest, for this reason Dasein, which can be powerless (metaphysically) only as free, must hold itself to the condition of the possibility of powerlessness, to the freedom to ground. And it is for this reason that we essentially place every being, as being, into question regarding its ground. We inquire into the why in our comportment toward beings of every sort, because in ourselves possibility is higher than actuality, because with Dasein itself this being-higher becomes existent.[46]

The passage on *mögen* (and its relation to love) in the "Letter on Humanism" must be read in close relation to this primacy of possibility. The *potentia* at issue here is essentially *potentia passiva*, the *dynamis tou paskhein* whose secret solidarity with active potentiality (*dynamis tou poiein*) Heidegger emphasized in his 1931 lecture course on Aristotle's *Metaphysics*. All potentiality (*dynamis*), Heidegger writes in his interpretation of Aristotle, is impotentiality (*adynamia*), and all capacity (*dynamis*) is essentially passivity (*dekhesthai*).[47] But this impotentiality is the place of an original event (*Urgeschehen*) that determines Dasein's Being and opens the abyss of its freedom: "What does not stand within the power of freedom is *that* Dasein is a self by virtue of its possibility—a factical self because it is free—and *that* transcendence comes about as a primordial happening. This sort of powerlessness (thrownness) is not due to the fact that being infects Dasein; rather, it defines the very Being of Dasein as such."[48]

Passion, *potentia passiva*, is therefore the most radical experience of possibility at issue in Dasein: a capacity that is capable not only of *potentiality* (the manners of Being that are in fact possible) but also, and above all, of impotentiality. This is why for Dasein, the experience of freedom coincides with the experience of *impotentiality*, which is situated at the level of the original facticity or "original dispersion" (*ursprüngliche Streuung*), which, according to the 1928 summer course, constitutes the "inner possibility' " of Dasein's factical dispersion.

As passive potentiality and *Mögen*, passion is capable of its own impotentiality; it lets be not only the possible but also the impossible, thus gathering together Dasein in its ground, to open it and, possibly, to allow it to master what exists in it and around it. In this sense, the "immobile force of the possible" is essentially passion, passive potentiality: *mögen* (to be able) is *lieben* (to love).

But how can such mastery take place if it appropriates not a thing but simply impotentiality and impropriety? How is it possible to be capable not of possibility and potentiality but of an impossibility and impotentiality? What is freedom that is above all passion?

THE PASSION OF FACTICITY

Here the problem of love, as passion, shows its proximity to that of the *Ereignis*, which constitutes the central motif of Heidegger's thought from the 1940s onward. Love, as passion of facticity, may be what makes it possible to cast light on the concept of the Ereignis. We know that Heidegger explains the word *Ereignis* on the basis of the term *eigen* and understands it as "appropriation," situating it with respect to *Being and Time*'s dialectic of *eigentlich* and *uneigentlich*. But here it is a matter of an appropriation in which what is appropriated is neither something foreign that must become proper nor something dark that must be illuminated. What is appropriated here and brought not to light but to "lighting" (*Lichtung*) is solely an *expropriation*, an occultation as such. "Appropriation is in itself expropriation. This word contains in a manner commensurate with Appropriation the early Greek *lēthē* in the sense of concealing" (*Das Ereignis ist in ihm selbst Enteignis, in welches Wort die frühgriechische lêthê im Sinne des Verbergens ereignishaft aufgenommen ist*).[49] The thought of the *Ereignis* is thus "not an extinguishing of the oblivion of Being, but placing oneself in it and, standing within it. Thus the awakening [*erwachen*] from the oblivion of Being to the oblivion of Being is the unawakening [*entwachen*] into Appropriation."[50] What now takes place is that concealment no longer conceals itself but becomes "the attention of thinking" (*die Verbergung sich nicht verbirgt, ihr gilt vielmehr das Aufmerksam des Denkens*).[51]

What do these enigmatic sentences mean? If what human beings must appropriate here is not a hidden thing but the very fact of hiddenness, Dasein's very impropriety and facticity, then "to appropriate it" can only be *to be properly improper*, to abandon oneself to the inappropriable. Withdrawal, *lēthē*, must come to thinking as such; facticity must show itself in its concealment and opacity.

The thought of the *Ereignis*, insofar as it is the end of the history of Being, is therefore in a certain sense also a repetition and completion of the thought of facticity that, in the early Heidegger, marked the reformulation of the "question of Being" (*Seinsfrage*). Here it is an issue not simply of the many manners (*Weisen*) of Dasein's factical existence but of the original facticity (or transcendental dispersion) that constitutes its "inner possibility" (*innere Möglichkeit*). The *Mögen* of this *Möglichkeit* is neither potentiality nor actuality, neither essence nor existence; it is, rather, an impotentiality whose passion, in freedom, opens the ground of Dasein. In the *Ereignis*, original facticity no longer retreats, either in distracted dispersion or historical destiny, but is instead appropriated in its very distraction and borne in its *lēthē*.

The dialectic of the proper and the improper thus reaches its end. Dasein no longer has to be its own *Da* and no longer has to be its own *Weisen*: by now, it definitively inhabits them in the mode of the "dwelling" (*Wohnen*) that in §12 of *Being and Time* characterized Dasein's Being-in (*In-Sein*).

In the word *Ereignis*, we should therefore hear the Latin *assuescere*, "accustoming," on the condition of thinking the "suus" in this term, the "self" (*se*) that constitutes its core. And if one remembers that the origin of Dasein's destinal character was (according to §9 of *Being and*

Time) its "having to be," it is also possible to understand why the *Ereignis* is without destiny, *geschickslos*. Here Being (the possible) has truly exhausted its historical possibilities, and Dasein, who is capable of its own incapacity, attains its own extreme manner: the *immobile* force of the possible.

This does not mean that all facticity is abolished and that all e-motion is effaced. "The lack of destiny of Appropriation does not mean that it has no 'e-motion' [*Bewegtheit*]. Rather, it means that the manner of movement most proper to Appropriation, turning toward us in withdrawal [*Zuwendung in Entzug*], first shows itself as what is to be thought."[52] This is the sense of the *Gelassenheit*, the "abandonment," that a late text defines as *die Offenheit für das Geheimnis*, "the openness to the mystery":[53] *Gelassenheit* is the e-motion of the *Ereignis*, the eternally nonepochal opening to the "ancient something [*Uralte*] which conceals itself in the word *a-lētheia*."[54]

We may now approach a provisional definition of love. What man introduces into the world, his "proper," is not simply the light and opening of knowledge but above all the opening to concealment and opacity. *Alētheia*, truth, is the safeguard of *lēthē*, nontruth; memory, the safeguard of oblivion; light, the safeguard of darkness. It is only in the insistence of this abandonment, in this safeguarding, which is forgetful of everything, that something like knowledge and attention can become possible.

Love suffers all of this (in the etymological sense of the word passion, *pati, paskhein*). Love is the *passion of facticity* in which man bears this nonbelonging and darkness, appropriating (*adsuefacit*) them while guarding them as such. Love is thus not, as the dialectic of desire suggests, the affirmation of the self in the negation of the loved object; it is, instead, the passion and exposition of facticity itself and of the irreducible impropriety of beings. *In love, the lover and the beloved come to light in their concealment, in an eternal facticity beyond Being*. (This is perhaps what Hannah Arendt means when, in a text written with her first husband in 1930, she cites Rilke, saying that love "is the possibility for each to veil his destiny to the other.")

Just as in *Ereignis*, the appropriation of the improper signifies the end both of the history of Being and of the history of epochal sendings, so in love the dialectic of the proper and the improper reaches its end. This, finally, is why there is no sense in distinguishing between authentic love and inauthentic love, heavenly love and *pandemios* love, the love of God and self-love. Lovers bear the impropriety of love to the end so that the proper can emerge as the appropriation of the free incapacity that passion brings to its end. Lovers go to the limit of the improper in a mad and demonic promiscuity; they dwell in carnality and amorous discourse, in forever-new regions of impropriety and facticity, to the point of revealing their essential abyss. Human beings do not originally dwell in the proper; yet they do not (according to the facile suggestion of contemporary nihilism) inhabit the improper and the ungrounded. Rather, *human beings are those who fall properly in love with the improper, who—unique among living beings—are capable of their own incapacity.*

This is why if it is true that, according to Jean-Luc Nancy's beautiful phrase, love is that of which we are not masters, that which we never reach but which is always happening to us, it is also true that man can appropriate this incapacity and that, to cite Hölderlin's words to Casimir Ulrich Böhlendorff, *der freie Gebrauch des Eigenen das Schwerste ist*, the free use of the proper is the most difficult task.

NOTES

1. W. Koepps, *Merimna und Agape, Seeberg Festschrift* (1929).
2. Ludwig Binswanger, *Grundformen und Erkenntnis menschlichen Daseins* (Zurich: M. Niehans, 1942).
3. Karl Jaspers, *Notizen zu Martin Heidegger* (Munich: Piper, 1978), 34.
4. Karl Löwith, "Phänomenologische Ontologie and protestantische Theologie," in *Heidegger: Perspektiven zur Deutung seines Werkes*, ed. Otto Pöggeler (Köln: Kiepenheuer und Witsch, 1970), 76.
5. See Elisabeth Young-Bruehl, Hannah Arendt: *For the Love of the World* (New Haven: Yale University Press, 1984), 247.
6. Martin Heidegger, *Being and Time*, trans. John Macquarrie and Edward Robinson (New York: Harper and Row, 1962), 492; the original is in Martin Heidegger, *Sein und Zeit* (Tübingen: Niemeyer, 1928), 139.
7. Martin Heidegger, *The Metaphysical Foundations of Logic*, trans. Michael Heim (Bloomington: Indiana University Press, 1984), 134; the original is in Martin Heidegger, *Gesamtausgabe*, vol. 26: *Metaphysische Anfangsgründe der Logik im Ausgang von Leibniz* (Frankfurt am Main: Klostermann, 1978), 169.
8. Ibid., English 13.0–31; original 163–64.
9. Heidegger, *Being and Time*, 88; original in Heidegger, *Sein und Zeit*, 61.
10. Oskar Becker, "Mathematische Existenz, Untersuchung zur Logik und Ontologie mathematischer Phänomene," *Jahrbuch für Philosophie und Phänomenologische Forschung* 7 (1927): 621.
11. In Heidegger's *Gesamtausgabe* (vol. 63), the title of the course appears as "*Ontologie: Phänomenologische Hermeneutik der Faktizität*." According to the note on p. 72 of *Sein und Zeit* (*Being and Time*, 490), Heidegger was already concerned with "the hermeneutics of facticity" in his 1919–20 winter semester lectures.
12. See the entry under *facticius* in the *Thesaurus linguae latinae* and the entry under *factio* in Ernout-Meiffet's etymological dictionary.

13. Otto Pöggeler, *Der Denkweg Martin Heideggers* (Pfullingen: Neske, 1963), 36–45. See also Oskar Becker, *Dasein und Dawesen* (Pfullingen: Neske, 1963), and K. Lehmann, "Christliche Geschichtserfahrung und ontologische Frage beim jungen Heidegger," in *Heidegger: Perspektiven*, ed. Pöggeler, 140–68. [Since the first publication of the present essay, Heidegger's 1921 lecture course has been published in Heidegger, *Gesamtausgabe*, vol. 60: *Phänomenologie des religiösen Lebens* (Frankfurt am Main: Klostermann, 1995), 160–299, under the title "Augustinus and der Neuplatonismus."—Tr.]

14. The Augustinian opposition between *uti* (using something with a view to other ends) and *frui* (enjoying something for itself) is important for the prehistory of the distinction between *Vorhandenheit*, "present-at-handness," and *Zuhandenheit*, "ready-to-handness," in Heidegger's *Being and Time*. As we will see, Dasein's facticity is opposed both to *Vorhandenheit* and to *Zuhandenheit* and therefore cannot properly speaking be the object of either a *frui* or an *uti*.

15. Saint Augustine, *Confessions*, trans. R. S. Pine-Coffin (London: Penguin Books, 1961), 229–30.

16. Martin Heidegger, *Gesamtausgabe*, vol. 61: *Phänomenologische Interpretationen zu Aristoteles: Einführung in die phänomenologische Forschung* (Frankfurt am Main: Klostermann, 1985), 99.

17. See the observations in H. Tietjen, "Philosophic und Faktizität," *Heidegger Studies* 2 (1986).

18. Heidegger, *Phänomenologische Interpretationen zu Aristoteles*, 130.

19. Ibid., 131.

20. Heidegger, "Problem der Faktizität—'kinesis'-Problem" (Problem of facticity, *kinesis*-problem), ibid., 117. If one recalls the fundamental role that *kinesis*, according to Heidegger, played in Aristotle's thought (in his seminars at Le Thor, Heidegger still spoke of *kinesis* as the fundamental experience of Aristotle's thought), one can also evaluate the central place of facticity in the thought of the early Heidegger.

21. Heidegger, *Being and Time*, 82; original in Heidegger, *Sein und Zeit*, 55–56.

22. Ibid., English 174; original 134–46.

23. Ibid., English 175; original 136.

24. The analogy is, of course, purely formal. But the fact that Heideggerian ontology coincides with the territory of psychology is important for its position in the history of the "question of Being" (*Seinsfrage*).

25. Heidegger, *Metaphysical Foundations of Logic*, 136; original in Heidegger, *Metaphysische Anfangsgründe der Logik*, 171.

26. The word *Weise* (which derives from the same root as the German *wissen* and the Latin *videre*) must be considered as a *terminus technicus* of Heidegger's thought. In his 1921–22 winter lectures, Heidegger plays on all the possible meanings of the verb *weisen* and its derivations: "Leben bekommt jeweils eine Grundweisung und es wächst in eine solche hinein. . . . Bezugssinn je in einer Weise ist in sich ein Weisen und hat in sich eine Weisung, die das Leben sich gibt; die es erfährt: Unterweisung." Heidegger, *Phänomenologische Interpretationen zu Aristoteles*, 98.

27. Heidegger, *Being and Time*, 67; original in Heidegger, *Sein und Zeit*, 42.

28. In the "Letter on Humanism," Heidegger explicitly refutes this interpretation of the *essentia/existentia* relation: "It would be the ultimate error if one wished to explain the sentence about man's ek-sistent essence as if it were the secularized transference to human beings of a thought that Christian theology expresses about God (*Deus est suum esse*); for ek-sistence is not the realization of an essence nor does ek-sistence itself even effect and posit what is essential" (in Martin Heidegger, *Basic Writings*, ed. David Farrell Krell [New York: Harper San Francisco, 1977], 207; the original is in Martin Heidegger, *Gesamtausgabe*, vol. 9: *Wegmarken* [Frankfurt am Main: Klostermann, 1976], 158–59). Another passage in the same text shows that the relation between existence and essence remained a fundamental question in Heidegger's thought even after *Being and Time*. "In *Being and Time* no statement about the relation of *essentia* and *existentia* can yet be expressed since there it is still a question of preparing something precursory" (*Basic Writings*, 209; original in *Wegmarken*, 329).

29. A genealogy of the contraction of *essentia* and *existentia* effected by Heidegger would show that this relation has often been conceived in the history of philosophy as something far more complex than a simple opposition. Without discussing Plato (who in the Seventh Letter explicitly states that *on* and *poion* are indissociable), we may consider Aristotle's *ti en einai* from the same perspective. Moreover, the notion of Stoic substance, *idios poion*, implies precisely the paradox of a "being-such" (*poion*) that would be proper. Victor Goldschmidt thus shows that the "manners of Being" (*pos ekhein*) do not constitute an extrinsic determination of substance but instead reveal substance and exemplify it (they "do its gymnastics," according to Epictetus's beautiful image). The relation between Spinoza's definition of *causa sui* (*cuius essentia involvit existentiam*) and Heidegger's determination of Dasein (*das Wesen des Daseins liegt in seiner Existenz*) remains to be considered.

30. The observation is L. Amoroso's; see his "La *Lichtung* di Heidegger come lucus a non lucendo," in *Il pensiero debole*, ed. Gianni Vattimo and Pier Aldo Rovatti (Milan: Feltrinelli, 1983), 137–63.

31. See Jacques Derrida, "Geschlecht," in *Martin Heidegger: Cahiers de l'Herne* (Paris: Éditions de l'Herne, 1983), 571–96.

32. Heidegger, *Metaphysical Foundations of Logic*, 137; original in Heidegger, *Metaphysische Anfangsgründe der Logik*, 173. In the same text, Heidegger relates Dasein's facticity to its spatiality (*Räumlichkeit*). If one considers that the word *Streuung* derives from the same root as the Latin *sternere* (*stratum*), which refers to extension and horizontality, it is possible to see, in this *ursprüngliche Streuung* one of the reasons for the irreducibility of Dasein's spatiality to its temporality, which is affirmed at the end of "Zeit und Sein" ("On Time and Being").

33. One thus reads "Faitisse estoit et avenante / je ne sais femme plus plaisante," in the *Romance of the Rose*; "voiz comme elles se chaucent bien et faitissement," in Jean de Meun; "votre gens corps votre beauté faictisse," in Baudes; "ils ont doubt regard et beaulté / et jeunesse et faitischeté," in Gaces.

But the true meaning of the word *faitis* can best be seen in Villon's text, in which he writes, "Hanches charnues, / eslevées, propres, faictisses / a tenir amoureuses lisses."

34. The word *Urfetischismus* is obviously to be taken in an ontological, and not a psychological, sense. It is because facticity originally belongs to Dasein that it can encounter something like a fetish in the strict sense of the term. On the status of the fetish in §17 of *Being and Time*, see Werner Hamacher's important observations in "Peut-être la question," in *Les fins de l'homme: A partir du travail de Jacques Derrida* (Paris: Galilee, 1981), 353–54.

35. "Dasein exists factically. We shall inquire whether existentiality and facticity have an ontological unity, or whether facticity belongs essentially to existentiality" (Heidegger, *Being and Time*, 225); "Das Dasein existiert faktisch. Gefragt wird nach der ontologischen Einheit von Existentialität und Faktizität, bzw. der wesenhaften Zugehörigkeit dieser zu jener" (Heidegger, *Sein und Zeit*, 181).

36. Ibid., English 264; original 222.

37. Ibid., English 224; original 179.

38. Ibid., English 345; original 299.

39. Martin Heidegger, *Nietzsche: The Will to Power as Art*, trans. David Farrell Krell, 45; the original is in Martin Heidegger, *Nietzsche*, vol. I (Pfullingen: Neske, 1961), 55.

40. Ibid., English 47; original 58.

41. Ibid., English 47–48; original 58–59.

42. Heidegger, *Basic Writings*, 238; original in *Wegmarken*, 360–61.

43. Ibid., English 196; original 316–17.

44. Martin Heidegger, *The Essence of Reasons* (Evanston: Northwestern University Press, 1969), 115; original in *Wegmarken*, 168–69.

45. Ibid., English 129; original 174.

46. Heidegger, *Metaphysical Foundations of Logic*, 215–16; original in Heidegger, *Metaphysische Anfangsgründe der Logik*, 279–80.

47. Martin Heidegger, *Aristotle's Metaphysics Omega 1–3*, trans. Walter Brogan and Peter Warnek (Bloomington: Indiana University Press, 1995), 94; the original is in Martin Heidegger, *Gesamtausgabe*, vol. 33: *Aristoteles; Metaphysik Theta 1–3: Vom Wesen und Wirklichkeit der Kraft* (Frankfurt am Main: Klostermann, 1981), 114.

48. Heidegger, *Essence of Reasons*, 129–31; original in Heidegger, *Wegmarken*, 175.

49. Martin Heidegger, *On Time and Being*, trans. Joan Stambaugh (New York: Harper and Row, 1972), 41; the original is in Martin Heidegger, *Zur Sache des Denkens* (Tübingen: Niemeyer, 1969), 44.

50. Ibid., English 30; original 32. The thought expressed here is so disconcerting that the English, French, and Italian translators did not want to admit what is, nevertheless, clear: namely, that the word *entwachen* in this context cannot mean the same thing as *erwachen*. In this passage, Heidegger establishes an opposition that is perfectly symmetrical with that between *Enteignis* and *Ereignis*.

51. Ibid., English 41; original 44.

52. Ibid.

53. Martin Heidegger, *Discourse on Thinking*, trans. John N. Anderson and E. Hans Freund (New York: Harper and Row, 1966), 56; the original is in Martin Heidegger, *Gelassenheit* (Pfullingen: Neske,1959), 24.

54. Heidegger, *On Time and Being*, 24; original in Heidegger, *Zur Sache des Denkens*, 25.

5

The Being-with of the Being-There

JEAN-LUC NANCY

With this admittedly baroque title, I would like to identify the following problem: Heidegger's Dasein, which French readers know as *l'être-là* (being-there), includes in its definition the constitutive or originary property of "being-with" (*Mitsein*). More precisely, Heidegger also introduces the term Dasein-with (*Mitdasein*). This latter term certainly does not resonate for anyone who is not already familiar with *Being and Time*, and the former even less. In fact, although duly attested to and repeated in this work, neither of these concepts belongs to the ordinarily accepted "idea" of its "system" or its "economy" (in contrast to, not only Dasein, but also "care," "anxiety," "world," or "being-toward-death"). This is not accidental: it is due to the text itself. Despite the presence of these terms, the text does not devote extensive analyses to them—far from it—that would be comparable to those addressed to the major concepts. And, nevertheless, *Mitsein* and *Mitdasein* are presented as equiprimordial to the essence of Dasein, that is to say, to its character as a being in which being is not an ontological ground but a putting into play of its own meaning of being as the proper meaning of being. Being-with, and more precisely, Dasein-with, form an essential condition for the essence of Dasein. How? This is not easy to uncover because of the limits of the analysis presented by the text (in addition, Heidegger's later work does not offer any further advances, even if it does not completely neglect the motif in question). Why this point of resistance and relative obscurity? Why doesn't the analytic of Dasein offer an access to one of its essential dimensions in an express and developed manner?

No doubt my question itself should first be refined and unfolded because it engages nothing less than an attentive rereading of the entire work, which could indeed lead to a complete reformulation of its stakes, namely, the "meaning of Being." But for the moment I would like in these pages to give the outline of a future analysis. I will do so as economically as possible without going into the detail of the text. It seems desirable to me to first identify the principle of a subsequent commentary.

DASEIN

Dasein is characterized by the fact that its proper being in its very being is an issue for it. Or, for Dasein, to *be* means to have its being at issue for it, exposing it to having "to be" and not to becoming what it is, since, it "is" its "to be," or its *"ex-being"*, its "being-outside-of-itself" (*son "à-être" ou son "ex-être," son être-hors-de-soi*). It does not have to become (*à devenir*) but to come to be (*à advenir*) in the very act of taking the responsibility for an essential non-essence whose meaning is the being-ahead-of-itself, the being-exposed, and hence at issue. This is Dasein's property insofar as it is da-sein, being-the-there (*être-le-là*): it is, or rather, it has to be the "there" of an opening, that is to say, of a proper way ("each time its own") (*"chaque fois sienne"*) of letting oneself be or of deciding one's being according to the very ex-position that forms as well its proper being-in-the-world. To let/to decide: two sides, two possibilities or two aspects of the same exposition. It has to be the singular "there" of a proper manner of world forming (*faire monde*), that is, to form and/or to open onto a totality of meaning. The *Da* of *sein* constitutes its exposition.

One can thus say that Dasein is a singular, unique possibility of forming/letting a proper meaning of the world, and/or the world of a proper meaning open. The essential character of this meaning ultimately entails its own suppression. Death, the cessation of the "there," is also a there that no longer opens onto anything, if not onto its own abyss. To take on this horizon that precisely is not a horizon, this finite *horos* of an *infinite apeiron*, such are the stakes in what is at issue (*l'enjeu de l'enjeu*). This means, in brief, to appropriate (*faire mien*) that which cannot be appropriated, or, to let oneself be disappropriated at and from the height of mineness (an inverse version of Hegelian death).

MITSEIN AND THE PROBLEM

Furthermore, Dasein is essentially *Mitdasein*. From the outset *Mitsein* is essential for it: a being-with which is not a collection of things but an essential with.[1]

This draws our attention to the problem that we want to address. I would characterize this problem from the outset in broad strokes. Heidegger consistently maintained this essential character of the *with* and the first characteristic of his intent is the refusal to understand the simple "with" as a collection of simply contiguous things. Its ultimate characteristic, as we will see, will be the introduction of the category of the *people* through which Dasein's possibility of being historical will crystallize. Now, we know well that this motif of the people will lead later to involvement with Nazism. And it is moreover around this motif that he pursued, after 1933, an intense debate with Nazism, which he condemned, but insistently referred to a deeper thinking of the people and of history: the *Beiträge* and the courses of the same years testify to this.

Where, how, and why does the dangerously decisive moment occur? This question I also want to indicate straightaway did not concern Heidegger alone. Far from it. It concerns the whole of Western thought in its manner of grasping or failing to grasp in general what Heidegger first revealed: the essential character of the existential *with* (that is to say, of the *with* as a condition of the possibility of human existence—if not the very existence of all beings, something I cannot address here). We could rephrase it in the following way: *Being and Time* shows how coexistence forms an *experimentum crucis* of our thinking.

OF THE COMMON

Let us return to the problematic of *Mitdasein*. It is noteworthy that Heidegger does not develop an analysis that would seem necessary, namely, an analysis of the way several Dasein are able to be the *there together*. The question could be posed in the most elementary way: What *there* would there be for several Dasein? A common there, or perhaps it would a there for each? In the latter case, how would several Dasein be brought together?

How is *Mitdasein* possible and how can it be represented? As a being-with of several Dasein, where each opens its own *there* on its own account? Or, as a being-with-the-there, or perhaps more clearly, as a being-the-there-with, which would imply that the openings, as it were, intersect, cross, mix, and let their properties interact, yet without conflating them into one unique Dasein (in which case the *with* would be lost)? Or, in a third sense, as a common relation to a there which would be beyond the singularities (but what would such a *there-beyond* mean)?

We have, then, basically, three possible modes of the "common": the common daily interactions (common as ordinary, vulgar), the common as a sharing of properties (relations, interactions, blendings), and the common as a proper agency in itself, hence communal or collective.

In other words, there are two extreme poles, pure exteriority and pure interiority, while between the two another regime that is difficult to identify is suggested. But it is necessary to note immediately that the two extreme regimes are a priori at least capable of escaping the essential character of the *with*: the first seems to fall back into the mere contiguity of things, while the second seems to assume, as Dasein, a community that would lie beyond singularities. It is in fact this twofold possibility that is mobilized in *Being and Time*, precisely to the extent that the intermediary regime remains undeveloped in the work and would remain so throughout Heidegger's work.

When I employ the term *regime* I also want to stress its political connotation. The first regime corresponds to democracy, at least in the way Heidegger and others from his time understood it. The second regime corresponds to that which impends in the same epoch, and moves more or less visibly toward a form of "totalitarianism." With this comment I want to emphasize that the political is a result of, and not a cause of, a fundamental disposition of thought or of civilization in the age of its "discontent." One must not forget that the discontent was as *common* to that epoch as it is to ours.

It is true—to make a general remark about the rest of Heidegger's work—that after *Being and Time* most of the motifs of the "existential analytic" are absent and that Heidegger wished to make a turn that was decisive for the fundamental disposition of his thinking (no longer proceeding from man to being but from being to man). But it is all the more striking to note the latent and at times explicit presence of the motif of the "people" in the rest of his work (for example, in the "foundations" evoked in particular in the *Origin of the Work of Art*, or in Hölderlin and in his thematics of language and poetry—subtended by the idea stated in the *Beiträge* that "the people is a voice"). In a symmetrical manner, one could easily show that the theme of the common/vulgar permeates or impregnates—without being newly thematized in the name of the "they"—many of the analyses on technology (but not all, a fact that would merit further development).

THE UNTHOUGHT

It is therefore all the more striking that a specific interrogation of what was at stake with the terms of *Mitdasein* and Being-with-others

(*Miteinandersein*) has never been attempted, given that the *with* was declared essential to the very essence of the existent (nothing in the later work allows us to believe it was forgotten or minimized: Heidegger never ceased to think in a collective or communal dimension and nothing in his work even approaches solipsism).

Some will say on this point, "That's exactly where the problem lies!" They will say that Heidegger has always been a communitarian or communalist thinker in the hyper-national or hyper-heroic style that Lacoue-Labarthe calls "arch-fascism" and in which the individual counts for nothing except to be subsumed under the Gest (*la Geste*) and the Legend of a common foundation and inauguration, that is, under the greatness of destiny and of civilization.

That is true, but it is no less true that no other thought has penetrated farther into the enigma of *being-with,* and that in Heidegger's time as well as today no object of thought has been more neglected than this enigma (this is enigmatic precisely because thinking has kept it at a distance for so long).

In our time—at least for the last twenty years—the decline of the political as well as the resurgences of various communitarianisms testify to the presence of an unthought in this register. This lack, no doubt, speaks volumes about a fundamental disposition of our entire tradition: between the two subjects—on the one hand "the person" and on the other hand "the community"—there is no place for the "with," nor more generally for what would not be a "subject" (in the sense of self-constitution) without for that matter being a mere thing (in the sense of things simply posited side by side, a meaning of the *with* that Heidegger specifically wants to avoid).

This is why I want to return, albeit schematically, to the economy of *Being and Time* to examine the manner in which, between the *"they"* and the *"people,"* the *with* has been hidden, lost or repressed.

COLLABORATION OR CO-PROPRIATION

Let us begin with the *they*. The *they* constitutes the improper (*uneigentlich,* too often translated as "inauthentic") mode of being-with: *common* existence in the sense of the "ordinary." In this type of existence, the *They* behaves like everyone and effaces and levels down value distinctions (nobility, greatness). It is not necessary to say more about this well-known description.

Rather, it is necessary to emphasize the following: while the proper (*eigentlich*) modalities of Dasein are analyzed early on in the work, the proper mode of being-with, in contrast, had to wait until much later (fifty paragraphs later) to be discussed in the context of historicity and historicality. The *they* is not historical and consequently, since it merely concerns the *everyday*, everydayness lacks historicity, which will only be addressed much later.

But then, in order to posit itself, historicity must break from everydayness. The difficulty of recognizing everyday existence—which is also the difficulty of recognizing that the each day can involve the each time mine (*je-mein*) of Dasein—constitutes an essential resistance, a veritable guiding thread of the entire tradition. How can the ordinary be raised to have meaning, value, or truth? And how can one take on a meaning, a value, or a truth that would not include the ordinary? This *double bind* has never been so apparent as in Heidegger's work, even if he does not confront it as such. He declares, nevertheless, in several instances, that the proper does not detach from the improper but consists in a modified grasp of the very world of the improper.[2]

Nevertheless, we are given an indication that points toward what is proper to being-with. In paragraph 26 the mode of relation specific to the *with* is analyzed: "caring for " or "solicitude" (*Fürsorge*). "Caring for" is distinguished from "to make use of," which forms the mode of relation with non-Dasein entities. (Let us note that, on the one hand, the separation between human entities and other entities remains as clear-cut and impermeable as in any other classical thinking, and, on the other hand, the relation to "nature" remains treated in a manner that is allusive and elusive. This twofold remark will eventually have consequences for our current topic: that is, for that which engages the *with* straightaway in a distinction that I will deem ontologically lofty from the supposed simple and dull coexistence of things. But this is not the place to develop this aspect.)

There are two positive species of "caring for" (the negative species, those of the refusal or the rejection of the other, only confirm the following: even in the negative mode the *with* is affirmed as essential. Heidegger clarifies that solitude and isolation are both modes of the *with*). The first species consists of caring for, in the sense of taking *the place* of the other, and relieving him or her of the burden of care. This assistance relieves the other of his or her own care: it is *disappropriative.* (As has been often noted, "welfare work" is here among others the target of Heidegger's critique, which corresponds already to a certain political tonality.)

The second species, on the contrary, involves returning the other to its own proper care: that is, to the logic of its own being as a decision for existence, that decision being a decision for the proper engagement of the meaning of being. (We can here make an analogy—

which can at least be helpful and suggest other directions of thought: between the two kinds of solicitude, the difference resembles the distinction between psychological therapy and a psychoanalytic relation, particularly such as conceived by Lacan.)

How one can orient oneself toward decision and toward the opening of the other—toward, when all is said and done, its *there*—in order to "return him or her to it," is not clearly established. Nor is it established how it is possible that the proper is returned to the proper from an exteriority. It must be possible, and, in the terms already posed, a regime of nonexteriority between the existents (and not simply between entities) must be necessary. The *with*, understood in terms of existence, must therefore be elaborated as a quite particular space—the word *space* being understood here both in the literal sense, since the existents are also bodies, extended beings, and in a figurative sense, which would answer the question: "What takes place *between us*?"(However, how can we differentiate between the literal and figurative meaning?: that would be a supplementary question that would compound the problematic of the proper. For the moment it will be set aside.)

The question of the "between us"—which would be in fact the question of the "between," according to which there can be a "we"—would present itself in terms of the two possibilities given by Heidegger's text: on the one hand, a common occupation defined by an external task (making substitution possible), on the other hand "a common engagement for the same thing" (*Sicheinsetzen für dieselbe Sache*), which would take place on the basis of each proper existent. On the one hand, the *with* remains in exteriority—itself *common* in two senses of the word—and on the other hand, it is transformed into the commonality of a relation to a unique thing or cause. On the one hand, mere cooperation, on the other hand, *co-propriation*. On the one hand, occupation, on the other hand, preoccupation: this also amounts to saying that genuinely concernful "caring for," only happens in the second case.

But how can *co-propriation* occur? We are not told. We know only that it must involve a common thing or cause.

FROM DEATH TO DESTINY

Before we learn much later that this thing-and-cause is none other than that of the people as a common or co-destiny, we will have to go through the central and most celebrated part of the work, the long path of the analytic of the existent in terms of care, concern, anxiety, decision, and the exposure of its being to its own being at issue. In the end, as we know, the issue is the putting into play of the proper itself in its ultimate possibility, which happens as the impossibility of positing this proper, of ceasing to expose or appropriate it. Death brings the abandonment of any position of a proper meaning of being (one could even say, of a *meaning* in general) and represents the freeing of the improper will for such a meaning.

This death is different from *perishing*: the latter, by itself, is only the common fate of the cessation of life. But death offers the supreme possibility: that of maintaining the exposure of the existent right up to its own extinction. For that very reason, it is strictly proper, and no one can substitute for my death. Here, "caring for" reaches its limit. Or rather, we discern better how the height of concern for the other consists in returning him or her to his or her own death. In a way that, itself, is also not made explicit (and not even evoked), it would be a question of properly designating to the other its most proper and inalienable property of dying.

To decide oneself for freedom, or, to be properly delivered over to the freedom of being "toward" death (*zum Tode*), thus understood as essential finitude—that is, as an infinity of exposure—is the meaning of the putting into play of the meaning of being that the existent *is*, and that it is each time properly for itself in a singular way that cannot be shared. My death is that for which no one else can substitute his or her care. The other can only care to return me to my care: but once again, the nature of such an operation is not presented explicitly. Whatever the case may be, the outcome is the same: absolute solitude in death. In this sense, there is an essential limitation to the principle of the essentiality of the *with*. However, Heidegger never states this in these terms.

We are told later in paragraph 74 that the existent, according to this rigorous isolation of its death, has not yet attained the level of its *destiny*, and similarly—in a parallel and corollary sense—it still has not partaken of a *being-there-with* in any way "properly" speaking. On the contrary, the freeing for death proper takes place on the basis of the constantly improper being-with. *One commonly* perishes, whereas *I* die alone. If nothing of death is shared, everything remains around it in exteriority (in the same way that the corpse returns to being a material object among other things).

But it is different if one achieves (if one is capable of achieving . . . —but nothing is said of such a capacity) the height and the intensity of destiny. *Destiny* means a sending toward, a destination for certain possibilities that are no longer concerned with the supreme possibility of the existent alone, but through which a *history* occurs (*Geschick, Geschichte*). A history, that is, a non-ordinary event.

CAN THE THEY BECOME THE PEOPLE?

How does the They accede to the dimension of destiny? Through essential being-with. Only the existent who is exposed to the blows of fate (*Schicksal* and not *Geschick*) can assuredly welcome in its decision of existence the whims of fate. The existent can make its being "transparent" therein, that is, let its being-decided play through this contingency. It is then said to be fateful (*schicksalhaft*). That does still not endow it with a destiny. One can say that it is susceptible to having a destiny without yet being destined or destinal. Heidegger writes in §74: "But if fateful Dasein, as Being-in-the-world, exists essentially in Being-with-Others its historicizing [*Geschehen*, also a word for event] is a co-historicizing [*Mitgeschehen*], and is determinative for it as *destiny* [*Geschick*]"(BT, 436). In the case of the essential *with*, the event is transformed from mere fate into a destinal event. And it is precisely the dimension of the essential *with* that makes possible, indeed, effectuates this transformation.

Heidegger continues: "This is how we designate the historicizing of the community, of the people. Destiny is not something that puts itself together out of individual fates, any more than Being-with-one-another can be conceived as the occurring together of several Subjects" (Ibid). (Reference is made in a footnote to §26 where the principle of the essential *with* as distinct from juxtaposition was posited.)

There is thus no transition from the *they* to the people, except that at the same time the *they* and the *people* appear very clearly as two poles of being-with, that is, the improper and the proper. From the one to the other, then, there is no passage and there is nothing which allows us to understand the modality of a "modified grasp" of the improper *with* by the proper *with*.

The *they* remains improper because it is in pure exteriority and each one remains there delivered over to or open to its singular fate, unique as proper death, and banal as the common cessation of life. The *people* is proper because in it, or as it, the *with* is prior as the *common* of a *community*. In either case there is a transcendental priority of the proper or the improper. Consequently, the community of the people offers a priori "determinate possibilities," which are not the possibility of proper death as impossibility. Although these possibilities of the people—that is, the people as possibility—are neither specified nor represented, they are nonetheless clarified sufficiently "in communicating and in struggling": it is a common cause for which there is a reason to fight, which supposes that the people becomes itself above all in conflict with other people.[3]

In a surprising way in the context of *Being and Time*, yet in a very classical manner (Fichtean or Hegelian, for example), common destiny alone sanctions, in truth, the fate of each one, or more precisely the meaning of that fate. The *common fate* of death disappears twice, as it were: first as a banal demise that remains external in relation to the abandonment to the supreme possibility of existence, and a second time according to the sublimation of individual death brought about by *common destiny*.

In both cases, the *with* has preceded any individuality and succeeds it. But in one case it precedes and succeeds as a mutual anonymity and indifference of all juxtaposed existents, while in the other case it precedes and succeeds as a community endowed with its own destinal possibilities. In the end, there are two constitutions of the being-there-with: an impossible one, in the crowd where the very essentiality of the *with* dissolves; and a hyper-possible in the people where the essentiality of the *with* is determined and made possible. From one to the other there does not seem to be any passage (*one* hardly sees it, and neither *I* nor *we* can find it).

BETWEEN THE PROPER AND THE IMPROPER

Between the two, there is nothing less than the *being-the there-with*, which has been overlooked. In fact, *Mitdasein* should determine the *with* as proximity (contiguity and distinction) of the multiple *there*, therefore suggesting the following: multiplicity is not an extrinsic attribute of Dasein, since the concept of the *there* implies the impossibility of a unique and exclusive there. A *there* can only be exclusive—for it is necessarily so insofar as it is "mine"—if it also involves the inclusion of multiple other *there*. The analogical model here should be understood according to Leibniz's *Monadology*, or according to one of the topological schemas initiated by the Möbius strip, and in which the concept of "proximity" (*voisinage*) present in the topology proposes a suggestive metaphorical connection between mathematics and the ontology of the *with*.

The intertwining of the limit and of the continuity between the several *theres* must determine proximity not as pure juxtaposition but as *composition* in a precise sense, which must rest on a rigorous construction of the *com-* . This is nothing other than what is made necessary by Heidegger's insistence on the character of a *with* that cannot be reduced to an exteriority. For the *being-with-the-there* there must be contact, thus also contagion and encroachment, however minimal, and even an infinitesimal derivation of the tangent between the openings in question. There must be a relative indistinction of the edges of the opening, and at least a tangential intersection of their aims or horizons. *I* can only open myself *there* by also opening onto other *theres*, as one says that a door opens onto a *garden*. The *with* must compose the nature of the "onto," the "against" (as in "stuck against"), and the "trans," (as in "transsexual"). (This also means that the *with* is itself endowed with a complex, com-posed and inter-twined nature.)

But if such is the case, then neither the *they* alone nor the *people* alone can meet this condition. The condition in question is indeed the existential condition of a being-with, which is not secondary in the constitution of existence, but truly and essentially co-originary in the existent.

As much as Heidegger felt the necessity of the primordiality of the *with* with particular acuity (he was no doubt the first to see this point so clearly since the relation between consciousnesses constitutive of the Hegelian subject), he also himself suppressed the possibility that he opened, that of thinking the *with* exactly as he indicated: neither external nor internal; neither masses nor subject; neither anonymous nor "mine"; neither improper nor proper. The limit, the impasse or the failure are thus inscribed quite precisely at the place of and owing to the very opening of the text of *Being and Time*.

. . . AND THE SHARING OF DEATH

The death to which Heidegger subjected the being-there, or the existent, has also been surreptitiously suppressed or sublated. That is to say, to a certain extent in spite of himself, he has sublimated, sublated, and heroicized in destiny the infinity of the end or the absolute finitude that "death signifies"—or rather *de-signifies* (*in-signifie*). In an unexpected way, "being-toward-death" is *destined* to the extent that the essential *with*, understood in its proper sense as *community* and not as the improper *they*, leads, carries, and lifts each existent up to a historical possibility that confers a kind of supra-existence on it—a supra-existence certainly concealed as such in the text, but which it inevitably follows from the opposition between the historicality of the community and the improper history of everydayness.

This supra-existence—which I designate in this way by analogy with the supra-essence of the God of negative theology—can be seen in §75, where Heidegger undertakes to oppose the immediate nature of "Resoluteness"—in which the veritable "loyalty of existence to its own Self" takes place—to the duration and connectedness in the order of the they (to the flux of the *they*). It is not according to the time of a lived experience, but according to the moment of resoluteness, that this loyalty to the self "steadies itself" (in opposition to the inconstancy of the *they*) by making itself "a moment of vision for what is world-historical." It is in this way that the statement, resoluteness as fate "is freedom to *give up* . . . in accordance with the demands of some possible Situation," must be understood.[4] In other words, sacrifice is the last word of the encounter in the Moment of the singular being-toward-death with the common being-to-destiny. Consequently, the proper *caring-for* the other consists in its exposure or its disposition to this sacrifice. *The* sacrifice, or the dialectic, which can only be said following Bataille . . .

Much later, and after the Nazi episode, in his commentary on Hölderlin's hymn *The Rhine*, Heidegger would still speak of the community of soldiers at the front, while the theme of Dasein, and even that of *Mitdasein*, was less central. One in fact can see, in the *Beiträge*, a persistence of the first without a development of the second, while at the same time a new insistence on the people appears, which is concerned with producing an understanding of the people opposed to Nazism (in a word, the people as "voice" and not as "race"). In other words, Heidegger will have persisted—and even beyond the period of the war as I have suggested in passing—in thinking a *with*, with the same essentiality as before.

I will not go farther here in this analysis: I only wanted to reveal its principle. I want at this point to indicate another level of analysis that can be developed from there.

This other path must largely go beyond Heidegger, but nonetheless begin from him, because one must above all avoid rejecting in its entirety that which harbors within itself an intimate connection between an indispensable essentiality of the *with* and a redoubtable destinality of community. We must then pose this question: Why this leap from the *with* to the people, thus understood?

There are two possible responses:

1. This leap does not belong to Heidegger alone but to a determination that is extremely central to Western thinking, if not perhaps broader than it. The fate of an individual never suffices to make a destiny—unless tragic (or absurd, in the modern version of the tragic).

We can even advance the hypothesis that Greek tragedy responds to the effacement of destinal community (families, genealogies, people) in favor of a common destiny of humanity unknown by prior cultures. Contrary to all appearance, the individual bears the despair of Western consciousness (and it is not by chance that Western monotheism wants to save the individual by reintegrating it with a *people* of God).

But no doubt it is the destination itself that must be questioned, for even the destiny of the people, or as people, in Heidegger's work, does not offer any final destination. He does not take account of the destination of destiny, and it is the entire composition of history that is put into play. This is an old matter, as we know, begun with the rationalism of progress and then simply mirrored by the catastrophic thinking of the decline. As we know, in Heidegger's work, there is a vision of the history (of Being) that comes to an end and exhausts itself in a "final sending" destined to the ultimate "forgetting" of being, therefore of meaning, or of the meaning of its meaning. In a way, it is always—whether negatively or positively—Hegelian in the most general sense of the term.

But this means that the ahead-of-itself of the ex-istent remains to be thought in another way than as destination, that is to say, very precisely, as ex-posure, and that ex-posure itself remains to be thought as co-ex-posure: as exposure of and to the essential *with* of its co-constitution.

This indeed *remains*, as a task to which neither sacrifice, nor community, tragedy, or salvation can respond.[5] In a paradoxical manner, Heidegger has remained himself inadequate with respect to his task. But this paradox is common to all of philosophy.

2. In a collorary sense, it appears thus that the *with* suffers from this operation. By another paradox, even more embedded within the very course of *Being and Time*, the claim of the essentiality of the *with* turns out to be insidiously undermined in favor of another category, namely, community, which appropriates the *with* to a destinal unity in which there is no place for the contiguity of the *theres*, nor consequently any place, whether logical, ontological, or topological, for the *with* as such. This shortcoming cannot be imputed to Heidegger alone and an ethico-political condemnation does not suffice—far from it—to account for it.

Indeed, the issue is to wonder how to give thought to a co-exposure that in the end exposes itself to nothing other than itself and not to the supra-existence of a community; how to give thought to a communication (*Mitteilung*)[6] that does not constitute a message for the community; how to give thought to a moment when the exposure to death does not lead to a sacrifice but shares out (*partage*) between all, between us, the eternity of each existence.

For, if it is exactly at the site of the *with* that both the opportunity and risk of existence are manifest, then one must also accept—still in accordance with the Heideggerian paradox—that this site is the site of death. Between the unsurpassable death of solitary dying and the sacrificial death in the struggle for the cause of the people—and incidentally, without simply excluding these two extreme possibilities—how are we to give thought to the sharing of death? How can we give thought to death between us, indeed, to death as the very co-opening of the *there*?

CODA

Or should another name be set alongside death, a name that Heidegger does not use in the text, in his work, but which is found in his thought during the time of *Being and Time*?

In the correspondence with Hannah Arendt from 1925–28[7] one finds very precise elements, undeveloped but quite explicit, of a thinking of love that could very precisely be situated between the improper and the proper of the *with* in *Being and Time*. Love is indeed identified as the true site of a "we," and of a world that would be "*ours*"[8] at the same time that it represents the genuine "caring for" the other, since its definition, borrowed from Augustine, is "*volo ut sis*":[9] "I want you to be what you are." Thus, love is *mitglauben*, a shared faith in the story of the other and *mitergreifen*, a shared grasp of the "potential of the other,"[10] in such a way that love is always a singular *with*: "*your* love. Love *as such* does not exist, of course."[11]

One finds, then, in these letters, an existential analytic determined by a sharing according to which love would not substitute for death, but coincide with it. I do not want to undertake here a reading of these letters, a task for another time. But it is indispensable to establish that the exclusion of love outside of the general sphere of the *with*, of which it is nonetheless the truth—an exclusion that Hannah Arendt herself had perpetuated throughout her work, where "*amor mundi*" leaves out and in a state of exception the passionate love of two existents—is not specific to Heidegger, and is on the contrary axiomatic for any thinking of the "common" throughout the tradition—a tradition that, incidentally, is constantly counterexposed in its own structure to the Christian commandment of love. We are far from being finished with our consideration of this paradox and its enigma.

Translated by François Raffoul and David Pettigrew.

NOTES

We would like to thank Professor Nancy for his generosity in making his essay available for this volume.

1. Paragraph 26 of Martin Heidegger, *Being and Time*, trans. John Macquarrie and Edward Robinson (New York: Harper and Row, 1962) will serve as our guiding thread. Hereafter referred to as BT.

2. On this particular point I refer the reader to my essay "The Decision of Existence," in the *Birth to Presence*, trans. Brian Holmes et al. (Stanford: Stanford University Press, 1993), and on the whole discussion, to "Heidegger's 'Originary Ethics,' " in *Heidegger and Practical Philosophy*, ed. François Raffoul and David Pettigrew, trans. Duncan Large (Albany: State University of New York Press, 2002), as well as *Being Singular Plural*, trans. Robert R. Richardson and Anne E. O'Byrne (Stanford: Stanford University Press, 2000).

3. This is a motif that one finds much earlier in the history of ideas concerning the people (e.g., Johann Gottfried von Herder in his "Treatise on the Origin of Language" [1772], second book, third law, in *Philosophical Writings*, trans. and ed. Michael Forster [Cambridge: Cambridge University Press, 2002]). Languages, cultures, and people are posited in opposition while individuals are posited through differentiation.

4. BT, 442–443.

5. I can only mention this in passing, with respect to all of Husserl's work regarding intersubjectivity: whatever its merits, it always fails to touch upon the *with* as such, its allure or its texture as a between, a *with* that the intersubjective presupposes and conceals as opposed to revealing its modality.

6. This word ordinarily means "communication," but it would be too ambiguous here. "*Sharing*" (*partage*) would be closer to its meaning. But one must also understand that it is a matter of sharing an announcement or a call: a "communication" addressed to the community in order to indicate its destination, and to have it shared. Hence, my transposition of the word into "message." Only a commentary on the term *Mitteilung*, in its connection with *Kampf*, could clarify the stakes of the question of the *mit*. It is not a "communication" where it is a matter of speaking between us, but an address that sends us all to our destiny.

7. Ursula Ludz, ed., *Letters 1925–1975: Hannah Arendt and Martin Heidegger*, trans. Andrew Shields (New York: Harcourt, 2003). Hereafter cited as L, followed by the page number and date of the letter.

8. L, 19, Letter of 8 May 1925.

9. L, 21, Letter of 13 May 1925.

10. L, 25 Letter of 22 June 1925.

11. L, 27 Letter of 9 July 1925.

6

Heidegger and the Ethics of Facticity

ERIC SEAN NELSON

> Zilu asked about serving ghosts and spirits. The Master said, "You are not even able to serve people, how can you serve ghosts and spirits?"
> "May I inquire about death?"
> "You do not even understand life, how can you understand death?"
>
> —Confucius, *Analects*, 11.12

> Releasement [*Gelassenheit*] toward things and openness to the mystery belong together. They grant us the possibility of dwelling in the world in a profoundly different way.
>
> —Martin Heidegger, *Discourse on Thinking*

> [T]he transcendence of Dasein's Being is distinctive in that it implies the possibility and the necessity of the most radical individuation.
>
> —Martin Heidegger, *Being and Time*

INTRODUCTION

Martin Heidegger's *Being and Time* has been repeatedly criticized for ignoring the social and ethical dimensions of human existence. After discussing the possibility of an "ethics of individuation" based on passages from *The Fundamental Concepts of Metaphysics*, I argue that

Heidegger is not concerned with developing a social or moral philosophy as such but with the question of how individuation (*Vereinzelung*), within the horizon of the question of being (*Sein*), is possible given the predominance of the social and the fallenness of the public sphere.[1] The priority of the question concerning the individuation of Dasein—and its explication through the *alterity* of uncanniness, facticity, and death in relation to the *identity* of tradition and the "they" (*das man*)—provides a basis for rethinking the significance of the ethical in *Being and Time*, especially in light of Heidegger's earlier project of a hermeneutics of facticity and related works of the late 1920s. Insofar as Heidegger unfolds the finitude and *facticity of the ethical*, as a question to which ethical thinking must needs respond, Heidegger intimates an *ethics of facticity*.

Heidegger's reversal of ethics in *Being and Time* is not done in the name of another ethical position or view, such as egoism, nor for the sake of the unethical—despite his later political engagement of the 1930s. It is instead a performance and staging of the very question of ethics in its facticity. Heidegger interrogates ethics as embodied in tradition and everyday life in order to disclose possibilities that remain hidden in discourses appealing to axioms, principles, values, and virtues. These unnoticed and suppressed possibilities are intimated in Heidegger's discussions of the existential structures of Dasein such as conscience, guilt, solicitude or concern for others, and care. The coming to freedom and responsibility involved in the individuation of Dasein—with its threefold equiprimordial structure of being-itself, being-with others (*Mitsein*), and being-amidst things—occurs or is enacted as a response to the facticity of one's own existence, especially as disclosed in the inescapability of one's death.

ETHICS AND INDIVIDUATION

In investigating the significance of individuation in Heidegger, we are confronted with the initial problem that it is often not seen as an issue at all. Individuation is already self-evident, since we are all already individuals. If it is questioned at all, it is interpreted as the particularization of a universal, the instantiation of a type, differentiation according to a category, and affiliation with or alienation from some given authority or identity. It is accordingly either reduced to numerical, physical, and spatial differentiation or a belonging to a pregiven genus or fixed essence for which "becoming oneself" is a redundant question.

For Heidegger, the question of individuation is an issue concerning not "what" but "who" one is. It is bound up with the enigma of how the self can know itself in its facticity, that is, that which resists the self and its appropriations, including its own self. Heidegger described such questions, in which the self questions itself concerning itself and as a whole (GA 29/30, 20),[2] as existential or metaphysical. They disclose myself as a question to myself.

Heidegger's employment of the German word *Vereinzelung* (individuation) suggests a break or separation involved in "becoming one" or in being reduced onto oneself. Although they need not coincide in ordinary German, Heidegger identifies *Vereinzelung* with loneliness and solitude (*Einsamkeit*) in *The Fundamental Concepts of Metaphysics*:

> This individuation is rather the *solitariness* in which each human being first of all enters into a nearness to what is essential in all things, a nearness to world. What is this *solitude*, where each human being will be as though unique? (GA 29/30, 8)

Why does this individuation, the singularity that is not just a particular instance of the universal in being as though unique, require solitude? In this need, is it nothing but a flight and escapism, such as that attributed to the Daoist hermit, into the illusory tranquility of the rural solitude of some mountain stream or forest path? Perhaps. Yet more significantly, for Heidegger, solitude is a condition not of escaping the world but of encountering it. Solitariness is a prerequisite of individuation because the latter breaks with the constant noise of normal indifference in order to near and hear the world. Individuation is a kind of transcendence (SZ, 38), a stepping out of oneself toward the world. The break of immanence (transcendence) is necessary for the happening of a "step back from" that is equally a "stepping out into" and allowing to be seen. Solitude, as separation from participation in the continuous hum of everydayness, is the breakdown of connection through encountering finitude. The uniqueness of self and things does not arise from the imposition of a view, prescription, or imperative (i.e., "ethics" in the traditional sense) but emerges in the event of letting world be encountered (i.e., "ethics" in a phenomenological sense).

As a response to finitude, including the facticity that one is, individuation is a becoming finite. Since finitude is the way in which humans exist or dwell, it is not a mere "fact" about human nature. Nor is encountering one's own finitude equivalent to idealistically reducing the world to the ego and its concerns, as such egoism is part of the average everydayness that is in question. On the contrary, according to Heidegger:

> Finitude is not some property that is merely attached to us, but is *our fundamental way of being*. If we wish to become what we are, we cannot abandon this finitude or deceive ourselves about it, but must safeguard it. Such preservation is the innermost process of our being finite, i.e., it is our innermost becoming finite. Finitude only *is* in truly becoming finite. In becoming finite, however, there ultimately occurs an *individuation* of man with respect to his Dasein. Individuation—this does not mean that man clings to his frail little ego that puffs itself up against something or other which it takes to be the world. (GA 29/30, 8)

This taking-up, safeguarding, and preserving of finitude can be seen as an "ethics of finitude." It is not ethics in the standard sense of prescribing universal rules and systems of axioms, values, or virtues to follow, since Heidegger rejected "ethics" as legislation and calculation. Such an ethics is not about the formation of a set of values, worldview, or ideology at all, much less some supposed "spiritual" and "cultural" warfare, but opening up their questionability in exposing the self to its world.[3] The possibility of this ethics should be separated from while confronting Heidegger's own notorious "fallen" ideological engagement, which was perhaps due to blindness to the pervasiveness and power of ideology and value thinking.

Heidegger's emphasis on the event and enactment of conservation, not of the dominion of custom and opinion but of responding to the world out of its openness and givenness, can be thought of as an attempt to trace that which throws views, values, and constructs into question in order to let the world, self, and other be encountered. However, this is not ethics in the conventional sense of legislating laws, moralizing about virtues, or prescribing values. It is an ethics that confronts and potentially releases its own tradition, historicity, and hermeneutical situation. The prospect of such a phenomenological ethics depends on whether individuation, as a break that opens and discloses other possibilities, is even thinkable.

INDIFFERENCE AND INDIVIDUATION

The orienting issue of *Being and Time* is the sense and truth of being. Yet rather than providing a classical philosophical analysis of being, or ontology, Heidegger interrogates the sense of being via the issue of that being who examines its own way or mode of being. *Being and Time* asks the question of being but does so by addressing that being which questions itself. He calls this being, which we in each case are, Dasein.

Being and Time, at least the published fragment, consists of the analytic of Dasein. Far from being the philosophical anthropology that Husserl feared, much less an encyclopedic or systematic account of human nature, Heidegger's analysis focused on a sparse number of aspects of human existence and in an eccentric way from the perspective of modern social philosophy. Heidegger did not begin with the individual as an essence or atomic fact from which to construct society through power, markets, contracts, and convents. His analysis takes as its point of departure Dasein in its "neutrality," in what he calls the "indifference" of everydayness, and proceeds to examine situations that broach the significance of being and the self by placing this indifference in question.

Average everyday life is not indifferent in the Kantian sense of being disinterested or Stoic impartiality. It is not the absolute indifference experienced in profound boredom, unconcerned with all affairs, which Heidegger described in *The Fundamental Concepts of Metaphysics*. Instead, through its self-interested concern with everyday things and affairs, it is indifferent to that which would throw light on the character and plight of its own existence. It is in these situations, where the everyday and the ordinary become questionable, that the grip of everyday indifference is broken. The difference indicated in this breaking, in which the "one" of the "they" (*das man*) is doubled into two in order to become the "one" of oneself (*vereinzelt*), is the possibility of individuation. Individuation as the break with indifference can take place because Dasein's neutrality is already broken by the facticity of its existence: "The being that we in each case are, the human is in its essence neutral. We call this being Dasein. Yet it belongs to the essence of neutral Dasein that it has a necessarily broken neutrality, insofar as it in each case factically exists" (GA 27, 146).[4]

The transition from being lost in the facticity of the indifference, conformity, and compulsion of the "they" (*das man*) to the self-individuation involved in what Heidegger calls authenticity (*Eigentlichkeit*) requires that Dasein can be a question to and for itself precisely in and through its facticity. Heidegger accordingly contends in §9 that the analytic of Dasein cannot begin with Dasein in its difference, qua actually existing concrete individual, but rather with its common indifference or averageness. For Heidegger, Dasein's being "must be developed from the existentiality of its existence. This cannot mean, however, that 'Dasein' is to be construed from out of a concrete possible idea of existence. At the outset of our analysis it is particularly important that Dasein should not be interpreted in the difference of a definite way of existing, but that it should be uncovered in its *indifferent character which it is proximally and for the most part*. This *indifference* is not nothing, but a *positive* phenomenal characteristic of this being" (SZ, 43, emphasis added).[5] Although the goal of the analytic of Dasein will be Dasein in its difference (individuation), its factical possibilities (existence) are not straightforwardly available in average everydayness.

Difference remains invisible to the indifference of the they.[6] Dasein dwells in the familiarity of its self-understanding without seeing its possibilities or hearing "who" (not "that") it is. The familiarity and compulsion of common life presents itself as certain, obvious, and unquestionable. This habitual and customary reproduction of power is all the more coercive because it is not superimposed by some system upon the "innocent" lifeworld but already comprises the lifeworld itself. Although Heidegger was not interested in ideology-critique or prescribing authenticity as a normative end or standard, since he rejected ethics and critique in this sense, his thought still has consequences for such thinking given this account of inherent non-innocence of everydayness. Hegemony achieved through the public sphere and civil society, through everyday beliefs and practices, is consequently much more unquestioned and pervasive than any dominion based on institutions alone.

It is often forgotten that fallenness, according to the logic of temporalization at work in *Being and Time*, is not so much spatial—fallen from heaven—as it is temporal. Everyday existence is not simply a "social reality" but is itself a mode of being in time, it is fallenness into the present. For fallen everydayness, according to its temporality of existing in the present without encountering the moment, everything is an extension of its own present. Although it understands and lives the past and future as extensions of the present, and as guaranteed by history, memorializing tradition, and expected progress, the absolutized perspective of the present is itself historically formed and finite. The *Augenblick*, the instant or moment, is an encounter with one's own temporal finitude and, as such, potentially a break in which decision and individuation can occur. Yet Dasein is not only challenged by its present. Being related to a past that cannot fully be mastered and a future that is not simply a reproduction of its own present, the identity of the lifeworld and common sense are always implicitly questionable. Everyday existence avoids such questionability in its "flight" from this unknown past and unknowable future, because exposure to this temporality, to the ecstatic character of time, throws its self-certainty and self-understanding into question.

Dasein is first of all to be understood out of the social indifference in which it is usually affected and moved. Yet, via the very affectivity and motility indicated in average everydayness, Heidegger articulated Dasein's possibilities for understanding being and enacting its existence in its difference and singularity. This is done through the interruption of everyday indifference, which allows the releasement of the everyday. These interruptions occur through experiences of limits, which Karl Jaspers had described as "limit situations."[7] These disruptions are not merely negative and inconvenient, but disclose the very character of existence in its facticity and possibility. The differentiation of existence occurs through the possibilities disclosed in the breaks and disruptions of everydayness itself. It is difference itself that reveals possibilities for the individuation of Dasein. Although alterity is hinted at in Jaspers's notion of "limit-situation," it remains inadequate for Heidegger's analysis of individuation insofar as it fails to enact the questionability of existence. As merely other, alterity and difference can always be reintegrated back into the indifference of everydayness, just as there is a kind of "newness" and apparent variety that is actually more of the same. Indifferent everydayness involves a repetition without difference. The broken hammer can be replaced, anxiety can be forgotten, and the strangeness of the stranger can be integrated or excluded according to the norms of everydayness. Interruption alone cannot individuate, but rather how Dasein responds to interruption is the key to its individuation: Whether the break itself is recognized as such and its questionability intensified or whether it is excluded as nonsense—as the "nothing" disclosed in human existence often is—or—like death—integrated into the identity of everydayness. The questionability of such experiences and situations needs to be embraced and deepened if radical individuation is to occur. This is why Heidegger emphasized the moment of being pushed and shaken (*Stoß*) in his description of the call of conscience: "In the disclosive tendency of the call, lies the moment [*Moment*] of a push [*Stoß*], of an abrupt arousal [*Aufrütteln*]. The call is from afar unto afar" (SZ, 271). This being called is a being pushed and shaken in the call, since ordinary hearing does not listen to it. Dasein, as being-with others, can listen to others and does so in the manner of everydayness. Losing itself in the undifferentiated talk of everydayness, such that it hears yet fails to listen, Dasein "fails to hear in that it listens away to the 'they' " (SZ, 271). The call of conscience interrupts ordinary hearing and discloses another possibility for hearing: "This hearing-to [or "listening away" (*Hinhören*) to the they] must be broken; i.e., the possibility of another kind of hearing that interrupts it must be given by

Dasein itself. The possibility of such a break consists of being called-onto [*Angerufen*] without mediation" (SZ, 271).

The individuation of Dasein, which is in each case a being with others in the world, is not enacted in the everyday relationship between self and other. This relationship is itself usually characterized by the indifference of everydayness. Instead this enactment occurs only when the questionability of Dasein in its being-with is enacted. It is precisely such experiences of interruption and uncanniness that individuate human existence, when it hears the claim addressed to it in such experiences, and thus lets difference appear (SZ, 276–77, 280, 307).[8]

The call of conscience is a call by oneself onto being oneself. As such it interrupts the identity of everydayness to let singularity and responsibility appear. Angst, however, does not proceed from and back to oneself insofar as it, as possibility, interrupts the very being of the self. Angst individuates Dasein in relation to the nonrelational that can at any time strike (SZ, 188–89, 191). That is, it singularizes Dasein in regard to the ownmost (*eigensten*), nonrelational (*unbezüglichen*), and unbeatable (*unüberholbaren*) possibility of its own death (SZ, 250–51). The unavoidable possibility of death confronts each Dasein as its own death, as a death that addresses "me" by ending and thus radically placing into the question the very mineness of my existence. This possibility is nonrelational in that it cannot be ordered in the relationality of the world but places relationality itself into question. Death is not another relation, it appears as the relationless as such, as something that cannot be "outstripped" or "beaten."

Dasein runs in after or away from death, yet it does not overcome the death it is expecting or avoid the death it is fleeing. Rather than being something it can master, death masters Dasein each time. Death remains in its difference something that cannot be sublimated (*unaufhebbar*), mediated (*unvermittelbar*), and thought relationally (*unbezüglich*; SZ, 250).[9] It thus indicates the fundamental thrownness into facticity of Dasein. Dasein is incapable of conceptualizing or mastering death, since death withdraws from being understood (SZ, 250). It is in this sense that the death of the other cannot be represented (SZ, 240–42). For Heidegger, it is only in the shadow of one's own death in which this nonrelationality occurs and the nexus of worldly significance is broken.

At first it seemed that average everydayness had the first and last word, and that interruptions could always be reappropriated and integrated back into the same. Yet, with the disclosure of fundamental nonrelationality in anxiety, the direction of Heidegger's analysis is reversed. It is not uncanniness and questionability that are derivatives of everydayness; it is everydayness that presupposes the uncanniness and questionability that it suppresses: "That kind of being-in-the-world which is tranquilized and familiar is a mode of Dasein's uncanniness, not the reverse. From an existential-ontological point of view, the 'not-at-home' must be conceived as the more primordial phenomenon" (SZ, 189). Heidegger would insist on the fundamental homelessness of "man" almost ten years later in his *Contributions to Philosophy*: "Be-ing is the hearth-fire in the midst of the abode of the gods—an abode which is simultaneously the estranging of man (the 'between' in which he remains a (the) stranger, precisely when he is at home with beings)" (GA 65, 486–87/343).[10] Dasein is primordially strange and foreign, we do not even know what "man" is (GA 29/30, 10), and we remain strangers to ourselves (ibid., 6). It is not the identity and indifference of everydayness that is primary. Singularity and difference are constitutive of Dasein through its openness as well as its uncanniness and questionability such that Dasein is each time a question to itself.

DASEIN AND ITS OTHER

Levinas criticized the primacy of one's own death in Heidegger and proposed an alternative approach in which the death of the other always takes precedence.[11] Is there not after all a testimony of/to the other in her death, one that suggests the ethical relation to the other rather than absorption in the egoism of self-concern? One could even formulate Levinas's point in a way such as to alleviate some "Heideggerian" concerns: Could there not be a testimony to the other that is outside of the conceptuality and relationality of representational thinking; could there be a witnessing that does not undermine the nonrelationality and nonidentity of the other's death as in each case its own? This last question raises the point of Heidegger's reference to Tolstoy: "In his story 'The Death of Ivan Ilyitch' Leo Tolstoy has presented the phenomenon of the disruption and breakdown of having 'someone die' " (SZ, 254, fn). A simple statement, yet one that indicates that testimony and witnessing are not necessarily the average everyday response to the death of the other, although they can occur through the disruption and breakdown of death. The "ownness" of death is not ownership and its "mineness" is not egoism, since own and mine indicate that they are questions for oneself (myself) that place oneself (me) into question and not some other person somewhere else. Perhaps, following the structure of care, one needs to await one's own death in order to care for the other's death, since this breaks the uncaring indifference of everydayness that does not care for the self or the other. In that sense it is more than the recognition of not being able to live the other's death. Death places me into question, addresses me as a question, precisely by being my death. If death escapes representation and relationality, the other's death can be a question for me although I do not experience or live through what it was like for her from her perspective. This is because death is a limit to experience rather than some content that could be reproduced from one mind to another. It is mine in that it occurs to every "I" each time alone. It is not mine in the sense of a possession that I control since it controls me. Dasein does not possess itself in death but is, on the contrary, "shattered" (SZ, 385). Heidegger would repeat and transform this claim in the mid-1930s. In his *Introduction to Metaphysics*, the human being, who responds to the violence of being through violence, shatters on death (IM, 121/168),[12] and the violence-doing of Dasein "*must* shatter against the excessive violence of being" (IM, 124/173). Heidegger also commented in his *Contributions to Philosophy* on the role of understanding and its being shattered in *Being and Time*: "But understanding of being is throughout just the opposite, nay even essentially other than making this understanding dependent upon human intention. How is being still to be made subjective at that place when what counts is the shattering of the subject?" (GA 65, 455–56/321).

Dasein cannot have itself then as a possession, according to Heidegger, since it is already thrown into a world in which it is not the center and in which it is being decentered. Dasein is not only ek-static, it is essentially decentered or "ek-centric" (GA 27, 11). Even if Levinas's objection is unconvincing, the problem runs deeper than the one he posed. Dasein is not an identical subject that can only be interrupted by another. It is distant and foreign to itself, such that the alterity and difference of uncanniness constitutes its very mode of being. Dasein is thrown into facticity not as a general subject (GA 27, 5) but as "each time" (*je-weilig*) and "in each case its own" (*je-meinig*). It is therefore one's own death, not the death of the other, that indicates the most radical alterity and singularity. Dasein is in each case "my own" each singular time without sublimation, mediation, or relationality (i.e., *Unaufhebbarkeit*, *Unvermittelbarkeit*, and *Unbezüglichkeit*).[13] Death as the most extreme possibility determines the facticity of Dasein.[14] As facticity, it cannot be overcome or withstood.

Dasein is constituted as being outside of itself and outside in a world, existing as thrown beyond itself as ek-static and outside itself as ek-centric (GA 27, 11), which literally means being out of orbit. The self is then both near and distant to itself. This familiar and unfamiliar self occurs in and through everydayness and the individuation of uncanniness. Individuation as *Vereinzelung* is a singularization through the interruption of the identity of the they, the opening of the difference that Dasein already is as each time its own. Yet this singularization of Dasein as thrownness in a specific situation does not necessarily imply isolation if it brings Dasein into the entirety of its relations in the midst of beings (GA 27, 334). The separation and solitude of individuation might be isolating but this does not by itself make it egoism or solipsism.

One can describe *Being and Time* in terms of an inappropriable connectedness, that is, a contextuality that centers and decenters Dasein. In this relationality, including its "relation" to the nonrelational, Dasein is both dependent and free in its relations to things, others, and the world. The relation to the other exemplifies this inappropriable relationality in that Dasein cannot take the place of the other. The other's existence withdraws from appropriation insofar as it is each time and in each case its own. Thus, "I am *never* the Dasein of the other, although I can be *with* him."[15] For Heidegger, "time is the principle of individuation" and Dasein is its own way of being its time.[16] Dasein is inherently singularizing from the start, since it *is* its time. It is temporal. It is not only in the moment but is each time its moment.[17]

In the relation of Dasein to its other, it can attempt to take this away from the other by leaping in, taking over, "understanding better," or it can promote the other's individuation. Thus, Heidegger indicated a different kind of relation in which the other is to remain free. In solicitude or caring-for (*Fürsorge*) the other, as authentic care, Dasein does not leap in for the other in order to take the other's care away, but rather is affected by it in order to give it back to the other. Caring for the other in its "care" does not imply taking the other's care away (*abzunehmen*), but instead means to overtake it (*übernehmen*) in order to return it (*zurückzugeben*). Insofar as Dasein leaps ahead for the other instead of leaping in, it does so for the sake of the other rather than for itself. It takes up the other not to appropriate her but precisely in order to bring her to her own being as care. Solicitude or caring for the other's care is not the reduction of my responsibility to promoting the responsibility of the other instead of, for example, helping someone in genuine need. It is more than the moral minimalism of abstract individualism insofar as it indicates the possibility of a reciprocal individuation in which each has its own being, as freedom and care, promoted.

Individuation involves differentiating oneself from common life—in its averageness and fallenness—while taking up the responsibility of sharing with the other from out of this difference. This difference is a between that separates and binds, suggesting that individuation cannot be fulfilled. It happens only out of its impossibility. As Heidegger already argued in 1924, fallenness is constitutive of Dasein's facticity.[18] As such, it remains inappropriable. If human existence never overcomes, much less outlasts, its confrontation with its own death, then authenticity can at most only be a modification of facticity: "The authentic being of Dasein is what it is only insofar as it is inauthentically authentic, that is, 'preserved' in itself. [Authenticity] is not anything that should or could exist for itself next to the inauthentic" (GA 64, 81). Instead of transcendence being an otherworldly condition or the formation of an isolated sovereign individual, authenticity indicates an altered way of relating to one's inauthentic everydayness. It is not to "shake off" tradition and everydayness, which is constitutive of the very finitude of Dasein and thus inescapable, but to appropriate it more primordially (SZ, 220). Yet, as this appropriation is always related to the inappropriable, transcendence can only be a response to—and taking up of responsibility for—facticity. That is, freedom is taking up one's responsibility in its facticity (GA 64, 54). If responsibility is inevitably each time one's own yet enacted in relations with others, and freedom is a response to facticity (the awakening of possibilities in the facticity that one is), then ethics is always only the ethics of facticity.

The "giving back" of care also clarifies the idea of an inappropriable relatedness by revealing a relation in which the other is not mediated by one's own but is promoted precisely as being other than myself: "This solicitude which essentially pertains to authentic care; that is, the existence of the other, and not to a *what* which it takes care of, helps the other to become transparent to himself *in* his care and *free for* it" (SZ, 122). Heidegger clarified this "being-for-the-other" further in his 1928–29 lecture course *Introduction to Philosophy*. There he described how the essence of being-with-one-another consists of being-open-for-one-another (*Für-einander-offenbar-sein*), an openness *for* the other that allows reciprocity and its lack to be possible (GA 27, 88). As Heidegger later maintained, understanding (*verstehen*) is not an indifferent mutuality but a reciprocal placing into question. Understanding is not an encounter between two fixed positions that somehow remain unchanged in their communication, or concludes in conversion, but is differentiation through addressing and questioning both oneself and the other out of care (GA 13, 17, 20).[19] Understanding is enacted through a confrontation and conflict in which the other places one's own in question, and vice-versa, transforming those who engage in it (GA 13, 20). Understanding thus requires both (1) the long lasting will of listening to the other and (2) the courage to one's own determination (GA 13, 21).

THE BEING-WITH OF DASEIN

Levinas and others have criticized Heidegger for subjectivism and individualism[20] and argued that Heidegger's thought is inherently unable to think the social and ethical. In response, I have argued that Heidegger's work hints at an "ethics of facticity" or finitude in proceeding from an indifferent commonality to the possibility of individuation through the difference in/of experience itself. This individuation requires the unfolding of what Heidegger describes as conscience, freedom, and responsibility. Although Heidegger rejected the term *ethics* for various historical reasons, it is clear that his project has an ethical dimension and significance. In addition, rather than excluding sociality, his account of individuation shows how it is possible as free from domination (i.e., taking the other over) and as promoting the other's Dasein as care, freedom, and responsibility.[21]

One should not forget that Dasein is "always already" being-with and that being-with is a fundamental equiprimordial determination of the being of Dasein. The "with" occurs not because of identity or because Dasein is made alike but rather because of the "there" (GA 27, 137). Dasein encounters others and things in how they give themselves because it is the opening of the there (GA 27, 136). Because Dasein is being-with, being-with cannot be derived from the idea of the subject (GA 27, 133), nor the self from the other (GA 27, 135), nor in the "I/you" relation that simply doubles the solipsistic subject (GA 27, 141, 146). Sociality and community, and every form of "I/you" relation, is only possible because Dasein is each time in its own way already with others and is, as such, a being-with-others (GA 27, 141). Insofar as Dasein is being-with-others, Dasein is always already spoken to and addressed by the other (GA 29/30, 301). The self, insofar as it listens to and hearkens to the other, is always already placed into question by the other and pulled out toward responsibility for the other in care: Care as care for the self inherently is bound to the care for the other. Authentic Dasein cannot step in, take over, and occupy its place but can only promote the other's self-care. The answer, the binding responsibility that brings Dasein to choice and decision (WDF, 169),[22] is care. Care discloses the difference of the average being-with and the authentic possibility of being-with, in which Dasein first stands in relations directed toward others.[23]

The question of community and individuation is not then a question of inferring a collective subject from an individual one or of deducing the individual from the collective. It is neither about an ahistorical and worldless self nor a social organism that allows no difference.[24] Heidegger had already suggested this in his winter semester 1921–22 lecture course, when he made the case that the self-world is neither identical to the ego nor can it be isolated from being-with and the environing world (GA 61, 96).[25] The question of being-with cannot be one of the phenomenological constitution or construction of being-with from out of one's own self considered as an isolated ego or subject (GA 29/30, 302). Insofar as being-with is to be understood as a structure of everydayness, it too must be transformed in the modification of everydayness that occurs through individuation. Dasein is in each case my own such that I am never the Dasein of the other but only *with* the other. Consequently, Dasein never becomes the other but is rather individuated in such a way that in becoming itself it becomes otherwise than itself and in becoming otherwise than itself authentically becomes itself. Individuation is not a closed isolated process such that the nearness to the "they" would be lost. Dasein cannot comport itself as being-with without listening to the they and without cultivating its ability to hear beyond what is usually and for the most part said in order to achieve a responsive hearing that takes into consideration a being-*with* the other that is also a being-*for* the other (SZ, 122, 163). Responsiveness thus implies responsibility, and, yet, it cannot occur without the confrontation and conflict with the other for the other (GA 27, 22–23, 327).

BEING-WITH OTHERS AND THE RESPONSIVENESS OF HEARING

Following the interpretation staked out in the previous sections of this chapter, Heidegger did not turn to the question of the self or self-sameness to the exclusion of the other as well as the alterity of the world and one's own self. The individuation of Dasein in its being-with unfolds through hearing. This does not occur as a process of identification or empathy, but rather it only occurs through differentiation and becoming other. All understanding is therefore in this sense differentiating confrontation (*Auseinandersetzung*). Dasein transforms itself in its being-with precisely through the responsibility for the other in encountering and differentiating the other. Individuation signifies more than recognition of difference and alterity. The individuation and differentiation of existence occurs not as a progressive teleological development but through its own questionability and uncanniness. Heidegger's thinking is thus a questioning-answering responsiveness in relation to the facticity of the thrownness of human existence. The historicity of thrownness into one's own generation and world signifies the impossibility of a pure responsiveness that would occur without interruption and conflict, without the historicity and destiny in which Dasein finds itself. This means that Dasein cannot recognize another without differentiating itself and its other. Difference occurs not as indifferent lack of contact and isolation, but rather as and in the crossing of the between. Difference shows the fundamental questionability of Dasein, which is both itself and not itself, and indicates the ownmost interruption and placing into question of one's own. Dasein is referred to an originary unified phenomenon, but this unity belongs to difference itself—it is the transcendence of Dasein in its nothingness and lack of bearing (GA 27, 354). Dasein is thus in each case already betrayed and endangered in its transcendence-in-the-world (GA 27, 358). It belongs to "the each time of the facticity of transcendence" (GA 27, 367). As such, Dasein does not first of all observe and inquire. It understands others and "intuits the world" through encounter and confrontation (GA 27, 367–68, 382–90). As noted earlier, ontological difference opens up the radical diversity of ontic differences in being its formal indication.

The authenticity of Dasein is only possible as addressing and being addressed, hearing and responding; that is, as a responsive hearing of the other. Heidegger therefore claims in *Being and Time* that "[l]istening to . . . is the existential being-open of Dasein as being-with for the other. Hearing even constitutes the primary and authentic openness of Dasein for its ownmost possibility of being, as in hearing the voice of the friend whom every Dasein carries with it. It hears because it understands. As being-in-the-world that understands, with others, it 'listens to' [*hörig*] itself and *Mitdasein*, and in this listening [*Hörigkeit*] belongs [*zugehörig*]" to these (SZ, 163). Listening to others is a belonging to them. Yet there could be no belonging as listening without difference, since otherwise nothing would need to be said or communicated. The necessity of language is based in the nonidentity of its participants. Since Dasein listens to *Mitdasein* (the being there of the other in all of its facticity and possibility) in addition to itself, it cannot simply be a listening to oneself. Despite the fragmentary character of *Being and Time* and the undeveloped character of *Mitsein*, being-with as constitutive of Dasein's existence is repeatedly implied.

Dasein always already belongs to others, it is already with others in the world as a common significant with-world, out of which it understands and acts. Hearing and listening inform and attune a comportment that is directed toward the other, insofar as Dasein is open for the world in standing out in the world, that is, is ecstatic (SZ, 164). This means that the question is not whether but how we go along with and don't go along with others, and how the alterity of the other can be recognized. Heidegger answers this question by pointing toward the possibility of genuine hearing. This hearing and hearkening indicates the passivity of a letting occur. Both are necessary conditions for a responsive relation with the other. This problematic will be transformed after the change of direction called the "turn" in Heidegger's thinking. The listening confrontation occurs out of the "between" and the abyssal divide, as the answer and question concerning the violence and uncanniness of the human. Heidegger explored in his *Introduction to Metaphysics* this nexus of address and conflict, of *logos* and *polemos*. Heidegger speaks "*Wege zur Aussprache*" (1937) of the possibility of interpretive confrontation (*verstehende Auseinandersetzung*)—a phrase he already used in the early 1920s. Heidegger is concerned here with a recognition of the other, which does not forget the question of difference between self and other. This is understood as a conflict (*Streit*), not for the sake of strife but for understanding the other (GA 13, 15–21). This is because difference (*Unter-schied*) is announced in hearing.[26] But, to tweak a statement of Heidegger, we are not simply inexperienced in such hearing. Rather, our ears are overcome by what prevents responsive hearing and interpretive confrontation.[27]

NOTES

1. I retain "fallenness" as a translation of *Verfallenheit*, because (1) the word does not mean "falling prey" and (2) Heidegger intentionally transforms reified theological concepts such as conscience, fallenness, and guilt by phenomenologically relating them to concrete phenomena. Avoiding a word because of its previous religious meanings misses the point Heidegger made by using it. Giorgio Agamben shows in chapter 4 of this volume how fallenness and thrownness are both modes of facticity and articulates their "religious" context. Facticity as fallenness emerges from Heidegger's early interpretation of Saint Augustine, where facticity as "the made" is explicated according to the non-originariness and fallenness of man, and hence is fetish and idol, as opposed to that which is made and done by God. Non-self-originary, human *facticius* is opposed to the self-originariness of the divine *nativus*. In phenomenologically rearticulating fallenness and facticity, Heidegger suggests the

positivity of the original non-originariness of Dasein in characterizing it as "ruination" and "fallen" in opposition to the theological understanding of facticity as mere fetishism and sin.

2. *Die Grundbegriffe der Metaphysik* (Frankfurt: Klostermann, 1992). Second Edition. Translated as *The Fundamental Concepts of Metaphysics*, trans. William McNeill and Nicholas Walker (Bloomington: Indiana University Press, 1995).

3. Heidegger's works of the late 1930s, in part informed by his own failed involvement in National Socialism (1933–34) and his growing insight into its character, deepens this critique of ethics, life-philosophy, value-thinking, worldviews, and their supposed "conflict" as symptoms of more fundamental problems with modernity.

4. GA 27: *Einleitung in die Philosophie*. Second Edition (Frankfurt: Klostermann, 2001). Translation forthcoming: *Introduction to Philosophy*, trans. Eric Sean Nelson and Virginia Lyle Jennings (Bloomington: Indiana University Press, forthcoming).

5. All Heidegger references are to the pagination of the *Gesamtausgabe* (Frankfurt: Klostermann, 1976–ongoing) unless otherwise noted. SZ: *Sein und Zeit* (Tübingen: Niemeyer Verlag, 1985) Sixteenth Edition. Translations: *Being and Time*, trans. J. Macquarrie and E. Robinson (New York: Harper and Row, 1962) and *Being and Time*, trans. Joan Stambaugh (Albany: State University of New York Press, 1996).

6. Interestingly, the question of naming difference remains deeply problematic for Heidegger. See, for example, Peter Trawny's investigation of the "inappearance" or "invisibility" (*Unscheinbarkeit*) of difference in Heidegger's thought. Trawny's essay explores the complexity of difference, the multiple ways in which difference is enacted, in Heidegger's thought. Difference is itself no longer difference when it is understood, according to the logic of identity, as a first principle or ground. This presents Heidegger with the impossibility of identifying and naming difference, since difference *as* difference withdraws and withholds itself. Peter Trawny, "Die unscheinbare Differenz," in *Phénoménologie Française et Phénoménologie Allemande*, ed. E. Escoubas and B. Waldenfels (Paris: L'Harmattan, 2000).

7. Heidegger developed the issue of death in proximity to Jasper's notion of "Grenzsituation" but increasingly differentiates them. See, for example, GA 64: *Der Begriff der Zeit* (Frankfurt: Klostermann, 2004), 48. I discuss in greater detail the importance and inadequacy of Jaspers' "limit-situation" for Heidegger in "Questioning Practice: Heidegger, Historicity, and the Hermeneutics of Facticity," *Philosophy Today* 44 (2001): 150–59.

8. The intersection of familiarity and unfamiliarity (proximity and distance) is already a topic in 1919. The disruption of the familiar presupposes the stability of the familiar that is thrown into question. Compare, for example, GA 58: *Grundprobleme der Phänomenologie* (Frankfurt: Klostermann, 1992), 251.

9. Compare David Wood's argument that death and angst "make significance tremble" in Heidegger rather than being the naive virile mastery of

death that Levinas suggested. *The Deconstruction of Time*, second edition (Evanston: Northwestern University Press, 2001), xxiii.

10. GA 65: *Beiträge zur Philosophie: (Vom Ereignis)* (Frankfurt: Klostermann, 1989). Translated as *Contributions to Philosophy: From Enowning*, trans. P. Emad and K. Maly (Bloomington: Indiana University Press, 1999).

11. Heidegger's presence haunts Levinas's thought such that it is often present even when Heidegger is not explicitly discussed. Levinas's most extensive discussion and critique of Heidegger on issues such as death can be found in his later work *God, Death, and Time*, trans. Bettina Bergo (Stanford: Stanford University Press, 2000). Also compare the discussions of Levinas and Heidegger by Bernasconi, Raffoul, and Wood in *Addressing Levinas*, ed. Eric Sean Nelson, Antje Kapust, Kent Still (Evanston: Northwestern University Press, 2005).

12. IM: *Einführung in die Metaphysik* (Tübingen: Niemeyer, 1976). Fourth Edition. English translation: *Introduction to Metaphysics*, trans. Gregory Fried and Richard Polt (New Haven: Yale University Press, 2000).

13. See François Raffoul's analysis of the "each time mine" of *Jemeinigkeit* in his *Heidegger and the Subject* (New Jersey: Humanities Press, 1998), 215–21. Also compare John van Buren's account of *haecceitas* in the context of difference, facticity, and singularity in Heidegger's habilitation on Duns Scotus. *The Young Heidegger* (Bloomington: Indiana University Press, 1994), 105–107.

14. Heidegger already connected facticity and death in 1924. See, for instance, GA 64, 51.

15. I cannot *be* the other but only *be with* her, this entails that Dasein cannot overcome the asymmetry of self and other. This not due to the "irrationality of lived experience" or "the limitedness and uncertainty of knowledge" but is constitutive of the way of being that Dasein is (GA 64, 47). The alterity seen by Levinas in the death of the other does not have the same power for Heidegger. Rather than placing the self into question, the other's death is indifferently reintegrated according to the maxim that "one dies" (GA 64, 49). However, as in his examination of *The Death of Ivan Ilyich*, Heidegger's description of such indifference does not entail that he is advocating it.

16. GA 64, 57, 82–83.

17. Compare Frank Schalow's analysis of temporality as diversity and plurality in Heidegger in his article "Decision, Dilemma, Disposition: The Incarnatedness of Ethical Action," *Existentia* XII, no. 3–4, especially 249–50. I would argue in addition that this follows Heidegger's early strategy of the formal indication of facticity: Ontological difference opens up the plurality of ontic difference, time the singularity of the moment.

18. GA 64, 51.

19. GA 13: *Aus der Erfahrung des Denkens* (Frankfurt: Klostermann, 1983).

20. Levinas, of course, interprets Dasein as a fundamentally non-intersubjective subjectivity. See Bernhard Waldenfels, *Phänomenologie in Frankreich*. Second Edition (Frankfurt: Suhrkamp, 1998), 236.

21. The authentic (*eigentliche*) is related back to one's own (*eigene*). Authenticity had an explicitly social as well as temporal dimension in the early1920s,

since the relation to "one's own" means opening up the possibilities available to one to individuate oneself "in one's own time and generation" (PIA, 248): "Phänomenologische Interpretationen zu Aristoteles (Anzeige der hermeneutischen Situation)," ed. H. U. Lessing, Dilthey-Jahrbuch 6 (1989): 237–69.

22. WDF: "Wilhelm Diltheys Forschungsarbeit und der gegenwärtige Kampf um eine historische Weltanschauung. 10 Vorträge." Dilthey-Jahrbuch 8 (1992–93): 143–80.

23. Dasein is, as Nancy and Raffoul have established, a singular-plural indication. See Jean-Luc Nancy, *Being Singular Plural*, trans. R. Richardson and A. O'Byrne (Stanford: Stanford University Press 2000), 6–7 and Raffoul, 1998: 215–21. Bringing into consideration Kisiel's and Van Buren's work on the logic of formal indication only strengthens this argument. See Theodore Kisiel, *The Genesis of Heidegger's Being and Time* (Berkeley: University of California Press, 1993) and van Buren, 1994: 324–47. The formal indication of Dasein points toward the singularity of its enactment, a temporalizing singularity indicated in the "each time" of *Je-weiligkeit* and the "each time my own" of *Je-meinigkeit.*

24. Heidegger not only rejected the idea of a "worldless 'I,' " but also would later criticize the more dangerous shapes in which this worldless subject is absorbed into "something greater" such as life or the *Volk* (GA 65, 321/225; also compare IM, 54/74).

25. GA 61, *Phänomenologische Interpretationen zu Aristoteles.* Second Edition (Frankfurt: Klostermann, 1994).

26. Compare, in addition, the following discussions of the significance of hearing in Heidegger—GA 55: *Heraklit.* Third Edition (Frankfurt: Klostermann, 1994), 238–60; pp. 162–63 of Charles Scott, "*Zuspiel* and *Entscheidung*: A reading of sections 81–82 in *Die Beiträge zur Philosophie*," *Philosophy Today* 41 (1997): 161–67; and Peter Trawny, *Heideggers Phänomenologie der Welt* (Freiburg: Alber, 1997), 90–96.

27. I would like to thank François Raffoul and Jeanne Marie Kusina for their comments and criticisms.

7

Intransitive Facticity?

A Question to Heidegger

Rudi Visker

It is no secret that for some time now the wind blowing through contemporary philosophy has changed direction. It comes from an angle that is known as "the other," with or without a capital O, neutral or personal, inside or outside the "subject." And it is generally considered to be a good wind: as long as it blows in the "subject's" face, its effects can only be positive. Skies will clear up, and all sorts of problems will drift away. Thus, a book with the fashionable title, *Strangers to Ourselves*, ends with the promising conclusion that "by recognizing *our* uncanny strangeness"—the "other" in us—"we shall neither suffer from it nor enjoy it from the outside." The foreigner, Kristeva triumphantly continues, "is within me, hence we are all foreigners." From which would follow a "cosmopolitanism of a new sort": "If I am a foreigner, there are no foreigners."[1] Needless to say, Lacan thought differently, which is why the famous article on "The Mirror Stage" ("I am an other"), was followed in the *Ecrits* by a paper on "Aggressivity in Psychoanalysis," in which he argued that aggression had its origin in an intrasubjective source, that is, in just that fission that forever marks a subject that is "an other" and will never manage *to be* it.

This should suffice to draw our attention to a number of presuppositions that seem to characterize what one could call the "alterity" turn in contemporary philosophy. There are at least two: that which is other to the "subject" seems somehow to be in "accord" to it—if it changes the "self," as is generally assumed, it changes it for the better. The Other may be a trauma, as in Levinas, but then a trauma that liberates—that alterates "without alienation."[2] The second presupposition is implied in the first: there must be an other-in-me, of which I was hitherto unaware and which somehow is activated or awakened by the other outside me, grateful for this outward help to undo it from a self (a "subject") that suppressed it. Hence, a corollary: the otherness-in-me is generally assumed to be only a threat to that part of me that stands in the way between me and the other outside of me. In other words: it is an otherness that does not threaten me from within me; it will always allow for there to remain a me to which, or in which, it is other.

I will refrain from showing here how this confidence in the theme of "alterity" gets its most serious and rigorous articulation in the philosophy of Levinas, who was perhaps more lucid than others in understanding that what these three presuppositions commonly presuppose is a "theologization of the self";[3] they have their common basis in our "last reality" which would be "religious" precisely in the sense that, as created beings, we are "initially for the other," bound to and vowed to him or her, *before* we are bound to ourselves.[4] The point I want to make is more general: when I spoke of a new wind blowing through contemporary philosophy, I was not exclusively thinking of Levinas's increasing popularity. I was also referring to how that wind had been blowing against whatever stood in its way in the landscape of Heidegger's texts. The catchword here seems to be "existential solipsism" (SZ, 188/233). Just a few quotes, almost at random:[5] "In its essence *Entschlossenheit* is linked with what Heidegger calls 'existential solipsism' (SZ, 188): *doxa*, relationship to other human beings, and plural debate are excluded from it and relegated into the orbit of concern, i.e., the inauthentic comportment of Dasein. Consequently, the very distinction between inauthentic and authentic seems to coincide with the distinction between public and private. We are justified to suspect here the echo of the Platonic disdain for human affairs." Whether one agrees or not with this suspicion, its message is clear: Dasein would still be too much of a subject, too "monadic," or too autarkic, even when reaching out to others: "[A]uthentic solicitude is a paradoxical relation in that, while seemingly uniting people, it refers them to their radical unrelatedness." One can, of course, wonder whether people are not in fact radically unrelated. But the point is that, even if one were to do so (as Heidegger himself did), one has already transgressed the boundaries set by a contemporary sensibility. As is shown by another quote. Its author proudly announces that he is "deliberately twisting Heidegger's words" with the aim of opposing his idea that "the fundamental experience of finitude is nonrelational, and all relationality . . . rendered secondary because of the primacy of *Jemeinigkeit*." This author confesses himself "shocked": "Authentic Dasein cannot mourn. One might even say that authenticity is constituted by making the act of mourning secondary to Dasein's *Jemeinigkeit*. Heidegger writes, shockingly in my view, 'We do not experience the death of others in a genuine sense; at most we are just "there alongside" (*nur "dabei"*)' (SZ, 239)." How then should we mourn? What is implied in mourning that Heidegger overlooked or excluded?

Here is the twist our author wishes to put on Heidegger's words who claimed that the corpse of the dead other is " *'more' than* a lifeless material thing" (SZ, 238/282): "I would say that the fundamental experience of finitude is rather like being a student of pathological anatomy where the dead other *'ist ein lebloses materielles Ding.'* . . . one watches the person one loves . . . die and become *a lifeless material thing*. . . . This is why I mourn." The misunderstanding implied here is too obvious to merit comment.[6] Mourning, as Derrida has shown[7] (and nothing in Heidegger's text seems to go against this), has precisely to do with the difficulty to "let the other go," to let him/her be dead, and this difficulty would not even arise if his/her corpse would *only* be "a lifeless material thing," and not refer, beyond itself, to the idea of life. I would not have given this quote were it not for the eloquence with which it opposes the primacy of *Jemeinigkeit* in Heidegger to what it would prefer instead: a primacy of relationality. As if there is something intolerable about nonrelationality and as if changing primacy, like one changes currency, could help us solve the problem. Intersubjectivity against the subject—no loss and only profits to be gained! Clearly, in suggestions like this we meet again the idea of the loss of all foreignness, but this time without recurrence to something other to/in ourselves—without resorting, that is, to that part of ourselves which, *for Heidegger, could help explain why there is alterity as such*. For in my incapacity to die the death of the other—to take it over—I experience myself as not being the other, and the other as not being me. Which is to say that not everything is accessible by me, that I am not "everywhere and nowhere" (SZ, §36) and that, to my grief perhaps, I am bound to my being in a different and more irreversible way than I am bound to the being of the other. And perhaps *this* is finitude. At least for Heidegger who did what he could to show that death "throws" Dasein "back" upon itself (SZ, 437/385), but who also did his utmost to understand why Dasein is the kind of being that "dislikes" the company of its being and is constantly on the run from it. It is not just that death, for inauthentic Dasein, is something that only happens to others, so that it could escape its mortality and its finitude. For it would not be any less inauthentic for Dasein to think that it can die the death of others, by, for example, properly mourning that death in being there *otherwise* than "just alongside." Without the experience of this radical unrelatedness, Dasein could never "open up" to the other; it would take the other's place, which amounts to saying: it would not let him/her be other—dead for example, or mortal or finite, that is, burdened by a weight no one can take over. To truly meet the other, that is, Dasein needs to accept a certain priority of its *Jemeinigkeit* over its *Mitsein*. For, as is well known, it is through the existential *Mitsein* that Dasein first and foremost manages to avoid its task of having to be the being that it is. This was, of course, the famous lesson on the "They": Dasein's tendency to not be itself—to be anyone in fact, except itself.

As these last paragraphs have suggested, I do not intend to sail with the wind that is blowing in contemporary thought. Indeed, I intend to sail against it. For it seems to me that what is now considered to be unfashionable in Heidegger, and in need of revision, is precisely what must be defended, and perhaps even fortified. "Intransitive" facticity would be just such a fortification—more in line, that is, with the spirit of Heidegger's argument than those who propose "to rewrite *Being and Time*" in order to adapt its ontology to the ethics we seem to be in need of: "[I]t is necessary to refigure fundamental ontology (as well as the existential analytic, the history of Being, and the thinking of *Ereignis* that goes along with it) with a thorough resolve that starts from the plural singular (*du singulier pluriel*) of origins, from being-with."[8] Instead of an existential analytic, we would need a coexistential analytic. Being would be being-with and this "with" would not simply be an addition to Being, but what constitutes it. It would be "at the heart of Being" (ibid., 30). One would need to go beyond Heidegger who only went as far as positing being-with as constitutive of being-there but waited to introduce "the co-originarity of *Mitsein* until after having established the originary character of Dasein" (ibid., 31). In preserving the order of classical philosophical exposition, Heidegger would have failed to "thematize the 'with' as the essential trait of Being and as its proper plural singular coessence" (ibid., 34). Admirable as this attempt to go beyond Heidegger seems to me, it nonetheless seems to opt for a course that is exactly contrary to the one I intend to set (which does not mean, since the earth is round, that the two would never meet, if only because I share and respect Nancy's worries about the fate of a community that would be more than a mere assemblage of parts).[9] Contrary to what seems to be Nancy's intention, I do not think that we should try to understand what Levinas insists on calling an "otherwise than being" as "the ownmost of Being," and thus try to think "being-with rather than the opposition between the other and Being" (ibid., 199 n. 37). What I shall put forward as "intransitive facticity" would rather seem to point to an opposition between the other and Being, which is not the "opposition" Levinas tried to thematize in terms of a Good (or a God) Beyond Being, and which tries to link the problem of singularization to something that seems to fall between the folds of either ethical or ontological difference.[10] But before we come to that, we should take not one, but more than one step back and make sure that we understand what exactly brought Levinas to oppose an "otherwise than Being" to Heidegger's "Being."

UNTRANSLATABLY MY OWN

Let us start, then, at the beginning, with this untranslatable term "Dasein" which, because of its untranslatableness, seems to invite us to take it for granted. Dasein is a verb. But it refers to a being. And yet, Heidegger never speaks of *a* Dasein. The reason is, of course, that the kind of "being" involved is not a being that one has, but a being that one is (GA 17, 287). In the expression "Dasein *is* its being," the "is" does not function as a copula that links Dasein to a predicate ("its being"). It has a transitive meaning. One is *one's being*, like one lives *one's life*. But not quite like one cooks *one's dinner*. For the relation between the subject of the verb *to be* and its direct object is more intimate than in the latter example. One can choose not to cook one's dinner and eat out instead, but one cannot choose not to be one's being. For Dasein *to be* means to conjugate the verb *to be* in the first person singular—"I am" means: I have to be the being that I am (SZ, 42/68). Whatever I do, it will be a way to be that being. Nothing can be said about my being, no content given to it, that will not be adverbial: referring to a *how* (*ein Wie*) I am that being (GA 17, 45). Perhaps one could also say that being is not just a transitive (GA 63, 7) but also a reflexive verb—but one cannot say it as well in English as one can in French: "*on n'est pas, on s'est,*" Levinas comments (EE, 38/28), which misleadingly translates as "one is not, one is oneself," as if there would be a content to this "self" ("just be yourself!"). Heidegger says it like this: "Dasein ist das Seiende, das *ich je selbst bin*, an dessen Sein ich als Seiendes 'beteiligt' bin" (GA 20, 205). A being in whose being I as an entity "share" (HCT, 152), or as I propose to translate: in which I play a part. I always play a part in my being, which is why Dasein "does not signify a what, (but) the way to be" (ibid.) of the being it designates. And there is only one way to be this being: "[T]o be it—is essentially to be it in each instance mine, whether I expressly know about it or not" (GA 20, 206/153). "To be it" translates the German *Zu-sein*, which also connotes: having to be this being, being unable not to be it. Hence the famous *"daß es ist und zu sein hat"* of which *Being and Time* tells us that this "that" is "naked" (e.g., SZ, 134/173)—for it is not a "what," and hence Dasein seems to miss something other beings have. It misses a *quidditas*, an "essence," a *"Wesen"*: "the 'essence' (*Wesen*) of Dasein (*des* Daseins) lies in its existence," in its "having to be (*Zu-sein*)" (SZ, 42/67). If its *"Wesen"* would not be the kind of verb we have been referring to, but a noun (*essentia*), Dasein would not be the being "for which its proper mode of being in a certain sense is not indifferent" (GA 26, 171/136). Which is to say, and we will come back to it, Dasein would not transcend (GA 27, 323 ff.).

Dasein is thus indeterminate, its being offers it no content, it can only give, indeed: it *cannot but* give content to its being. But this indetermination is not a simple lack. It is not a privation. It is a chance: what seems to be a void (*Nichtigkeit*) is in fact the most positive (*das Positivste*) in Dasein (GA 27, 332). It means that for Dasein, to be is *to be able to, "Seinkönnen."* In Dasein, *possibility is higher than actuality*[11]—Dasein is free, it has a leeway not just added to its being, but in its very being! In other words, in not being fixed by an essence or accidental properties, Dasein does not fall together with itself. It is "opened up," not just to its being, for which it is responsible, but also to the "contents" it cannot but give to this being. Or more precisely, for there is a complication: since Dasein's being implies a certain openness, it is not just "something" that *can* be filled, but something that always already is filled. Heidegger uses the verb *preisgeben*, which means to surrender (e.g., a city under siege), to give up (e.g., one's honor), to be helplessly exposed to (e.g., famine), and even to sacrifice (e.g., one's life). Let me quote a long passage from Heidegger's first course upon his return to Freiburg (WS 1928–29, the course Levinas must have attended)—I will quote in German and give the translation in note: "Weil das Dasein ein solches Seiendes ist, dem es in seinem Sein um dieses selbst geht, ist es an das Seiende preisgegeben, und zwar wesensnotwendig. Denn wir hörten, das Dasein ist erschlossenes; Seiendes, das es nicht ist, ist ihm offenbar; aber jetzt zeigt sich: nicht im Sinne einer bloßen Kenntnis, sondern, weil das Dasein wesenhaft aus sich herausgetreten ist, ist es dem Seienden und dessen Übermacht preisgegeben, und zwar nicht nur der Übermacht etwa der Naturgewalten, sondern auch den Machten und Gewälten, die das Dasein als Seiendes in sich selbst bringt" (GA 27, 326).[12] It is almost as if Dasein's being in its indeterminateness leaves Dasein in the lurch, surrenders it to powers higher than its own—including, Heidegger adds, those powers that it carries within itself. And thus, as he also adds, "transcendence as transport over beings [*das Seiende*] in the understanding of Being [*Seinsverständnis*] has lost completely the indifference one is tempted to credit it with, when one unfolds the problem of the understanding of Being in the frame of traditional ontology" (ibid.). "*Transzendieren das Seiende, d.h. In-der-Welt-sein, heißt, an das Seiende preisgegeben sein*" (ibid.). There is a sense of drama here: man is alone although he is surrounded by beings. This "metaphysical isolation" (GA 26, 172/137) of Dasein is thus ontological, not ontic: it means that Dasein's being has entrusted it with a task for which it provides no answer. Man is no longer that creature that under the eye of his/her creator had to travel the path set for it, thus accomplishing its essence. Dasein is "given up": no longer *homo viator*, but "a lieutenant of the nothing" (*Platzhalter des Nichts*), which traverses its being (BW, 108).

Not finding an answer in its being as to how it has to be its being, Dasein will find its answers elsewhere: in that to which it has been surrendered. *Being and Time* will thematize this as Dasein's tendency to fall (*Verfallen*). But the lecture courses that preceded it and prepared for it are, in a way, much more thrilling when it comes to describe Dasein's "problem" with its being. Thus, the famous *Widerschein* or *Reluzenz*, mentioned only once or twice in *Being and Time* (e.g., SZ, 21, cf. 16 and 247) (*Widerschein*) finds itself in the company of a host of other Latin terms (*Praestruktion, Larvanz, Ruinanz, Horrescenz, das Tentative, das Quietive, das Alienative, das Negative*) that all turn around the same problem: life—as it is then still called—misses something and it is not going to accept that condition. One could even say: it is not going to be grateful for it. And then one could add that if there is an ethics implied in this ontology, it is precisely the ethics that follows from learning to see in what we supposedly "miss," that which makes us possible: our dwelling place, our *Aufenthalt*, our ethos. But we are not quite as far as that. Life, Heidegger tells us, "constantly eludes itself as such," it avoids meeting itself (*sich aus dem Wege gehen*) (GA 61, 107/80) and tries "to let itself . . . be carried [*tragen*] by beings which it is not" but with which it can "identify," since it is open to them, and, in fact, always already occupied by them (GA 26, 174/138—transl. corrected). Dasein, as it were, profits from the fact that, being open, it is always already taken in by other beings, "human" or not, which will always give it things to do, to be occupied with, to engage itself in, to have plans with or for: "This very multiplicity of possibilities . . . always implies an increase in the possibilities of *mistaking* [*Vergreifen*] oneself in ever new ways. . . . insofar as these *interminable mistakes* [*Verfehlbarkeiten*] are all of the character of meaningful things in which, as meaningful-wordly objects, life lives, this interminability becomes what is formalistically characterized as infinity and infinite abundance, inexhaustibility, that which can never be mastered, the 'always more of' life, and the 'always more than' life" (GA 61, 107/80). "Mistakes" should be understood literally here: not as errors, but as mis-takes—ways not to grab the thing itself, but to grab past it.

"Life" does its utmost to mistake itself for something else. For example, life tends to "miss" the fact that it is finite. It misses that "fact" like a shot misses its target, by first "missing" the meaning of this finitude (taking it to mean: "not infinite") and then (in the same breath) reappropriating it by its ever new possibilities: "This infinity is the disguise (*Maske*, mask) factical life factically places upon and holds before itself and its world. . . . With this infinity, life blinds itself [*blendet*], puts out its own eyes. In the sequestration [*Abriegelung*], *life leaves itself out*; life comes up too short. Factical life leaves itself out precisely *in defending itself explicitly and positively against itself*. . . . In its taking of directions, factical *life places itself on a certain track* [*bahnt sich die Spur*] and does so specifically by inclining [*Neigend*], suppressing distance [*Abstandverdrängend*], sequestering itself [*sich abriegelnd*] within a directionality toward the easy" (GA 61, 107–108/80–81). Let's repeat the underlined: (factical) life leaves itself out in defending itself explicitly and positively *against itself* by placing itself on a certain track. We'll come to the "factical" (*faktisch*) later. Let us first ask why "life" (later: Dasein)[13] needs to defend itself *against itself*.

UNDOING DASEIN'S SELF-DEFENSE

Heidegger would dismiss the question. There is no "why," for there is no *need* for such a defense. It just so happens that with the kind of Being that we are analyzing here (life, i.e., Dasein), the structure of this being is such that it is always already distracted from what its being demands of it: to be this being in the first person singular. But, as we have seen, this demand is empty and even not listening to it—being distracted—is a way to pay heed to it. "Whether I expressly know about it or not," we heard Heidegger say, I am the subject of my Being in the grammatical sense of the term *subject*. We touch here upon the status of doing philosophy for the Heidegger of the 1920s. Let us not forget that *Being and Time* explicitly said that the analytic of Dasein that it was offering was meant to provide us with "possibilities for a more primordial [*ursprünglichere*] existentiell understanding" than we would have had without it (SZ, 295/341), and that, in the same book, Heidegger describes his project as "an interpreting liberation of Dasein for its utmost possibility of existence" (SZ, 303/350). Fundamental ontology is not meant to be neutral. It is revolutionary. Its task is not just to *describe* Dasein, but to help the Dasein that it addresses *to become* Dasein. How so? Why could fundamental ontology not restrict itself to a neutral description of the ways in which Dasein is busy being its being, of the ways it moves about in its being—a being that has, Heidegger tells us in an early text, a "peculiar kind of movement" (*Bewegtheit*) to it (GA 63, 65/51)? How could the thematization of Dasein's "movement" be not neutral?

There are at least three elements in Heidegger's writings that one should take into account here—and, as we shall later see when we turn to Levinas's early discussion with Heidegger, none of them follows directly from an analytic of Dasein *as such*, but they all involve a certain articulation of that analytic—a kind of "decision" imposed on it by Heidegger. The three *topoi* I am thinking of are the following: Dasein *flees*; but that from which it flees, will always have left a *trace* that can help Dasein to find its way back to itself; provided it grabs the occasion and pays heed to *the call*, which it can, however, always refuse to hear. Heidegger seems to think of philosophy as a certain practice that can help Dasein recognize such a call. Thus, after a lengthy analysis in which he gives seven points of comparison to set off the two types of boredom (being bored by/being bored with) he had been lecturing on, Heidegger ends his lecture with a characteristic warning: "It would, however, be a *misunderstanding* if we were merely to take what is summarized in these seven points as a result, instead of demonstrating all this to ourselves in a living manner by now retracing the various interwoven paths taken by our investigation hitherto. For, to point it out once more, in case you have not yet noticed: it is not a matter of taking a definition of boredom home with you, but of learning and understanding [*verstehen lernen*] to move oneself in the depths of Dasein" (GA 29/30, 198/131, transl. corrected). Philosophy can only prepare for such an understanding, which is not intellectual but is rather, as all *Verstehen* in Heidegger, a matter of knowing one's way about a certain x or y, in this case: "boredom." "Philosophizing," Heidegger tells his students in a later lecture of the same course, "always remains something penultimate" (257/173). Philosophy prepares for a "complete transformation" (*Umstellung*, ibid. 95/62) of (our conception of) man, but it cannot succeed by itself. It will only succeed if those it seeks to address will revolve around their own axis: "Nor will we be tempted to believe that these questions and the answers we give to them will eliminate the need [*Not*] of contemporary Dasein. Such need will at best be rendered more acute [*verschärft*], more acute in the sole possible sense that this questioning will bring us to the brink [*Rand*] of possibility, the possibility of restoring to Dasein its actuality, that is, its existence. Yet between this uttermost brink of possibility and the actuality of Dasein there lies a very fine line. This is a line one can never merely glide across, but one which man can only leap over in dislodging his Dasein" (ibid.).

Seinem Dasein einen Rück geben—to give it a push or a pull, can only happen in "solitary action" (*einzelnes Handeln*). It cannot be taught—but it can be facilitated, and this is what philosophers or poets do by "helping bring to word that which Dasein wishes to speak about in this fundamental attunement [i.e., boredom—R.V.]" (249/167). For it is "by means of words" that "the attunement of Dasein can be made visible in such a way that certain new possibilities of Dasein's being are set free" (GA 20, 375/272). Philosophy's task is "not to describe the consciousness of man but to evoke the Dasein in man" (GA 29/30, 258/174).

Instead of "evoke," Heidegger writes *beschwören*, which is what one does with snakes, spirits, demons. But he immediately discards all reference to magical enchantment or mystical vision and insists that philosophy has at its disposal only "sober conceptual questioning" to "form" and "keep open" "its own interrogative space" (ibid.). Yet, it is within that, almost (?) therapeutic space, that the call must be heard or received. Better still: in which it can resound. For there is a call, and the only problem is that Dasein's normal comportment is such that it does not hear what is nonetheless there, reaching out to it. Here we find again the basic structure behind the three themes I previously mentioned. Dasein is *on the run* for something it *need not* run from and which it *cannot outrun*. It is this co-presence of a "need not" and a "cannot" that explains the opposition which is underlying all of the lecture courses leading up to *Being and Time* and well beyond it: the opposition between *Feigheit* (cowardice) and *Mut* (courage).

Dasein, as we know from *Being and Time*, has a tendency to take it easy and to make it easy for itself (SZ, 165/128; GA 61, 109). It tries to avoid taking up "the burdensome character" of its Being—the "that it is and has to be" we discussed before. What is threatening about this burden is that it does not tell Dasein what to do with it, how to carry it. But Dasein *wants answers* and it finds them in what surrounds it, in its *Umwelt*. The things Dasein is engaged with *reflect back* on Dasein a certain kind of image as to who it is and what it needs to do. This is the famous *Widerschein* or *Reluzenz*—reflection in an optical sense: "To reflect means, in the optical context, to break at something, to radiate back from there, to show itself in a reflection from something. . . . Dasein does not first need to turn backward to itself [i.e., re-flect—R.V.] as though, keeping itself behind its own back, it were at first standing in front of things and staring rigidly at them. Instead, *it never finds itself otherwise than in the things themselves,* and in fact in those things that daily surround it. It *finds itself* primarily and constantly *in things* because, tending them, distressed by them, it always in some way or other *rests* in things. Each one of us is what he pursues and cares for" (GA 24, 226/159). Dasein prefers, as it were, to have its own self reflected to it from things, rather than to face the fact that it *is* this self and that this self can only have the content Dasein gives to it, without ever coming to a "final" content, for to actualize one possibility is to leave out others one could have actualized instead (possibility, remember, is higher than actuality—and this is a consequence of that thesis). Dasein thinks of itself, for example, as a future professor, it writes a PhD thesis and hopes to find a job, to be invited to conferences, to outdo other competitors, to get tenure track, to become important, etc. This is what surrounds it and provides it with *answers* and a path to follow—Dasein's future is prestructured by its *Umwelt*: it "comes toward itself from out of the things" (GA 24, 410/289). Instead of being "answerable" for its self, Dasein gratefully *takes over the answers* that make it "forget" (ibid.) its questions: "[L]ife, possessing relucence in care, is precisely intent on having something surrounding itself, having the world *in such a way that this world* makes up the surroundings [*Umgebung*] for the activity of life and *answers or at least listens, watches or comments such activity*" (GA 61, 129–30/96, underlined corrected!). Transcendence, one could say, instead of being dramatic, *but mute* (i.e., not answering, not responding, irresponsive), becomes a charade in which it is not us who transcend beings, but beings that move over into us and submit us to a force we unknowingly provided them with. There is some sort of *fetishism structure* to what seems to be happening here: "as though Dasein's can-be were projected by the things, by Dasein's commerce with them, and not primarily by Dasein itself from its own most proper self" (GA 24, 410/289). We've lost our *Seinkönnen* in or to the mirror held out to us by things. But only because we expect, like the evil queen in *Snow White*, the mirror to be able to give us an answer to the question that plagues each of us: "Who am I?" And because like the queen we are satisfied with an answer to a different question ("Who am I not?") as long as it gives us some hold, for example the hold of the comparative (you are a more promising student than . . .) or of the superlative (you are the best).

Heidegger thus *understands* how Dasein can come to lose track of itself, but he doesn't approve, does not think this is inevitable, although it is happening all of the time. He insists on calling it *a flight* (*Flucht*): "Aussein auf etwas, was begegnet in der Welt ist nichts als der Ausdruck des Wegkommens aus der Unheimlichkeit" (GA 17, 317). To be intent on something that one can come across in the world is *nothing but* the expression of getting out of the uncanny. Nothing but! And Heidegger immediately gives an example that may function as an eye-opener to what in fact he is claiming here: "From this basic phenomenon of uncanniness one also has to explicate what we designate as language [*Sprache*]. Sprache: a specific way of man's being. Sprache means . . . as speaking in the uncanny: *sich aussprechen, lautwerden in der Unheimlichkeit*" (GA 17, 317). And he adds, between brackets: "a well-known phenomenon, that one starts to speak loudly [*laut zu reden*] in the uncanny." And a bit farther: "Das Dasein spricht sich gewissermaßen aus sich heraus—von sich weg." One could render this as: Dasein talks itself out of it. And then the question becomes: what is this "it" and how or in what sense is it uncanny? It is on this question that Levinas and Heidegger disagreed. As least on first sight.

TALKING ONESELF OUT OF "IT'

The passage with which we ended the previous section comes from a 1923–24 lecture course—this by itself is remarkable for in these few lines much more seems to be said about language than we come to know in *Being and Time*, where the most significant thing that is said about it is that it is the "worldly Being" of *Rede*: "Die Hinausgesprochenkeit der Rede ist die Sprache" (SZ, 161/204). With or in language *Rede* becomes "verlautbart" (SZ, 163)—it is put into words and these words sound—they are sounds one can encounter within the world: "Language is a totality of words—a totality in which discourse [*Rede*] has a 'worldly' Being of its own; and as an entity within-the-world, this totality thus becomes something which we may come across as ready-to-hand" (ibid.). Thus, *Being and Time* has the idea that language (*Sprache*) should be thought of in terms of an ex-pression (*Sichaussprechen*) of *Rede*. But it no longer seems to have what, in 1923–24, Heidegger was suggesting when linking such "sich aussprechen" (to express oneself) to a "sich *aus sich heraus* sprechen" (to talk oneself out of oneself) and to a "von sich weg sprechen" (to talk away from oneself), which I tried to render as "to talk oneself out of it" and for which Heidegger himself gave the example of "becoming loud" in the uncanny. In speaking, Dasein *turns away* from what is uncanny about itself! Which means that Dasein, as it were, seeks to escape the confrontation with its "self" by seeking the company of words—just as we heard Heidegger explain that Dasein is fleeing its own mute transcendence by turning to what in the world seems to provide it with answers. In other words, it would seem that language qua "*Verlautbarung*" is considered by Heidegger in 1923–24 as itself some sort of flight. If this "flight" were somehow necessary, this would have amounted to an unprecedented existential grounding of language: something in Dasein (the "it" Dasein talks itself out of—the uncanny) would have driven it out of itself . . . into language! Heidegger would have been on the brink of discovering something—an "on the way to language"—that he never retrieved.

It is no coincidence that this potential insight into the Being of language did not prevail. What prevented such breakthrough is precisely the theme, already present in 1923–24, that got the upper hand in *Being and Time* and in the inaugural Freiburg lecture, "What is metaphysics?" Loudness, in these texts, is seen as a way *not to hear*, to *outcry* a message that silently announces itself (*Gerede* in *Being and Time* is essentially "vociferized" *Rede* [*verlautbarte Rede*], and the voice of conscience, as is well known, does not resort to sounds, but says nothing, speaks in *silence*).[14] Thus, we read in *What is Metaphysics?*: "[I]n the malaise [*Unheimlichkeit*] of anxiety we *often* try to shatter the vacant stillness with compulsive talk only proves the presence of the nothing" (BW 103, my italics to indicate that such a flight is not necessary). It is this "nothing" that makes Dasein feel ill at ease (malaise = *mal à l'aise*), for it robs Dasein of its usual "holds" and confronts it with the "nakedness" of "the Being that it is and has to be." In other words, what is characteristic for the moods Heidegger will analyze as "*Grundstimmungen*," such as anxiety and boredom, is that they take away what is usually present as something to hold onto for Dasein. The mirror things hold out to Dasein and from which a certain picture of itself reflects onto Dasein is, as it were, shattered in anxiety or in boredom. Or perhaps more exactly: it is still there, but no longer reflecting anything, like a fogged mirror in the bathroom after having taken a hot shower. In other words: the *Reluzenz*-structure drops out. Standing-out-toward "nothing," Dasein is left "hanging" in the very movement that characterizes it qua ex-istence, "hovering," as it were, "above" the nothing (BW, 103) of which we heard Heidegger say that it is not a privation (the absence of *something* that ought to be there), but "the most positive" (*das Positivste*) about Dasein (that through which it is not closed onto itself, but a being that is "opened up," that "lacks" an essence, and that *is* its possibility).

One could think of this "lautwerden in der Unheimlichkeit" in terms of what happens when "whistling in the dark."[15] If one thinks of darkness as a kind of disappearance (what is normally there to be seen is now not visible), then darkness does away with (at least part of) the *Reluzenz*-phenomenon: Dasein is thrown back upon itself, alone with itself. And it doesn't withstand this, it breaks up that loneliness by singing or talking or whistling to itself. It thus seems to provide itself with the means to distract itself from itself—as Heidegger puts it in a different, and more familiar context to those who read *Being and Time*: "Dasein speaks about itself and sees itself in such and such a manner, and yet this is only a mask which it holds up before itself *in order not to* be frightened by itself. The warding 'off' of anxiety" (GA 63, 32/26). In other words, what I am suggesting is that "idle talk" and "whistling in the dark" both resort to language as a "sound system," both serve the same purpose of breaking Dasein's uncanniness, as it were, by placing something (the worldly Being of *Rede*: sounds, *Sprache*) *between* Dasein and itself. With this fall *into* the world—*into* language—Dasein puts itself off track (*sich verführen*). It mis-takes itself. It fails to hear (*überhört*, SZ, 279) its "own" message for which it substitutes a more telling story and thus gives in to its tendency to "have itself objectively there for itself," to "bring itself objectively into its there," that is: "to take possession of itself," that is in turn: "to make itself certain and secure about itself" (GA 63, 64–65/51). Language, one could conclude on the basis of this 1923–24 passage, is Dasein's last resort. When all else fails, when all escape routes are blocked, Dasein can still speak to itself or whistle a tune that will calm it down. Language is Dasein's most reliable pacifier.

One only needs to compare this "take" on language with one single sentence from Levinas's 1947 *From existence to Existents* to immediately see both how this text—Levinas's "first" "real" book—is at once very different from and extremely close to the Heidegger of the twenties. Here is the passage I have in mind: "One has to find something to say to one's companion."[16] To be sure, the stakes of this passage are easily overlooked, for Levinas continues the phrase: "[One has to] exchange an idea, around which, *as around a third term*, social life necessarily starts" (ibid.). This reference to a third term suggests that Levinas, here as elsewhere, is merely pointing out that the kind of other we meet in "the world," is but an other who is "dressed" in a "role" or a "function" or a "form" that covers up what is genuinely other about him/her: that which Levinas in his other works will refer to as "the face of the Other" which "breaks through" or "rends" all such forms, functions, or roles: "Form is that by which a being is turned toward the sun, that by which it has a visage [the French *face* and not: *visage*, transl. corrected!], through which it gives itself, by which it comes forward. *It conceals* the nudity in which an undressed being withdraws from the world" (EE, 61/31, my italics). Polite, "formal" conversation, in which one exchanges *n'importe quoi*, be it some meaningless comment about the weather or about the dentist who is once more lagging behind schedule, would be but a way to *avoid* meeting the Other: "Social life in the world does not have that uncanny [*inquiétant*, transl. altered] character that a being feels before another being, before alterity" (ibid.). Read in this way, there would be no break with the structure of Heidegger's argument—indeed, there would be a formal parallel: social life, for example, formal conversation, would be but a means to flee the confrontation with what is uncanny. And the disagreement with Heidegger would restrict itself to the *a quo* from which one tries to distract oneself—Dasein's nothingness, for Heidegger; the Other's nakedness, for Levinas: "[T]he basic timidity that affects one . . . is banished from the world" (EE, 61/32), precisely by resorting to the "form-al" holds the world offers us to hold on to (EE, 63/33).

But this would be misunderstanding Levinas's aim here and completely missing the point he is making—precisely against Heidegger. "To say that clothing (and thus, by extension: 'form,' 'function,' 'role') exists *for* covering oneself up is not to see how clothing *frees* man from the humbleness of his naked state" (EE, 65/34, my italics). It is not just that "not everything that is given in the world is a tool" (EE, 65/34) and would thus display the *Um-zu* structure (in order to, e.g., cover oneself up) Heidegger famously analyzed. It is, above all, that Heidegger failed to realize—if he ever overlooked anything (TA, 45/63), as Levinas adds elsewhere, perhaps not without humor—that "in the ontological adventure the world is an episode which, far from deserving to be called a fall, has its own equilibrium, harmony and positive ontological function: the possibility of extracting oneself from anonymous being" (EE, 69/37). Social conversation, "idle talk," is not just an escape that takes the place of a more genuine communication, of a *Verschwiegenheit* (a telling silence) that, without resorting to formulas without content, says all there is to say.[17] It is a *liberation*! It *frees* from an embarrassment that would be mortifying—both to oneself and to the other. Like in Heidegger, something is put *between* oneself and the other—a third term is inserted between the parties, but this term, unlike in Heidegger, is seen as what "provides the possibility of existing in a withdrawal from existence" (EE, 70/38).

Time, then, to go backstage and wonder how Levinas can come to formulate as a problem—existing in a withdrawal from existence—what to a Heideggerian ear would be, at best, a confusion of terms. Here is a parallel statement, from a contemporary text: the world "offers the subject a liberation from itself. [It] permits it to exist at a distance from itself. The subject is absorbed in the object it absorbs, and nevertheless keeps a distance with regard to that object" (TA, 51–52/67). Let me try to comment.

THE WORLD—A FIRST LIBERATION

What for Heidegger is a flight, a falling into the world (in an ontic sense) and a turning away from one's being-in-the-world (in an ontological sense) by clinging to the relucent and prestructured contents Dasein comes across *in* the world—in short: Dasein's absorption into what it is not is characterized by Levinas as a liberation. Instead of losing itself *to* the world, what Levinas calls "world" here is what *permits* the subject to lose itself! Instead of seeing in everyday life a lack of courage, Levinas reads it as "a preoccupation with salvation" (TA, 39/58)! Instead of an inauthentic flight, a necessary one! And thus a parting of ways, where Levinas chooses to follow the track Heidegger "decided" to ignore—for example in the passage concerning language's "birth" out of the uncanny, which we discussed in the preceding section. What happens, in fact, is that Levinas's path leads him back to a point situated this side of Heidegger's primitive (i.e., underived) concepts—Dasein, *Jemeinigkeit*, existence, being-in-the-world. Indeed, Levinas starts from a notion he knows to be "absurd" to Heidegger: "The most profound thing about *Being and Time* for me [E. L.] is this Heideggerian distinction [between *Sein* and *Seiendes*, *Being* and *being*, between *existence* and *existent*]. But in Heidegger there is a distinction, not a separation. Existence is always grasped in the existent, and for the existent that is a human being the Heideggerian term *Jemeinigkeit* (mineness) precisely expresses the fact that existing is always possessed by someone. I do not think that Heidegger can admit an existence without existents, which to him would seem absurd" (TA, 24/44–45).

Levinas knows what he is doing. He knows that he is parting ways with Heidegger, who indeed did not hesitate to correct the one passage in which, to my knowledge, he had dared to suggest the idea of a Being without beings.[18] I am not going to take the reader through all the stages that Levinas follows in *Existence and Existents* and *Time and the Other* after having chosen as his starting point precisely this notion which, to Heidegger, could make no sense. Let it suffice to point out what the obvious consequences of such a move must be. Once one accepts a Being without beings, the next step, of course, is to introduce *a being*—a step that Levinas, who knows his classics, calls hypostasis: the transition of a verb into a substance. A transition giving rise to something that stands on its own (sub-*stance*) and that cannot, of course, be the initiative of what will result *from* it: a subject that exists in a withdrawal from existence (Being). It is as if a certain fissure is opened up in the continuum of such anonymous Being that Levinas also calls the *"il y a,"* a *"there is,"* as indistinct as can be. Distinction presupposes a setting apart, a caesura, a certain between, and thus, so to speak, the transition from the analogous to the digital, from continuity to discontinuity. The *il y a* opens up (*s'ouvre*: EE, 171/104), recedes and as it were, gives "birth" (EE, 26/8) to an ontological privacy: to *a* being that has a certain mastery over Being (its Being). An atheist version of creation—without creator, without generosity: it just so happens that "there is" a rent in what hitherto was seamless.[19] A strange "contract" where one of the parties only comes into existence as a result of the contract it was never given occasion to sign (ibid.). The hypostatic subject has contracted its being, almost as one contracts a disease. Like something it didn't ask for, but was infected with. Loaded with a weight it is not quite fit to carry and which nonetheless (Levinas thinks of what happens in effort, fatigue, weariness, or indolence) it is unable to let go, "holding on to what it is letting slip" (EE, 42/18). The subject's delay in its contract with being, its always having arrived too late for it to cancel that contract which already obliges it, seems somehow to keep pursuing it. The delay continues, being is portrayed as an effort to catch up with oneself: "Existence drags behind it a weight—if only itself—which complicates the trip it takes. Burdened with itself . . . it does not purely and simply exist. Its movement of existence, which might be pure and straightforward, is bent and caught up in itself, showing that the verb 'to be' is a reflexive verb: it is not just that one is, one is oneself [*on s'est*]" (EE, 38/16).

On s'est—we used this formulation before when commenting on Dasein's "that it is and has to be." But then we (ab-)used it to clarify Heidegger's insight that being is a transitive verb: one is one's being. But it is not so for Levinas—as one of the few commentators on these early texts pointed out: "Heidegger, when saying that existence is a burden [*Lastcharakter des Daseins*] does not have the means to take into account its doubling into a being and a having."[20] It is precisely this mixture of something transitive and something "absolutely intransitive" (TA, 21/42) that Levinas seems to be pointing to. One is one's being, for sure, but this being is more than the direct object of the verb *to be*. It sticks to the one who is supposed to conjugate it in the first person singular, but who in fact never achieves that mastery, constantly hindered by it, stumbling over it, as one stumbles over one's feet. Inevitably so, according to Levinas, for in being oneself (*on s'est*), there is already a self that is, as it were, too much: "The relationship with oneself [*soi*] is, as in Blanchot's novel *Aminadab*, the relationship with a double chained to the ego [*moi*], a viscous, heavy, stupid double, but one the ego [*le moi*] is with precisely because it is me [*moi*]" (TA, 37/56). There is, in other words, a price to be paid for mineness, for escaping from Being without beings: the "inability to detach oneself from oneself," the inevitability of "returning to oneself," of being "riveted to oneself" (TA, 36/55). "Ontological relationships are not disembodied ties. The relationship between ego [*moi*] and self [*soi*] is not the inoffensive reflection of spirit upon itself. It is the whole of human materiality" (TA, 37–38/56–57).

This should suffice to catch the gist of what is happening here: not so much a critique of Heidegger than a different starting point which then, of course, will lead to endless disagreements. As we will clarify in the next sections, what Levinas is doing is in fact shifting the weight between the terms of Heidegger's existential analytic—one could say that by risking the hypothesis of a fall into being before there is a thrownness into the world, Heidegger's analysis is rendered more dynamic. And the source of this dynamism is a desire in the subject to escape . . . itself. To get rid, that is, of its double—which also means: of its materiality, of its being stuck to itself, of its being doomed to be its own company. *Jemeinigkeit* in Heidegger is a task, not a desire. Whereas in Levinas it is, from the start, the longing for a releasement—which is why whatever meets that longing halfway will not be seen as a mere distraction, but as an attempt at liberation. Thus, the world, which,—precisely because it is not just an ontological function, but also an ontic content, not just a void that allows things to appear, but also these appearances themselves—will be portrayed as what "nourishes" this desire to part company with itself: "[T]he world and our existence in the world constitute a fundamental advance of the subject in overcoming the weight that it is to itself, in overcoming its materiality—that is to say, in loosening the bond between the self [*soi*] and the ego [*moi*]" (TA, 44/62). Hence, Levinas's polemical remark that "Dasein in Heidegger is never hungry" (TI, 134): "Human life in the world does not go beyond the objects that fulfill it. It is perhaps not correct to say that we live to eat, but it is no more correct to say [as Heidegger would, according to Levinas] that we eat to [*um zu*] live. The uttermost finality of eating is contained in food. When one smells a flower, it is the smell that limits the finality of the act. To stroll is to enjoy the fresh air, not *for* health [cf. *das Worum-willen* of SZ §18] but for the air. These are the nourishments characteristic of our existence in the world. It is an ecstatic existence—being outside oneself—but limited by the object" (TA, 45–46/63). Limited—and not seduced into inauthenticity. The world is a resting place, a first stop for that endless desire of the subject to transcend itself—to find itself engaged by a movement at the end of which it will have been transformed. Which is to say: redeemed. And this, as is well known, will presuppose an event that prevents the everyday transcendence of life in the world "from falling back upon a point that is always the same" (TA, 48/66). Such a transcendence "without a return to its point of departure" (ibid.) will need to come from Outside. It will need the ethical Other—the face and not its worldly form.

THE MESSAGE OF BOREDOM

Let us see where this excursus into Levinas has brought us. Recall our starting point: Heidegger's idea that being is transitive and that the being he calls Dasein should not flee from the task implied in this transition. Levinas may have helped us to realize that in thus putting forward the verbal Dasein as the name by which to refer to the human being's Being, Heidegger may have left out what he should not have missed—not just to come to a "full-fledged anthropology" (which was, of course, not his intention: SZ §10), but to raise the question of Being. And of Time. Again, let us refrain from following Levinas in the reasoning that leads him to conclude that "time" should not be linked to Being, but to the Other (*Time and the Other* thus already in its title announces Levinas's disagreement with *Being and Time*). The "differend"[21] with Heidegger can be formulated at less cost—by simply focusing on an analysis they both share: the analysis of boredom.

As was pointed out before, what makes boredom such an interesting mood for Heidegger is that, not unlike anxiety, it seems to do away with the obfuscation to which Dasein tends to fall prey by way of its very ek-sistence. Instead of being taken in by things, in boredom Dasein finds itself disengaged: nothing seems to interest it any longer, everything becomes pale and indifferent. Consequently, when in *The*

Fundamental Concepts Heidegger analyzes and describes various types of boredom, his interest seems to lie precisely in the kind of boredom for which Dasein can no longer "blame" anything or anyone. This boredom leaves Dasein no escape, it seems to force a phenomenological reduction onto it in which it *cannot but hear* the message concerning its own Being that is addressed to it.[22] Here, it is not just a matter of a train coming late, of a teacher giving a boring class, or of a wasted evening in a not so engaging company that lies at the heart of boredom. Boredom no longer seems to come from outside (reflecting back on us through *boring* things, persons, situations), but from the depths of Dasein itself. Everything becomes, in one sole stroke (*mit einem Schlag*), indifferent to Dasein, including itself. This is, as Boris Ferreira has wonderfully shown.[23] what seems to make this type of boredom even deeper than anxiety: for in anxiety, Dasein's *Umwillen-seiner-selbst* (for the sake of itself) still stands (it is anxious *for itself*), whereas in deep boredom Dasein seems no longer even to care for itself. One could perhaps add that the difference with a full-fledged depression is that Dasein, even here, still cares about this no longer caring for itself (the transition to depression then being a matter of degree). Hence the desperation, the ultimate nonindifference with being bored. Be that as it may (GA 29/30, 211/140 may not be dealing with the same "despair"), what is striking is that Heidegger returns, to describe what is happening here, to the formulation he used in *Being and Time* (and elsewhere) to describe anxiety (*es ist einem unheimlich*, SZ §40): *es ist einem langweilig*. It is this *"einem,"* which suggests a certain anonymity (as does the *"es"*), that interests us here.

Here is Heidegger's commentary on the meaning of "it is boring for one": "For whom then? Not for me as me, not for me with these particular prospective intentions and so on. For the nameless and undetermined I, then? No, but presumably for the self [*dem Selbst*] whose name, status and the like have become irrelevant" (GA 29/30, 215/143). The quote goes on, but the English translation manages to make Heidegger say the exact contrary of what he in fact says: "wohl aber dem Selbst, dessen Name, Stand und dergleichen belanglos geworden, *selbst in die Gleichgültigkeit mit hineingezogen ist*"—it is the name, status, etc. which are *themselves* drawn into indifference, and not, as the translators have it, the Self "which is *itself* drawn into indifference" (FCM, 143). This is crucial, if only because, as we shall see, Levinas will disagree on precisely this point! The rest of the passage should be understood accordingly—what drops out is the inauthentic self, *Being and Time*'s They-self (*Man-Selbst*), the self as one has it through *Praestruktion* and *Reluzenz*: "Yet the self of Dasein that has lost its stakes in all these areas [*das in all dem belanglos werdende Selbst des Daseins*] does not thereby lose its determinacy, but rather the reverse, for this particular *impoverishment* [*Verarmung*] which sets in with respect to our person [*Person*] in this 'it is boring for one,' first *brings the self* in all its nakedness *to itself* as the self that is there and has taken over the being of its Da-sein. For what purpose? To be it [i.e., Dasein]" (ibid., translation corrected). The point is clear: we lose our public selfhood, our *persona* (name, status, function, etc.), but we do *not* lose all selfhood. To the contrary, we are reminded of what truly being a self amounts to: to be the being that each of us is (*jemeinig*) and has to be. For Heidegger, what is characteristic of deep boredom is the link between this de-*persona*-lization and its reverse, extreme singularization, metaphysical loneliness: no one (and certainly not the public "one" [*Man*]) can take over my "*Zu-sein*" from me. If one misses this point, one has missed everything (as, for example, H. Dreyfus does in making the same mistake as our translators, with regard to anxiety).[24] One will have missed, for example, the structure of the revelation (*offenbaren* is a verb that keeps coming up in these lectures) Heidegger is trying to uncover here. He resorts to a play on words that, again, is almost untranslatable. "Alles Versagen ist ein Sagen, d.h. ein Offenbarmachen" (e.g., GA 29/30, 216) ("all telling refusal is in itself a telling, a making manifest," FCM, 140).

Let us analyze the structure of this formula first, before wondering what is said in deep boredom, by whom and to whom. Surprisingly, Heidegger, who is normally very wary of what I elsewhere called "the privative approach,"[25] resorts to a full-fledged privative reasoning. The dominant term is *Sagen*. *Ver-sagen* means that something is with-held, not given, refused. It is a sort of active negation. One is deprived (cf. *privation*) of something. Privative negations refer to the absence of something *that ought to be there* (e.g., a wingless bird). Thus, in Heidegger who continues the passage: "What do beings in this telling refusal of themselves as a whole tell us in such refusal? What do they tell us in refusing to tell? It is a telling refusal of *that which somehow could and was to be granted to Dasein*. And what is that? The very possibilities of its doing and acting. The telling refusal tells of these possibilities of Dasein. This telling refusal does not speak about them, does not lead directly to dealings with them, but in its telling refusal it points to them and makes them known in refusing them" (GA 29/30, 211–12/140). This is, then, deep boredom's message: "[I]n telling refusal there lies a reference to something else. This reference [*Verweisung*] is the telling announcement [*Ansagen*] of possibilities left unexploited [*brachliegenden Möglichkeiten*]" (212/141).

In deep boredom Dasein comes to understand itself as *Seinkönnen, possibilitas*—precisely because boredom is the kind of mood in which no single possibility is attractive enough to engage in and thus to identify with. Boredom, then, is an im-possibility, or one could better say: it im-possibilizes Dasein, that is, it paralyzes (inauthentic) Dasein's tendency to always engage itself in possibilities which it is intent to actualize and out of which it understands itself.[26] By not leaving Dasein any *such* possibilities, boredom confronts it with its being-possible as such. But, over and above that, it also confronts Dasein with the fact that it is not the sole master or origin of its possibilities—as it tends to think every time it is engaged in one of them, planning and projecting ahead. "Something" else is pointing to itself in this telling refusal, "something" that Heidegger calls "that which properly makes possible the Dasein in me" (*das eigentliche Ermöglichende des Daseins in mir*) (216/143), "something that makes possible, sustains and guides [*führt*] all essential possibilities of Dasein" (ibid.).

This "something" else is, for Heidegger, time. Time is what withholds itself in boredom and thereby points to itself and to its "link" with Dasein—and thus: to its "link" with Being. For *Dasein* is, for Heidegger, the kind of being that, because it is such that it always plays a part in (its) Being, carries in itself the privilege of being able to raise and listen to the question of Being . . . and Time. And just as Being "kann unbegriffen sein, nie aber völlig unverstanden" (SZ, 183/228), just as Being, however forgotten it gets, always has left a trace that points to its having been forgotten (*Being and Time* could not have been written, the question it asks could not have been raised, were it not for such traces which it diligently tracks), so time too cannot hide without leaving a trace: "What entrances in telling refusal *must* [my italics!] at the same time be that which gives something to be free in its telling announcing and which fundamentally makes possible the possibility of Dasein" (GA 29/30, 223/148). "Why must?" Levinas will ask. And he won't be impressed by Heidegger's answer. Indeed, why should it be the case that "Alles Versagen ist ein Sagen"?

DOES BOREDOM TRULY HAVE A MESSAGE?

Let us first summarize, before we take up Levinas's question. For Heidegger boredom seems to be a kind of purgatory in which Dasein is ultimately forced to come to terms with the kind of being that it is and has to be. Dasein, that is, is not just suffering from boredom. Boredom, painful as it may be, is also an occasion for Dasein to wean itself from its tendency to cling to whatever can help it not meet itself. In this respect boredom operates on Dasein not unlike anxiety: "Anxiety discloses an insignificance of the world; and this insignificance reveals the nullity of that with which one can concern oneself—or, in other words, the impossibility of projecting oneself upon a potentiality-for-Being which belongs to existence and which is founded primarily upon one's objects of concern. *The revealing of this impossibility, however, signifies that the possibility of an authentic potentiality-for-Being is allowed to lit up* [*Aufleuchten-lassen*]" (SZ, 343/393, transl. corrected). Anxiety qua impossibility points to a possibility, it "reveals the possibility of an authentic *Seinkönnen*" (SZ, 343/394). One finds the same structure in Heidegger's analysis of boredom: what im-possibilizes is *at the same time* what possibilizes. *Alles Versagen ist ein Sagen*: there is a withholding—a putting out of order of what tends to hold us, gives us something to hold on to (some sense of purpose, a project) and, simultaneously, a pointing toward what truly holds us. Thus, in boredom, time somehow doesn't seem to pass and we, who are bored, seem to be stuck, held up, unable to continue. We are "aufgehalten"—as if paralyzed by something that has put us under its spell. As we have seen, this "something" is time: "The time that thus entrances [*bannt*] Dasein, and announces itself as thus entrancing [*Bannendes*] in boredom, *simultaneously announces itself and tells of itself as that which properly makes possible*" (GA 29/30, 223/148). Thus, for Heidegger, what goes wrong in boredom is due to time and it can only be "fixed" by time—"[T]he spell of time can only be broken by time" (226/151, transl. altered): "It is boring for one [*einem*]. In this, the time that entrances [*bannende*] as a whole announces and tells of itself as that which is to be ruptured [*gebrochen*] and can be ruptured solely in the moment of vision [*Augenblick*] *in which time itself*, as that which properly makes possible Dasein in its actions, is at work" (224/149). Boredom is time *out of joint*, bidding Dasein to open itself up (*sich erschließen*) to the element that makes its "Da" possible and to take up its responsibility for the freedom it has thus been granted, by *being* its past and its future, which is to say: by *joining them* in an active, transitive sense: "The moment of vision [*Augenblick*] breaks the spell of time [*Bann der Zeit*], and is able to rupture it, insofar as it is a specific possibility of time itself. It is not some now-point that we simply ascertain [*feststellen*], but it is the look of Dasein in the three perspectival directions we are already acquainted with, namely present, future and past . . . the look of resolute disclosedness [*Entschlossenkeit*] for action in the specific situation in which Dasein finds itself disposed in each case" (226/151).

Heidegger's reasoning is thus not only privative (*Alles Versagen . . .*), but also homeopathic (time is both the poison and the cure)! One can wonder, as Michel Haar does in a fine commentary on this text, "whether Heidegger is not resorting to a metaphysical topos when turning the negativity of boredom into the principle of a rediscovery of time and of what seems to be a total self-appropriation of Dasein."[27] Indeed, as Haar adds, "Heidegger does not take into account the case where boredom would no longer give way, where time would indefinitely continue to fall apart without pulling itself together again" (ibid., 135). There seems to be in Heidegger an implicit premise that there is "a necessary link between the accomplishment of an extreme degree and the overcoming of such limit" (ibid.). Indeed, the problem for Heidegger is that Dasein always seeks to escape boredom, instead of letting it take its full swing (ausschwingen lassen, GA 29/30:216) and letting it tell what it has to tell. Hence, his whole analysis is directed toward a situation where boredom is at its deepest and the possibilities not to hear its message minimal—toward the "*es ist einem langweilig*" that we analyzed in the previous section. There is a revelation and philosophy—"*das Vorletzte*"—is to accompany it in order to secure the chances of Dasein becoming Da-sein by listening to what is revealed—to the *Sagen* behind or in the *Versagen* (123/82). And thus one also understands why Heidegger, although constantly referring to such willingness to listen as courage (*Mut*) and to its negation as cowardice (*Feigheit*), will nonetheless emphatically deny that his is a philosophy of heroic deeds:[28] for Dasein does not have to do something heroic, it only has to stop doing what it usually does, and instead of suppressing boredom, let it be and let it take Dasein into its own element (GA 29/30 § 19).

Not unlike Michel Haar, who never refers to him, Levinas contests just these two moments—privation and homeopathy—which get Heidegger's analysis going. Boredom, for him, is not a *Versagen* in which what withholds at the same time announces itself. It is a *Versagen* that should be understood on its own terms—not in reference to a *Sagen* that provides it with its intelligibility and with its way out. In boredom, what paralyzes and puts under a spell, is not time, but the *il y a*—the Being without beings from which man's being arose in a transition that was never secure. Boredom is a kind of limit-situation in which the *il y a* announces its return: "In the hypostasis . . . in which a subject's mastery, power or virility are manifested as being in a world, in which intention is the forgetting of oneself in light and a desire for things . . . we can discern the return of the *there is*. The hypostasis, in participating in the *there is*, finds itself again to be a solitude, in the definiteness of the bond with which the ego [*le moi*] is chained to itself [*soi*]" (EE, 143–43/84). Accordingly, for Levinas, the problem of boredom is not a confrontation with one's true solitude, but its contrary. In not feeling engaged by anything outside itself, the subject is not alone: "It is, as it were, a dual solitude: this other than me accompanies the ego like a shadow. It is the duality of boredom, which is something different from the social existence we know in the world to which the ego turns in fleeing its boredom; it is also something different from the relationship with the other which detaches the ego from itself" (EE, 151/90). There is, then, not so much something lacking in boredom (what Heidegger refers to as a mixture of "*Hingehaltenheit*" and "*Leergelassenheit*"), but something too much: the ego is suffocated by itself—by its self. To the point of being threatened by its "extinction" (EE, 113/64): "What we call the I is itself submerged . . . invaded, depersonalized, stifled. The disappearance of all things and of the I leaves what cannot disappear, the sheer fact of being in which *one* participates, whether one wants to or not, without having taken the initiative, anonymously" (EE, 95/53). To be sure, "what one calls the I" is not what Heidegger calls Dasein—it refers to the mineness of a me that, as we have seen, is portrayed by Levinas as having fallen into Being before it falls into the world (EE, 173/105). Consequently, boredom for Levinas is not the ontological mood that Heidegger takes it to be (the mood that brings Dasein to its ontological purity): it "puts into question not the existence, but the subjectivity of the subject; it prevents the subject from gathering itself up, reacting, being someone. What is positive in 'the subject' sinks away to a nowhere" (EE, 121/68). But this "nowhere" is not the Heideggerian nothing—it is, so to speak, rather a nothing that *no longer* "nothings,"[29] that no longer, one could translate, provides beings with appearance by holding them apart. The *il y a* "lacks rhythm" (EE, 111/62), it is a continuum in which all distinctions are lost, including those "boundaries" that one needs to speak of *a* being (which as *this* being must be distinct from *that other* being). What happens in boredom is as it were the undoing of the hypostasis, and thus the transition of a noun (a substance, standing on its own) into a verb—nothing appeals to us any longer, but "this nothing is not that of pure nothingness. There is no longer *this* or *that*; there is not 'something.' But this universal absence is in its turn a presence, an absolutely unavoidable presence" (EE, 94/52), which Levinas likens to "a field of forces, a heavy atmosphere belonging to no one" (EE, 95/53) and which slowly, but irresistibly, seems to suck us in.

It should come as no surprise that, given this different starting point, Levinas will, as it were, reverse whatever Heidegger, in his analysis of boredom, wishes to bring to the fore. Thus, instead of trying to bring Dasein to the point where it lets boredom take its full swing, Levinas will rather applaud all attempts to turn away from boredom by seeking whatever distraction one can have: smoking, for example, is analyzed by Heidegger as a socially acceptable "inconspicuous possibility of passing the time" (GA 29/30, 169/112), whereas for Levinas, the cigarette, as a worldly object of enjoyment (TI, 133), would be one of those screens the world puts on offer to loosen the bond with oneself—smoking is a way for a being that is burdened with its own company, to be *more alone* than it would be when "merely" with itself. True, we do not smoke *in order to* escape boredom, but while smoking we are typically engaged in just that rhythm (inhaling/exhaling) that is absent from the *il y a*. Smoking, one could say, is indeed good for nothing: it is a way for the nothing to "nothing" (*nichten*), to create an interval, a distance between the self and itself. But, of course, like all worldly activities, it is *not* a successful "liberation." One will have to light up, again and again, and at the end of each butt one will again find that "silent association with oneself" (EE, 150/89) that for Levinas is the tragedy of existence, its incapacity to successfully leave itself behind, to truly transcend itself. Nothing in man's being "replies" to such desire. "Being is without reply": "Being is essentially alien and strikes against us. We undergo its suffocating embrace . . . but it does not respond to us" (EE, 28/9, transl. corrected!).

Unlike time for Heidegger, which is both the cause and the liberator of boredom, Being for Levinas is indifferent to the indifference it afflicts us with. There is no generosity in the *il y a*, no *Sagen* behind its *Versagen*—as Levinas keeps stressing by opposing it to (the later) Heidegger's *Es gibt*: "*There is*, in general, without it mattering what there is, without our being able to fix a substantive to this term. *There is* an impersonal form, like in *it rains*, or it is warm. Its anonymity is essential" (EE, 95/53). But we are not at the end of our surprises—here is Heidegger: "It is boring for one. What is this 'it'? The 'it' that we mean whenever we say that it is lightning, it is thundering, *it is raining*. It—this is the title for whatever is indeterminate, unfamiliar" (GA 29/30, 203/134). But the attentive reader will not be led astray by the striking coincidence that Levinas should have chosen the "*il pleut*" to set off the *il y a* from Heidegger who himself refers to "*es regnet*." For Heidegger's whole consecutive analysis will go on to determine what at this point in his lectures remains indeterminate. As we know, the *es* for Heidegger is, of course, not a determinate being—it will turn out to be the intimate horizon of all beings (220,226/146,150), including Dasein: time! And in taking and withholding, time will give and be at the center of a remarkable *sacrificial structure*, which makes one wonder whether there is not an intertext that, at a deeper level, is shared by both Heidegger and Levinas, who are supposedly each other's antipodes: "The temporal spell that becomes manifest in this 'it is boring for one' can be broken only through time. Only if the temporal spell is broken do beings as a whole no longer refuse themselves, *only then do they give up their own possibilities, make themselves graspable* for each specific Dasein and *give this Dasein itself the possibility* of existing in the midst of beings in one particular respect, in one particular possibility in each case"(226/151).[30] Time, by "impelling Dasein into the extremity [*Spitze*] of the *Augenblick*" (151/227) arranges for its own spell to be broken and, in its wake, for a generalized economy of donation where it seems that beings as a whole *offer themselves* to Dasein by giving up their own possibilities, in a sort of imitation of time which "did what it could" to give itself up—calling on the one banned to break its spell . . .

This is certainly not the only place where Being (of which Time is "the first name," GA 9, 376) seems to be engaged in a part Levinas would have liked to reserve for the Good or even for God. The whole structure of Heidegger's argument—in deep boredom Dasein is *forced* to hear a message (GA 29/30, 209/139) it nonetheless is called upon to receive (and thus, could possibly not receive)—reminds one of Levinas's appeal of the Other which the I *cannot* not hear (i.e., it is forced to hear it), and yet has the freedom to ignore (to not receive). As if Levinas's formula for revelation—"revelation is carried through [*se fait*] by the one who receives it" (OB, 156)—could equally well hold for Heidegger's "*Offenbarung*." Indeed, the same tension one finds in Levinas between, on the one hand, an appeal that has always arrived, and on the other hand, a revelation that only arrives for the one who is open to it, seems to be at work in Heidegger's text, who resorts, in fact, to a solution that is entirely parallel to the one proposed by Levinas. Received or not, there is always a trace—one will always already have been struck by that which one flees from. Fear is suppressed anxiety (Heidegger). Shamelessness suppressed shame (Levinas, OB, 192 n. 21). Undeep boredom suppressed boredom—but boredom still. The three *topoi* that we earlier signaled to form the backbone of Heidegger's analysis—a flight, a trace of that from which it flees, a message that can be heard—may have been discarded by Levinas, as far as the analysis of boredom is concerned. Nonetheless it would be easy to show (it is shown in *Truth and Singularity*) how they make up the backbone of the ethics he opposes to ontology. And with a similar aim, or at least a similar result: a purification of the human such that it falls into "accord" with its element—Being (Time) for Heidegger, the Good for Levinas—to repeat a passage I commented elsewhere:[31] "Being's *esse*, through which an entity is an entity, is a matter of thought, gives something to thought, stands from the first in the open. In that there is indeed *a kind of indigence in being*, constrained to an other than itself, to a subject called upon to welcome the manifestation. . . . [It] follows that, outside of the part subjectivity plays in the disclosure of being, every game that (it) would play for its own account would be but a veiling or an obscuring of being's esse" (OB, 132). Indeed, this was the point of undoing Dasein's "self-defense": to distract it from its distraction and bring it into its own element such that it could welcome the manifestation. But when Levinas puts another distractor to the fore—the ethical Other whose appeal finally breaks the bond with which I am tied to myself—the result seems to be the same: a kind of indigence of the Good (of God) who can only manifest itself (Himself) indirectly—that is, through that appeal, which leaves me no game to play for my own account that will not be a kind of foul play: irresponsibility, as the (impossible) refusal to be responsible, is not an alternative, but the confirmation of a prior responsibility.[32] Just as Heidegger's fleeing Dasein, Levinas's irresponsible subject is an impurity, a stain on the script that is written for it—a false note in the harmony it was supposed to join as the element where it "belonged."

These similarities are not mentioned here to cancel the difference between Heidegger and Levinas. They are meant to put it into perspective—into a different perspective, that is, than the one that would prefer to simply portray Levinas as the first critic of fundamental ontology.[33] Not that there is no critique! But it shares a certain soil with what it criticizes: firstly, because it takes an opposite starting point—the one that we saw Heidegger "decided" not to take (third section); and secondly, because it ends up with a solution that seems formally analogous to what it opposes. Foucault had a name for such a situation: he called it the "tines" of a fork,[34] and what interested him was the stem that held them together and above all, the soil into which it was planted. Perhaps what we have here, then, is another of these passionate discussions in urgent need of deflation. For it could be that by thus refusing to take sides, in thus "bracketing" the parties' right or wrong, we may come to spot what perhaps was not entirely unhidden to each of them. Time, then, to finally raise the question we have been trying to make audible all along—the question of an intransitive facticity.

BETWEEN THE TINES OF A FORK

It is no coincidence that we took so long to come to the issue we promised to raise. For it has been traveling with us for some time now and we had to make an effort to let it go unnoticed so that it could make the journey on its own terms instead of being forced on the Procrustean bed Heidegger specialists would no doubt have accused us of preparing for it. Facticity is, in fact, simply Heidegger's technical term to distinguish what one could call "concrete" Dasein from the kind of concreteness one meets in other beings. "Factical" Dasein is, of course, a situated Dasein in many ways: it is born in a certain place, at a certain time, in such or such a family, it is a boy or a girl, with a certain physiognomy (color of skin, of eyes, of hair . . .), growing up in a town or on the countryside, speaking the local dialect or not, etc. But, as we have seen, Heidegger has a number of terms that eliminate the need for such a list of specifics: Dasein is always *jemeinig* (it is the Dasein of a specific person), it is *jeweilig* (it "has" its own "time"), it is "thrown" into a specific world (it is thus not *causa sui*, not its own origin, and always situated in a certain setting—for instance, the twentieth century, which is, of course, not the twelfth and thus "prevents" Dasein from taking part in the second Crusade). One could say that, whenever Heidegger writes *faktisch* (factical), he was simply, by abbreviation, referring to all the above. But the point is that there is a difference, characteristic for Dasein, between what is *faktisch* and what belongs to mere factuality (*Tatsächlichkeit*). Whatever "facts" one can enlist for this person's *Dasein* will be "facts" that are taken up in his or her Dasein: not predicates, but adverbs, modalities of his/her being. In other words: each Dasein will *be* its facts in a transitive sense. They are not just outward characteristics (qualities an outward observer can state about this or that Dasein), but, if you wish, characteristics that are "lived" by the one supposedly so characterized. Unlike animals, Dasein is not simply sexed.[35] It "is" gendered: sexual difference is a difference that it lives and "understands" (in the very wide sense that *Verstehen* gets in Heidegger: to know one's way about). Unlike stones, Dasein does not simply "have" weight, it watches its weight (or it doesn't). Unlike plants or flowers, Dasein is not simply "colored," its "color" is not indifferent to it—it will *be* its color, for example by taking pride on it (*black is beautiful*) or by thinking that it should not play a role when applying for a job (and thus rejecting either positive or negative discrimination; either of which, of course, it could also support). Thus, for Dasein, facticity (*Faktizität*) should be distinguished from factuality (*Tatsächlichkeit*): "Facticity is not the factuality of the *factum brutum* of something present-at-hand, but a characteristic of Dasein's Being. . . . The 'that-it-is' of facticity never becomes something that we can come across by beholding it" (SZ, 135/174). I will return to what I have left out in this passage in a moment. Let us first seek confirmation in a much earlier quote: " '*Facticity*' is the designation we will use for the character of the being of 'our' 'own' Dasein. More precisely, this expression means: in each case (*jeweilig*) this Dasein . . . insofar as it is, according to its being (*seinsmäßig*), 'there' in the character of its being. *Seinsmäßig Dasein* means: not, and never, to be there . . . as an object of which we merely take cognizance and have knowledge. Rather, Dasein is *there* to itself in the *how* of its ownmost being. . . . Being—transitive: to be factical life! Being is itself never the possible object of a having, since what is at issue in it, what it comes to, is itself: being" (GA 63, 7/15). One understands how this can be the opening passage of a 1923 course titled: *Ontologie. Hermeneutik der Faktizität*—for given the kind of Being Dasein is (a being "that it is and has to be"), what needs to be done in such an ontology is, of course not to objectively describe such a being by taking an outward look at it. It is, to the contrary, to understand how such a being "makes sense" of its being, how it "moves" about (in) its being. Consequently, "the common thesis that Heidegger has no ethics, appears from the perspective of a hermeneutics of facticity to be a plain misunderstanding."[36] For at the center of Heidegger's enterprise is the distinction between facticity and factuality—a distinction that points to the fact that Dasein is in each case interested in its own being, that it plays a part in it, that its being is not indifferent to it. As Grondin continues his comment, "[T]he task of such a hermeneutics is to destroy the concept of humans as objects for an indifferent theory and to substitute for it the human being as a *Seinkönnen* that each such being has to take upon itself" (ibid.). Indeed, as we have seen, ontology for Heidegger was not meant to be neutral! It was meant to be practical through and through, a reminder to each Dasein of the task implied in its having to be its being. Hence, the quote we abbreviated from *Being and Time* reads in its full version: "Facticity is . . . a characteristic of Dasein's Being—one which has been taken up in existence, even if proximally [*zunächst*] it has been thrust aside" (SZ, 135/174).

We have seen how this 'thrusting aside' (*Abdrängung*—an almost Freudian term!) brings a certain unrest into Dasein in which it fails to see its own doing. Instead of seeing in this unrest the suppression of a movement at the heart of Dasein—the movement of transcendence opening its *Da*, Dasein only sees in it a lack of rest. And it will blame time for withholding from it what it truly needs: more time! It will see time as merely *versagend*—depriving it of the time it lacks (even in boredom where there is, in a sense, too much time, this "too much" is precisely what seems to hold Dasein up and to prevent it from catching up with its plans, projects, activities, thus introducing a delay into its being for which it believes time is to blame). Always short of time, Dasein will perceive itself as doomed to a lesser element, and it will long for what transcends that element: the supratemporal, the eternal, the objective, the transhistorical (even if, like Spengler,[37] one decides to look for it in the historical itself).

Whereas Heidegger believes Dasein can and should overcome this unrest,[38] for Levinas man's existence inspires him/her with an unrest that does not derive from a movement he/she tries to suppress, but from the fact that the existence of a being necessarily implies that the anonymous flow of a being without beings has somehow *been brought to a stop* in *this* being which no longer flows along with that anonymity, but breaks (*rompt*) it (EE, 169/103). This interval is "the present"—the instant: that which stands on its own, without being the result of what precedes it, nor being linked to what follows it. The instant is *the separation* of a being which has a name out of the anonymity of being in general. It is what we earlier encountered as the hypostasis: the birth of an independent subject, the transition of a verb into a substance—a transition that now appears as a certain freezing of what flows: the instant stands, it does not move. It does not come from somewhere and it does not go somewhere. "Not having received its being from past" (EE, 170/103), it will not cede it to either past or future. It is, thus, "an event," a "pure present" (ibid.), not "included in the dynamism of time" (EE, 168/102). But as such, it points to a "deeper drama" (EE, 143/85) that one misses, if, like Heidegger, one thinks that "ecstasy is the original mode of existence" (EE, 139/82): "To the notion of existence, where the emphasis is put on the first syllable, we are opposing the notion of a being *whose very advent is a folding back upon itself,* a being which contrary to the ecstaticism of contemporary thought, is in a certain sense a substance" (EE, 138/81). To which Levinas adds, in full awareness of his originality: "Hypostasis, the apparition of a substantive, is not only the apparition of a new grammatical category; it signifies the suspension of the anonymous *there is*, the apparition of a private domain of a *name* [un nom]. On the ground of the *there is* a being arises. *The ontological significance of an entity in the general economy of Being, which Heidegger simply posits alongside of Being by distinction, is thus deduced*" (EE, 141/83).

But with this "deduction" everything that is supposed to follow from it in the Heideggerian universe of thought will be changed. Including facticity, of which it can precisely no longer be affirmed that it is "taken up into existence"—a formulation that we already came across in Heidegger and which he also uses with regard to birth (SZ, 391/443). Indeed, for Heidegger, Dasein's proper way to relate to its birth is not to see it as something of the past that lies behind its back: "Understood existentially, birth is not and never is something past in the sense of something no longer present-at-hand" (SZ, 374/426). Factical Dasein *is* its birth, *"es existiert gebürtig"* (ibid.), its birth is not a fact, but a matter of facticity, for which the existential term is thrownness: "As being, Dasein is something that has been thrown, it has been brought into its 'there,' but *not* of its own accord. . . . As existent, it never comes back behind it as some event which has . . . factually befallen and fallen loose from Dasein again; on the contrary, as long as Dasein is, Dasein, as care, *is* constantly its 'that it is' " (SZ, 284/330). One has rightfully seen in these passages the basis for a Heideggerian ethics of responsibility. As François Raffoul has shown, it is the very opacity, the finitude, and the expropriation implied in Dasein's birth—its thrownness—which brings Heidegger to the expression of a "Faktizität der Überantwortung" (SZ, 135)—factical Dasein as delivered over to its "that it is." As Raffoul writes, not without a certain sense for paradox: "What Dasein has to be, and what it has to be responsible for, is then precisely its very facticity, its being thrown as such. What I have to make my own is thus what can never belong to me, what evades me, what will always have escaped me."[39] That is, in other words: I have to appropriate my birth—take it up into my existence, in spite of its preceding me. I have to take up this predecession into my existence, I have to be "my own thrown basis," by "projecting myself upon possibilities into which I have been thrown" (SZ, 284/330). Which means that, instead of "getting dragged along in thrownness" (SZ, 348/400), I will have to take it upon my own shoulders, "catch" the throw of my Being-thrown-into the world, and "achieve some sort of position" in which I stand on my own (*Selbständig*) and no longer seek to avoid the task of having to be this my being which, for all its concretion, never determines me (SZ, 322/369).[40]

Levinas's views on what it means to be born could not be more different. Whereas for Heidegger birth qua thrownness does not rule out transcendence, but on the contrary calls for it ('become what you are!"), for Levinas "transcendence is not the fundamental movement of the ontological adventure"—it is, he adds, *"founded* in the non-transcendence of position" (EE, 172/105),[41] which is yet another name for what we met as "hypostasis," "substance," "instant"—the birth of a being *whose very advent is a folding back upon itself.* A folding back that, for Levinas, is an incapacity to leave, a being stuck to one's being, something "absolutely intransitive" (TA, 21/42), something that rules out all transcendence: "The act of taking position does not transcend itself. This effort which does not transcend itself constitutes the present or the 'I' " (EE, 138/81). There is something final, something irrevocable or irremissible about being born—one is inscribed into a being into which one is locked. Birth is an event, for sure, but "to not receive its being from a past, is not the gratuitous evanescence of a game or a dream. A subject is not free like the wind, but already has a destiny *which it does not get from a past or a future,* but from its present" (EE, 170/103). The instant, we have seen, stands on its own, but if it "thereby escapes the weight of the past (the only weight that was seen in existence [Levinas is referring to Heidegger among others]), *it involves a weight of its own* which its evanescence does not lighten, and against which a solitary subject, who is constituted by the instant, is powerless" (EE, 170–71/104). And Levinas concludes: "Time and the other are necessary for the liberation from it" (*ibid.*).

Transcendence will, then, for Levinas, need to come from outside. As does time—"a mode of existence where nothing is irrevocable, the contrary of the definitive subjectivity of the 'I' " (EE, 152/91). Whereas the instant remains out of time—severed both from past and future—time for Levinas redeems the unredeemable: "the work of time" (EE, 158/94) is a resurrection! Not the "destruction" of the instant, but "the unraveling of the knot which is tied in it, the definitive, which its evanescence does not undo" (EE, 195/95). Whereas Heidegger called upon Dasein itself to be the transition between its proper past and future in the *Augenblick* (the moment of vision), Levinas will need other eyes—the eyes of an Other to introduce "a future where *the present* will have the benefit of a recall" (EE, 156/93). Hence, his conclusion, which already announces *Totality and Infinity*: "To simply say that the ego leaves itself is a contradiction, since, in quitting itself the ego carries itself along—if it does not sink into the impersonal. A symmetrical intersubjectivity is the locus of transcendence in which the subject, while preserving its structure of a subject, has the possibility of not inevitably returning to itself" (EE, 164–65/100). For me to be somewhere else than my self, to be pardoned, to not be a definite existence, presupposes that one moves out of ontology, which can at best understand that there is such a need, but not that this need is truly a Desire.[42] A need will not be able to undo the bond that ties me to myself, whereas Desire is precisely such undoing—giving oneself up for the other. As *Existents and Existent* puts it, very soberly: "Reaching the Other is not something justified by one's own self. It is not a matter of shaking me out of my boredom" (EE, 144/85).

INTRANSITIVE FACTICITY, THE PREHISTORY OF "THE PRIMACY OF ETHICS"

At least two things should have become clear by now. The first point to remember is that Levinas's dismissal of the primacy of ontology and his subsequent turn to ethics and to "the Other" results from his early confrontation with ontology. More specifically, Levinas seems to have concluded that matters are worse—that the drama is "deeper"—than Heidegger would like them to be. Dressing up in the gown of the "methodological atheist," Levinas tries to show that Heidegger gives the game away by claiming what he would have to "prove": that being is transitive, that the cause and cure of boredom are the same, that Dasein can and should stop fleeing itself and, finally, that facticity can be taken up into existence. As we have seen, Levinas denies each of these claims and specifically points to a facticity that cannot be taken up into existence—the whole drama of the hypostasis being that its thrownness into being turns it into "a monad": "[I]t is by existing that I am without windows, and not by some content in me that would be incommunicable" (TA, 21/42). Which brings us to a second point: *it is precisely by insisting on the subject's solitude*, on its being inscribed in its own being—the one thing one cannot "exchange" (ibid.) between beings—*that Levinas finds his way toward intersubjectivity*. Far from blocking off the road to others, as the wind of our times would have it, it is precisely an even more radical unrelatedness between people than one finds in Heidegger ("existential solipsism"), which seems to eliminate "the disdain for human affairs" Heidegger found himself accused of. Social conversation, for Levinas, testifies to a "joy of communication" that is more than a "Pascalian diversion" (TA, 40/59): "By connecting solitude to the subject's materiality—materiality being its enchainment to itself—we can understand in what sense the world and our existence in the world constitute *a fundamental advance* of the subject in overcoming the weight that it is to itself, in overcoming its materiality—that is to say, in loosening the bond between the self [*le soi*] and the ego [*le moi*]" (TA, 44/62). Being, that is, far from being a co-Being and a Being-with in which beings would be exposed to one another, is precisely what works against all such exposure, to the point of triumphing over all such "worldly" advance, which is, ultimately, unable to move the *stasis* of the hypostatic subject into the ex-tasis and the ex-istence of Heidegger's Dasein. As bearer of a *Da*, the imminent implosion of which it is incapable of successfully warding off, the being that Levinas calls "subject" is marked by a facticity that time and again seems to rub out the "ex-" in which or by which it seeks asylum for its "-sistence." But, as we have seen, this "atheist" pessimism—a sobered up version of Heidegger—is but a starting point from which to fully appreciate the unworldly appearance of an Other who is more than the form s/he turns toward us, but is "the bearer of his own light"—a light that will finally come to save the subjectivity of the subject (cf. TI, 26) by allowing it to truly transcend itself, and thus to not find itself unaltered when arriving at the other shore. Sociality is an excellence, as Levinas will later say. It redeems a hope that, within the element of ontology, would long since have petered out, given its endless disappointments.

Where does this leave us? Except with a "differend"? With a "discussion," that is, where the terms that go to and fro between the parties constantly change meaning and where there is no reason, except idiosyncratic sympathy or *per baculum* argumentation, to choose one side rather than the other? We can, of course, patiently document, as we indeed did, such "conversation" and try to bring order to Babel. But this would be to reduce ourselves to the silence of the witness or, if we are more ambitious, to take up the role of a referee who, at least, still has the illusion of partaking in the game. Or we could ask, instead, whether this game is still ours. . . . Indeed, as we had occasion to point out, there seems to be something in that game that only regards us, and does not seem to be of any concern to the players.

I am referring to the fact that, however opposed Levinas and Heidegger may have come to be, they also seemed to share, as it were, a common "soil," which did not do away with their differend, but strangely seemed to allow for it. Let us, instead of repeating what was noted before (near the end of the sixth section), simply recall that, however different ("differend") the diagnosis of the predicament of our "*Zu-sein*" may have been, there was at least a formal agreement over what could be considered a cure: a part for the subject to play, such that it could leave behind its "unrest." And such a part presupposes a script in which the subject would find just those lines that were only meant for itself. Lines that could invest it with a singularity it could, in principle, affirm or bear, without being crushed by the demands they put on it. And if ethics, for Levinas, constitutes the better script, one should not forget that it has stolen its lines from the "not-so-fundamental" ontology it was meant to trump: "no one can take my responsibility from me" being substituted for "no one can die my death in my stead." Responsibility will purify the subject to the point of it becoming invested with "an interiority without secret" (OB, 138)—an expression that recalls, to say the least, that strange "impoverishment" that, according to Heidegger, time was offering to

Dasein, as it invited it to take up *its* time and carry through time's self-sacrifice, which time itself was calling for.

Both Dasein and the Levinasian "subject" have to give up something—have to "impoverish"—for them to embrace time and settle in the folds where they ultimately belong. They have to give up "eternity"—a denial of time for Heidegger, who sees in it the inauthentic longing for an im-mortality where mortality is privatively misunderstood as what lacks the "im-"; a condition that is *not yet* in time for Levinas, who portrays "birth" and "the instant" as being "out of time," independent but suffering from their own weight—a terrible price to pay, but still worth paying, if one thinks of what it allows one to leave behind: the thick, suffocating presence of the *il y a*, an "atmospheric density" (TA, 26/46) that one feels sometimes approaching in the nightmarish "consciousness that it will never finish" (TA, 27/48), that one is going to die *forever* (EE, 100/56), entirely in the grip of a past "that renews nothing" (ibid.) and from which there is *no escape*—indeed, from which death itself would be a liberation.

It is too late to question this unexpected agreement. Let us be satisfied with a hint: perhaps one way to make sense of this debate is to see it in terms of the a-cosmic situation that characterizes "modernity." Indeed, the Heidegger of the twenties has been read and understood by many a reader as either giving expression to such "acosmism" or trying to curb it (or failing to do so, as some have concluded).[43] Let us not forget the passage in *Being and Time* where Heidegger speaks of "the sole authority which a free existing can have": a "loyalty to its own self," which consists in "revering [*Ehrfurcht*] the repeatable possibilities of existence" (SZ, 391/443). One can see Levinas as disagreeing with such "anti-nomism" (as Hans Jonas calls it). A disagreement that made him return to Plato in his "own" way—which was perhaps still a "modern" way, reacting, like Heidegger, to modernity from within the boundaries of modernity. Indeed, Levinas, in a sense, tries to save the kosmos without restoring it: he puts it in our own hands, the hands of "adults" whose only way to God or to the Infinite is through an infinite responsibility of an endless bleeding ("a haemorrhage," OB, 92) for the other(s). In the end, Parmenides may have been killed, but ethics—circling around the one Good, the one Infinite, and the One God—nonetheless seems to retain the essential traits of *henology*.[44]

It is these traits that should make us wonder whether that discussion can still be ours—and whether what one called, with a terrible word, "postmodernity" (terrible because it became fashionable by—not just for—not being understood) should not be understood in different terms than the acosmic ones put forward to understand the modern predicament. Instead of the demise of the old order, one would have to face an "increase" of orders: what was considered *un*-ordered turned out to be a *different* order—and not just one, but many! The problem of postmodernity, then, is not that an order fell out, but that, in its wake, there was an endless multiplication of competing orders. Not an a-cosmism, but a poly-cosmism that one can perhaps compare to an explosion of the transcendental (Being; the Good) that somehow in Heidegger and Levinas still retained its unity.[45] And in its wake a sort of rediscovery that there is something in us that "does not move"—and that this something is not the same for each of us, indeed that there may be more than one such "Thing" to have taken in each "single" person. I am referring to all these differences for which people are prepared to bleed as for what in their lives is higher than life. Would it be wrong to see them as ever so many infinities coming to replace the once exclusive Infinite; as the many go(o)ds replacing the one Go(o)d; as particularizations of the Absolute turning into particular ab-solutes? Thus the feeling of an unclear "belonging"—for one is not bound to *all* of them, and those one feels "attached" to have nothing about them that could explain why it is *to them* and not to others that we feel thus attached.[46] Hence the discovery of a silence that is not voluntary, nor telling in the sense of Heidegger's *Verschwiegenheit* and that should not be understood as what suppresses speech. This infancy—this silence in us that refuses to give way to adulthood—is, Lyotard suggested, something like our soul.[47] Something not taken in by time, and not to be rendered to it. Let us say that it perhaps points to an infra-temporality that is not inferior to time, but perpendicular to it, like supra-temporality was before modern philosophy taught us to see in it something that could and should be reduced to its true origin: temporality. Postmodernity, then, is perhaps the name for a condition in which the intemporal insurrects against its undue temporalization. Something does not move—some "Thing" in us "more us than us," as the (Lacanian) saying goes. We bump into that some "Thing" every time we are unable to join a common practice, to disappear in a certain social metabolism. The "subject" is an indigestion. The subject, that is, is confronted with its subjectivity in the "this is not me" in which it is thrown back upon itself as if "throwing up" or being "thrown up by" an element in which it does not belong. But I am thrown back to some "thing" about me that remains opaque *to* me: I couldn't possibly *prove* the worth of my attachments. They have me before I have them. They are, as Rorty puts it somewhere, "the lights I work by." Or as the later Heidegger said, there is an untruth at the heart of truth, which Derrida famously rendered as: there is darkness at the heart of light, a shadow cast inward.[48] A closure, that is, that unlike in the Heidegger of the twenties, can no longer be seen as what comes to close off a more primordial openness.

There might be, then, still another kind of intransitive facticity: the one by which we introduced the term (the opening pages of the seventh section) and which we gradually lost sight of, as we came under the spell of the debate between the "early" Heidegger and the "early" Levinas. Could it be a coincidence that the only time in these lectures of the twenties Heidegger gives the example of skin color, he leaves it to *das Man* to mention it whilst forgetting it: "Of course, *people will say*, attunement is perhaps something other than the colour of the hair and skin of human beings . . ." (GA 29/30, 90/60)? But what if the *Grundstimmung* which is ours, should be understood from out of such differences that turn us into subjects that are "not without" qualities[49]—not reducible to them, nor detachable from them, but "attached" to them, decentered by these differences we cannot give up, nor stay alone with. Lacan had a name for such a "mood." He called it, like Heidegger, "anxiety"—but he significantly added that it was "*not without* object." And he related it to an "embarrassment" that he refused to see as the reverse of a shortcoming vis-à-vis an Other who is asymmetrically above us. "Embarrassment," he said, comes from the Latin *imbaricare* (to impede). And Lacan, being Lacan, compliments himself for this find which, as usual, he does not really explain. Manifestly, he says, the wind is blowing with me (*manifestement le vent souffle sur moi*).[50] He may have been right—manifestly, the wind that carried him is not the one against which we have been trying to set our course.

NOTES

Whenever available I have consulted the English Heidegger translations (English pagination after the solidus); other translations will be my own. Small changes are not specified, and all italics are mine.

1. J. Kristeva, *Strangers to Ourselves*, trans. Leon S. Roudiez (New York, etc.: Harvester Wheatsheaf, 1991), 192.

2. E. Levinas, *Otherwise Than Being or Beyond Essence*, trans. A. Lingis (Dordrecht, etc.: Kluwer, 1991), 114–15 (henceforth cited as OB)—on trauma and the "other-in-me" in Levinas and Freud, my "The Price of Being Dispossessed: Levinas's God and Freud's Trauma," *The Face of the Other and the Trace of God: Essays on the Philosophy of Emmanuel Levinas*, in ed. J. Bloechl (New York, Fordham University Press, 2000), 243–75.

3. E. Levinas, "Discussion Following 'Transcendence and Intelligibility,' " in *Is It Righteous to Be? Interviews with Emmanuel Levinas*, ed. J. Robbins (Stanford: Stanford University Press, 2001), 271: "the psyche is originally theological."

4. All these expressions can be found in Levinas (e.g., *Totality and Infinity. An Essay on Exteriority*, trans. A. Lingis) [Dordrecht, etc.: Kluwer, 1991], 178–79, 253, etc.—henceforth quoted as TI). For an analysis, see chapter 11 of my *Truth and Singularity. Taking Foucault into Phenomenology* (Dordrecht, etc.: Kluwer, 1999), esp. 330ff. I will refer to this book as T and S.

5. I will not reference these quotes, since I give them as tokens of "the said" of our times—that is, as what Foucault in his archaeology named *énoncés* (statements). Their anonymity is, in a sense, essential: what matters is not who said it, but that these are the things that are being said (or written).

6. It would suffice to read the corresponding passage in *Being and Time* (SZ, 238–39/282–83). But, again, the point is not to polemicize, but to take notice of its being said.

7. E.g., J. Derrida, *Mémoires pour Paul De Man* (Paris: Galilée, 1988), 57 ("invivable").

8. J.-L. Nancy, *Being Singular Plural*, trans. Robert D. Richardson and Anne E. O'Byrne (Stanford: Stanford University Press, 2000), 26.

9. In my "Enfance, transcendance et mortalité des valeurs. Pour un républicanisme actuel," in *Le pluralisme des valeurs. Entre le particulier et l'universel*, ed. A.-M. Dillens (Brussels: Facultés Universitaires Saint-Louis, 2003), I try to show how what I call here "intransitive facticity" leads to a certain existential *derivation* of being-with and to a corresponding notion of community and public space(s).

10. The present article is a sequel to my "Is ethics fundamental? Questioning Levinas on Irresponsibility," in which I question "ethical difference" from the same perspective as the one I am adopting here and elsewhere, notably in T and S (see the conclusion, pp. 390 ff.).

11. Cf. SZ, 143–44/183: "As a modal category of presence-at-hand, possibility signifies what is *not yet* actual and what is *not at any time* necessary. It characterizes the *merely* possible. Ontologically it is on a lower level than actuality and necessity. In contrast to this, possibility as an existential is *the most primordial and ultimate positive way* in which Dasein is characterized ontologically" (last italics mine).

12. This roughly translates as: "Because Dasein is the kind of Being for whom its Being is at issue in its Being, it is surrendered to beings, and essentially so. For we heard, Dasein is opened up; beings, that it is not, are revealed to it; but now we see: not in the sense of a mere cognizance, but (in a different sense): because Dasein essentially has stepped out of itself, it is surrendered to beings and their superior forces—not just those of nature, but also the powers and violences that Dasein as a being carries in itself."

13. For this evolution from "life" to "Dasein," see e.g. H. Tietjen, "Philosophie und Faktizität. Zur Vorbildung des existenzial-ontologischen Ansatzes in einer frühen Freiburger Vorlesung Martin Heideggers," *Heidegger*

Studies 2 (1986): 11–40. Also Th. Kisiel, "Das Entstehen des Begriffsfeldes 'Faktizität' im Frühwerk Heideggers," *Dilthey-Jahrbuch* 4 (1986–87): 90–120.

14. For an analysis of *Rede/Gerede* in *Being and Time*, see my T and S, 30–39, in which I ask the sort of questions that Derrida's early readings of Husserl have taught us not to neglect.

15. See my "Whistling in the Dark," *Ethical Perspectives* 8, no. 3 (2001): 168–78 where I confront the Kierkegaard-Heidegger tradition on escaping anxiety with the different understanding of such "whistling" one finds in Blanchot, Lacan, and the early Levinas.

16. E. Levinas, *From Existence to Existents*, trans. A. Lingis (Pittsburgh: Duquesne University Press, 2001), 32. I will henceforth quote this as EE with the French pagination (Paris: Vrin, 1943), here p. 61, preceding the English one. I will also refer to *Time and the Other*, trans. R. Cohen (Pittsburgh: Duquesne University Press, 1987) as TA with the French pagination (Paris: P.U.F., 1979) given first. With TI I refer to the English text of *Totality and Infinity. An Essay on Exteriority*, trans. A. Lingis (Dordrecht etc.: Kluwer, 1991).

17. For *Verschwiegenheit* as a cure for the ambiguity that is introduced by vociferation, see my analysis referred to in note 14.

18. I am referring to the famous 1943 "Nachwort zu: 'Was ist Metaphysik' " where Heidegger originally wrote "daß das Sein wohl [corrected 1949: nie] west ohne das Seiende" (GA 9, 306). See J.-L. Marion, "L'angoisse et l'ennui. Pour interpréter 'Was ist Metaphysik?' " *Archives de Philosophie* 43 (1980): 121–46, esp. 134.

19. As will become clear below, I am not implying that the author of EE was an "atheist." I am suggesting that, for strategic reasons, he adopts the "methodical atheist" standpoint Heidegger had claimed to take, in order to show it to be untenable.

20. D. Franck, "Le corps de la différence," *Philosophie* 34: 75.

21. I use the term in the sense in which Lyotard introduced it in his book with the same title: as a "discussion" where there is no neutral language in which both parties can formulate, without distortion, what they have to say. That such is the case, will become clear as we proceed.

22. I see no reason for not extending the Heideggerian phenomenological reduction to what happens in "boredom," after a broad consensus has been built that anxiety, in Heidegger, can be seen as such a reduction (for that point: J.-Fr. Courtine, *Heidegger et la Phénoménologie* [Paris: Vrin, 1990], 218–47).

23. See his excellent *Stimmung bei Heidegger. Das Phanomen der Stimmung im Kontext von Heideggers Existenzial-analyse des Daseins* (Dordrecht: Kluwer, 2002), esp. 265 ff.

24. This remark goes back to a long discussion I had with Dreyfus—the core of our disagreement comes down to my protesting his comment that "In the face of anxiety the self is annihilated" (*Being-in-the-World. A Commentary on Heidegger's Being and Time. Division I* [Cambridge: MIT Press, 1991], 304 and the analysis that then follows).

25. See the article in note 10 above.

26. In this respect, boredom could be called, like death, the possibility of impossibility—provided one reads that expression as *genitivus subjectivus*: it is the impossibility that possibilizes (see T and S, 246 ff.). Correlatively, Levinas's alternative formula for death (the impossibility of possibility) will also be the matrix for his competing analysis of boredom.

27. My translation of M. Haar, "Le temps vide et l'indifférence à l'être," in *La Fracture de l'Histoire. Douze essais sur Heidegger* (Grenoble: Jérôme Millon [Krisis], 1994), 128. Further references to this analysis will be given by simple pagination in the text.

28. For "courage" and "cowardice," just a few passages, almost at random: GA 63, 103; GA 20, 436; GA29/30, 117, 248, 255; "What is Metaphysics," passim. For Heidegger's feeling that he has been misunderstood: "Afterword" to "What is Metaphysics" and the long retrospective complaint in 1941: GA 49 (§11).

29. For this variation on Heidegger's famous "das Nichts nichtet" in "What is Metaphysics," see my article quoted in note 15 above.

30. The corollary in Levinas would have to do with the Good's self-abdication (it interrupts the desire it arouses and deflects it to the nondesirable other) and the self-contraction of God who doesn't *impose* his creative "authorship" on creatures (TI, 58, 77–79, 105) and runs the risk of being ignored (OB, 161). For an analysis of these themes in Levinas: T and S, chapters 9 and 10 (esp. 282 ff.).

31. See T and S, 17–19.

32. For an analysis of this move, see the article quoted in note 10 where I also point to a nonprivative notion of "irresponsibility" which one can defend against this privative definition.

33. Almost the title of an important article by J. Taminiaux ("La première réplique à l'ontologie fondamentale," in *Cahiers de l'Herne: Emmanuel Lévinas*, ed. C. Chalier and M. Abensour [Editions de l'Herne, 1991]).

34. My attention was drawn to this expression by Ian Hacking's "Michel Foucault's immature science," *Noûs* 13 (1979): 39–51. Hacking claims it to be his own ("a teasing device that I call Foucault's fork which surprises us by stating that competing bodies of belief have the same underlying rules of formation," 41), but one can find it in *The Order of Things. An Archaeology of the Human Sciences* (New York: Vintage, 1973), e.g., 299.

35. See my "Demons and the Demonic. Kierkegaard and Heidegger on Anxiety and Sexual Difference," in *Immediacy and Reflection. An International Kierkegaard-Symposium*, ed. P. Cruysberghs (Leuven: Leuven University Press) (in print).

36. J. Grondin, "Die Hermeneutik der Faktizität als ontologische Destruktion und Ideologiekritik. Zur Aktualität der Hermeneutik Heideggers," in *Zur philosophischen Aktualität Heideggers. Bd. 2. Im Gespräch der Zeit*, ed. D. Papenfuss and O. Pöggeler (Frankfurt a.M.: Vittorio Klostermann, 1990), 163–78, quote p. 169.

37. Interestingly, in GA 60 Heidegger portrays Spengler as some sort of Platonist: "Denn bei Spengler ist die geschichtliche Welt die Grundwirklichkeit,

die *einzige* Wirklichkeit" (46). Spengler's "absolutization" of historical reality is a mere "opposition" to Plato, but not a real break (47–48).

38. It is not for nothing that anxiety is described as a state of "peculiar calm" (BW, 102) and self-compunction, totally different from the "bewildering" "drifting back and forth between 'worldly' possibilities," characteristic of fear (SZ, 344/394).

39. Fr. Raffoul, "Heidegger and the Origins of Responsibility," in *Heidegger and Practical Philosophy*, ed. Fr. Raffoul and D. Pettigrew (Albany: State University of New York Press, 2002), 212.

40. I have elsewhere argued that what this means is that one cannot, according to Heidegger (another "decision"!) authentically "fall." "Falling" is what I called a "disappearing existential" (in contrast to other existentials where there is both an authentic and an inauthentic way of taking them up, authenticity with regard to falling implies that one stops falling and takes up "a position," etc. See T and S, chapter 1 and pp. 175–76).

41. The "founded" refers to the way ethics will come to redeem this longing (cf. infra).

42. The distinction between "need" and "Desire" is made at the beginning of TI (see section I.A.1. Desire for the Invisible). Ethics, one could say, replies to a need by changing it into a Desire (without that alteration the whole enterprise would be open to the Nietzschean suspicion that I only help my neighbor out of self-interest).

43. E.g., H. Jonas, *Zwischen Nichts und Ewigkeit. Zur Lehre vom Menschen* (Göttingen: Vandenhoeck and Ruprecht, 1963), 5–25.

44. As I argued in chapters 5 and 9–11 of T and S.

45. See my "De sterfelijkheid van de transcendentie. Levinas en het kwaad [The mortality of the transcendent. Levinas and evil]," *Tijdschrift voor Filosofie* 65, no. 1 (2003): 59–92 (English summary: 91–92).

46. See my article quoted in note 9.

47. J.Fr. Lyotard, "A l'insu," *Le Genre Humain* 13 (special issue *Politiques de l'oubli*): pp. 37–43, citation p. 39.

48. J. Derrida, *Edmund Husserl's Origin of Geometry. An Introduction*, trans. J. P. Leavey Jr. (Stony Brook: Nicolas Hays Ltd., 1978), 105: "But, so that history may have its proper density . . . must not the 'critical' forgetfulness of origins be *the faithful shadow* that accompanies the movement of truth rather than its accidental aberration?" (my italics). This remark paved my way to the later Heidegger and to Foucault (T and S, chapter 2). I have turned it against Rorty's "let's stick to our own lights" in " 'Hold the Being.' How to split Rorty between Irony and Finitude," *Philosophy & Social Criticism* 25, no. 2 (1999): 27–45.

49. On the meaning of this "not without qualities," see the article quoted in note 10. If one accepts the nonprivative notion of irresponsibility that I develop there (singularization as having the structure of being attached to some "thing" that does not respond to us), it becomes less evident to affirm, as François Raffoul does (*art. cit.*, 217) that "everything takes place as if it was precisely the disruption of this commonality between the I and others, as Jean-

Luc Nancy has emphasized, which provided the basis for the very emergence of the other and *therefore for the very possibility of an ethics of responsibility*." I would tend to disagree with Raffoul and Nancy over this last clause. My disagreement comes from a notion of irresponsibility that is not ethical but mè-ontological (and which, as such, points to "metaphysical solitude" that is not incompatible with a notion of community, but is perhaps putting it under less strain than is "otherwise" done).

50. J. Lacan, *L'angoisse, Séminaire 1962–63*, unauthorized text published by the "Association freudienne internationale," 17. For an illustration of such "embarrassment," see my "In Respectful Contempt. Heidegger, Appropriation, Facticity," in *Appropriating Heidegger*, ed. J. Faulconer and M. Wrathall (Cambridge: Cambridge University Press, 2000), 137–54, esp. 150–51.

Part III

Race, Embodiment, and the Unconscious

8

Can Race Be Thought in Terms of Facticity?

A Reconsideration of Sartre's and Fanon's Existential Theories of Race

Robert Bernasconi

The thesis that race is a social construction is something of a dogma in the humanities and social sciences today. According to this thesis, race is not a natural kind, but instead finds its basis in society. Social constructionist views of race emphasize its contingency.[1] They understand themselves as answering the racial essentialism that maintains that one's race biologically determines one in the sense of delimiting one's capacities and thus one's possibilities, unless, of course, one happens to be white, in which case one might believe, as Kant did, that one belongs to the race that has all the talents.[2] Social constructionism, therefore, has a liberatory intent, but there is a growing sense that it has largely failed to meet its emancipatory goal: most philosophical accounts of social constructionism, far from empowering a marginalized group that has historically been seen as a race, leaves that group deprived of agency and the specific kind of identity that it needs in order to combat racism. Races on these accounts are products of racism, but this knowledge threatens to break down some of that solidarity that is necessary if the historical effects of racism are to be redressed. The current debate over affirmative action offers ample evidence of how a certain form of social constructionism, that form that understands itself as denying the reality of race, can be used to leave in place the gross inequalities of opportunity that are now thoroughly institutionalized, for example, the United States of America as a result of first de jure and then de facto segregation and the uneven distribution of resources that that has allowed.

In a recent essay entitled "Sartre and the Social Construction of Race," Donna-Dale Marcano attempts to enrich the social constructionist account of race and make the process of the constitution of racial identities intelligible, by applying the resources of Sartre's late philosophy as found in the *Critique of Dialectical Reason,* which she judges vastly superior to the account he gave earlier in *Being and Nothingness* and *Anti-Semite and Jew.*[3] By focusing on historically oppressed groups, she shows that social constructionism, as usually understood, leaves out of account what might make certain identities worth preserving. This indeed is what happens when in *Anti-Semite and Jew* the early Sartre says that the anti-Semite makes the Jew.[4] Sartre's first model highlights the way a group identity is constituted from the outside by the gaze without much reference to the group's history or its agency. It is this version, together with the account of acting under descriptions that Sartre provides in *Being and Nothingness* in his discussion of the waiter who is a waiter by playing at being waiter that has inspired a number of the philosophical versions of the social constructionist view of race, including that proposed by Anthony Appiah in *Color Conscious.*[5] She argues that it is only the second model, that found in the *Critique,* which allows for an explanation of how members of an oppressed group create an identity for themselves (SS, 225).

Although I might disagree with her slightly on that last point and will argue that there is some evidence of such an account in "Black Orpheus," I find myself in full agreement with Marcano's argument: I agree that there are significant differences between the accounts of group formation offered by the early and the late Sartre, and also that the second of their two accounts can deeply enrich the application of social constructionism to the question of racial identities. However, I want here to highlight a concept more prominent in the early Sartre's discussion of social identity than that of the later Sartre, but not absent from the latter, a concept that in my view maintains a certain abiding value for a discussion of these issues. That notion is the idea of facticity. However, my reintroduction of the idea of facticity is not so much intended to enrich social constructionism, which is what I take to be the main task of Marcano's essay, as it is intended to contribute to a different inquiry, one that she also is engaged in, for example, with her remarks on agency, and that is to develop an account of the existential reality of racial existence within a racialized society.

It should be understood that Sartre, the great apostle of freedom, insists, even in *Being and Nothingness,* that one cannot choose one's identity. This does not sit well with certain sensibilities nourished by modern theories of individualism, particularly as one finds them in the United States, according to which one is supposed to have an inalienable right to choose one's identity or perhaps even refuse all identities and be seen in one's singularity (cf. CC, 99). The existential conception of race operates always in the tension between, on the one hand, the meanings—here the identities—which others impose on me on the basis of what he calls, perhaps somewhat misleadingly, "objective characteristics"[6] and, on the other hand, my inability to realize that identity without remainder. Any attempt by me to reduce myself to my race would, like trying to deny it in a racialized world, be in bad faith. Race is in his terms an unrealizable (EN, 610; BN, 527). I can never coincide with this identity: I always escape it: "Human reality as for itself is a lack and that what it lacks is a certain coincidence with itself" (EN, 139; BN, 95). This conclusion follows from Sartre's ontology and specifically his conviction that human reality is what it is not and is not what it is (EN, 103; BN, 63), but it leaves him with the problem of authenticity.

What would it mean to have an authentic relation to one's social identity? So long as Sartre asks the question, he never seems to have a good answer. He negotiates the problem eventually, I suspect, only by refusing the question. Hence, it is not surprising that, at the time of *Notebooks for an Ethics,* he treats the idea of race, along with class and nation, as a form of alienation that hinders concrete human relations.[7] Hence too, his argument in "Black Orpheus" that blacks on their own should renounce their race as a prelude to the classless society, something Frantz Fanon objected to having a white man tell him, although he did not seem to object when Aimé Césaire said something similar.[8] This is an indication of how in the realm of political praxis issues arise that do not seem always to occur to a certain kind of philosopher: questions about how the truth-value of a statement depends on who says it, questions about what beliefs about identity, for example, are conditions for the possibility of action. The path that Sartre treads from *Being and Nothingness* to *Critique of Dialectical Reason* has much to do with his efforts to negotiate those questions of which he was initially largely ignorant, by his own admission. Although I am not aware of any direct evidence that Sartre's revision of his early thought on race was in part a consequence of Fanon's critique of it in *Black Skin, White Masks,* I believe we can see, in addition to the example I have just given, other places in the later Sartre where Fanon's fingerprints are visible, and that is why I shall focus on both thinkers.

It is worth recalling that Fanon embraced most enthusiastically those aspects of Sartre's account of race that have been taken up by the social constructionists, and also that, after the one-sided view of *Anti-Semite and Jew,* where we hear nothing about Jewish history and Jewish agency, both Fanon and the early Sartre offer an account of how an oppressed group contributes to its own identity formation. One sees this already in "Black Orpheus" where Sartre was explicit that Aimé Césaire's words do not describe negritude, "they create it."[9] It is an acknowledgment that even in a racist society, it is not only the racist who plays a role in the construction of the meaning of a race. It is in terms of their "basic experience of suffering," their "collective memory" of slavery, their collective past that is to say, that, according to Sartre, the poets of the negritude movement theorize black identity (A, xxxvi–xxxix; BO, 134–36). Frantz Fanon agreed. In the context of a discussion of Sartre's claim about the anti-Semite making the Jew, Fanon not only proclaimed *Anti-Semite and Jew* to be among the best books that he had read, he also reiterated its major conclusion, transferring it to the question of antiblack racism: "The black soul is a white man's artifact."[10] However, he subsequently observed in *A Dying Colonialism* that "[i]t is the White man who creates the Negro. But it is the Negro who creates negritude."[11] This is not said by Fanon against Sartre, as is often thought; it is a faithful paraphrase of what Sartre had explicitly noted in "Black Orpheus." Nevertheless, even in this expanded form, social constructionism still does not succeed in theorizing the experience of racial minorities who live race as a destiny that is constantly to be negotiated. This is not surprising if one recognizes that that is not the question social constructionism was designed to address.

Social constructionism is a thesis about the ontological basis of certain categories, such as race. It leaves open the question of how race works in society.[12] If we want as an answer more than just a taxonomy of race in the sense of an account of how the classification system operates in any given context, then we need to bring a richer philosophical lectionary to bear. Anthony Appiah in *Color Conscious* proposes a "sociohistorical" account of the construction of race and thereby finds himself drawn into a discussion of "a process of identification in which the [racial] label can shape the intentional acts of (some of) those who fall under it," but he lacks the philosophical resources to take this much farther than saying that being raced is unlike being a waiter because we *can* ask whether someone is really of the black race, whereas it makes no sense to ask someone who has a job as a waiter, whether that is what they really are (CC, 79–81). Here in my view is where Sartre has something valuable to contribute.

Sartre does not so much present a social constructionist account of the term *race* within an alternative idiom, that of continental philosophy, so much as he offers an existential account of what it means to live in a racialized society, a society that is organized in such a way that many people say that race is the most real thing in their lives. One sees this very clearly when in *Being and Nothingness* he explicitly warns against seeing race as "purely and simply a collective fiction" (EN, 607; BN, 524). Indeed, he explains that to declare race a collective fiction, is not unlike the gesture of the bourgeois who make themselves bourgeois precisely by denying that classes exist (EN, 614; BN, 531). That is a measure of how Sartre would be suspicious of at least some of the applications of certain forms of social constructionism, such as we have seen in the affirmative action debate. Furthermore, the key to understanding the early Sartre's account of freedom lies in his claim that "[i]t is impossible to grasp facticity in its brute nudity, since all that we will find of it is already recovered and fully constructed" (EN, 126; BN, 83). In any given situation it is impossible to say what comes from freedom and what comes from the brute existent: the situation is, in a phrase that suggest that Sartre had already anticipated Merleau-Ponty's philosophy of ambiguity, "an ambiguous phenomenon" (EN, 568; BN, 488). This means that for Sartre the question of what belongs to race according to my choice and what is imposed on me from the outside is in principle unanswerable. That is why he is on certain occasions inclined to emphasize our lack of freedom, even though he more often highlights our choices. Facticity refers ultimately to the ambiguity of the situation whereby one cannot tell for sure what is my or my society's contribution and what is already given, what is and what is not socially constructed.

I believe that Sartre's *Being and Nothingness* should be read as a book that from the outset was directed to the questions of ethics and politics. Although Sartre in *Being and Nothingness* postponed these questions, the publication of the *Notebooks on Ethics* provides some of the missing pieces that enables us to see the larger argument of which *Being and Nothingness* is only one part. The much-misunderstood chapter on freedom and facticity reads differently as soon as one recognizes that its final brief section on responsibility is not an afterthought, but the conduit by which Sartre hopes to pass from a phenomenological ontology to a politics and thence to an ethics. This is clearest when one turns to the questions of social identity that permeate *Being and Nothingness*, as one sees from the examples he offers. Consider Sartre's example of the Jew who is excluded from a restaurant on account of his or her race. Sartre uses that example to show that one's possibilities in a specific society are always dependent on one's place in that society. They are a function of how society sees one, and to deny that amounts to "a total alienation of my person" (EN, 607; BN, 524). Sartrean freedom does not mean that one chooses one's identity independently of society. It means that one chooses it by taking responsibility for the situation in which one finds oneself, indeed for the whole world, including the freedom of others, and that certainly includes the identity that in any given context one is assigned.

Sartre explores race in *Being and Nothingness* in the section on "My Neighbor" in the course of the chapter on Freedom. He distinguishes three layers of reality which come into play as I constitute my concrete situation in a world that is not simply mine, that is to say, in a world whose meaning is not simply revealed by my own ends. First, there are the meanings that are independent of my choice: Sartre offers as examples, stations, signposts, warning sounds, and so on. The second layer is constituted by meanings that I discover as already mine. The third layer is the Other as a center of reference to which these meanings refer. Sartre allocates race, along with nationality and physical appearance, to the second layer (EN, 591–92; BN, 510). Even though these identities are not primarily for ourselves, but for the Other, and even though I cannot see myself as others see me (see also RQ, 90–91; AJ, 74–75), I am responsible for those identities. Take a case that is close to home for many of us: white privilege. While I applaud the efforts of the Race Traitor movement to disrupt society's categorization and its arbitrariness, in a racialized society such as our own, one is, in Sartre's terms, as much in bad faith if one renounces race in favor of individualism as one is if one reduces oneself to one's race as something simply assigned to one. In either case one tries to be something that one has not chosen to be, but one's responsibility lies in the fact that one has always already chosen: that is what Sartre means by the original choice. It is not that I choose my situation or my race as if I was presented with a variety of options, but that I am responsible for it. To be sure, what it might mean in practice to take responsibility for white privilege is not always clear, and Sartre at the time of *Being and Nothingness* not only had an inadequate ontology stemming from an ill-conceived method, but also was hampered by his own flawed descriptions of how the oppressed experience racism, so that his account of their responsibility is especially deficient. For this reason, Fanon's intervention in *Black Skin, White Masks* is indispensable for any attempt to think race as facticity.

This is not the place to explore the extraordinary complexity of Fanon's critique of Sartre, but it is significant that from the outset Fanon gave a greater weight to materiality than Sartre was willing to do in his early work. Like many black intellectuals from the Caribbean, Fanon's diagnosis was that blacks who encountered white society internalized its racism and in consequence suffered from an inferiority complex, but he insisted that its cause was primarily economic and only subsequently internalized (PN, 8; BSWM, 11). Nevertheless, this meant that the inferiority complex would be perpetuated until the economic disparities had been addressed. It was only because Sartre subsequently in the *Critique of Dialectical Reason* proposed a complete rewriting of his ontology around the notion of scarcity, including economic scarcity, that an intellectual reconciliation with Fanon became possible. That is why, although I must inevitably devote the most space to the analysis offered in *Being and Nothingness* where Sartre speaks most about facticity, it is the account given in the *Critique of Dialectical Reason* that I am ultimately proposing for consideration.

However, another issue that Fanon raised has even more implications for my efforts here. Fanon complained that Sartre had forgotten that a black suffers in his body differently from the way whites do (PN, 112; BSWM, 138). I believe that Fanon is doing more here than proposing a revision of one aspect of Sartre's phenomenological description. It is to be understood, on my interpretation, as one of a number of reminders that Sartre, as white, lacks a certain access to the issues. What Sartre forgets is something no black person could "forget": that he or she lives his or her body differently from the way whites live their bodies. Mindful of Fanon's criticism of Sartre on this point, I shall try in what follows to keep what I say within appropriate limits. I will first outline Sartre's account of race as facticity in *Being and Nothingness*; I will try to clarify what Fanon found valuable in this account and what he found questionable; I will end by showing how in the *Critique of Dialectical Reason* Sartre accepted Fanon's proposed revisions and presented an account of race that it seems they largely shared. It is this account, not the early account, that I am proposing we adopt when I advocate the concept of facticity as a tool for understanding how race works in racialized societies such that are called upon to change society. It should never be forgotten that, for Sartre and Fanon, to recognize race as a facticity is to recognize it as something for which we must all take responsibility (EN, 638–42; BN, 553–56).

The question is whether the term *facticity* is a useful resource for an existential account of race. The notion of facticity employed by Sartre has its roots in Heidegger's use of the same term in *Being and*

Time, but the reference to Heidegger is not very helpful here as Sartre uses the term in his own way. Even though some commentators have recently asked whether Heidegger's notion of facticity might not also serve as a basis for a thinking of race, as of gender, it is possible that it is not a thick enough notion in Heidegger.[13] It seems that his idea of facticity, understood both as thrownness and as the "that it is" of human existence, is still too thin to accommodate a notion such as "race."[14] Sartre's notion of facticity is much thicker. Indeed, one problem with Sartre's use of the term is how much he tries to pack into it.

One finds no single definition of facticity but rather a layering of the term as Sartre develops his ontology in the course of *Being and Nothingness*. For Sartre, the "that it is" of facticity is necessary, but what I am—my race, my class, my rationality, my character, my past, my physiological structure—are contingent (EN, 392–93; BN, 328). My facticity is a necessary contingency. Or, as he puts it in his own inimitable way, it is "the invulnerable contingency of the in-itself which I have to be without any possibility of not being it" (EN, 162; BN, 118). Even if one has no choice but to assume one's facticity, one has an infinite number of ways of taking it up, including evading it, which is, on this account, simply another way of assuming it. Facticity is thus not opposed to freedom, or introduced by Sartre only in order to restrict his otherwise unquestionably exaggerated claims about freedom. There is no freedom without facticity and vice versa. However, it is because one's existence as body in the midst of the world is one's facticity (EN, 428; BN, 361) that Sartre highlights the idea of race as facticity, alongside other facticities, such as sexual difference (EN, 452; BN, 383), class, nationality, and physiological structure (EN, 392–93; BN, 327–28). He explains in "Materialism and Revolution":

> It is not that man is outside Nature and the world, as the idealist has it. . . . He is completely in Nature's clutch . . . from the very beginning, for him being born really means "coming into the world" in a situation not of his choice, with *this particular body*, *this* family, and *this* race, perhaps.[15]

The misleadingly called "objective characteristics" that define me in the context of the United States at the beginning of the twenty-first century as white, just as other "objective characteristics" define others as black or Chicano, do not mean that my race is determined entirely from the outside, even though I have not chosen the terms in which I am seen. However, on Sartre's account I am responsible for the meaning I give to the labels attached to me. One of Sartre's examples is the prohibition

"No Jews allowed here." He suggests that it is only by recognizing the freedom of anti-Semites and by assuming this being-a-Jew that I am a Jew for them, but he offers the possibility that I might also reduce anti-Semites to the status of pure objects through recognizing the power of my gaze or one accepts that the recognition of others and the assuming of Jewish identity is one and the same (EN, 610; BN, 526–27).

Nevertheless, this gives rise to a series of problems that Sartre seems unable to resolve at this time. He is clear that the Jew does not successfully negotiate the problem by assimilation or by renouncing his or her Jewishness, and that what Jews want is to be integrated into the nation as Jews (RQ, 175; AJ, 145). However, this leads to the problem of what it would mean to be an authentic Jew. Sartre's answer is that this will only be possible after "the radical liquidation of anti-Semitism," that is to say, after the socialist revolution and the entry into a classless society (RQ, 181–82; AJ, 149–50). However, as we saw from Fanon's response to "Black Orpheus," that has its own problems. Nor is that the end of the matter as we see when we read, in *Notebooks for an Ethics*, that "[i]n the very idea of *race* (nature) there is an ought-to-be. One has to construct one's race, realize it in oneself" (CM, 485; NE, 469). Had we not already been told in *Being and Nothingness* that race is an unrealizable? The question of the realizability or unrealizability of race is not a fundamental ambiguity for Sartre as is the relation of freedom and what is given. It is an unresolved problem in the early Sartre that Fanon made a decisive contribution to resolving.

Fanon saw the potential of the concept of facticity for the discussion of race: he employed it twice in *Black Skin, White Masks*, although it is not to be found in the English translation. Both uses of the term occur in the second chapter in the course of his controversial discussion of the novels of Mayotte Capécia.[16] Although Fanon subsequently rejected the idea that one can use her novel as a basis for a discussion of the woman in color in general (PN, 65; BSWM, 81), that concession does not occur until the next chapter, thereby enhancing the impression that he was here being insensitive to women of color. In any event, Fanon announced with respect to the condescension shown by her by the rich Martinicans of Didier: "It is because she is a woman of color that she is not accepted in these circles. It is on the basis of her facticity that her resentment is elaborated" (PS 35–36; BSWM, 44. Trans. modified). Mayotte Capécia's facticity is not her skin color or her race as a biological fact: it is her situation, the fact that as a woman of color she is rejected by society. What matters is how she responds to that situation, how she takes up this facticity. By being resentful, she accidentalizes the fact of her "absolute blackness" instead of recognizing it (PN, 37; BSWM,

46). It is important to understand that, however critical of Mayotte Capécia Fanon appears to be, the point of the discussion is ultimately to show that she cannot address her problems on her own, that they arise out of society and that society must be changed, if she is to be able to change. Having identified the way in which blacks are attacked in their corporeality, Fanon declares that "[t]here is no reason now to be surprised that Mayotte Capécia dreamed of herself as pink and white. I should say that was quite normal" (PN, 132n; BSWM, 163n). That is to say, Fanon regards it as "normal" for black Martinicans to be anti-black, because the European archetypes of the Negro are pervasive throughout society (PN, 154; BSWM, 191).[17]

It is important to understand what Fanon is saying here. He is saying that Mayotte Capécia should not see her exclusion from white society as a contingency, as a social constructionist would want her to do, because that leads to an unproductive resentment that arises from the thought that she could take a place in such a society, as could have happened if she had been born "pink and white," if her light skin allowed her to be seen as "pink and white," or if the boundary line was drawn differently so that so-called mulattos were placed among the biké and not on the other side. Mayotte Capécia's problem is that she wants to enter into society, whereas what she should want is the destruction of society as presently constituted, including especially the high society of the rich Martinicans of Didier. Fanon sees Mayotte Capécia's response as perfectly normal, given the nature of society, but entirely unproductive, because she identifies the problem as existing outside herself and so she denies her agency.

If this first use of the term *facticity* in *Black Skin, White Masks* helps to show what Fanon found productive in Sartre's use of the term, its second occurrence takes us beyond Sartre. The second reference to facticity in *Black Skin, White Masks* occurs when Fanon speculates on various ways in which the educated mulattress, who rejects the advances of a black man, might be engaging in doubly equivocal behavior, that is to say, bad faith. One of the forms of bad faith, which is described as the abstract point of view, would consist in the mulattress seeing this black man as a savage; another—"the point of view of facticity"—is for her to reject black aesthetics and declare that blacks are ugly (PN, 47; BSWM, 58). In the third chapter Fanon returns with a similar example, although now in the context of a novel by René Maran. Fanon writes: "Jean Veneuse is ugly. He is Black. What more is needed?" (PN, 64; BSWM, 80). Whether the focus falls on the one issuing the judgment or on the one judged suddenly seems less important, as, from this perspective, is Sartre's idea of identities as unrealizables.

Fanon's success in forcing the issue is apparent if one returns to Sartre's discussions of ugliness as a facticity in *Being and Nothingness*, which must have been on Fanon's mind as he discussed it with reference to these novels. Sartre there explains that the assertion "I am ugly" is not the pure establishment of my ugliness but, employing a phrase of Gaston Bachelard's, the apprehension of "the coefficient of adversity" presented by society to my enterprises as it can be discovered only through the choice of these enterprises (EN, 536; BN, 459).[18] On Sartre's account, my ugliness, or my beauty, and my race, belong to my body as "the contingent form which is taken up by the necessity of my contingency" (EN, 393; BN, 328). My race is an unrealizable that I cannot identify with either as a contingency or a necessity. It is something I can be only by assuming it through my existence. "For-myself I am not a professor or a waiter in a café, nor am I handsome or ugly, Jew or Aryan, spiritual, vulgar or distinguishable. . . . I who *am* them can not realize them" (EN, 610; BN, 527). What is at stake for Fanon is apparent in another example that goes to the very heart of *Black Skin, White Masks* and its thesis that the black is locked in a vicious circle because he or she is suffering from an inferiority complex that can be addressed neither at the individual level nor the societal level, because an individual "cure" can accomplish little or nothing when the economic structure of society still reinforces that inferiority, and yet the societal change cannot be accomplished without the individual also being changed.[19] By contrast, Sartre presents the inferiority complex as the free and global project of myself as inferior before others (EN, 536–37; BN, 459). Hence, he says in *Being and Nothingness* that the fact that I do not receive the meaning of my race passively is expressed "but by completely reversing the terms—when it is said that the fact of being of a certain race can determine a reaction of pride or an inferiority complex" (EN, 612; BN, 528). Fanon's objection would seem to be that Sartre is taking the obstacles to resisting the judgments of an alien aesthetics or the imposition of an inferiority complex too lightly. It is hard not to sympathize with that conclusion when one reads Sartre's proclamation that "if it pleases me to consider the anti-Semites as pure objects, then my being-a-Jew disappears immediately to give place to the simple consciousness (of) being a free, unqualifiable transcendence" (EN, 610; BN, 527). Fanon could not identify with the ease of this "if it pleases me . . ."

For Sartre, however much society might oblige me to act in accordance with an identity to which I might from time to time be reduced from the outside, nevertheless for myself I escape it. Even in a racist society my identity is an "unrealizable" (EN, 610; BN, 527).

Fanon's response emerged most clearly when he wrote: "I am not a potentiality of something, I am wholly what I am" (PN, 109; BSWM, 135). The implied contrast is with the account in *Being and Nothingness* that consciousness is what it is not and is not what it is. Similarly, when Fanon wrote that "[m]y Negro consciousness does not hold itself out as a lack. It *is*. It sticks to itself" (PN, 109; BSWM, 135.), he was challenging Sartre's account of human reality as a lack, a lack of a certain self-coincidence (EN, 139; BN, 95). Fanon agreed with Sartre that "the Jew can be unknown in his Jewishness. He is not wholly what he is" (PN, 93; BSWM, 115), but he considered himself as a black man "overdetermined from without," the slave not of an idea, but of his appearance (PN, 93; BSWM, 116). However, Sartre's position on this issue would change. In *Being and Nothingness,* Sartre insisted that one never *is* this or that: facticity cannot constitute me as *being* a bourgeois or being a worker (EN, 126; BN, 83). By contrast, in *Critique of Dialectical Reason* he expressly revises that claim: in order to make oneself a bourgeois, one must first be bourgeois (CRD, 289; CDR, 231). To be sure, one could find isolated texts that support the idea that Sartre already knew that. In the section on "My Neighbor" in the course of his discussion of freedom and facticity in *Being and Nothingness,* Sartre highlights certain determinations that I *am* without having chosen them: "Here I am—Jew, or Aryan, handsome or ugly, one-armed, etc. All of this I am for the Other with no hope of apprehending this meaning which I have outside and, still more important, with no hope of changing it" (EN, 606; BN, 523–24). However, within a couple of pages he seems to have taken it back. "I do not limit myself to receiving passively the meaning 'ugliness,' 'infirmity,' 'race,' etc., but, on the contrary, I grasp these characteristics—in the simple capacity of a meaning—only in the light of my own ends" (EN, 612; BN, 528). In the *Critique,* my facticity is not qualified or relativized in that way.

The notion of facticity may not play a prominent role in *Critique of Dialectical Reason,* but it nevertheless does play a decisive role. Sartre shows how human beings, while never being able to transcend their bodies altogether, still find ways in which to overcome its limitations in reference to specific aims. Thus, the fact that I do not have eyes in the back of my head means that, on my own, I am vulnerable to attack from behind, but a military platoon by forming itself into a square can organize itself to cover all directions at once.[20] Sartre describes this, a little mysteriously, as a dissolving of the facticity of the living being, but he later explains that even though this "basic facticity . . . as a special biological determination of unworked materiality" is eliminated, nevertheless it is encountered again in another form through the "contingent determination of the practico-inert field" (CRD, 536; CDR, 542). Although the discussion is introduced in order to highlight the fundamental obstacle to unification that is represented by dispersion—in Sartre's example, a group can dissolve as a result of circumstances that intervene and do not derive directly from the objective it has set itself—the example confirms that in the late work, as in his early writings, one's facticity is not something simply given, but is always to be renegotiated. This is how Sartre throughout thinks of race as facticity. The difference between the early Sartre and the late Sartre on this issue is that only for the latter did facticity include the way that past actions are now embedded in the material conditions. That is to say, he came to offer a thicker, richer, notion of facticity.

Sartre's early accounts of race tend to focus on direct relations between blacks and whites, Jews and Gentiles. As a result, his analyses of racism highlight the actions, speech, and thoughts of individuals. In his later work, Sartre's attention moves on a larger canvas. The existential notion of a "situation" gave way to the dialectical notion of a system operating as a totality. It is in consequence of this insight that Sartre in the *Critique* tended not to talk of races as such but of the colonizer and the colonized. There is, of course, a similar displacement of race into a discussion of colonialism early in Fanon's *The Wretched of the Earth*, insofar as the racial dimension is insisted upon, but yet, at the same time, the basic terms of the analysis are the colonizer and the colonized.[21] For Sartre, this shift of focus from racism to colonialism as a system mediated by materiality is his way of saying that racism is not a system of thought or even a thought at all. "Racism is the colonial interest lived as a link of all the colonialists of the colony through the serial flight of alterity" (CRD, 344; CDR, 300). Sartre offers an example drawn from Algeria, but one that can readily be extended to other times and places. He observed how the colonized are denied an education either in their culture or that of the colonizers:

> The activity of racism is a *praxis* illuminated by a "theory" ("biological," "social," or empirical racism, it does not matter which) aiming to keep the masses in a state of molecular aggregation, and to use every possible means to increase the "sub-humanity" of the natives. . . . (CRD, 477; CDR, 721)

The attempt to reduce racism to a prejudice, a state of mind of individuals, so that direct proof of racism has to be sought in someone's pronouncements as evidence of their intentions, is one of the ways a racist society perpetuates itself.

Neither Sartre, nor Fanon, think of racism as a set of beliefs that may or may not be manifested in action. They construe racism primarily as a set of practices supported by institutions. These practices and institutions might under certain conditions call for racism as a set of beliefs to justify it, as when it is attacked, but that is a subsidiary effect. In his still unpublished 1964 lectures in Rome on ethics, Sartre argues that racism, the exclusion of the oppressed from "the club of men," should be understood as the resolution of the contradiction embodied in colonial praxis.[22] One finds similar examples elsewhere in Sartre. In "Colonialism Is a System" he argues that one of the functions of racism was to compensate for the latent universalism of bourgeois liberalism, in the sense that if all human beings have the same rights, then some must be made subhuman (SV, 44; CN, 45). Similarly, in his Preface to Fanon's *The Wretched of the Earth*, he proclaims that "nothing is more consistent . . . than racist humanism" (SV, 187; CN, 151). That is to say, if you are going to treat a man like a dog, one must persuade oneself that he is a dog. But, of course, that presupposes that one has first recognized him or her as human, as Sartre is fond of pointing out (CRD, 190; CDR, 111).[23] In other words, one is in error if one focuses on the apparent contradiction between racism on the one hand and moral universalism or bourgeois humanism on the other hand. The decisive contradiction is that between the colonial practices on which one relies for one's continuing economic well-being or one's status and the beliefs to which one appeals to claim certain rights for oneself. This contradiction is resolved by racism in one or other of its various forms. To that extent moral universalism, which analytically opposes racism, can be seen dialectically as producing it. Racism is the consequence, not the cause. It is produced by the colonial system, when it determines that the colonized is not simply other; but the "other than man" (CRD, 672; CDR, 715), "the Enemy of Man" (CRD, 676; CDR, 720).

In the *Critique of Dialectical Reason* one finds a clear awareness that racial identities in any given context belong in reciprocal relation to each other so that one cannot look at any racial identity in isolation, an insight that was no doubt enhanced by Fanon's *Black Skin, White Masks*. Briefly, Sartre addresses the question of reciprocity in terms of an-Other being, a primary alienation that for the most part subsists as what he calls seriality, a collectivity in which there are no intrinsic relations among members of the group so that they relate to each other only in their relative alterity as members of this series, like people standing in line to catch a bus. It is only in a context where a race, like a class or other form of collective, lives their unity that race escapes seriality and becomes a group. But the group cannot sustain itself and will always be small. Furthermore, it is not the racist but the passive constitution of things, that creates the black, just as it is now the colonial system rather than the colonizer who produces the colonized (CRD, 698; CDR, 738). Fanon responds in *The Wretched of the Earth* that it is the colonizer who makes the colonized, but that the colonial system is the truth of the colonizer (DT, 66; WE, 36). Fanon thereby agrees with the later Sartre in placing emphasis on the system while at the same time trying to keep his earlier analysis intact.

Sartre not only highlights the antagonism between the two parties, he also underlines their reciprocity. He understands the colonist and the colonized as a couple, "produced by an antagonistic situation and by one another" (CRD, 677; CDR, 721). Sartre is here in danger of perpetuating a dichotomy of races, but his decisive insight is that racism can be sustained without being owned: it can be sustained by a collectivity through always being the attitude of another (CRD, 622; CDR, 652). Sartre illustrates this Other-being with the case of the employer who beats a worker because this is what one does. And the employee submits to the beating for the same reason. Sartre explains, "*[T]hrough the two individuals*, the Other relates to the Other" (CRD, 485n; CDR, 731n). Each class finds its unity not in itself, but through the Other (CRD, 735; CDR, 792). This is also how it is with race. One can easily see how segregation has been perpetuated by this Other-being: it does not need any whites to say that they do not want families of another race on their street to create white flight. It is enough that they believe that their presence might impact house prices, and, that the belief is at once reflected in house prices.

The impact of that on the conception of race can best be explained by contrasting the account in the *Critique* with the account given in *Anti-Semite and Jew* some fifteen years or so earlier. In the earlier text the focus was on the individual Jew in isolation, so that the unity that the Jew feels with other Jews is understood as arising from the similarity of their individual experiences in relation to non-Jews, an account that is hard to sustain and always seems to allow for exceptions, as when some member of a group denies these experiences. The account in the *Critique* is fuller: the being-Jewish of every Jew is lived in his or her relations with all other Jews, insofar as he or she is constituted, through all Jews, as Other for non-Jews.[24] Sartre explains:

> To the extent that, for the conscious, lucid Jew, being-Jewish (which is his statute *for non-Jews*) is interiorized as his responsibility in relation to all other Jews and his being-in-danger, out there, owing

> to some possible carelessness caused by Others who mean nothing to him, over whom he has no power and every one of whom is himself like Others (in so far as he makes them exist as such in spite of himself), *the* Jew, far from being *the type* common to each separate instance, represents *on the contrary* the perpetual *being-outside-themselves-in-the-other* of the members of this practico-inert grouping. (CRD, 318; CDR, 268)

Sartre uses as his example the Jewish doctor who, on being told that there are too many Jewish doctors, finds the other doctors dispensable (CRD, 318; CDR, 268).

Underlying membership of a race, as of a class, are passive syntheses of materiality. We are born into a world where race and class already exist; they are "the *crystallized practice* of previous generations," so that individuals find an existence sketched out for them at birth (CRD, 289; CDR, 232). What is petrified in past being also serves as a future sentence that has been imposed on one from the outside: that is to say, it is experienced as having a certain necessity (CRD, 302; CDR, 250). However, it should be recognized that in the course of the *Critique* Sartre refines this conception, so that although he refers initially to the way class as a collective being is in everyone to the extent that everyone is in it, such that class is a matrix, a milieu, a sort of passive weight (CRD, 305; CDR, 252), at a later stage of the account he concedes that "*common class-being* is no longer, for everyone, *being-in-the-milieu-of-class*" (CRD, 356; CDR, 315). The milieu is dissolved insofar as class is a serially structured multiplicity of multiplicities. To that extent "class-being is practico-inert, and defines itself as a determination of seriality" (CRD, 649; CDR, 686). The same would be true of race-being except in those perhaps rare moments when certain people who share this race-being for a time act as a group, for example, in demonstrating for a cause. Sartre seems to have been guided here by the Marxist idea that it is only under certain specific circumstances that the workers cease to be the masses, living "a false unity of isolations," and form the proletariat as a unity.[25]

The focus of Sartre's early analysis of racism and of anti-Semitism fell on the individual and his discussion of race similarly resulted in a discourse of authenticity and inauthenticity with all its inherent problems. While not abandoning the notion of authenticity altogether, Fanon, in *Black Skin, White Masks*, perhaps taking a clue from certain remarks at the end of *Anti-Semite and Jew*, postponed the question of authenticity to a future society (RQ, 171; AJ, 141). As a result the focus fell on society, the need to change it, and the difficulty of so doing given the reciprocity of colonizer and colonized within the colonial system. That is also the basis on which Sartre came to highlight what he saw as a problem among some members of the African American middle class in May 1966. He attacked them not because he regarded some of them as "inauthentic" or "not really black" but for seeking only their integration into the American bourgeoisie. He acknowledged that they reprove whites for their racism but he claimed that they did not know the real causes of racism: "[T]hey do *not see* the infrastructures on which racism is founded because they are conditioned by these infrastructures and *live* them blindly."[26] One can raise the question as to whether Sartre was in a position to issue this kind of judgment, whether he had not, as Fanon had already pointed out with reference to certain remarks in "Black Orpheus," once again overstepped the limits of what he, as a white man, could legitimately say, but at the same time one can recognize in what Sartre is saying, an objection of the kind Fanon issued against Mayotte Capécia: they both warn against a focus on individual advancement, as if racism could be overcome at that level, one person at a time. The richer, thicker, fundamentally less individualist and more political notion of race as facticity developed by the later Sartre with Fanon's help exposes such illusions and it is my opinion that it is high time that philosophers pass beyond the formula that "race is a social construction" to address at a deeper level the question of how race functions in society, and how it is lived, so that we better know how to identify and combat racism in its various forms. My argument has been that there is good reason why some of us who try to do so turn to the conceptual resources provided by Fanon and the later Sartre, and one of the singular advantages of doing so is that they supply us with the kind of emancipatory discourse that people have mistakenly thought that social constructionism provides.

NOTES

1. See Ian Hacking, *The Social Construction of What?* (Cambridge: Harvard University Press, 1999), 1–34.

2. Immanuel Kant, *Vorlesungen über Anthropologie*, Akademie Ausgabe vol. xxv, part II (Berlin: Walter de Gruyter, 1997), 1187.

3. Donna-Dale Marcano, "Sartre and the Social Construction of Race," in *Race and Racism in Continental Philosophy*, ed. Robert Bernasconi (Bloomington: Indiana University Press, 2003), 214. Henceforth SS.

4. Jean-Paul Sartre, *Refléxions sur la question juive* (Paris: Gallimard, 1954), 84; *Anti-Semite and Jew*, trans. George J. Becker (New York: Schocken, 1976), 69. Henceforth RQ and AJ respectively.

5. K. Anthony Appiah, "Race Culture, Identity: Misunderstood Connections," in *Color Conscious* (Princeton: Princeton University Press, 1996), 78–80. Henceforth CC.

6. Jean-Paul Sartre, *L'être et le néant* (Paris: Gallimard, 1943), 606–607; *Being and Nothingness*, trans. Hazel Barnes (London: Macmillan, 1956), 524. Henceforth EN and BN respectively.

7. Jean-Paul Sartre, *Cahiers pour une morale* (Paris: Gallimard, 1983), 430; *Notebooks for an Ethics*, trans. David Pellauer (Chicago: University of Chicago Press, 1992), 414.

8. Robert Bernasconi, " 'The European knows and does not know': Fanon's response to Sartre," in *Frantz Fanon's 'Black Skin, White Masks,'* ed. Max Silverman (Manchester: Manchester University Press, forthcoming).

9. Jean-Paul Sartre, "Orphée noir" in *Anthologie de la nouvelle poésie nègre et malgache*, ed. Léopold-Sédar Senghor (Paris: Presses Universitaires de France, 1948), xxviii; "Black Orpheus," trans. John MacCombie, in *Race*, ed. Robert Bernasconi (Oxford: Blackwell, 2001), 128. Henceforth A and BO respectively.

10. Frantz Fanon, *Peau noire, masques blancs* (Paris: Seuil, 1952), 11; *Black Skin, White Masks*, trans. Charles Lam Markmann (New York: Grove Press, 1967), 14. Henceforth PN and BSWM respectively.

11. Frantz Fanon, *Sociologie d'une revolution* (Paris: Maspero, 1982), 29; *A Dying Colonialism*, trans. Haakon Chevalier (New York: Grove Press, 1967), 47.

12. See, for example, Naomi Zack, *Philosophy of Science and Race* (London: Routledge, 2002), 106.

13. See Tina Chanter, *Time, Death, and the Feminine: Levinas with Heidegger* (Stanford: Stanford University Press, 2001), 12.

14. Although the reference is by no means decisive, it is worth recalling that one of Heidegger's close associates, Oskar Becker, publicly criticized the philosophy of *Being and Time* on the grounds that it could not accommodate a concept of race: "Nordische Metaphysik," *Rasse. Die Monatasschrift der Nordischen Metaphysik* 5 (1938): 88; and "Para-Existenz. Menschliches Dasein und Dawesen," *Blätter für Deutsche Philosophie* 17 (1943/44): 86–87. Clearly, there is a great deal more that could be said here, particularly if one introduces Heidegger's accounts of the *Volk* from the 1930s. I address these issues in "*Rasse* and *Erde* in Heidegger's *Beiträge zur Philosophie*," a lecture delivered in Wuppertal in June 2002.

15. Jean-Paul Sartre, "Matérialisme et revolution," *Situations*, III (Paris: Gallimard, 1976), 220; "Materialism and Revolution," in *Literary and Philosophical Essays*, trans. Annette Michelson (New York: Criterion Press, 1955), 236. Henceforth S III and LPE respectively.

16. See T. Denean Sharpley-Whiting, *Frantz Fanon, Conflicts and Feminisms* (London: Rowman and Littlefield, 1998), 31–52.

17. Fanon's questioning of the concept of normality should be noted at this point (PN, 116n; BN, 142n).

18. Gaston Bachelard, *L'eau et les rêves* (Paris: José Corti, 1942), 213; *Water and Dreams*, trans. Edith R. Farrell (Dallas: Dallas Institute of Humanities and Culture, 1999), 159.

19. Robert Bernasconi, "Eliminating the Cycle of Violence: *The Place of A Dying Colonialism* within Fanon's Revolutionary Thought," *Philosophia Africana* 4, no. 2 (2001): 17–25. The correct title of this essay is "Eliminating the Vicious Circle," but this and a number of other changes were made without authorization in the course of publication.

20. Jean-Paul Sartre, *Critique de la raison dialectique* (Paris: Gallimard, 1960), 521; *Critique of Dialectical Reason, vol. one, Theory of Practical Reason,* trans. Alan Sheridan-Smith (London: NLB, 1976), 524. Henceforth CRD and CDR respectively.

21. Frantz Fanon, *Les damnés de la terre* (Paris: Gallimard, 1961), 70; *The Wretched of the Earth,* trans. Constance Farrington (New York: Grove Weidenfeld, 1991), 40. Henceforth DT and WE respectively.

22. Robert V. Stone and Elizabeth A. Bowman, "Dialectical Ethics: A First Look at Sartre's Unpublished 1964 Rome Lecture Notes," *Social Text* 13–14 (1986): 205.

23. See also Jean-Paul Sartre's Introduction to Albert Memmi's *The Colonizer and the Colonized,* reprinted in *Situations* V (Paris: Gallimard, 1964), 55; *Colonialism and Neocolonialism,* trans. Azzedine Haddour, Steve Brewer, and Terry McWilliams (London: Routledge, 2001), 52. Henceforth SV and NC respectively.

24. Thomas R. Flynn, *Sartre and Marxist Existentialism* (Chicago: University of Chicago Press, 1984), 95–97.

25. Jean-Paul Sartre, "Les communistes et la paix," *Situations* VI (Paris: Gallimard, 1964), 363; *The Communists and Peace,* trans. John Kleinschmidt (New York: George Braziller, 1968), 216.

26. Jean-Paul Sartre, "La conscience de classe chez Flaubert," in *Les Temps Modernes* 240 (May 1966): 1923. The concern raised here reflects a similar ambiguity about the Jew and other racial minorities that can in certain circumstances be both oppressed and a member of the middle class, so that "as they share the privileges of the class which oppresses them, they are unable, without contradiction, to work for the destruction of these privileges" (S III, 177; LPE, 209).

9

Merleau-Ponty on Fact and Essence

BERNARD FLYNN

In *The Will to Power* Nietzsche writes, "Facts are precisely what there is not, only interpretations."[1] Merleau-Ponty's position is far more radical, in that for him, there are neither facts nor interpretations; which is to say, neither independently given facts nor interpretations, but rather a fundamental *écart*, or fissure, where Being gives itself in the register neither of the factual nor of the intelligible. If this is the case, then the problematic of subsumption is fundamentally short-circuited. The classical notion of intelligibility in Western philosophy is the process by which the "given," in itself unintelligible, is subsumed under a concept that is itself inherently intelligible. This relation is well expressed in Kant's famous remark in the *Critique of Pure Reason* that percepts without concepts are blind and concepts without percepts are empty. According to Nietzsche, it is this "true" world, the second or intelligible world, which has served as the basis for the intelligibility and value of the apparent world. Thus, the crisis of European nihilism is engendered by the process in which the "true world has become a fable," that is to say, the process by which the superior values of the intelligible world have devalued themselves. Merleau-Ponty as well is sensitive to the radical disjunction between fact and essence; and he is well aware of the pernicious consequences that it entails. Concerning this displacement, he writes:

> It is on account of having begun with the antithesis of the fact and the essence, of what is individuated in a point of space and time and what is from forever and nowhere, that one is finally led to treat the essence as a limit idea, that is, to make it inaccessible. For this is what obliged us to seek the being of the essence in the form of a second positivity beyond the order of the "facts," to dream of

> a variation of a thing that would eliminate from it all that is not authentically itself and would make it appear all naked whereas it is always clothed—to dream of an impossible labor of experience on experience that would strip it of its facticity as if it were an impurity. Perhaps if we were to re-examine the anti-thesis of fact and essence, we would be able on the contrary to redefine the essence in a way that would give us access to it, because it would not be beyond but at the heart of that coiling up [*enroulement*] of experience over experience. . . .[2]

At the end of Nietzsche's story of Western philosophy, "How the 'True World' Became a Fable: The History of an Error,"[3] he tells us that the devaluation of the supersensible world does not at all confer value on the sensible world, since the sensible world has been systematically impoverished to the profit of the supersensible world. It is positivism that attempts to construct a philosophy on the basis of the debris of the collapse of the true world—the facts. Merleau-Ponty's response is to seize upon neither pole of this opposition, but rather to put into question the opposition itself. Is the bifurcation of fact and essence really faithful to our experience of the world?

In the first volume of Proust's *Remembrance of Things Past*, Marcel is seated in the carriage of Dr. Percepied, as it approaches the village of Martinville, when he describes his perception of three steeples as follows:

> In noticing and registering the shape of these spires, their shifting line, the sunny warmth of their surfaces, I felt that I was not penetrating to the core of my expression, that something more lay behind that mobility, that luminosity, something where they seemed at once to contain and to conceal. . . . Without admitting to myself that what lie hidden behind the steeples of Martinville must be something analogous to a pretty phrase, since it was in the form of words which pleased me that it appeared to me. . . .[4]

At this point Marcel takes a pencil and paper and writes a draft of the description of the steeples that is similar to the one we have just read. Proust's description of the three steeples is far removed from the quintessential gesture of the philosophy professor who points his hand to a something, a "that," a *fact*, and then says that it is a chair, a what, a *concept*. In Proust's description there is an intertwining of surface and depth, of word and perception, of intelligibility and pleasure. But let us not jump to the conclusion that Proust's description is a composite of what the philosopher has analytically distinguished. Perhaps the radical disjunction between fact and essence is not something we find at the most primitive rung of experience, but rather something that we create as an effect of a philosophical presupposition. To experience the real, the visible, as opaque chunks of being, or as a wandering troupe of sensations in need of a transparent system of ideal significations (essences) lest they descend into utter unintelligibility, is a consequence of having made of myself a pure power of knowing. It is a consequence of what Merleau-Ponty calls a "frontal confrontation with Being." This *frontal* conception of Being, whereby an object is thrown before a subject that is itself the pure power of representation, constitutes the basis of the modern doctrine of subjectivity. For him, this thought reaches its apotheosis in the philosophy of Sartre, where subjectivity, the for-itself, is identified with Nothingness. In opposition to this frontal encounter with Being, Merleau-Ponty writes, "Being no longer being *before me*, but surrounding me and in a sense traversing me, and my vision of Being not forming itself from elsewhere, but from the midst of Being."[5] Merleau-Ponty wishes to think the relationship between fact and essence in such a way that it could not be thought of in terms of any possible permutation of the relationship of a duplicate to an original, a copy that has the quality of consciousness to an object that does not. For him, vision is a relation to Being which is formed within Being. According to him, "The perception of the world is formed in the world, the test for truth takes place in Being."[6] Vision is engendered by a fold of the visible on itself. As his thought moves away from the problematic of perception as adequation, he approaches, in his own way to be sure, something like Heidegger's conception of Being as self-revelation, as revealing and concealing itself; and perception as the place of this self-revelation of the sensible. Let us focus on the consequences of this nonfrontal relation to Being in terms of our discussion of the problematic of subsumption, which is inextricably linked to the bifurcation of fact and essence, the immediate presence of the fact and the spatially-temporally nonlocalizable essence. Merleau-Ponty writes:

> Like the screen memory of the psychoanalysts, the present, the visible counts so much for me and has an absolute prestige for me only by reason of this immense latent content of the past, the future, and the elsewhere, which it announces and which it conceals.[7]

Let us reflect for a moment on the psychoanalytic concept of a screen memory. Laplanche and Pontalis in their *The Language of Psychoanalysis*, define a screen memory (*souvenir-écran; Deckerinnerung*) as follows:

> The childhood memory characterized both by its unusual sharpness and by the apparent insignificance of its content. The analysis of such memories leads back to indelible childhood experiences and to unconscious phantasies. Like the symptom, the screen memory is a formation produced by a compromise between repressed elements and defence.[8]

The mechanism that is prevalent in the formation of a screen memory is displacement. Freud writes, "Not only *some* but *all* of what is essential from childhood has been retained in these memories."[9] The screen memory is an apparently trivial childhood memory, which survives with remarkable clarity. Since it is a product of displacement, its analysis takes the form of a decomposition of its apparent unity in the direction of multiplicity. What appeared as unified and immediately given must be connected with what is not given as present. For example, in *The Interpretation of Dreams*, in the "dream of dreams," the dream of Irma's injection, Irma's complexion leads us to Irma's friend who is not present in the dream at all. Displacement introduces a sliding movement which undercuts the immediacy of the given in person; it decomposes the compact identity of the given. Not to recognize the operation of displacement in the screen memory would be to think that this irrelevant memory simply records a fact of early childhood, a fact that remains vivid for no particular reason, while the rest of our infantile experiences succumb to "childhood amnesia." The unanalyzed screen memory is an *apparent given* that analysis decomposes into one moment of a sliding continuum. When Merleau-Ponty writes that the *present* is *like* a screen memory, he certainly does not mean to suggest that all of our experiences of the present must be analyzed in terms of repressed childhood experiences. The salient point of the analogy is that the present, like the screen memory, has an illusory independence or *Selbständigkeit*, and that it too is a moment of a continuum. It is not an atom of presence, an absolute "here and now." What we encounter in the visible is not "a multiplicity of individuals synchronically and diachronically distributed, but a relief of the simultaneous and of the successive, a spatial and temporal pulp where the individuals are formed by differentiation."[10]

After contesting the primacy of the present by introducing the notion of the screen memory, which both announces and conceals a past, a future, and an elsewhere, Merleau-Ponty writes:

> There is therefore no need to add to the multiplicity of spatio-temporal atoms a transversal dimension of essences—what there is is

> a whole architecture, a whole complex of phenomena "in tiers," a whole series of "levels of being," which are differentiated by the coiling up of the visible and the universal over a certain visible wherein it is redoubled and inscribed. Fact and essence can no longer be distinguished, not because, mixed up in our experience, they in their purity would be inaccessible and would subsist as limit-ideas beyond our experience, but because—Being no longer being *before me*, but surrounding me and in a sense traversing me, and my vision of Being not forming itself from elsewhere, but from the midst of Being—the alleged facts, the spatio-temporal individuals, are from the first mounted on the axes, the pivots, the dimensions, the generality of my body, and the ideas are therefore already encrusted in its joints. There is no emplacement of space and time that would not be a variant of the others, as they are of it; there is no individual that would not be representative of a species or of a family of beings, would not have, would not be a certain style, a certain manner of managing the domain of space and time over which it has competency, of pronouncing, of articulating that domain, of radiating about a wholly virtual center—in short, a certain manner of being, in the active sense, a certain *Wesen*, in the sense that, says Heidegger, this word has when it is used as a verb.[11]

Farther on he adds: "We never have before us pure individuals, indivisible glaciers of beings, nor essences without place and without date."

What *there is (il y a, es gibt)* is neither facts nor essences but "a certain style." Merleau-Ponty displaces the problematic of fact and essence by the notion of *style*. Every style, unlike the traditional concept of essence, is encrusted with the thickness of Being and "not only in fact but also by right, could not be detached from it, to be spread out on display under the gaze."[12] In our ordinary usage of the "style," we see that this is the case. One speaks of the style of Flaubert: and someone well read in his works recognizes his style in a passage lifted out of context; or one speaks of his style in comparison to that of Balzac or Stendhal. But it is unimaginable that one could form a concept of his style; and then view his individual works as instances, or instantiations of the abstract concept *Flaubert's style*. His style is not an idea but a *way of writing*. It is a power of engendering texts. The notion of style suggests itself to Merleau-Ponty as a replacement for the fact-essence opposition precisely because a style, unlike an idea, is not definable, or conceivable, apart from the thickness of Being. A style is encrusted in the field of the Visible, a field characterized by displacement and sliding. It is a notion that does not have clearly delineated boundaries. Merleau-Ponty begins *The Visible and the Invisible* with a section entitled "The Perceptual Faith and its Obscurity." The first line of the text reads: "We see the things themselves, the world is what we see: formulae of this kind express a faith common to the natural man and the philosopher."[13] It is interesting to note that this experience of the "natural man *and* the philosopher" (emphasis added) is characterized as *faith*. The faith that Merleau-Ponty evokes is perhaps the contrary of Kierkegaard's agonized "leap of faith." This is a faith the commitment to which has always already been made and which we are in no danger of losing, except by a philosophical interpretation that misconceives it as a form of knowledge. For Merleau-Ponty, the position of an object held certain before one is an effect of making the knower a pure power of revelation, a subject that as pure power of knowing is nowhere. When Merleau-Ponty characterizes natural experience not as certainty but as faith, one is reminded of what Augustine said of time, that it is clear only if one does not reflect on it. Nevertheless, to practice philosophy is precisely to reflect on it. Merleau-Ponty constantly returns to natural experience, and in a sense it will function as the touchstone against which constituted philosophy will be tested. It cannot have a founding function because it itself is obscure, since it is not a knowledge but a faith. There can be faith only if there is an absence of certainty, only if there is doubt. According to Merleau-Ponty, who in this respect is in accord with Stanley Cavell, the history of Western philosophy has attempted to exorcize this doubt precisely by exacerbating it. The exorcism of doubt is the devise, the method, by which one installs oneself in certainty. However, Merleau-Ponty characterizes this project as an insurance policy, the premiums of which are more onerous than the loss that it indemnifies us against. Which is to say, by this project we lose the "there is" of the world, our very insertion into Being. When one begins philosophy by refuting skepticism, one takes up the position of the skeptic. As both Merleau-Ponty and Cavell show us—by generalizing the common question "How do I know that?" to everything, one fundamentally changes its meaning. If I ask, "Do I know if the dog living across the street is a golden retriever?" there are any number of ways that I can find out. I can: go across the street and look; ask the owner; look in a Dog Book, and so forth. But if I ask, "Is my body and the table before me real?" there are no procedures that I can follow, nobody that I can ask to respond to this question. The first question is situated within an ontological context, whereas the second is not. Geographically it makes sense to ask, "Where is Chile?" but it makes no sense at all to ask, "Where is the world." Thus, it must be concluded that doubt and ambiguity are ineluctably linked to both natural experience and philosophy.

What is the source of this ambiguity that philosophy has tried in vain to extricate us from? It is the Body. It is my perception that gives me the conviction that I encounter being; it is because I see the tree that I firmly believe that it really exists. However, "as soon as I attend to it this conviction is just as strongly contested, by the very fact that this vision is *mine*."[14] My vision of the world is in some sense or other in my body. Merleau-Ponty opens a vertiginous labyrinth by evoking the other and his perception.

> If perhaps there is for me no sense in saying that my perception and the thing it aims at are "in my head" (it is certain only that they are "*not elsewhere*"), I cannot help putting the other, and the perception he has, *behind his body*. More exactly, the thing perceived by the other is doubled: there is *the one he perceives*, God knows where, and there is the one I see, outside of his body, and which I call the true thing—as he calls true thing the table *he sees* and consigns to the category of appearances the one I see.[15]

To further complicate the issue: since the claim is that seeing is our fundamental relation to reality, he must recall that we see with our eyes and that we have two eyes. And as we know that binocular perception is in some sense "formed" by, if not a synthesis, a "metamorphosis" of monocular images and, nevertheless, the monocular images cannot be compared to the true vision. "They are phantoms and it is the real; they are pre-things and it is the thing: they vanish when we pass to normal vision and re-enter into the thing as into their daylight truth."[16] Merleau-Ponty is not suggesting that real vision is constructed out of phantoms, but rather that like the evil fairies, they are present at its birth.

> Thus the relation between the things and my body is decidedly singular: it is what makes me sometimes remain in appearances, and it is also what sometimes brings me to the things themselves; it is what produces the buzzing of appearances, it is also what silences them and casts me fully into the world. Everything comes to pass as though my power to reach the world and my power to entrench myself in phantasms only came one with the other; even more: as though the access to the world were but the other face of a withdrawal and this retreat to the margin of the world a servitude and another expression of my natural power to enter into it.[17]

It is in order to occult this fundamental obscurity that the domain of essence, and the pure epistemic subject that is its noetic correlate, was constructed. And indeed the world of essences does deliver us from relativism and solipsism. But if Merleau-Ponty's desire to remain close to the obscurity of perceptual faith forecloses this possibility, then how can he avoid these positions? Without an appeal to God, or an essential insight, or a transcendental subject, how does he avoid absolute relativism or solipsism? His response is ambiguous. If philosophers have sought to transcend the domain of phantoms to which the body seems to deliver us, by leaving the body behind or somehow compensating for its "deformation" of the true, Merleau-Ponty, on the other hand, will not try to "get around" the body, to encounter the true in spite of it. For him, the relation between the body and the things seen is not an ontic relation between things. To say that the body is not a thing, is not to surreptitiously introduce a sort of carnal subjectivity; rather, it is to radically displace the ontology of subjectivity. For if the body were a subject, in any recognizable sense, then it would have to interpose between itself and the world a representation in need of interpretation. To think the relation of seer and seen, Merleau-Ponty needed to create a new concept—the flesh. The thickness of the body is not an impediment to a vision of the true. Rather, it is that "the thickness of flesh between the seer and the thing is constitutive for the thing of its visibility as for the seer of his corporeity; it is not an obstacle between them, it is their means of communication. It is for the same reason that I am at the heart of the visible and that I am far from it: because it has thickness and is thereby naturally destined to be seen by the body."[18] Transcendental philosophy in moving from the "body" to the "mind" seeks to move from *thickness* to *transparency*.

The opposition between the thick, the opaque, on the one hand, and the transparent, on the other, is not metaphoric. Derrida has *read* major figures in the history of philosophy in terms of this hierarchical opposition. According to him, the place, the site, of metaphysics is the inner voice—the voice that remains silent. This site is privileged as the place of the essence due to the transparency perceived—or more properly, desired to be perceived—there between signifier and signified. The opacity of the signifier is dissolved in the diaphanous media of the living breath, the relation of the voice to itself. To be diaphanous means to be without layers, without depth. If Derrida is right to read the tradition in terms of its desire to occult the idea of thickness and layers, one recognizes the novelty of Merleau-Ponty's contention that "the thickness of the body, far from rivaling that of the world, is on the contrary the sole means I have to go unto the heart of things." Furthermore,

> It is the body and it alone, because it is a two-dimensional being, that can bring us to the things themselves, which are themselves not flat beings but beings in depth, inaccessible to a subject that would survey them from above, open to him alone that, if it be possible, would coexist with them in the same world.[19]

The relationship of the body to the world is not an ontic relation between two things. It is a relationship of Being. The body is an "*exemplar sensible*."[20] The visible itself, having depth and layers, would be inaccessible to a being totally transparent to itself, and thus totally other than the visible. As vision reveals the visible, it is itself revealed as inscribed within the visible. Vision is not an act of pure revelation of its object, since it is at the same time revealed as itself visible, as visible in principle. The body is a being of layers: as vision and visible, as inside and outside. Merleau-Ponty writes:

> [V]ision is a palpation with the look, it must also be inscribed in the order of being that it discloses to us; he who looks must not himself be foreign to the world that he looks at. As soon as I see, it is necessary that the vision (as is so well indicated by the double meaning of the word) be doubled with a complementary vision or with another vision: myself seen from without, such as another would see me, installed in the midst of the visible, occupied in considering it from a certain spot.[21]

The vision cannot possess the visible without at the same time being possessed by it. The duality of the vision, which is the contrary of any dualism, poses the body as "a being of two leaves, from one side a thing among things and otherwise what sees them and touches them."[22] To see the world is to see the place from which I see it marked out within the visible, which revealed by it also subtends it. To see without being visible, as in the story of the magic ring that Plato evokes in the *Republic* or the scandalous peeping Tom crouched over the keyhole in the hotel corridor in Sartre's *Being and Nothingness*, is a phenomenon not without interest from a psychoanalytic point of view, but it is not a faithful description of perception. The visibility of the vision is "visible by right," and not simply in fact.

> If it touches them and sees them, this is only because, being of their family, itself visible and tangible, it uses its own being as a means to participate in theirs, because each of the two beings is an

> archetype for the other, because the body belongs to the order of the things as the world is universal flesh.[23]

Regarding his description of the body as a being of two leaves, of sensing and sensible, Merleau-Ponty hesitates. Rather, he insists it is "neither thing seen only nor seer only, it is Visibility sometimes wandering and sometimes reassembled."[24] On another level, in the *Phenomenology of Perception* he claims that rather than saying that "I" perceive, one should say one *(on)* perceives. The sense of the prepersonal life of the body is deepened in *The Visible and the Invisible* where he tells us that we should not say that "my body perceives" but rather that I cannot perceive without it, that perception dawns through it. There is a generality of the sensible, an "anonymity innate to Myself that we have previously called flesh, and one knows there is no name in traditional philosophy to designate it."[25] The flesh is not some sort of subtle matter, and it is not spirit. It is not a representation of mind. Merleau-Ponty tells us that a "mind could not be captured by its own representation."[26] Let us consider one of the "characteristics" of this notion of the flesh, namely, its being a "general thing." Already it is a problem to speak of "characteristics" because Merleau-Ponty insists that it is not a substance; being a "general thing" it consequently eludes identity. The flesh is "a *general thing*, midway between the spatio-temporal individual and the idea, a sort of incarnate principle that brings a style of being wherever there is a fragment of being. The flesh is in this sense an "element" of Being. Not a fact or a sum of facts, and yet adherent to *location* and to the *now*. . . . And, at the same time, what makes the facts have meaning, makes the fragmentary facts dispose themselves about 'something.' "[27] It is as a crystallization, a condensation, of this general thing that fragments of being come to be given as a style. The flesh is a spatial and temporal pulp where individuals are formed by differentiation. What there is, is neither facts nor essences, but rather crystallizations in the field of the flesh—a spatial-temporal pulp. In traditional philosophy, the concepts of both fact and essence are defined by the notion of identity. The notion of identity is temporal: the fact is conceived of as an indivisible atom of time, absolutely unique and individual; the essence as identical with itself is repeatable, and therefore dissociable from any point in time. On the contrary, a "general thing" does not exist in terms of the identity that it has with itself. We have to pass from the thing (spatial or temporal) as identity, to the thing (spatial or temporal) as difference, for example, as transcendence, as always "behind," "beyond, far-off . . . the present itself is not an absolute coincidence without transcendence; even the

Urerlebnis involves not total coincidence, but partial coincidence, because it has horizons and would not be without them, the present, also, is ungraspable from close-up, in the forceps of attention, it is an encompassing."[28] The concept of the flesh is his attempt to forge a notion that is not based on, or does not imply, the distinction between the intelligible and the sensible, the fact and the essence.

Since the time of Plato, mathematics in general and geometry in particular have been presented as models of genuine knowledge. Often the aspect of geometry that is brought center stage for the philosopher to emulate is the disjunction between fact and essence, the opposition between the triangle drawn on the blackboard and the essence of the triangle which has no spatial or temporal location. In 1960 Merleau-Ponty gave a course at the Collège de France on Husserl's essay, "The Origin of Geometry." At this time, we cannot follow in any detail these rich notes. I want only to indicate that even faced with the paradigmatic instance of the opposition between fact and essence, Merleau-Ponty endeavors to show the inherence of ideality in the sensible and in history. He tells us that "it is necessary to excavate below ideal identity"[29] and he continues, "[O]bviously, this is going to require a total remanipulation of the distinctions between fact and essence, *real and ideal*" (emphasis in text).[30] Husserl claims that it is through language that the insight of the proto-geometer becomes more than events in his or her mental life; however, it is not as though language were merely an exterior envelope containing an idea. Merleau-Ponty writes:

> Language is virtual communication, the pre-existence and permanence of ideality, because what is expressed changes its *Seinmodus* <"ontic mode"> in it: the words, the texts exist objectively in the fashion of physical things, and, in this permanent existence, they convey their sense as an activity which has fallen into obscurity but which is reawoken and which can again be transformed into activity.

It is writing that completes the process of disassociating the ideal meaning from the thought that produced it for the first time. Through writing the thought comes to exist in the world. "The ideal world supported by the sensible world."[31] As incarnated in the written word, the ideal meaning is subjected to reactivation and at the same time it is subjected to forgetfulness. It becomes part of tradition and, for Merleau-Ponty, tradition is a double movement, "being other in order to be the same, forgetting in order to conserve, producing in order to receive, looking ahead in order to receive the entire force of the past."[32] We do not survey tradition from the outside, we are *in* it and *of* it. Merleau-Ponty, commenting on Heidegger, underwrites his statement that "we do not have language, rather language has us." In a similar way we might say that both our thinking and the ideal meaning that we think are encrusted in a tradition.

As Merleau-Ponty deconstructs the opposition between fact and essence, on another level he problematizes the opposition between the authentic, the proper, and the inauthentic, the improper.

We have already evoked the one (*on*) as the anonymous perceiver in the *Phenomenology of Perception* and the deepening of this notion of anonymous in *The Visible and the Invisible*. This dimension of the pre-personal, of the intersection of the person and nature, is presented without *pathos*, with no rhetoric of loss or fallenness and correlatively with no imperative of salvation through resoluteness. All of the above, being Merleau-Ponty's opposition to Heidegger. One might also note a certain opposition to Levinas as well. Merleau-Ponty's conception of the *il y a* into which we are all inserted prior to any consent on our part, does not share the ominous, almost sinister, quality of Levinas's *il y a*: the faceless gods, the rumbling before separation that seems to exist, not simply prior to but in opposition to, the world of ethical responsibility. For Merleau-Ponty, Nature, rather than being a threat to Ethics, is its condition of possibility.

NOTES

1. Friedrich Nietzsche, *The Will to Power*, trans. Walter Kaufmann (New York: Random House, 1968), 267.

2. Maurice Merleau-Ponty, *The Visible and the Invisible*, trans.Alphonso Lingis (Evanston: Northwestern University Press), 112–23.

3. Friedrich Nietzsche, "How the 'True World' Finally Became a Fable: The History of an Error," *Twilight of the Idols*, in *The Portable Nietzsche*, trans. Walter Kaufmann (New York: Penguin Books, 1959), 485–86.

4. Marcel Proust, *Remembrance of Things Past*, trans. Moncrieff and Kilmartin (New York: Random House, 1982), 196–97.

5. *The Visible and the Invisible*, 114.

6. Ibid., 253.

7. Ibid., 114.

8. J. Laplanche and J.-B. Pontalis, *The Language of Psychoanalysis*, trans. Nicholson-Smith (New York: W.W. Norton, 1973), 410–11.

9. Ibid., 411.

10. *The Visible and the Invisible*, 114.

11. Ibid., 114–15.
12. Ibid., 119.
13. Ibid., 3.
14. Ibid., 5.
15. Ibid., 9–10.
16. Ibid., 7.
17. Ibid., 8.
18. Ibid., 135.
19. Ibid., 135–36.
20. Ibid., 135.
21. Ibid., 134.
22. Ibid., 137.
23. Ibid.
24. Ibid., 137–38.
25. Ibid.
26. Ibid.
27. Ibid., 139–40.
28. Ibid., 195.
29. Maurice Merleau-Ponty, *Husserl at the Limits of Phenomenology*, trans. and ed. Leonard Lawlor with Bettina Bergo (Evanston: Northwestern University Press, 2002), 16.
30. Ibid., 19.
31. Ibid., 57.
32. Ibid., 31.

10

The Chiasm and the Remainder

(How Does Touching Touch Itself?)

Jacob Rogozinski

Philosophical questions have a strange fate. As remarkable as they are, they are nevertheless sometimes blurred or toned down, and slide into the background as if they had definitively stopped mobilizing thought. But inversely, sometimes there is an apparently devalued or disinvested question that, no longer of interest to anyone except historians, suddenly returns and imposes itself anew as a fundamental stake. Such is the case with the question of the touch and of the tactile chiasm. There was a time when problems relative to perception, to the proper body (*le corps propre*) or the flesh,[1] to the relations between the different senses (and notably between touch and sight) were at the center of phenomenological research, as Merleau-Ponty's work attests in France. But then, starting in the 1960s, these problems almost totally disappeared from our intellectual horizon. Now we see that the question of the touch has resurfaced in, and provided the title for, one of Derrida's recent books.[2] A sign of the times? A sign, maybe, that "French phenomenology" has begun to emerge from its long eclipse, and that the questions that animated it have recently seen the light of day again.

We know that Husserl gave a great importance to the phenomenon of tactile auto-affection, to the singular experience of *the touch touching itself*. When one of my hands touches the other, it perceives it at first as a physical thing; but this hand-thing also senses itself being touched. Tactile impressions awaken in it, and "it becomes flesh" (*Es wird Leib*), a hand of living flesh that also touches the hand that touches it. In this way, "the flesh is originarily constituted in a double mode," as both flesh and material thing.[3] Merleau-Ponty designated this experience as an "intertwining" or a "chiasm," the name of a rhetorical figure implying a crossing-over and an inversion of terms. For Husserl, the chiasm did not seem to be a *problem*: he took for granted that the touching hand and the touched hand recognize each other spontaneously like two members of the same body, and that each hand can perceive itself as both flesh and bodily thing without difficulty. Everything happens as if what is to be constituted (namely, the unity of the proper body, the identity of the flesh and the body, the temporal simultaneity of their givenness) were given in advance. But here, Husserl does not practice the *epokhe* in a sufficiently radical manner: he situates the chiasm only on the plane of mundane reality and considers the flesh as a sort of body, an organic and already unified body. Moreover, it suffices to speak of one "hand" touching "another hand" in order to falsify the analysis totally—for it then seems obvious that the same hand can be both touching and touched and that the two hands belong to one sole body. This is the overwhelming obviousness that I want to call into question. We must be more Husserlian than Husserl himself on this point, we must be more faithful than he to the radicality of the *epokhe*: we must suspend the naive certainty of being in the world and having a body; and confront both the strangeness of a primordial flesh that does not yet have eyes and hands, but only carnal poles, and the strangeness of an ego that is not yet a subject or an individual human, but that is, rather, dispersed into innumerable splinters of one or more selves. The problems of the unification of poles, of the auto-identification of the self-flesh,[4] of the possibility of these syntheses in which the self-flesh incorporates itself in space and subjects itself to time, are thus posed in all their difficulty. The question of knowing how the chiasm is possible thus emerges as an enigma.

There is another manner of sketching the difficulty—by decreeing that the question is not posited, that the chiasm does not take place. "I can touch my hand only insofar as it touches," declared Sartre: touching and being-touched are for him "two radically distinct phenomena" that "exist on two incommunicable planes."[5] Sartre thus installs himself in a rigid dualism, an insurmountable opposition between the "for-itself" and the "in-itself," between the body and the flesh, the subject and the object, the self and an other. In order to overcome these cleavages, to retrieve an "interworld," a milieu common to myself and to others, Merleau-Ponty (after having taken some distance from Sartre) was going to abandon dualisms in favor of the thesis of Husserl. Not only does he recognize that the carnal chiasm is possible, but he even gives it a universal weight: according to him, it is no longer only my touching hand and my touched hand that are joined in the chiasm, but also my own hand and that of the other, when I discover that the hand of the other possesses "the same power to espouse the things that I have touched in my own," so well that the other and myself "function as one unique body."[6] Not only does the chiasm "encroach" the difference between myself and the other, but it also traverses the divergences between me and the things and between me and the world. For "my body is made of the same flesh as the world,"[7] and what we call the flesh thus ceases to be my singular flesh in order to become the ultimate element of being, the place of a generalized exchange, of a limitless effusion where are the planes intersect and intermingle, and where I ground myself (*se fonder*)[8] with all others in the immense flesh of the world. For each one of us, this universal intertwining is rooted in an "exemplary sensible," a privileged experience that is that of *one's own* flesh when it touches itself in the midst of touching: the singular chiasm of my flesh would be the "measure" of all flesh, the matrix in which all the chiasms of the world are grounded. But am I *truly* capable of touching myself touching? In fact, nothing is less certain, and Merleau-Ponty confirms Sartre's objections when he recognizes that the hand of flesh can never coincide with the hand-thing, that "the right hand as an object is not the same as the touching right hand: the first in an intertwining of body, muscle, and flesh squashed into one point of space, the second traverses space like a rocket in order to reveal the exterior object in its place."[9] If this is the case, if the two sides or the two "lips" of my flesh do not manage to rejoin themselves, the thread of the world is unraveled, and I will never come to open myself to being or to unite with others in the common element of one and the same flesh. Obviously, Merleau-Ponty refuses to admit this, as it would be to avow that all his philosophy rests on a false hypothesis. He is constrained here to waver between two opposing points of view, insisting sometimes on coincidence, sometimes on divergence, reaffirming that the chiasm is possible while recognizing that it has never occurred.

Why is there no chiasm? What impedes my flesh from being joined to itself? Time makes a failure of it, and the temporal *simultaneity* of contact is confirmed as impossible: " the two hands are never *simultaneously* related to one another as touching and touched," and it is for this reason that their meeting remains "always imminent" but "is eclipsed at the moment of being realized."[10] We would be dealing here with a *virtual* synthesis, which would never really (*réellement*) be accomplished: endlessly delayed, the chiasm is missed each time. Merleau-Ponty cannot accept this failure. At this moment of his analysis—and in order to get around this difficulty—he invokes "the total being of my body," its originary unity in which the "hiatus" that traverses my flesh would have always been absorbed. Even if he was attentive to the differences that existed between the senses, between the tactile fields of my two hands or the perspectives of my two eyes, he nevertheless affirms that this multitude of divergent experiences is "sustained, subtended by . . . the unity of my body," and that it remains "the experience of one sole body before one sole world."[11] Like Husserl before him, Merleau-Ponty presupposes what he had to constitute, and his analysis is enclosed in a circle: that which would render the chiasm possible would be the unity of my body, even though the chiasm is supposed to be grounded on this unity. But by what right do we affirm that the body is a "total being," or that the body and the world are One? This naive certitude falls apart under the *epokhe*: like that of the world or of the self, the unity of the body is dissolved or splintered into a multitude of dispersed poles. Nothing allows prejudging any longer that the self and the world would succeed in uniting themselves in a chiasm. We can suppose that the solution that Husserl proposed would not have been satisfactory to Merleau-Ponty, and indeed, some of his working notes show that he was looking for another way out of the problem, and that he was oriented outside of the body, toward a "central blind spot" that could serve as a hinge between the two sides of the flesh: "[T]o touch and touch oneself . . . do not coincide in the body . . . something other than the body is needed for the junction to be made: it takes place in the *untouchable*."[12] What can be this point X that Merleau-Ponty designates as "the untouchable of touching, the invisible of vision, the unconscious of consciousness," and how does he succeed in assuring the "juncture," the knotting of the chiasm? Death interrupted Merleau-Ponty's work just as he was trying to elucidate this enigma.

His incomplete work leaves us with a question to which we should try to respond. More than any other, Merleau-Ponty's work confronted a difficulty that is still our own, and it challenges us as much by its failures and impasses as by its responses. Let's consider the principal obstacle he ran into, namely, the bogeyman of temporality: in his view, the impossibility of a *simultaneous* contact, of a perfect temporal coincidence between touching and being-touched, prohibits the chiasm from being knotted. Posed in these terms, the problem is no doubt unsolvable, because its shifts, its "overhangs," will inevitably persist between the different versions of my experience, impeding the two lips of my flesh from rejoining or clasping each other in the same moment. By formulating the question in this way, Merleau-Ponty prevented himself from giving an answer. He had not seen that the problem of simultaneity—of the punctual coincidence between two experiences—had meaning only on the plane of the world: only in mundane temporality, in the clock-metered time that regulates our daily lives, can two points of time coincide (e.g., two trains can arrive "punctually," simultaneously in the same station). If I engage in the *epokhe*, the world and the time of the world are put out of play, and I access an immanent temporality where the present no longer appears as a simple point in time, but rather as a cloth in movement, a fluent phase within a flux, *a field of presence*. What we call simultaneity is already announced in this immanent temporal flux, when several impressions are given "at the same time" to my consciousness, when their fields of presence are superimposed and overlap each other. And yet, as Husserl notes, these originary sensations that constitute simultaneity "are not themselves simultaneous."[13]

They do not put isolated events that may or may not coincide into relation; rather, they compose within the flux a temporal community, a synchrony; and this is in turn grounded "upstream" in the temporal flux on this side of the temporal synthesis, on a community of resonance to which the events appeal, respond, and associate themselves. The carnal chiasm provides a privileged example of this originary synthesis in which initially separated impressions are conjoined and resonate in unison: when the poles of my flesh come into a relation of identity, their fields of presence are joined together, and their differentiated temporal fluxes are unified in one unique flux. In wanting to ground the chiasm on a temporal simultaneity (which would prove to be impossible), Merleau-Ponty completely inverted the order of foundation: in truth, the carnal synthesis grounds the temporal synthesis; the chiasm thus renders the synchrony of the flux possible. Nothing authorizes us to affirm that this synchrony never happens, or that the two fluxes do not succeed in being unified themselves in an immanent manner.

The chiasm is thus possible—or at least temporality is not an obstacle for it—because the temporal synthesis is too "perfect," too synchronous to let the least hiatus subsist in it, and it is precisely in this way that it differs from an always incomplete carnal synthesis.[14] Paradoxically, Merleau-Ponty returns to the most "imperfect" syntheses in order to ground the other. But this does not mean that the chiasm has really occurred: it may be that another obstacle forbids the touching hand from identifying itself totally with the touched hand. If it is true that the two poles cannot be touching and touched at the same time, if they slide into one another like two foreign things without ever meeting up with and clasping one another, we would have to see here the index or clue of a more originary difference, which would be carnal rather than temporal. The flesh also takes precedence over time here, and a disjunction of time does not impede the flesh from uniting with itself: it is, rather, an internal divergence of the flesh that breaks the temporal synchrony. We would have to deal with an eidetic impossibility, an essential incompatibility that prohibits the self-flesh from traversing the divergence that tears it apart, from recognizing itself in this unknown entity, this non-I, this non-flesh against which he throws himself from the outside.

Derrida also confronts this aporia of the chiasm. He takes it, in effect, as the "metaphysics of the touch," the illusion of a coincidence without divergence, of an absolute presence in the fullness of contact that, according to him, still reigns in Husserl (and to a certain extent in Merleau-Ponty). We would have to recognize on the contrary that the "I touches itself by spacing itself, by losing contact with itself," that is, that it is *touched without touching itself*.[15] This divergence from itself would characterize the tactile experience just as much as the experience of vision: whether I see myself or I touch myself, I never give myself to myself in a pure auto-affection miraculously protected against all alterity. If Derrida revokes this privilege from touching, it is not in order to reestablish a privilege for vision: rather, this revocation is in the name of a more radical exteriority, that of "technical prostheses," of grafts, of mechanical substitutes that dissociate the body from itself, and expropriate it from its self-identity. The thesis of the chiasm would all too well play the part of contact without distance, of the immediate coincidence of two hands. It would fail to recognize that "a certain *exteriority . . . must* even be a part of the experience of the touching-touched."[16] In order for this experience to be possible, an absolutely exterior element must be insinuated between the two sides of my flesh, an element "foreign to both the touching version and the touched version of the impression," a "parasite," an "intrusion," that would nevertheless be the condition of the chiasm—the condition of its possibility, but also (and *above all*) of its impossibility. Certainly, Derrida never simply affirms that the chiasm is impossible, but rather that it occurs without occurring, that it "happens without happening," that the flesh "is touched without being touched," etc. But these "undecidable" formulae that he cherishes have only a purely rhetorical value here: they allow him to maintain an apparent equilibrium between the possible and the impossible and between coincidence and divergence, even though the balance always tips to the same side, namely, that of the impossible. The draconian conditions that he imposes on it prohibit the carnal synthesis from becoming knotted: destabilized, dislodged by this foreign outside, this intrusion that separates it from itself, the experience of self-coincidence "succeeds in interrupting itself," that is, that it occurs only by interrupting itself, by canceling itself immediately. *"There is not 'the' touch"*: this sentence borrowed from Jean-Luc Nancy is the *leitmotif* of the book entitled *Le toucher*. It signifies that there is more than one way of touching, but equally, it signifies that the sense of touch does not exist *as such*, that the flesh never succeeds in touching itself. The chiasm thus does not occur, it happens only by running aground.

Just like Sartre, but for very different reasons, Derrida contests that a meeting or identification between the two disjoined poles of my flesh is possible. But if the chiasm never happens (or only "happens by disappearing"), it follows that my flesh will never be able to make itself body, to come into the world, or to recognize itself in the body of the other: there will be for me neither body nor world nor other, nor even any longer a "self" or "flesh," but rather only a network of technical prostheses grafting and connecting themselves endlessly onto other prostheses. The greatest authors of science fiction have already given us a glimpse of this possibility. In *The Three Stigmata of Palmer Eldritch*, Philip K. Dick describes the intrusion of a foreign entity, maybe of divine nature, in our universe. This entity assumes the appearance of a certain Palmer Eldritch, endowed with a prosthetic hand, a metal nose, and artificial eyes. To the extent that the entity invades our world, it contaminates all flesh, making all humans into replicants or clones of itself, endowed with the same stigmata. Is Derrida ready to assume this kingdom of prostheses and simulacra? Is he ready to nihilate himself, to disappear totally as living flesh, or as an incarnated Ego? Is he ready to lose himself in the unworldly, unclean world (*monde immonde*) of Palmer Eldritch? But why does he refuse to allow the possibility of a carnal synthesis? Why implant this exterior Other in the flesh, this Outside that impedes it from rejoining itself? For reasons that belong to the very project of deconstruction, to fundamental motifs of his thought. According to Derrida, there can never be *pure* auto-affection or a purely immanent givenness, because "this auto-affection immediately leaves its inside," and reverts to a "hetero-affection."[17] We would thus be concerned with a philosophy of auto-*hetero*-affection in which an irreducible alterity (which is announced in multiple ways as "trace," "remains," "specter," etc.) always comes to worry the closure of the same, of the *auton*, prohibiting it from closing in on itself. And here again, the balance is not equal: in this knotting of the same and the other, the *heteron* in fact takes precedence over the *auton*. For Derrida, the Same (presence and self-identity, appropriation, coincidence, adequation, truth, meaning, etc.) can only be an effect of the Other (of *differance*, interruption, divergence) and it happens only by repressing this alterity that engenders it—an alterity that comes back, contaminating and destabilizing the Same that pretends to erase it. Derrida applies this schema to the question of the touch, and this leads him to support the claims that carnal contact (auto-affection) presupposes the "hiatus of non-contact" and that a hetero-affection comes forcibly to interrupt the chiasm and render it impossible. I wonder if this schema is suitable here, if it doesn't do violence to the phenomenon of touching, and if it doesn't disfigure the experience of which it is supposed to take account. Maybe we must envisage it otherwise, by inverting the primacy that Derrida accords to the Other, and by considering carnal auto-affection on the contrary as the originary condition of the *heteron*, of this Outside that alters it without ever succeeding in truly interrupting it. We could then conceive that the self-flesh manages to rejoin itself in a chiasm, despite the alterity that haunts it. This is how Merleau-Ponty understands it when he tried to think both the meeting and the divergence on the ground of an essential complicity, and when he tried to discern the "untouchable of touching" this enigmatic point where, despite everything, the whole "junction" is made, where the chiasm can *occur*.

How do we decide *in truth* between these two conceptions of the touch, these two versions of auto-hetero-affection? It is precisely the truth that will make the difference: we must wonder in effect if this Other, this foreign Outside, is truly foreign to the self-flesh, and if it is not instead a matter of blindness, of an auto-dissimulation of the flesh, of an *internal* fold or withdrawal, of a part of my flesh that forgets itself, and that is presented in an illusory manner, as if it came from the Outside and from the Other. Derrida would not be able to accept this, and first of all because he refuses to oppose the truth to non-truth: for him, "the truth is phantasm itself."[18] He thus risks mistaking a phantom for the truth, of letting himself get trapped by the *apparent* exteriority of element X that emerges in the heart of the chiasm, without apperceiving that this Stranger from the outside is in truth the flesh of my flesh. What is this phantom, this untouchable that haunts the touch? Here the Derridean analysis can no longer help us. According to Derrida, this heterogenous element proceeds simply from the *visibility* of the tactile surface: it is because "of the possibility of the hand being seen" that the gesture of touching "cannot be reduced to a pure experience of the purely proper body."[19] No alterity, no self-divergence would characterize the touch *as such*: they would affect it only from the outside, in the external perspective of vision. A strange and sudden change of fortune leads us to the classical position opposing the immanence of the touch to the exteriority of the look, the very position for which Derrida criticized Husserl. The deconstruction of the metaphysics of the touch comes up short. This is no doubt the consequence of a process that puts such a strong accent on the Outside, on hetero-affection, such that it no longer succeeds in retrieving the alterity that affects it *in* the tactile field, and instead can attribute it only to a totally foreign element, to the radical exteriority of the visible (or of the prosthetic). If we desire to understand how the chiasm is possible, we must be more Derridean than Derrida himself, at least on this point: instead of attributing it to vision, we must try to locate the birthplace of the Untouchable *in the touch itself*.

Philosophers who have approached this question of the chiasm seem to fall into an antinomy: either one presupposes (like Husserl) that the chiasm is possible and that it has always already occurred—but does not seek to know how it is produced and makes a good deal out of the divergence, the hiatus that tears it; or else one takes account of this divergence only to conclude from it (with Sartre and Derrida) that the chiasm is impossible, that it "happens only by interrupting itself"; or else one oscillates between the two terms of the alternative, sometimes accenting the coincidence, sometimes the divergence (as Merleau-Ponty did). At least one thing must be taken for granted: if there is an aporia of the chiasm, if it is true that a yet unknown element is an obstacle for it, this element can come from neither a temporal disjunction nor an exteriority of the visible, but rather from a carnal difference, from a divergence internal to the touch itself. In the tactile experience, each pole of the flesh attains the other pole only *from the outside*, it perceives it as a foreign thing on with which it collides without ever rejoining. It seems absolutely impossible that my touching flesh recognizes *itself* in my touched flesh: how would the self-flesh fuse itself with this insensible and inert thing without disavowing itself, without renouncing its singularity, its carnation, its life? The question here is one of an essential impossibility, of a radical demarcation that separates the I from the non-I, the flesh from the non-flesh: what is an obstacle for the flesh is the insurmountable divergence of the egological difference, of the carnal difference.

The chiasm does occur, however, and it would be absurd to inquire indefinitely about its possibility or impossibility. It is a fact that *there is the chiasm*: if not, I would have no body, and there would be for me neither the other nor the world, and all my experience would sink into a bottomless chaos. It depends here on an *archi-facticity* that no anterior condition, no superior principle would know how to ground. Not only death, but indeed every true event, can be defined as *the possibility of the impossible*, and this is also true for the inaugural event that is the chiasm. It seems impossible that my immanent flesh could enter into a relation of identity with that which is given to it as a transcendent thing, but this impossibility is exactly what happens at every instant. This does not mean that the two poles of flesh are always perfectly identified with each other. Let's risk a hypothesis: it may be that the chiasm performs only *a partial identification*, or that each time, it generates a leftover or remainder, a residue of the non-flesh, indissociable from my flesh yet resistant to all incarnation. We will henceforth call this element, which is both foreign to the flesh and yet within the flesh, the *remainder*.[20] Neither Husserl nor Merleau-Ponty—the only philosophers who truly confronted the enigma of the chiasm—thematized this phenomenon. By evoking the "dehiscence," the "overhanging" that impedes the two lips of my flesh from joining up, Merleau-Ponty nevertheless approached it, even if he interpreted it in a false manner as the effect of a temporal lag. And Husserl approached it very nearly when he remarked that in the experience of the touching-touched, the two tactile surfaces are initially separated but "can nevertheless overlap each other, fuse in a certain manner, but cannot however be mixed together." The concern here will be with a partial fusion that allows discontinuous zones of the tactile field to "enter into a sort of continuity," "to constitute one same surface," even though their "localities remain separated"; and this, Husserl adds, is "an entirely unique event on the phenomenological plane."[21] The experience of the chiasm attests that there is, at the very point of contact of the two zones, a heterogenous element that resists their total identification.

No direct approach to this "entirely unique phenomenon" is given to us. As the event of the chiasm, the existence of the remainder must be considered as a fact, but the question here again is one of a transcendental archi-facticity that is totally distinct from all the empirical facts. The remainder is untouchable for my touch, but also invisible for my vision, inaudible for my hearing: we will never meet up with it in the world, as one element among others in our daily experience, no more than we will ever meet up with the Being of beings or with absolute Life. Certain intraworldly phenomena sometimes seem to give us access to the remainder, but they are not confused with it, no more than is the Face of the Other confused with a visible face, nor the primordial Flesh with a physical body. If a phenomenology of the remainder is possible, it would be responsive to what Heidegger calls *a phenomenology of the inapparent*. This must be elaborated according to its own method: in a manner different from noematic phenomenology, and oriented toward perceptive experience, the moment of *phenomenological construction* will occupy a privileged place there.[22] What protects or conserves such a construction of the arbitrary and of the *Schwarmerei* is first of all the rigor of the eidetic analysis, but also the exigency of never losing sight of the "transcendental guide of the object," of settling on the "backwards-questioning" concerning the appearance of phenomena in the world, on the givens of our experience and of the worldly sciences. If it were not capable of shedding new light on the phenomena of love and hate, of death, faith, madness, sovereignty, persecution, sacrifice, and so many others, then the phenomenology of the remainder would not be worth one ounce of effort.

When we affirm that the carnal chiasm always generates a remainder, it is not a matter of a simple postulate, but rather of an eidetic necessity. What would happen if each pole of flesh managed to incarnate the other pole *without remainder*? Each of them would become for the other its own flesh, its own life: the other would become the same, or a sort of indiscernible "double" of it. The ensemble of poles would integrally fuse and the flesh would fold back on itself; by collapsing in on itself, it would implode without ever succeeding in objectivating itself as a body with differentiated organs. Husserl designates the site of my flesh as the Absolute Here, a "zero-zone, a hole of space (*Raumloch*), a non-constituted, non-intuited, unintuitable."[23] The tactile chiasm allows the flesh to be progressively constituted by pulling or extracting itself out of (*s'arrachant*) this Hole; but this implies that the *Raumloch* is inserted in space, that its gaping openness [*beance*] is converted into a local opening—an interval between my flesh and my flesh. This supposes that an element-X, a remainder, leaves open the divergence between each pole, saving the flesh from sinking into the Bottomless (*Sans-Fond*). The remainder guards my flesh against this disaster, this implosion to which certain psychoses testify. This disaster can become just as menacing and mortifying as it is ambivalent, but it is above all that which protects the flesh and renders its genesis possible—its ultimate condition of possibility, and not of impossibility. The eidetic analysis shows us that the phenomenon of the remainder is a necessary condition for the experience of the chiasm, and it is with this experience that we must begin if we want to describe its genesis more precisely. When I touch myself in the midst of touching myself, I am dealing with a double sensation that fuses in order to become a unique, redoubled sensation. As Husserl remarks, each of these two sensations is always already an object of an intertwined "double apprehension," and is given as both *Empfindung* (the sensation of a transcendent object), and *Empfindnis* (immanent "sensing" (*sentance*) where the flesh senses itself sensing, and is affected by its own receptivity).[24] If we place every transcendent sensation out of play, if we center the analysis on the sensing [*sentance*] alone, we will discover a still more originary double apprehension. The hyletic layer of the primary contents of sensation (in which the transcendence of the noema is already announced) is distinguished from a second layer (of motor kinestheses, drives, and originary impressions where my flesh is affected by itself, its mobility and its life). Husserl underlines often that kinestheses belong to the flesh of the Ego, that the Ego "is one with" them, but in fact it is this whole second strata that is lived as "mine," as "of my flesh."[25] We will say that this implies a *consciousness of mineness*, whereas the layer of hyletic data of sensation is accompanied by a *consciousness of foreignness*. At the moment of the chiasm, this double apprehension present in each pole is overlaid with the analogous double apprehension proper to the other pole and is identified with it. Consciousnesses of mineness fuse in order to be integrated into the consciousness of a single Ego-Flesh, while the consciousnesses of foreignness are also unified and thereafter present as the intention of a Thing foreign to, yet inseparable from, my flesh. The consciousness of this intimate Stranger then emerges in the Ego—this is the haunting of the remainder.

This haunting is thus rooted in what is most immanent within the *hyle*, in this un-conscious, in-apparent, archi-hyletic strata resistant to the thematization of noematic intentionality, which according to Husserl constitutes the *Ichfremde Kern*, the "nucleus" (immanent to me) of "the stranger in me." If the Ego is originarily incarnated, if it is my flesh, we can understand that this "first not-I" constitutes in my flesh a remainder that is foreign to my flesh. And yet this remainder has no consistency of its own: it is only a transcendental Appearance, an inevitable illusion. In the first contact, each pole of flesh is initially presented to the other pole as foreign to its flesh, even thought it is not *truly* so. The chiasm permits removing this originary auto-dissimulation, by revealing the flesh to itself in each of its poles, delivering it from its occultation. In this sense, the chiasm is the event of truth, *aletheia*. That part of my flesh that despite its disclosure, continues in each pole to give itself to the other pole as the non-flesh is the remainder. We would entirely mistake this phenomenon by considering it as a simply exterior element or as an "intrusion" from the outside. Certainly, the remainder presents itself in this way, but it dissimulates its true identity: in truth, it is the flesh of my flesh, but of a flesh that is blinded by and about itself, and that is presented to itself as foreign to itself. My flesh is thus the place of an *Urstreit*, a conflict between truth and non-truth, between the chiasm and the remainder, which will never end during my lifetime. Each unfurling of the flesh, each advance of the carnal synthesis coincides with a disclosure through which the Ego-Flesh is delivered (at least in part) from the Appearance that traps it. With every failure, with every crisis of the chiasm, the power of the remainder engenders new illusions, *transcendental phantasms* that will profoundly mark our relation to our body, the world, and others. We apprehend the remainder through these phantasms, as the anxiety of dying, by anticipating our becoming-cadaver; the abjection of the remainder becomes the target of our hatred, and its transfiguration constitutes it as the first object of love. It is this persecuting Thing with which delirium is obsessed, and maybe it may be that to which the mystic aspires in that moment that we strangely call "ecstasy." We will content ourselves here with sketching some traits of this intrigue of the flesh and the remainder that weaves (itself into) the thread of our life (*fait la trame de notre vie*).

According to Husserl, every hyletic datum exerts an affection on and excites the Ego, and the rays that the Ego directs to these phenomena only respond to this "adverse trait" (*Gegenzug*), to the "counter-rays" (*Gegenstrahlen*) that come from the object in the inverse direction. Through this game of missed meetings (*chassée-croisée*),[26] the phenomenon "is constituted as a pole of attraction" for the Ego by awakening such affects as desire, love, or hate.[27] A phenomenology of the remainder must not be limited to a static description, but rather must try to take into account this dynamic, affective, or drive-based dimension of the phenomena disclosed by Husserl. From this point of view, the remainder is not only what resists incarnation, but also that which exerts an affective attraction on the flesh, tries to capture it, to orient it toward itself, to absorb it in itself, whereas the flesh also tries to attract the remainder and to confer carnation upon it. A double-crossed attraction, where the flesh and the remainder are called by one another, stretched toward each other, each seeking to capture the other and absorb it in itself. When they are crossed and rejoined, the synthesis that they generate will keep the trace of their primordial combat, and we will have to deal with two opposed modes of synthesis, wherein either the remainder takes precedence over the flesh, or the flesh wins out over the remainder. The genesis of the flesh will be marked by crises, caesurae, and reversals of dominance in which these two syntheses are intertwined while overlapping and encroaching on one another. Let's specify that it is a matter of a *transcendental genesis* that does not unfold in the time of the world or according to a linear succession: it is, rather, unfurled within our immanent life, in this originary temporal flux that knows neither a before nor an after, neither succession nor simultaneity. To name such phenomena, "nouns fail us." We can figure their genesis only by starting from our worldly experience, describe it in the framework of a constituted temporality: as a *history*, a temporal "process" the different "phases" of which succeed one another. We can certainly consider this history as a fable, a fiction destined to figure the unfigurable genesis of the flesh—and yet *de te fabula narratur*: it is the drama of our life that this fiction tries to describe. Our analysis is situated on the plane of this transcendental archi-facticity, which is the condition of possibility of all ontic factuality. If, with the rigor that eidetic reduction and variation confers upon it, this fiction carries a response to certain fundamental questions of existence, if it allows for disclosing originary configurations of our flesh, it is because this fiction is true.

When the flesh takes precedence over the remainder, we see a *synthesis of incorporation* in which the flesh invests the remainder, offers its *Leiblichkeit* to this residue of the non-flesh and gives to it the meaning of being a living flesh; but on the other hand, by a gift in return, the remainder confers its *Dinglichkeit*, its thing-being, to the flesh, thus allowing it to be spatialized, to prepare itself a place in the objective space of things. What we call our body is the fruit of this synthesis under the dominance of the flesh, the product of this happy union between flesh and the remainder, in which the flesh recognizes itself and brings the remainder to life, delivers it from the Appearance that dissimulates it from itself. We designate under the name of the remainder the originary nucleus of all transcendence, an archi-transcendence immersed in immanence. Its synthesis with the flesh will always play a decisive role in the constitution of transcendent realities, of my body in the world, but also of the body of the other and of the *alter Ego* "appresented" by this body. The constitution of the other results in the same aporia as that of the proper body, since my flesh must be identified with a foreign entity, recognize itself in it (at least by analogy), and transfer its carnation to it—but without being confused with it, without fusing integrally, lest the other would be only a "double," a simple reflection of myself. Yet, this meeting with the Stranger, this synthesis of the Ego-Flesh and of its Other had already occurred in my own flesh: by touching the body of another, by coming up against this foreign thing, against the other that I will never touch—I retrieve on another plane this untouchable part that I had already felt in the other pole, and that I had recognized in the end as the flesh of my flesh.[28] Without the remainder of the chiasm, without the synthesis of incorporation by which it unites with the flesh, the constitution of the *alter Ego* would be impossible, would oscillate between the divergence of a total foreignness and a mortal fusion with my double. In a certain sense, the genesis of the other and of the community repeats the primordial genesis of my body of flesh, but in another mode, on the plane of transcendence and intersubjectivity, on which the flesh of the other is never given in "archi-presence," and remains forever separated from my flesh. The persistence of a remainder proves irreducible, and it prohibits the community from folding back on itself, from joining together with itself in the unity of one Great Body.[29] We must thus wait to retrieve this same haunting and these same dramas, these same crises that mark the life of my flesh on the plane of the community.

This fecund alliance of the flesh and the remainder undoes itself. All our experience shows us that the unity of the proper body remains incomplete and precarious, that a part of the remainder resists incorporation, continues to haunt the body as an unassimilable residue and to destabilize the synthesis that must reabsorb it. We must admit in effect that *the crises of the chiasm* occur during the genesis of the Ego-Flesh and try to describe their conditions of possibility. In truth, a transcendental analysis can only ever determine the *possibility* of such crises. Their effects in our experience, their phantasmatic repercussions show us that they really do occur: like the event of the chiasm and the phenomenon of the remainder, the occurrence of the crisis—with the concrete forms that it takes in each singular existence—refers to an archi-facticity. It would not be a matter in any case of a total dissociation, of a sort of interruption of the chiasm: the chiasm would cease only with life. But precisely because the chiasm is a synthesis of heterogenous elements, we can envisage that these elements dissociate and renew themselves in another mode, that they decompose themselves in an inverted synthesis, under the dominance of the remainder. The very meaning of the synthesis is thus perverted: instead of the flesh incarnating the remainder and giving it life, it is now the remainder that devours the flesh, transforms it into a fleshless Thing. The remainder is, however, only a part of my flesh, still opaque and blind to itself: in this perverted synthesis, the chiasm of death, it is always the unflagging movement of the flesh that is unfurled, but dissociated from itself and turned back against itself.[30] This is how the new modes of Appearance are constituted, these transcendental phantasms that are such disfigurations of the primordial flesh. In order to understand this crisis, it is important to distinguish the two dimensions of the chiasm, its two intentional axes. When the flesh meets up with itself and grasps itself, each pole overcomes the divergence that separates it from the other and identifies self with the other, according to a specific synthesis that we will call *horizontal*. This also implies that each pole is itself lived both as flesh and as body, and that each pole performs their identification *within itself*, according to another synthesis that will call *transversal*. Each of these two syntheses generates a specific mode of remainder, and their crisis is tested in very different manners.

At the moment when the transversal synthesis undoes itself, that which is given at the same time as flesh and non-flesh—as my body—is dissociated, is presented separately, *successively*, as the living flesh and as the remainder: it is no longer the flesh that gives life to the remainder but rather the remainder that disincarnates the flesh. The flesh senses itself collapsing in the non-flesh, becoming a fleshless thing, which amounts to passing from life to death. As soon as the flesh fails and inverts itself, the flesh feels itself dying, it *dies*, and this primordial agony is that which gives meaning to the anticipation of our death yet to come, and this grounds the possibility of our being-toward-death. However, this emaciation of the flesh, its absorption in the remainder, is only a phantasm in which the flesh is blind to itself to the point of living as dead; but it is necessary for it to remain in life in order to be able to live its death. In the distress of my archi-agony, I thought I was dying, but I could not really die: my flesh gave itself the appearance of death. Another possibility is then presented, at least as radical, at least as "impossible" as that of my death: that of an awakening, of a renaissance of my flesh, delivering itself from the captivity of the remainder. As its dissociation is never total, a renewal of the chiasm always remains possible, that is, a return of the perverted synthesis in which the flesh would come back to life, would begin again to incarnate the remainder, to deploy all the power of life in it. What to name this possibility? It resembles what the Jewish and Christian traditions designated as the *resurrection of the flesh* and seems madness for the wisdom of the world, of a world submitted to the law of death. Sometimes my "resurrection" (if this term is still appropriate) is not the work of a transcendent God, but rather of my flesh itself when it traverses the test of its archi-agony; and it is not an act of faith in a revealed religion, but rather a strictly phenomenological analysis that uncovers the apparent character of dying, and thus grounds the promise of a renaissance of the flesh, of its Eternal Return.[31] Certainly, what we call the archi-agony—this dying that has always already passed and that does not stop letting itself be overcome by an always reborn life—does not coincide with the final death of being-in-the-world, that we usually call "death." But the anticipation of our death-to-come teaches nothing other than this originary phenomenon of dying (in which every relation to death finds its meaning) by projecting it on a horizon of the future. What we naively call "death" would then be only the projection of a phantasm, the disfigured appearance of an Appearance.

If death, or rather dying, is rooted in the failure of the transversal synthesis, entirely different phantasms are engendered by the crisis of the horizontal synthesis. When this synthesis unknots itself, each of the two poles becomes foreign to the other again: where the flesh of its flesh was, there suddenly emerges an unknown Thing that devours its flesh. This menacing stranger is nothing other than the remainder, which is presented here in the mode of the "bad object," of the *abject*—a term to be heard in its literal sense, as waste to be expelled, rejected. And yet, this gesture of abjection is not sufficient to unstick the remainder from my flesh, since *it is of it*, since it is my own flesh when it is experienced as foreign to the flesh. It is also necessary for it to repeat ceaselessly in an always more violent rejection that always runs aground: the more one works desperately to expel the abject outside, the more it comes back to incrust itself in the heart of the flesh. This impotent rejection is accompanied by a particular affect that we call hatred. Hatred, of all the sentiments, is probably the most fraternal—because nothing is more hateable than my twin or my double, this stranger that *nearly nothing* distinguishes from me. In fact, it is always its own abjection that the one who hates hunts down in the Other: its nearly indiscernible proximity with the object of its hate only reinforces one's panicked fear of being it, and stirs up one's hatred again.[32] If there is, in every hateful relation to the other, a strange complicity, it is because it is rooted in a primordial relation of my flesh with itself, this perverted synthesis wherein each pole takes the remainder of the other pole as an object of hatred. Hating the other is a blind and crazy passion, a passion that in fact hates itself—hatred is thus an impotent passion, incapable of nihilating the Enemy that obsesses it, since it amounts to the same as it.

This passion is, like dying, a phantasm with which the flesh deceives itself about itself. When the chiasm will renew itself, when the return will have occurred, the flesh will begin to revive the flesh, its unfurling will win out over the resistance of the remainder and will give it life again. The illusion of being an abject Thing, foreign to itself, will end by being dissipated, as will the mortifying effects that it arouses. A *remission* is possible, which would, at least for a time, deliver us from hatred. This phenomenon is analogous, on the plane of horizontal intentionality, to the event of resurrection: the *transfiguration* of the remainder succeeds its abject *disfiguration* of it, and that which provoked disgust and hatred now awakens a fascinated attraction.[33] By transfiguring itself, the abject becomes *sublime,* in the exact sense that Kant gave to this term by defining it ingeniously as a "rapid succession of repulsion and attraction provoked by the same object."[34] What names can be given to the affects that emerge on the other side of hatred if not those of desire and love, without forgetting that they do not yet designate an affective relation to the other, but rather the attraction the flesh experiences for its own transfigured flesh? The mystery of affective ambivalence, the indissociable node of love and hatred (of which psychoanalysis hardly manages to take account) is thus clarified: these two opposed affects are rooted in two successive modes of carnal auto-affection, and are addressed to the same originary phenomenon, but to different phases of its manifestation. If the disfigured remainder unleashes my hatred, then by transfiguring itself it becomes the first unique "love" of my life. This miracle of a crystallization is repeated and completed on the intersubjective plane: by projecting the transfigured remainder in an *alter Ego,* the Ego erects the remainder as a sovereign figure whose brilliance subjugates the Ego, and the Ego does this without ever apperceiving that it is a part of its own flesh that it adores in this idol. Desire and love remain thus prisoners of the same illusion as hatred. It may be that this mode of transfiguration is not sufficient to break this infernal circle wherein the flesh lets itself be captured by the remainder: maybe it is only the reverse of disfiguration, its precarious and always reversible inversion, another lure of the fundamental phantasm wherein its influence is perpetuated in an opposed form. Hence the fragility of love, the ambivalence and instability that affect objects of desire, ceaselessly menaced by a reversion through which a trait of their past abjection reemerges suddenly and precipitates their failure. Love would thus not protect us against the eternal return of the abject and of hatred. A remission would be possible only on the condition(s) of breaking the cycle of disfiguration-transfiguration; of ceasing to erect the remainder as an object of hatred of love, as a persecutor-rival or as sublime idol, of recognizing its affective *neutrality,* its absolute indifference. On the condition of admitting that, as is the case with the Law of which the priest speaks in *The Trial,* the remainder "wants nothing from you," "takes you when you come and leaves you when you go." On the condition, finally, of disclosing in the double game of the remainder modes of non-truth, an illusion of our own flesh blinding itself about itself. Only truth can save us.

What is, and how do we attain, this truth that delivers us? It goes to work in our existence in diverse manners, none of which possesses a privilege over the others. Even if it never suffices for our deliverance, philosophy can open to us a way toward the truth, and in particular, this philosophy that we have mobilized here, namely, phenomenology. If we stop making of it an academic discipline limited to textual commentary, if we retrieve the first impulse that guided it, its orientation toward the "things themselves." Its brief history will already suffice to attest to the fecundity of this method, of its capacity to renew our approach to the most classic problems. This capacity is far from being exhausted, and we have tried, in an all-too-summary fashion, to put it to the test here, by showing how a phenomenology of incarnation and of the remainder could open new perspectives on the crucial questions of existence, death, desire, hatred, the genesis of the proper body, of the other, and of community. The renewal of this method will happen, however, only by being emancipated from the prejudices that continue to weigh on the destiny of "French phenomenology," including in its most potent elaborations. This can be accomplished by returning, first of all, to the lesson of Husserl, misunderstood and forgotten by his successors, of recognizing the primacy of touching, the carnal immanence of the tactile field that distinguishes it from vision and other senses of exteriority. Only on the plane of touching is a chiasm possible, is there reversibility (at least partial) of the two poles, and this authorizes us to designate the tactile chiasm as auto-affection.[35] This concern is not, however, for an absolute auto-affection, or for an undivided unity of only Life that never diverges from itself: not only does such a conception not give us access to transcendence (to our body, to the other, to the world), but it is also entirely mistaken about immanence and fails to recognize the crack that tears it apart, this remainder that is interposed between my flesh and my flesh. In truth, the flesh affects itself *as if* it were foreign to itself, under the form of an auto-hetero-affection—but this is only a mode of originary auto-affection through which the flesh is grasped by itself, and we must here consider the *heteron* as an alteration of the *auton*: as an internal reply of the flesh, an intimate divergence that it traverses by unfurling itself toward itself. We will be on guard against rejecting this heterogenous element to outside of the flesh, in the irreducible exteriority of the prosthesis or of the intrusion, by making here of hetero-affection the condition of all auto-affection, its "condition of impossibility" that, at the end of the account, prohibits it from taking place. This would amount to *taking literally the phantasm*, the appearance that the remainder gives of itself by disfiguring itself. It would amount to prohibiting these phantasms and all the living dead, all these internal persecutors and these familiar enemies that assail us from being delivered.

There will not be remission as long as we are under the influence of the fundamental illusion, that which the remainder engenders by dissociating it from the flesh, that is, as long as the Ego has not discovered that this malevolent or sublime Stranger is only a forgotten part of itself. This revelation of a *nonduality* between Ego and its Other, between the flesh and the remainder, does not lead us to the outside, under the horizon of an ecstatic transcendence, but rather toward the most immanent nucleus of our life: we will call it *instasy*. It can sometimes be presented as this extreme point of love that a poem of Hallaj evokes: *Ton souffle s'est mêlé à mon souffle comme l'ambre s'allie au musc odorant / Si l'on te touche, on me touche: tu es moi, plus de séparation*. And however, as we now know, this breach can only be partial: the alterity of the remainder will never disappear totally from my flesh—and, in truth, it cannot disappear without me nihilating myself as myself, without my flesh imploding and sinking in the bottomless of the *Raumloch*. Just as partial, just as provisory as it is, the breach nevertheless remains possible: it coincides with the most ample unfurling of the flesh, when this overcomes the crisis of the chiasm and gives birth anew by reincarnating the remainder. In this sense, it is the condition of our "renaissance," our re-birth, our "transfiguration," and it carries the promise of a neutralization of phantasms issued from the crisis, of their extenuation. This supposes that the emaciation of the flesh is not irreversible, that the chiasm can renew itself, that it is possible to go back to the source-point of the *Ur-impression*, to the origin of the entire temporal sequence, in order to repeat it in another mode. Without that, the Ego-Flesh would never manage to escape from the influence of the remainder. We touch here the limits of phenomenology. It can no doubt show that such a deliverance is possible, but its borders are those of philosophy and it would thus not be able to take us any further toward this truth that liberates us and that makes us give birth to ourselves.

Translated by Robert Vallier

NOTES

1. [It is worth noting from the very outset that much of Merleau-Ponty's effort to disclose a phenomenology of the body turns on the distinction in Husserl between *Leib* and *Korper*. In distinction from the corpse, a mere particle, or an astronomical body, all of which are named by *Korper*, a *Leib* is a living body or the lived experience of the body, and, as Derrida points out in *Speech and Phenomenon*, this concept belongs to a rich texture of words (e.g., *leibhaftig*, *Ichleib*) that all gravitate around and partake in Life

(*Leben*). In his first work, Merleau-Ponty translates the Husserlian *Leib* as *le corps propre*, which in turn has been translated into English as "the proper body," a translation we retain here for the sake of consistency. Starting in the mid-1950s, Merleau-Ponty begins to translate *Leib* as *la chair*, the flesh, in which one hears more clearly, though still somewhat distantly, the echo of life. Rogozinski's argument depends upon a clear understanding of the Husserlian heritage of "the proper body" and "the flesh" in Merleau-Ponty. For another account of the relation between body and flesh, one that is far less sympathetic to Merleau-Ponty's work, see Didier Franck, *Chair et corps* (Paris: Minuit, 1981).—Tr.].

2. Jacques Derrida, *Le Toucher, de Jean-Luc Nancy* (Paris: Galilée, 2000). The question of touch also reappears in one of the last works of Michel Henry, *Incarnation, une philosophie de la chair* (Paris: Seuil, 2000), where it occupies a more discreet, but just as decisive, place.

3. The *locus classicus* for this discussion is found in Edmund Husserl, *Ideas II*, section 36, trans. A. Schuwer and R. Rojcewicz (Dordrecht: Kluwer Academic, 1990).

4. [*Le moi-chair*. In philosophical French, *le moi* belongs to two traditions, the psychoanalytic and the phenomenological. In the former, especially in the Lacanian strain, it translates the Freudian *Ich*; in the latter, it designates the personal Ego, the ego in its personalistic mode. The two senses are closely related, but in that its difference from both "my flesh" and "the Ego-flesh" (both of which are used by Rogozinski in this article) needs to be maintained, we have opted to translate it as "the self-flesh."—Tr.].

5. Sartre affirms this at least three times in the chapter on the body in *Being and Nothingness*, no doubt to oppose himself to Husserl. I have analyzed the Sartrian critique of the chiasm in "Scotomes: Point de vue sur Sartre," *Les Temps Modernes* 531–33 (1990).

6. Maurice Merleau-Ponty, *The Visible and the Invisible*, trans. A. Lingis (Evanston: Northwestern University Press, 1968), 141 and 215.

7. Ibid., 248.

8. [The verb *se fonder* means to ground, to found, to base oneself. In that Merleau-Ponty was thinking the problem of ground throughout his work (most often under the sign of "institution," which is his translation of the Husserlian motif of *Stiftung*, one of the principle modalities of ground, which Derrida translates in his turn as *fondation*), it is worth noting that much of the author's subsequent argument refers implicitly to the problem of ground, as is evidenced in his deployment of related words such as *fondation*, le *Sans-fond*, etc.—Tr.].

9. Maurice Merleau-Ponty, *Phenomenology of Perception*, trans. C. Smith (New York: Routledge and Kegan Paul, 1962), 92. Translation modified.

10. Ibid., 93 (emphasis by JR; translation modified); see also *The Visible and the Invisible*, 147. We see that from one book to the next, Merleau-Ponty always encounters the aporia.

11. *The Visible and the Invisible*, 141–42 and 149. For him, the chiasm does not perform a true *synthesis* of heterogenous elements; rather, it connects only

"ensembles unified in advance by means of differentiation" (262). Translations slightly modified.

12. Ibid., 254.

13. On the formation of objective simultaneity starting from non-simultaneous originary impressions, see section 38 of appendix 8 in *Lectures on the Phenomenology of Internal Time Consciousness*, ed. M. Heidegger, trans. J. Brough (Dordrecht: Kluwer Academic Press, 1999). Husserl will consequently deepen the analysis by determining the co-givenness of impressions as a "community of resonance" constituted by a passive synthesis of association (see, among other things, appendices XIV and XXI) of *Analyses of Passive Synthesis*.

14. On the absolute synchrony of the Living Present, see appendix V of the *Phenomenology of Internal Time-Consciousness*. On the "perfection" of the temporal synthesis and the incompleteness of the carnal synthesis, see *Ideas II*, section 49.

15. Derrida, *Le Toucher*, 47, 51, et *passim*.

16. Ibid., 200. We find a similar critique of the chiasm in Michel Henry.

17. Jacques Derrida, *The Truth in Painting*, trans. G. Bennington and I. McLeod (Chicago: University of Chicago Press, 1987), French page 55. Here Derrida speaks of Kant, but the scheme is valid above all for his own thought.

18. Jacques Derrida, *Glas*, trans. J. P. Leavy Jr., and R. Rand (Lincoln: University of Nebraska Press, 1984), French page 251. I have tried to offer my explanation with respect to this question in "Il faut la vérité (notes sur la vérité de Derrida)," *Rue Descartes* 24 (1999).

19. Derrida, *Le Toucher*, 201. This is a surprising affirmation, repeated several times in the text.

20. Let us specify here that despite the homonymy, what we are calling the remainder (*le restant*) has nothing in common with the remaindering (*la restance*) evoked by Derrida. For him, this term designates above all the "survival" (*survivance*) of the trace of writing, the fact that it may persist beyond the death of its "author" and its destination. See "Signature, Event, Context," in Jacques Derrida, *Margins of Philosophy*, trans. A. Bass (Chicago: University of Chicago Press, 1982), as well as *Limited Inc.*, ed. G. Graff, trans. S. Weber and J. Mehlman, (Evanston: Northwestern University Press, 1988). Unless I am mistaken, Derrida never relates this motif to the question of the chiasm and of tactile auto-affection.

21. See Appendix XVII (written in 1931) to *Husserliana* XV (1973). This volume is not translated in English, but appears in French as *Autour des Méditations Cartésiennes* (Grenoble: J. Millon, 1998), 254–59. This is an essential text that shows that Husserl did not cede—or at least not always—to "the metaphysics of the touch" (i.e., of perfect coincidence, plenitude, and immediacy) that we sometimes too quickly attribute to him

22. We know that Heidegger designates "construction" as one of the three elements of the phenomenological method (along with the reduction and "deconstruction"): it is precisely because "Being is never accessible as a being" that one "must always be carried with respect to a free project," and

this is what he presents as a "phenomenological construction." See Martin Heidegger, *Fundamental Problems of Phenomenology* (1927), section 5, translation, introduction, and lexicon by Albert Hofstadter (Bloomington: Indiana University Press, 1988), 19–23.

23. In appendix IX (1916) of *Thing and Space*, trans. Richard Rojcewicz (Dordrecht: Kluwer Academic Publishers, 1997). Translation modified.

24. *Ideas II*, section 36. I have here adopted the translation of *Empfindnis* proposed by Levinas.

25. *Ideas II*, section 37. From 1907 onward, Husserl underlined that these kinestheses belonged originarily to the *Ichleib*, to the "flesh" of the Ego. See also *Thing and Space*, section 47.

26. [Everyone has had the experience named in the French *chassé-croisé*: you are supposed to meet a friend at 3 p.m., you wait for thirty minutes for the friend to appear, and then, tired of waiting, you quickly run around the corner to buy cigarettes; in the five minutes that you are gone, the friend appears, decides that s/he is too late, that you have gone, so leaves; thirty seconds later you return but the friend is not in sight. A game of missed meetings.—Tr.].

27. See the clues given in *Ideas* II, sections 22, 25, or 55 (taken up again and developed elsewhere, particularly in the *Analyses of Passive Synthesis*.

28. This is what Levinas did not understand. He knows how to describe admirably the position of an "Other in the Same," with the "denucleation of the Self," obsession, traumatism, the irreducible "dephasing" of the Living Present that it implies. But he dogmatically folded this alterity immanent to the Ego back on the relation *to the other* (*autrui*) without ever justifying such a decision.

29. The phenomenology of incarnation and of the remainder clarify the historical constitution of the human community as a *political body* and the no doubt reversible crisis of all representations of the body. We have presented a first sketch of it in "Chiasmus in the Polis: The Reversible Flesh of Community," in *Bodies of Resistance*, ed. L. Doyle (Evanston: Northwestern University Press, 2001).

30. We could apply what Heidegger said of the conflict between *Grund* and *Existenz* in Schelling to the relations between flesh and the remainder: their dissociability, which is the condition for the possibility of evil, signifies that they "can be moved in relation to one another, in such a way that one can take the place of the other," by a "reversal of what forms their unity in each, since they must always maintain themselves in unity." Thus, their "free mobility" is the condition of their discord and of the inversion of their relation. See Heidegger's 1936 seminar on Schelling, *Schellings Treatise: On Essence Human Freedom* (Athens: Ohio University Press, 1985).

31. Didier Franck's remarkable *Nietzsche et l'ombre de Dieu* (Paris: Presses Universitaires de France, 1998) invites us to understand the most abyssal doctrine of Zarathustra in this sense, as a non-Christian thought of the resurrection of the flesh

32. If an ontology of the remainder were possible, it would not be grounded on an analytic of "Being-there," but of "Being-in" in every sense—topological or trivial—of this expression, including that which the narrator of *A la recherche du temps perdus* gives it concerning the "two awful races" (Jews and homosexuals): "The baron was above all troubled by the words 'being in' . . . this expression took on an *extension* that M. de Charlus had not known."

33. Recall that these terms must be here understood in a purely phenomenological sense: in the perspective of a radical *epokhe* that suspends every religious belief. It is only thus that we will be able to approach (without leaving the domain of philosophy) more closely these enigmatic phenomena, for which *the madness of faith* gives us testimony.

34. Immanuel Kant, *Critique of the Power of Judgment*, section 27, trans. Eric Matthews, New Ed edition (Cambridge: Cambridge University Press, 2001).

35. This leaves open the possibility of the formation of "remainders" in the visual or auditory fields, but it is a matter of "transpositions" of the originary remainder, and this is rooted in the experience of the tactile chiasm.

11

The Unconscious Body in the Psychoanalytic Theory of J.-D. Nasio

DAVID PETTIGREW

The ambition of this chapter is to begin an exploration of the psychoanalytic contribution to the question of the body and its facticity. If Freudian psychoanalysis, as well as its later reformulation by Lacan, has provided a unique access to the body, this contribution has been overlooked or even denied by certain philosophers. Michel Henry, for example, in *Genealogy of Psychoanalysis*, takes issue with psychoanalysis in general, and in particular with what he considers to be its neglect of the body.[1]

Henry's critique stems in large part from his assumption that psychoanalysis, with its focus on the symptoms and signifiers of the unconscious, has somehow forgotten the body and its immanent experience of life, its facticity. In other words, for psychoanalysis, what matters is the unconscious, or "the psychical." The symptomatic bodily eruptions of the unconscious are merely indicators without substantial significance, except in terms of the underlying psychical cause. Henry holds such a psychoanalytic conception of the fragmented body to be particularly devoid of merit.

For Henry, affect, for example, is conscious and not unconscious (GP, 303). Henry does not speak of lack, gap, loss, or rupture, but rather of a kind of morphicity in immanence ("immanent transformation" [GP, 302]). For Henry there is no break or interruption: "[T]he movement of life is not interrupted" (GP, 305). He describes, moreover, a self-affectivity that amounts to an absolute and immanent subjectivity that cannot be interrupted or disturbed (GP, 307). On the basis of his emphasis on immanence and the constancy that is implied in his account of the uninterrupted movement of life, Henry undertakes a critique of the notion of unconscious "representation," (*Vorstellung*) and its attendant distortion (*Verstellen*) that are endemic to psychoanalytic interpretation. He writes:

> To confide to [representative] memory the reassembly of our being, of all the morsels of ourselves scattered throughout the absurd exteriority of ek-stasis, to re-stitch the infinitely broken thread of all those little stories, *is to forget that the reassembly is already accomplished*. It is the original inner reassembly in which the essence of all power and memory itself resides, the Archi-revelation of the Archi-body. (GP, 327, my emphasis)

On the face of it, Henry's concern or accusation is difficult to oppose. When we attempt to address the "psychoanalytic body" it appears indeed to have been unceremoniously disassembled. There is hardly a discussion, in psychoanalysis, of the living and breathing organism as a coherent whole. Recall, for instance, Lacan's essay on the mirror stage in which the infant sees its body image reflected in the mirror. The body that is seen is only an *image* of coherence, but there is no *bodily experience* of coherence. Rather, the body is in a state of motor incoordination. The image that the child sees and desires creates a *psychical rift* that can never be bridged. The ego begins its journey toward self-actualization upon a path or in a direction that is entirely fictional.[2] With such formulations, psychoanalysis seems to have already left the body behind, a body that was at best an inconvenient place of habitation and a means of transportation. The fictive nature of the image of the body becomes a motor force of desire, a desire that cannot be realized, and hence suffers from a constitutive instability and liability.

With this image of the body drawn from Lacan, we are no doubt operating under the authority of a psychoanalysis that began with Freud. However, I would like to consider, for much of the remainder of this paper, the work of a contemporary Parisian psychoanalyst, Dr. J.-D. Nasio, who has illuminated Lacan's theories by addressing the unconscious body in his work.

THE PSYCHOANALYTIC DISEMBODIMENT

Dr. Nasio recognizes and appreciates that the organic body or corporeal body of his patients is something that is worthy of study and care, but he is primarily interested in the psychical or unconscious causes of corporeal pain. Nasio asserts in *Five Lessons on the Psychoanalytic Theory of Jacques Lacan* that "the body with which psychoanalysis is concerned is *not the body of flesh and bone*, but a body taken to be a collection of signifying elements."[3]

Nasio appropriates Lacan's tripartite model of the symbolic, the real, and the imaginary in his thinking with respect to the imaginary body when he writes, "I perceive the image of my body first and foremost *outside* my body" (FL, 119). Moreover, for Nasio, we *psychically* incorporate these everyday objects from our world—our domiciles, lamps, clocks, and the house itself—insofar as they have an affective value. The house and its elements become no less than the extension of my body (FL, 119).

Such a body, on Nasio's account, is *partial* and not whole. For example, there is only but a *part* of a body that undergoes *jouissance*, a *jouissance* that, as Nasio puts it, is "condensed in one part or the other." He writes further that "*jouissance* [understood by Nasio as a bodily tension or pain] is nothing other than the thrust of unconscious energy when it is engendered by the erogenous orifices of the body" (FL, 117). The orifice is the fragmented and partial site of the passage of the *jouissance*, experienced as tension or pain. The body is considered, in the case of *jouissance*, and in general, as disassembled: in parts, localized, episodic, and non-immanent.

The psychoanalytic treatment of this body-in-parts is punctuated by the symptom. The symptom is a "disorder that causes suffering and manifests a pathological state," and moreover, on Nasio's account, the symptom seems strangely *dis*embodied (FL, 16). For Nasio, in psychoanalysis, the important aspect of the symptom is expressed in the patient's "speech," in the way "the patient speaks of his or her suffering, the unexpected details of the suffering, and, in particular, the impromptu nature of the speech" (FL, 16–17). Nasio asserts: "The symptom, properly speaking, is an event in analysis, one of the forms in which the experience occurs. . . . The experience is a momentary phenomenon, a uniquely privileged moment. . . . It has an empirical aspect as well which is presented at that moment when the patient speaks and *does not know what she or he says*" (FL, 15, my emphasis). One assumes that there is a bodily suffering, but the "symptom"—and with it the psychoanalytic body—is enacted in the analysand's speech as well as in the analyst's theory about the symptom (FL, 17).

Further, when Nasio states that the patient is "speaking" about the symptom, he means that, without his or her willful or conscious intention, signifiers are produced. In this case, the body is transformed into a speaking body; that is to say, a signifying body that "speaks" in parts. It would seem that the patient and his or her body is undone by, or subsumed by, the "speaking" of the symptom through the signifier.

Such a "disembodiment" is further indicated in Nasio's text, *The Book of Love and Pain: Thinking at the Limit with Freud and Lacan*,[4] in which it is said that a physical or bodily pain is eclipsed and reinvented through its psychical aspect. On this account, the pain begins, in a narrow sense, as a *physical* injury, but it develops, endures, and ramifies as *psychically* painful. The psyche produces an image of the injury, an image that is associated with the pain, or the memory of the pain. The pain no longer resides in the actual injury or wound, but in the mental representation of the wound. The psychical pain that is located in the mental representation of the specific corporeal location actually intensifies as the psyche fixates on the image and attempts to "bandage" it. The pain passes into the unconscious and the memory of the pain can reemerge in a unexpected manner that Nasio refers to as the symptomatic "resurgence of a forgotten suffering" (LP, 55).

In the Lacanian corpus the psychoanalytic body is further and irremediably fragmented by the phallus. The phallus operates from a place of detachment and involves the problematic of its loss. The agency of the phallus stems from the anxiety that it could be lost. It is around this anxiety that the castration complex is organized. For Nasio, following Lacan, human sexuality is determined not by the male genital organ but by its representation as phallus.[5] As concerns our motif of separation or fragmentation, the phallus involves the erasure of the penis and its separation from the body. That separation is a signature moment of the disembodied dissevering that is endemic to the psychoanalytic enterprise.

The phallus, in a sense, both threatens *and* carries out the castration in its imaginary and symbolic function as detachable and exchangeable (ESC, 52). The detached phallus operates in an economy of substitution, a system of continuous and repetitive exchange. Perhaps what matters more than the actual exchange or any particular exchange is the possibility of this exchange. For Nasio, the experience of castration is so crucial in the constitution of human sexuality that the central imaginary object around which castration is organized—the imaginary phallus—makes its mark on all other erogenous experiences, whatever body part is involved. Nasio emphasizes that lost objects, such as the breast or feces, gain their significance from the phallus (ESC, 53). The phallus stands within the symbolic series and outside it, outside as a limit imposed on the human being (ESC, 53). The phallus sets the standard for a series of other "objects of the drive," for Nasio, in the sense that they are unattainable. This limit on desire, this law means that all desire remains unsatisfied, or, if you will, in contraposition to Michel Henry, unfulfilled or unaccomplished.

To further elaborate on the psychoanalytic body-in-parts, whether as a collection of signifiers, symptoms, incorporated objects, the site of partial *jouissance,* or the phallus, I would like to address the relation between two concepts in the Lacanian corpus, as treated by Nasio: *objet a* and *jouissance.*

Objet a in a quite general sense designates a lost object. This "lost object" has an interesting relation to the body. That is to say, the object represents or stands in, in some respect, for parts of the body, or, for "the other." But one needs to say immediately that *objet a* is a conceptual placeholder for the object that, in psychical terms, is inaccessible. *Objet a* operates in an algorithmic circuit of desire: we seek the object, but it represents what cannot be attained. We seek it again, we repeat the attempt to regain the object that remains unattainable. *Objet a* is identified by Lacan as the cause of our desire. But as such a cause, *objet a* remains in a strange position. *Objet a* stands, as the cryptic *a,* for something that cannot be obtained or represented. If there is something that *objet a* represents, it is perhaps an impossibility or an irremediable absence. Nasio asserts in this respect:

> We think of *objet a* as a loss when it bears semantic figure related to the erogenous places of the body: the breast, the gaze, the voice, etc. All of these figures are in fact disguises of *objet a,* masks charged with a corporal signification, a cosmetic covering that Lacan categorizes as "dissimulations of Being." I insist, however, *objet a* itself is in itself an opaque real, a local *jouissance,* that is impossible to symbolize. (FL, 88)

What is particular to Lacan's *objet a* is that the object is lost and unattainable, an unattainability that perpetuates desire. Nasio emphasizes that, whether attained or not, the object involves an *identification,* indeed, an *incorporation* in which the subject identifies with the lost object, "to the point that one is assimilated to the other" (ESC, 173). This assimilation to *objet a* involves an "unconscious psychical tension" (ESC, 174). In the act of identification the *objet a,* while unattainable, remains a "constant surplus energy." The loss entails a *surplus,* a constant tension. This surplus tension suggests the psychoanalytic phenomenon of *jouissance,* as well as the connection between *jouissance* and *objet a.* However, what is interesting and perhaps most important in this context is that while the "object" is "incorporated" and assimilated in that limited and nuanced sense, it can never be fully absorbed but remains like a pebble or a wooden splinter under the skin. The inassimilability is underlined by the extent to which the object becomes the site of a *jouissance* that interrupts any unity of the body.

The body is displaced into this condensed and compact *a*. For Nasio, the body is condensed to such a vanishing point that we are no longer dealing with an object at all but rather with a hole. In other words, we arrive at the object as a kind of representation of loss, and the absent quality of the desired object leaves us in a gap. It is in this respect that Nasio describes the object as a *trou aspirant*, drawing on Freud's notion of an "in-drawing" hole.[6]

For Nasio, the place of this *trou aspirant* is a place of a *partial jouissance* that takes two forms. In one respect, the flow of desire, hindered by repression, is discharged in a symptom. This symptomatic discharge—whether in a somatic form, for example, as a *pain* (*not* as a pleasure) or as a fantasy—provides a *partial* relief (this is a so-called phallic *jouissance* with the phallus playing the role of a gatekeeper). Another part of the desire, in the second form, however, remains behind in a state of residual and constant tension or excitation (this is how Nasio understands *surplus jouissance*). *Surplus jouissance*, which is neither a relief nor a pleasure, remains "anchored" in the erogenous zones and orifices in the body.

Indeed, Nasio asserts that there is no signifier that represents *jouissance* in either a relative or an absolute sense. There is only a localization of *jouissance* in "signifying borders" that delimit the regions of the body that are the source of *surplus jouissance*. But the hole is more than a bordered opening, more than an orifice or a corporeal hole. In other words, for Nasio it is less a matter of a physical site than a matter of an unconscious interruption.[7]

As a cause of our desire, the in-drawing hole draws us out of ourselves into exile. We are exiled there as the object "extends and exceeds" us. Nasio speaks, in his book *L'inconscient à venir*, of the "inexplicable *jouissance* of exile."[8] As an interruption in the signifying system, the hole marks a conceptually impossible place that is always in intransitive excess. Such a being out of place in exile may be the proper locus of *jouissance*. But exile from what? Exile from the past. According to Nasio's formulation there is an impossible relation between the present and the past in the unconscious. This certainly seems paradoxical since it is the presence of the past in the unconscious that drives psychoanalysis itself. But Nasio specifies that, while psychoanalysis is organized around the intention of a return to an origin, an actual return cannot be accomplished. The possibility of the return, a "return" to what effectively never was, is foreclosed by the representations that hold sway in the unconscious. The certainty of the prevention of the return by repression is as certain as the attempt to return. Thus, what is "encountered" in the object-hole, *"above all, is the inability to return."*

For Nasio, this exile, this impossibility to return, is constitutive of our unconscious and is also constitutive of *jouissance*. We "return" through the repetition of a substitute formation and remain excluded nonetheless; this is an *aporia* that is constitutive of *jouissance*: a *jouissance* of impossibility, *jouissance* of pain, *jouissance* of frustration from a return that cannot be realized, a *jouissance* of dislocation.

For Nasio, yet another exile is formed out of the analyst's and analysand's exclusion from the real. What is common to these partners in the cure, Nasio writes, is their *common exclusion* (IV, 108). Against any expectation, according to this formulation, the analyst and analysand are outside of analysis, excluded from what they themselves fashion. This analytic exclusion from the real, this transferential "circling" is, for Nasio, a *jouissance* that he called suffering (IV, 110). What sort of place is this "place," this site of suffering and *jouissance*, this inaccessible site from which we are rejected? The theme of exclusion introduces yet another dimension to the non-immanence of the psychoanalytic body.

Where could *jouissance* be said to reside? Lacan said at one point that there is only *jouissance* in the body. But what body? In a corporeal hole, its unconscious representative, the interruption of signification, or in the transferential loop of an exilic desire? In each of these cases the hole or loop is a limit that breaks or encounters the break of the signifying order. It borders on the edge of the real at the limits of meaning. If *jouissance* is in the body, it is as an unconscious hole that is allegorical of an interruption or gap of that body. It is difficult to say that *jouissance* has a particular locus in a classical sense. For it is not in a container or in a particular space, but "occupies," if we can use that term, various localities.

Hence, *jouissance*, as described by Nasio, appropriates and alienates the lived body into a partial-body. Not only is the body disembodied and dissevered but it is also split as the psyche is divided from itself in exile: an exilic being. In fact, with Nasio it is not only the object of desire that is "en-holed," so to speak, but the subject itself. *Jouissance* is, and is not, in or of the subject: it carries and desubstantifies the subject. The subject cannot be "the who" of *jouissance* since it is undone in the event. Nasio writes that "[t]he paradox is that we are the subject of the act and that means that we are not; *that the "we are" during the act is a pure illusion*" (IV, 110, my emphasis). Where there is *jouissance*, we might say, there is no subject and no body. Hence Nasio's striking reference to the "subject-less hole of *jouissance*" (IV, 95). I would then, in the present context, attempt an approximation of the body's experience of its existence as a "body-less hole." Such a formulation could not be comforting to Michel Henry.

THE IMPOSSIBLE BODY OF PSYCHOANALYSIS

What is the fate of the psychoanalytic body thus described? The description we have thus far is of a *body in parts*, a disassembled body that is represented, fragmented, interrupted, and undone by the *jouissance* that courses through it and carries it in exile. What remains is a disembodied collection of signifiers. Such a body is the site of a certain nonaccomplishment marked by the failure of desire. Perhaps the psychoanalytic body could be characterized as an impossible body, in a way that remains to be considered.

Hence, the body is fragmented, incomplete, and even impossible, but is it accurate to say that psychoanalysis has forgotten the body or that there is no body of psychoanalysis? Psychoanalysis has engaged, after all, in a discourse that concerns the body's experience of its being, even if that experience is unconscious, intrinsically interrupted, divided, in exile, incomplete, and disaffected. In other words, it is a kind of embodied experience that is paradoxically disembodied. Even if the phallus or another unconscious signifier holds sway in the body, as psychically driven as the experience may be, whether the experience of the pathological symptom, the tension of the *jouissance*, or the frustration of the desire, those experiences take place nowhere else than in the body's experience of its existence. Perhaps the psychoanalytic body would need to be addressed precisely as such a body-in-parts as well as in terms of the psychical agency—the operation of the signifier—operating through and among those parts in their interrupted interrelation.

Recall that there is no subject (the subject-less hole of *jouissance*) that desires in virtue of a subject/object dichotomy. Indeed, in *Five Lessons on the Psychanalytic Theory of Jacques Lacan*, Nasio problematizes the relation of the subject to *jouissance*, writing, "When there is *jouissance* who undergoes it? His response, "[N]o one undergoes *jouissance*; . . . we do not undergo *jouissance* with something but *something undergoes jouissance within us, without us*" (FL, 40, my emphasis). We are *undone* by *jouissance* in the sense that we are undone by our desire. Perhaps what can be said of the subject with respect to *jouissance* comes from an expression Nasio uses in *L'inconscient à venir*: "subject-effect," ("*effet de sujet*"). With *jouissance* there is, then, but a subject-effect, a subject divided and exiled, expelled in a "signifying alterity" (IV, 30). The subject is sustained as a result of the repetition of the signifying order but always divided in that event. The abiding "place" that carries the subject-effect is, for Nasio, the "real"—albeit insubstantial—as soon as it is identified as underlying the subject-effect. If there is an in-itself, it has no meaning and no significance except as an *inconscient à venir*, an unconscious-to-come, or a subject-effect *to come*.

Perhaps if we cannot find an immanent or unified body in psychoanalysis we might locate what we could refer to as an episodic "body-effect" that is analogous to Nasio's notion of a subject-effect. The body-effect would be generated by the agency of the signifier and its symptomatic eruptions. The signifier would operate within and without the body, constituting an arc of desire. For Nasio, and his psychoanalytic treatment of the body, one can say that there is an extent to which there is a body-effect of desire that moves through and among objects: "objects" of desire that have been psychically incorporated and overdetermined. The body-effects would be marks of a field of psychical events that disrupts or exceeds spatial and temporal relations understood in a conventional sense. On this account the "body" would live ecstatically in a field shaped by unconscious memory and desire. The psychoanalytic body would be constituted in and operate in that field. The body would be extended, distended, and interrupted in and by the field of episodic and unpredictable eruptions of the body effect. By virtue of the interruption of this dissevered disembodiment, the body could be termed "impossible," but it is just such a paradoxically disembodied experience of being that suggests the contours of the psychoanalytic body. Such a body could not be whole, or fulfilled, but only ever a body "to come."

Nasio provides yet another model for conceiving of the body, namely the concept (borrowed from Lacan) of *le semblant*. The *semblant* emerges from the extent to which *objet a* resists symbolization or is impossible to symbolize. When Nasio writes of the *objet a* as a tension in the erogenous zones, he insists that the object is an "an opaque real, a local *jouissance* that is impossible to symbolize" (FL, 88). Why impossible to symbolize? It is impossible because what is sought is never a whole or unity. It is, rather, a hole around which a unity might circle without ever being capable of completing its journey.

Nasio suggests that while the object is impossible to symbolize it can be situated in the analyst as a fantasy. In other words, the analyst is a fantastic psychical appearance of *objet a*, an *incarnation of objet a*. It is in the analyst-as-fantasy that the *semblant* is located. But the analyst's "body" is not a geometrically localizable or measurable object. Rather, it is the hole, the enigmatic and unnamable *jouissance* that Nasio (after Lacan) calls the "*surplus-jouissance*." The *surplus* emphasizes that the "object" is always an excess, an excess of residual energy, that cannot be assimilated or managed, so to speak, by the subject.

Yet the analyst as *semblant* is not *simply* the site of an impasse. We recall that Lacan wrote that, "The analyst is the one who, by putting object *a* in the place of *le semblant*, is in the best position to do what must be done: to approach truth as [unconscious] knowledge."[9] Nasio, however, paraphrases this sentence in the following way, "*The analyst* is the one who by remaining silent [*semblance*], is in the best position to interpret, that is, to transform the symptom into a signifier which opens to unconscious knowledge" (FL, 76). For Nasio, then, it is the *analyst* who functions as *le semblant*. But Nasio asserts indeed that the analyst functions as *semblant* by taking the position of *objet a*. Nasio writes, "[W]hat is proper to the analytic experience lies in the singular position of the analyst as *objet a*" (FL, 97).

The analyst-*semblant*, like the *objet a*, then, would attract the analysand's desire, prolonging or extending him or her, activating the transference and the unconscious. Faced with the analyst-*semblant*, unconscious speech escapes the analysand, or, we can say that the analysand is drawn out of and beyond him or herself in the transference. For Nasio, however, the excess of the analyst in the face of the analysand is not just an analytic technique. The analyst serves, as in the case of *objet a*, as an in-drawing hole, or a void, if you will. The analysand is thrown or expelled from him or herself, against his or her will. Indeed, Nasio asserts that "the specificity of an analysis lies . . . in the event of a statement enunciated by the patient without knowing what he or she says" (FL, 98). The prolongation of the analysand proceeds to such an extent that Nasio asserts that there is a radical de-individuation of the analyst and the analysand. He writes:

> [T]he analytic relation will progressively cease to be a relation between two persons as it becomes a unique psychical place that includes conjointly the analyst and the analysand, or rather the place of the in between which envelops and absorbs the analytic partners. (FL, 98)

This liminal place at which the analytic partners arrive, this *entre deux*, is, for Nasio, the *surplus-jouissance*, a *jouissance* that is not expended but which remains in excess; an excess that destabilizes and portends the possibility of surprise engendered by the activation of the unconscious. The analyst "becomes the fantasmatic part (of the analysand's body) undergoing *jouissance*," extending and exceeding him or her. The nonsemblance of the analyst-*semblant* is, like *objet a*, the in-drawing void of erogenous energy that makes the unconscious work.

But for our purposes, a consideration of the psychoanalytic body would arrive here at a crucial juncture. With the de-individuation of the analyst and the analysand in the transference, Nasio thematizes an *inter*corporeality. We may think of this intercorporeality in two respects. The first mode of this intercorporeality results from the extent that the analyst takes on, shares, or becomes involved in, analysand's the symptom. Nasio writes:

> When in an analysis the patient interprets and explains their suffering, an essential phenomenon takes place: the analyst becomes, progressively and unnoticeably, the recipient of the symptom. The more I explain the cause of my suffering, the more the one who listens to me becomes the Other of my symptom . . . the symptom calls for and involves the presence of the psychoanalyst. (FL, 17)

For Nasio, this movement of the symptom points to the transference. He writes: "If you ask me about the transference in psychoanalysis, one possible response would be to define it as the particular moment of the analytic relation when the analyst becomes a part of the patient's symptom" (FL, 17). The implication of this aspect of the transference is that from the patient's point of view the analyst might be seen to be the source or the cause of their suffering. Such thinking suggests that the analyst is interwoven with the suffering of the patient—interwoven in the "body" of the patient. But how would we understand the "body" that is implicated in the transference, this second aspect of the de-individuation of the analytic partners?

By his or her listening, the analyst may take the place of the signifier that is missing from the chain, thereby resetting the loop of repetition and causing analysis to continue. At that moment, the signifiers arrange themselves through and without the knowledge of the analytic partners and, by gathering punctually in the act of a saying or a forgetting, weave the transferential bond. The analyst is implicated in an unconscious chain in order to launch the transference. One of the partners speaks, and, by not knowing what he or she is saying, activates the transference. By speaking, he or she attests to the fact that the signifiers are circulating and will continue to circulate between analyst and patient. This unconscious movement between the analyst and the analysand constitutes, for Nasio, an unconscious body. The analytic partners are de-individuated or de-individualized. The interwoven blending of the two partners could be referred to as a transubstantiation of the body of the analytic session. The event of the transubstantiation is an event that entails the activation of the unconscious and *jouissance*. The *jouissance* in this case is a body-*jouissance* because of the radicality of the transferential relation considered as a certain intercorporeality. For Nasio it is this very sort of unconscious intercorporeality that overturns the flesh and bone of the subject.

A CONCEPTUAL REORIENTATION OF THE IMPOSSIBLE BODY: THE FACTICITY OF PAIN

To think of the mode of existence that is described above as "bodily" would obviously require a certain conceptual reorientation suggested earlier, which we could call an ecstatic body. One could incorporate the eventful eruption of the *jouissance* that courses through the body, the temporal spread between present symptom and a past that is impossible to regain, and the eventful nature of the body effect that de-substantifies the body, renders it finite, and to come, under the auspices of the theme of ecstasis.

The ecstatic nature of the body in this psychoanalytic context reminds us of Henry's unambiguous rejection of the category of ecstasis (see GP, 317–27) but it also calls to mind the name of Heidegger. Heidegger offers an important resource for a conceptual reorientation with respect to our thinking of the body in the context of the current discussion. In a little-known lecture from 1964, *Bemerkungen zu Kunst-Plastik-Raum* (Remarks on Art-Sculpture-Space), Heidegger enters into a meditation on how we *body forth* (*leiben*) in space. In this lecture, Heidegger writes:

> The task is to see how human beings are in space. Human beings are not in space like bodies. Human beings are in space in such a way that they yield space [*den Raum einräumt*], that they have always already made room for space. . . . Human beings allow space as that which makes room and as that which opens, and they establish themselves and the things in this free space. They do not have physical bodies and are not physical bodies [*Körper*]; rather they body forth [*lebt seinen Leib*]. Humans live in that they body forth [*leiben*] and are in this way allowed into the open region of

> space, and through this passage [*Sicheinlassen*] already in advance stay in relation to their fellow human beings and things.[10]

In this essay, Heidegger differentiates between the "bodying forth" of human beings and the spatial location of physical objects. It is no surprise, then, when Heidegger writes, "Human beings are not limited by the surface of their putatively physical bodies" (KPR, 13). We do not move like objects but "stand" in the open or body forth as ecstatic. Heidegger writes, "When I stand here, I stand here as a human being only in so far as I am, at the same time, already there by the window, and that means outside on the street and in this city, simply stated: I am in a world" (KPR, 13–14). Perhaps we are in a world as what we could call the "ecstatic body." Consider Heidegger's remarkable formulation of this ecstasis when he writes, "We say, when a person has a free, joyous relationship with the world, that he or she is in an expansive mood [*aufgeräumt*]. A physical body can never be so expansive, the free space of joyousness is not proper to it" (KPR, 15).

The *Einräumt* of bodying forth could be understood as an agentless "yielding." Could this be analogous to the subject-less hole of *jouissance*? Heidegger writes, "The yielding of space that distinguishes human beings, the admittance [*Eingelassenheit*] in this space, this being-in-a-world, is even today hardly noticed in a sufficient enough manner" (KPR, 14). For Heidegger, this yielding speaks to a *mysterious* relation between bodying forth and space. The mysterious relation of bodying forth and space does not involve a subject and an object, or a subjective agency of any kind. In this relation, the experience of Being "yields, " that is, gives way and makes way: a yielding that is giving way and a yielding, as in a crop yield. Perhaps we can consider a psychoanalytic body that operates not as a consciously driven agent but as a bodily experience of its existence, or a bodying forth that "yields" in its ecstatic being in the world.[11]

However appropriate an ecstatic model may be, it may still be too conceptual or abstract for the matter at hand. For the body that psychoanalysis treats every day is not an abstract entity but is a body in pain. Whether the body is represented, imaginary, disassembled, or caught up in an impossible desire, pain is a phenomenon that accompanies the representations and divisions of the body-effect. The body-effect is itself the effect of psychical pain.

In its most primordial sense, for Nasio, pain is a rupture and exile from an origin. Whether represented or partial, pain perdures and intensifies as the unconscious memory of the exile. This pain is located, in part, in the symptoms that constitute the body-effect of what we have referred to as the unconscious, ecstatic-body. Moreover, this pain has an impossible or unthinkable quality that renders it unappeasable. In *L'inconscient à venir*, Nasio emphasizes the paradoxical, even impossible nature of the loss that perdures: as a result of the loss we desire to return to the past, must return to a past-producing signifiers and symptoms—the body-effect—but we cannot return to the past (IV, 28). There is, then, a necessary and impossible relation between the originary trauma and its symptomatic representative in the present. The symptom repeats the past but not in a faithful manner. In part, Nasio explains, this is because it is a memory event rather than a memory of an event (IV, 164). The impossible nature of the return produces the following paradox or *aporia* for Nasio. Each signifier-event of the unconscious is new but the unconscious is said to endure nonetheless. That is to say that the unconscious is defined, on the one hand, as a memory-in-act—not a memory *of* events but a memory-event, or as we have suggested, a body-effect—and on the other hand the unconscious is assumed to be something that remains, persevering and indestructible (IV, 165). Nasio writes, "If we accept that the unconscious is immanent to the act of saying (i.e., the symptom), if it is neither substance nor history, then we must conceive of the unconscious as the collection of representations articulated in the momentary saying of the narrative of the subject, the collection of these 'other words' in relation to which the saying comes to its place" (IV, 168). This recalls Nasio's remarkable formulation from *Five Lessons on the Psychoanalytic Theory of Jacques Lacan* that the unconscious only exists in analysis. Pushing the paradox, Nasio asserts that the unconscious "is " in the successive repetition of representations but is not the past, nor the substance of a person (cf. 169). This is the insubstantial phenomenon of the body-effect. Such would be the operation and the limit of the signifier. The remarkable and indeed paradoxical conclusion Nasio reaches is that *"the symptom is an act that repeats something that was not"* (IV, 169). The traumatic event is not a fact of the past that reappears in the current symptom. Perhaps the body-effect marks the impossible effort to repeat an originary body? As Nasio asserts, "The unconscious is neither the past nor the substance of a being" (IV, 169).

But how, then, can the unconscious or the past be said to exist if the signifier of the trauma is only immanent to the act? The paradox or trauma of which Nasio treats requires us to assume that the unconscious remains or exists. For Nasio, however, if there is a past, it is not chronological or historical past, but rather a primordial traumatic past of the threat of castration. This primordial threat has no place in time in the chronological or historical sense. It is, rather, perhaps mythical: a past that is empirically inaccessible. It is an originary scene that is forgotten and repressed (IV, 170). Hence, the "past" that abides is no more substantial than the unconscious as the event of the signifier. The symptom—the first part of the paradox—has a relation to the originary scene—the second part of the paradox—but it is an impossible relation. For Nasio, the name for the necessity and impossibility of this relation between the symptom and the past is *jouissance*; the *jouissance* of pain. The pain is produced by the event of the impossible relation: it is the impossible co-belonging of symptom and the originary past: an originary *jouissance* that remains the same, and always new. Psychical pain is in the constitutive event of the exile, an ecstasis, hence an interruption that abides. The originary trauma operates in the impossible conjunction of symptom and origin, symptom of an originary loss that can *only* be represented but which can *never* be adequately represented. The eruptions of the failure of representation, symbolization, symptoms, or signifiers are wound up with the body-effect in the psychoanalytic body. The psychoanalytic body would be a tear or a ripping between these two insubstantial poles: the eventual signifier and the myth of the originary trauma that endures.

For Nasio, the task of psychoanalysis would *not* be to resolve the paradox: to rejoin symptom and origin. This exile is not a pathology to be transcended or "cured." Indeed, in *L'inconscient à venir*, Nasio offers a response to the question of the ethics of psychoanalysis when he states: "analyst maintains the separation of the exile . . . " and steers the analysand to the unavoidability and the inescapability of the exile (IV, 33). Nasio continues, "With his or her interpretation . . . the analyst causes the analysand to encounter that which has never been missing, the real of the exclusion, the place of the exile" (IV, 32). Such an analytic function, he says, evoking both Freud and Lacan, is "our ethic."

Hence, the end of psychoanalysis is to preserve the memory of the originary pain and of the necessary and impossible connection to the symptom. That originary pain is in a sense all too immanent, in this admittedly insubstantial sense of immanent, but it perdures in a sense that is all too painful. That impossibility of coherence would be paradoxically constitutive of the psychoanalytic body.

Insofar as Nasio's work brings us to an encounter with this body-unconscious, through the unconscious signifier in its decisive event as body-effect, perhaps his work amounts to an unconcealment of the facticity of the psychoanalytic body; its very "accomplishment," to borrow the term from Henry.[12] Nasio brings us to encounter and interrogate the impossible relation between the bodily symptom and the archetypical past that is lost. The impossible relation is a hole that is a primordial *jouissance*, a *jouissance* that is intrinsic to our bodily being in its abiding non-immanence.

NOTES

1. Michel Henry, *The Genealogy of Psychoanalysis*, trans. Douglas Brick (Stanford: Stanford University Press, 1993). Henceforth cited as GP followed by the page number. One of the most telling aspects of Henry's general critique of psychoanalysis is that he challenges the theoretical and the practical validity of the idea of the unconscious.

2. Jacques Lacan, *Ecrits: A Selection*, trans. Alan Sheridan (New York: W. W. Norton, 1982), E 2.

3. Juan-David Nasio, *Five Lessons on the Psychoanalytic Theory of Jacques Lacan*, trans. David Pettigrew and François Raffoul (Albany: State University of New York Press, 1996), 118, my emphasis. Henceforth cited as FL, followed by the page number.

4. Juan-David Nasio, *The Book of Love and Pain: Thinking at the Limit with Freud and Lacan*, trans. David Pettigrew and François Raffoul (Albany: State University of New York Press, 2004). Henceforth cited as LP followed by the page number.

5. Juan-David Nasio, *Enseignement de 7 concepts cruciaux de la psychanalyse* (Paris: Editions Payot, 1992), 50. Henceforth cited as ESC followed by the page number. Translation mine.

6. Sigmund Freud, "Project for a Scientific Psychology," in *The Standard Edition of the Complete Psychological Works of Sigmund Freud*, trans. James Strachey (London: The Hogarth Press, 1974), 205–206.

7. As an "interruptive" hole in the signifying system *jouissance* can take many forms, or function in various sites. For Nasio, for example, the analyst occupies just such a "site" in the cure. That is to say that, for Nasio, the analyst occupies the place of surplus of *jouissance* (FL, 41). There is an interesting paradox here as to the locus or the agency of *jouissance*. The analyst is in the place of *jouissance*, in the sense of *objet a*, the impenetrable, the nonsignifying real that while nonsymbolic, is profoundly meaningful nonetheless for human existence. This site is a "nonplace," if you will, that is to say, it is not a place that can be occupied but that allows the possibility of an encounter with the real. *Jouissance* is, then, an interruption, a division, a parceling out of psychical tension. But this is not a tool that the analyst wields in order to handle the analysand. *The analyst as jouissance* is a tension, " a surplus that constantly maintains a high level of internal tension. This is the motor force of the cure, the core around which the analytic experience gravitates" (FL, 41).

8. Juan-David Nasio, *L'inconscient à venir* (Paris: Editions Payot and Rivages, 1993), 28. Henceforth cited as IV followed by the page number. Translation mine.

9. Jacques Lacan, *Book XX. Encore. The Seminar of Jacques Lacan. On Feminine Sexuality, The Limits of Love and Knowledge, 1972–1973*, ed. Jacques-Alain Miller, trans. Bruce Fink (New York: W. W. Norton, 1998), 95.

10. Martin Heidegger, *Bemerkungen zu Kunst-Plastik-Raum*, ed. Herman Heidegger (St. Gallen: Erker-Verlag, 1996), 13. Henceforth cited as KPR following by the pagination from the German text. The text of this essay was an address given by Martin Heidegger at the opening of the Bernhard Heiliger sculpture exposition on October 3, 1964, at the Erker-Gallerie in St. Gallen, Switzerland. Jedidiah Mohring translated this essay as part of his undergraduate Honors Thesis at Southern Connecticut State University in 2004. He received helpful advice from SCSU German Professor Marga Brockhagen as well as Professors Joseph O'Leary and Pierre Jacerme. Hakhamanesh Zangeneh and Susanne Schilz provided crucial assistance in the final preparation of the translation and his thesis manuscript.

11. Heidegger's treatment of the body in this passage is echoed in *Building Dwelling Thinking* (1954) and in the *Zollikon Seminars.* In "Building Dwelling Thinking" on page 335 of *Basic Writings*, trans. David Farrell Krell (New York: Harper and Row, 1977), Heidegger writes: "And only because mortals pervade, persist through spaces, by their very nature are they able to go through spaces. But in going through spaces we do not give up our standing in them. Rather, we always go through spaces in such a way that we already sustain them by staying constantly with near and remote locations and things. When I go toward the door of the lecture hall, I am already there, and I could not go to it at all if I were not such that I am there. *I am never here only, as this encapsulated body, rather, I am there, that is, I already pervade the space of the room, and only thus can I go through it* (my emphasis)." On pages 86–87 of the *Zollikon Seminars*, ed., Medard Boss, trans. Franz Mayr and Richard Askay (Evanston: Northwestern University Press, 2001), Heidegger distinguishes between the body as a corporeal object and the lived *bodying forth (Leiben) of the body.* Heidegger writes, "The bodying forth of the body, therefore, is a way of Dasein's being. But what kind of being? If the body as body is always my body, then this is my own way of being. *Thus, bodying-forth is co-determined by my being human in the sense of ecstatic sojourn amidst the beings in the clearing*" (my emphasis). It is interesting to find an earlier discussion of factical life in Heidegger's 1920–21 lectures on religion. In the lecture "Introduction to the Phenomenology of Religion," he engages the theme of factical life in order to undertake a phenomenological reorientation. Specifically, Heidegger is seeking an alternative to scientific thought. "Factical," he writes, on page 7 of *The Phenomenology of Religious Life*, trans. Matthias Fritsch and Jennifer Anna Gosetti-Ferencei (Bloomington: Indiana University Press, 2004), "does not mean naturally real or causally determined, nor does it mean real in the sense of the thing. The concept 'factical' may not be interpreted from certain epistemological presuppositions, but can be made intelligible only from the concept of the 'historical.' " Factical life experience is nothing less for Heidegger than the path to philosophy (cf. PhR, 8). Heidegger is attempting, at this relatively early stage of this thought, to thematize an experience of world that is not focused on

objective knowledge of a discrete object but rather on the milieu of the surrounding communal world (ibid.). " 'World' is that in which one can live (one cannot live in an object)," Heidegger writes suggestively (PhR, 8). The phenomena of that lived world are not discrete objects in this phenomenology but are richly relational. Hence, Heidegger's phenomenology of factical life experience in 1920–21 lectures had already attempted to encounter life not as an object but as a content-rich significance in connection with the surrounding world and its history in a way that is consistent with his terminology in the essay "Remarks on Art-Sculpture-Space."

12. Henry speaks on page 321 of GP of a "radical phenomenology": "Only a radical (i.e., material) phenomenology that does not simply designate appearance externally and formally but takes its concrete accomplishment into account is capable of recognizing the essential dichotomy of its actualization. . . . [O]nly such a phenomenology can grasp the ultimate significance of placing the idea's objective reality in the power that produces it since only such a phenomenology leads from phenomenality's ecstatic dimension and accompanying finitude to the original semblance in which life is life, which experiences itself in its whole being *and consists of that same self-experience.*" Perhaps J.-D. Nasio's elaboration of the impossible body of psychoanalysis moves in the direction of just such a radical phenomenology.

Part IV

Contemporary Perspectives

12

Keeping Art to its Edge

ED CASEY

On one side of the edge the vista beyond is hidden, and on the other side it is revealed; on one side there is potential collision, and on the other potential passage.

—J. J. Gibson, *The Ecological Approach to Visual Perception*

I think the major issue now in art is what are the boundaries.

—Robert Smithson, Interview with Anthony Robbin

Opening thoughts about "art" and "edge":

By the time we designate something as "art," it has lost its disruptive presence, its radical novelty, its challenge to our usual modes of classification, starting with those that belong to what we call "aesthetics," that is, the codification of primary directions of art in the last pertinent historical epoch. It has lost its edge. It has become institutionalized in keeping with the fateful sclerotization of fresh art—indeed, innovative action of any sort—as Sartre outlines when, in his *Critique of Dialectical Reason*, he traces the evolution of a group in fusion into a hierarchical social formation. Art, as "art," has lost its edge.

"Edge" disestablishes and upsets by its very structure: a structure whose effect is to obscure what is coming and to come—the sudden, the surprising, the new. Requiring a certain fixity in sight or touch (otherwise it could not serve as an edge at all), it opens onto what is un-fixed in time or space: in time, since we don't know just *when* a certain event, now unseen, will occur; in space, given that the layout we shall witness is yet unknown and can take many forms, none of them wholly predictable. Any situation or thing with such powers of concealment is apt to make us "edgy"—to put us "on edge," as we say revealingly in English.

Art and edge converge most obviously in art work that is *at the cutting edge*. Such work not only possesses striking features that draw our attention by, say, their sheer angularity. It is also work that creates its own edge—that becomes an edge of a new kind, a singular sort. This is part of what we mean by "avant-garde art," namely, art that is so far out on the edge of our usual expectations that we cannot anticipate its inception or control its course once it has emerged. As "avant-garde" literally says, it exists before habitual guard rails are erected—rails of tradition and formal expectation that prevent us from being caught surprised: anticipatory and defensive structures built from the repetition of what we already know, including what we know of previous artwork by the same artist or group of artists.

To break out of the bonds of previous styles, artists must break through encrustations of belief and history and practice. This is the perpetual struggle of the avant-garde: undermining accepted edges of the *cognoscenti*, "those in the know," so as to reach toward new edges never before realized or even recognized. The tried edges of what is all too well known give way to the evolving edges of what-is-to-come: the Event. Every coming event comes with double edges: those of the retained shadows of the remembered and those of the portended and about-to-happen. If remembered edges are essentially full—for they have been already experienced, already known—projected ones are just as essentially empty. "Empty" does not mean nugatory, much less meaningless, but empty of the definitely known and thus predictable. Edges proffer an emergent emptiness that points beyond itself in a transferential gesture toward what is not yet known: toward the surprising as what "takes hold upon" us rather than our taking hold of it. The principle is: *the emptily but actively intended lies beyond the edge of what we know*. Not because it is amorphous (*it*, the event, will have a perfectly determinate shape once it comes) but because, from a stance at the edge of the edge, it is uncertain what exact form it will take and, indeed, whether it will happen at all. But this is a position we assume in almost all circumstances, including those we think we know very well. Even the best known edge-world, say, that of our home-place, is still subject to surprise: do we really know, on any particular day, what will happen in the house? Of course not! The postman brings bad news when I had expected good; a fire breaks out in my daughter's bedroom around the corner from the living room where I am writing; the piece of fruit I am eating shows itself to be rotten at the core once I eat past its outer edge. The known comes perpetually bearing the unknown as its elusive other on its very back.

Considered in topological terms, an edge is a structure joining two surfaces whose outer shape is that of a convex dihedral angle—in contrast with a corner, which embodies a concave such angle.[1] A corner thus closes in—as when we are "cornered"—whereas an edge opens out: out into the new and the not-yet-known. But the convexity of an edge is never great enough to prevent the occultation of what lies on its other side. It is from within its very opening that it closes off in its own way, the unknown incubus indissociable from what is available: as if to warn us of any presumption to perfect knowledge, even in the most familiar or repetitive of settings. Despite their occlusive properties, edges are necessary to being in a place-world, where things and people and happenings continually emerge from behind edges, thereby offering new openings from the heart of occlusion itself.

A

Understanding edges in their inherent bivalency allows us to appreciate more fully certain features of artworks: frame, delineation, and representation. One of these features is the *frame* that acts as an edge for every work of art. Not only the outer frame that surrounds a given painting and serves to separate it from the wall, or the proscenium that comes between a theatrical production and its listeners, but the many sorts of inner frame found in artworks with a certain complexity of composition. I have in mind, for example, such things as John Marin's thick linear bands of paint or charcoal on canvas or paper that create a frame within the external frame.

Marin

These bands are extraordinarily effective, and they can be said to *edge-in* what is otherwise *edged-out* via the physical frame (often constructed for his paintings by Marin himself). Again, a double-edged circumstance—where the inner edges not merely mimic and repeat the outer edge but transform the painting as a whole. The same constructive character of such double edging obtains in the temporal arts: for example, the play-within-the play in many of Shakespeare's works, the plot-within-the-plot of Proust's *Remembrance of Things Past*, the narrative-inside-a-narrative so often operative in ordinary storytelling.

Edges can be as effectively temporal in these circumstances as they are saliently spatial on other occasions.

Beyond framing, *delineation* of any kind is an edge matter: if we don't see *some* edge, we can't make out what is delineated: every line is a certain kind of edge. Consider only the case of portraits, where the recognizable identity of the subject depends on a congeries of edges that, taken together, amount to an image that (within broad limits) resembles the person being portrayed. The degree of expected or required verisimilitude varies with the cultural and historical moment, ranging from the minute exactitude of a Holbein portrait (with virtually every pore of the skin represented) to a Chuck Close painting (wherein abstractly rendered details of a given face are in the service of an overall coherence). At either extreme, and however differently realized—Holbein employing the finest of brushes whose mark is minimal; Close setting up a visual pattern at the micro-level that makes no local sense—edges remain indispensable.

Holbein Portrait; Close Portrait

When we move from delineation to *representation*, the matter becomes more complex. Not all representations are linear in character, as we can see from many landscape paintings done in a broadly baroque mode in which the brush strokes do not aim at a linear depiction but figure for their own sake or as suggesting landscape features: from Turner to Monet to Soutine. Here the breadth of the stroke makes it into a pictorial entity in its own right—as does its sheer visual activism (as we see dramatically in Pollock or de Kooning). Mimetism as such, sheer resemblance, is no longer a goal in such cases: hence the comparative subordination of the line in such works. But representation is nevertheless aimed at, and in this enterprise edges remain of central importance: water lilies as painted by Monet, however fluid their shapes may be, are still distinct entities, distinguishable if not separable from the water on whose surface they float so intensely. The edges of each lily are seen as *there* in the painting even if they are not established by anything like a simple continuous line. It is the mass of paint as such that effects the representation; but this mass has its own peculiar edges, whether they are created by change of hue or value, or the texture of the paint.

Monet, Water Lilies

Even in the case of nonrepresentational art, edges continue to figure in decisive ways. The areas of color in Rothko's later works (what he called mockingly "objects") are as nebulous as painting gets.

Rothko; Mondrian

In place of the crisp abstract shapes of Mondrian or Albers, colors configure different areas of the overall painting, such that we can talk of different color "bands." Each such band has its own feathered, fluttering edge that allows it to be an intact and distinguishable entity. When edges reach this degree of nonlinear porosity, they become *boundaries* rather than *borders*. Where borders almost always call for linear representation—think of the way in which maps depict the borders between countries—boundaries do not. If boundaries are open to traversal at many points, borders actively discourage such traversal.

The distinction between borders and boundaries obtains for all arts in which edges figure—and that means all the arts. Borders exist in oral poetry as pauses between stanzas of verse or the repetition of epithets as they are read out loud, or in written poetry as the margins of the page that surround a given poem. Boundaries arise—and sometimes at the same time as such borders—when the reverberations of pronounced words are still heard as the poet goes onto the next line: the two lines are not confused with each other, their temporal edges being successive in character, but the *retentissement* of various words in their acoustic or alliterative (as well as their semantic) clustering calls for boundary conditions that do not close down or regiment the reading in any rigid manner.

Similarly, in architecture there are two kinds of edge that interact in much the same ways: borders as impermeable walls and roofs, boundaries as doors and windows—and at each juncture, corners as well as edges, the two operating as converse compatriots. Built structures are the ultimate edgeworks, especially those with a rectilinear pattern ranging from Renaissance palaces to exemplary cases of the International Style (e.g., Ludwig Mies van der Rohe's Seagram Building in New York); even those apparent exceptions such as Le Corbusier's Ronchamp Chapel or Frank Gehry's Bilbao Guggenheim present us with edges—the edges of the very curves that make up their manifest images, including the outer edges of these buildings as etched against the sky: the limits of any given look. Master architects are masters of the edge, as we can see in two such different instances as Frank Lloyd Wright's Prairie homes or in Paul Rudolph's aggressive late modernist work, in which carefully edged planes pivot around each other in pinwheel fashion.

Wright Houses; Rudolph Works

In poetry and in architecture—as in other arts such as sculpture and installations of several sorts—*there is no getting around the edge*, especially in its two primary forms of border and boundary.

A striking case in point is provided by Robert Smithson's celebrated "Spiral Jetty," the earthwork that was created from bulldozed gravel and earth by Smithson on the shore of the Great Salt Lake in 1969–70. In this work, which has recently reemerged from its unexpected submersion in the lake, we see a cosmographic symbol set squarely into the sea: a single spiral whose tail is connected with the shore and whose head disappears into the water:

Black and White Images of the SPIRAL JETTY

Intrinsic to the innovativeness of this work is the way it combines borders with boundaries in a new configuration. The shore is normally and naturally a border in the circumstance—it is the common limit of the land and the water, and retains a steady presence throughout—but the Jetty transforms it into a boundary: a band that acts as source and orientation for the earthwork that protrudes from it so audaciously. And the work itself acts as boundary for the shore: at once its elaboration and its outermost limit. At the same time, the edge of the Jetty acts as a boundary in relation to the salty water that invades it, submerges it, and by now has finally coated it with salt. The Spiral Jetty is a boundary for a border that becomes in turn a boundary of its own, just as it is a boundary in relation to the medium in which it is set—a medium that resists becoming a border (only a strict container of water acts as a genuine border for it: e.g., a river bank or dike, or a simple glass into which water is placed).

II

The Spiral Jetty—which I take to be exemplary of creative edgework (and which we are still trying to understand in its magical/mysterious working)[2]—points us to two crucial roles of the edge in artworks of all kinds:

1. Edges act as *limits* within which artistic freedom flourishes, as Smithson himself testifies: "There's greater freedom if you realize that you have these limits to work against and, actually, it's more challenging that way."[3] The freedom of any artist, his or her creative matrix, only occurs within the limits set up by the work itself. As Stravinsky remarks, "My freedom [as a composer] consists in my moving about within the narrow frame that I have assigned [to] myself."[4] A frame, as we saw earlier, is a form of edge, and edges, whether as borders or boundaries,

are the most crucial limits and those which the artist must respect even as he/she pursues the most groundbreaking of works;

2. The action of the edge in art is that of *intensification* and *amplification*; in the first case, the energies of the artist (and those of the admirer of his or her work) are gathered within the edges of the work itself, concentrating themselves there, while coalescing with the material media of which the work is composed; in the second case, a certain transcendent intentionality is evident as the work, once invested with the intense energies of creation, gestures beyond itself into its own periphery. We see both of these directionalities at work in the Jetty itself, whose spiral structure at once draws our perception or motion *into it* (this structure encourages us not just to look at, but to walk on, the Jetty), while simultaneously sending our look or step out beyond it into the surrounding Salt Lake or above, into the sun and sky: "[From the Jetty] you are sort of spun out to the fringes of the site . . . The shore of the lake [becomes] the edge of the sun, a boiling curve, an explosion rising into fiery prominence."[5] It is as if the intensification of the inward-moving spiral is such that it demands augmentation in the form of transcending its own boundaries.

Otherwise put, an artwork serves as a limit on itself and on our experience of it—a limit within which energies are gathered that themselves exceed the work itself in an ecstatic outflow. None of this would be possible without the operation of edges in their twofold action of intensifying and amplifying. Edges draw in even as they draw out in a powerful bidirectionality that has no equivalent in other human creations.

III

My claim concerning the role of edges in art is not that their presence guarantees artistic creativity, nor even that it is necessary to such creativity. Instead, I am pointing to the pervasive ingredience of edge in many artworks and many kinds of such works—an ingredience that is not often assessed as such. But I am also contending that attention to edges fosters and enhances the production (and eventually the appreciation) of art. This is especially so when edges occur as boundaries rather than as strict borders. When the latter happens—when edges act to prevent movement and innovation by being confining and excluding presences—they act to block significant artistic creation.

Borders, when exclusive and preclusive in their effects, confine artistic activity; only when they open up sufficiently to allow for the free passage of materials and ideas do they contribute positively to emergent artworks. But this is tantamount to their becoming boundaries—arenas for the kind of open-ended creativity that is essential to those artworks that establish their own form, style, or tradition. Boundaries are broadband regions with sufficient breadth to be more than literal lines or pure peripheries—that have the spatial width and temporal span to support creative work in their midst: indeed, to call for it.

Smithson has also said that an artist "does not *impose* but rather *exposes* the site."[6] On this conception, the artist should not force a plan or design on preexisting materials but find within these materials the nascent or tacit grounds for artwork newly directed and differently executed. But more than materials are here involved. Every site (I would prefer to say "place") comes edged: there is no edgeless place. The way in which a given place possesses its edges determines whether it will serve as a border or a boundary. Such edges are not only those of the materials from which a given artwork is fashioned nor even those elaborated materials of the finished work itself—important as both of these are for artmaking—but those that belong to the place of making itself: the studio, the plein-air scene, the place-of-working. In their essential porosity, these latter act as boundaries rather than borders. Once again, I am not saying that creative work *requires* boundary states rather than borders. Much such work has been done in prison cells and other constricted circumstances that offer no redemptive leeway: think of Solzhenitsyn writing in a gulag, or of Morandi, whose studio was also his bedroom in the modest bourgeois house of his mother and three sisters.

But when this is the case, the literal walls that otherwise constitute a border state are pierced by the artist's imagination or memory, transcending the disadvantages of physical confinement to become operative on another level. (Or when able to do so, the artist may just walk out of the studio toward the open landscape, as did Cézanne on an almost daily basis.) To transform a border into a boundary, that is, one set of edges into another, we need not have recourse to backhoe tractors and massive bulldozers, as did Smithson in the case of the Spiral Jetty. We can move beyond the enclosure of established borders—whether physical or geographical or architectural—by psychical means such as projections and visions, dreams and reveries, to realize artworks whose scope and import far exceed these constrictive circumstances. Such works create new boundaries of their own, whatever the restrictions of the borders that delimit them in earlier stages of their creation. When John Cage began recording ordinary street noises, he focused on what presented itself as a border-state of limited and limiting sounds. But the same noises, re-presented as music at a concert, encourage the audience to transform the aleatory and delimited content of sounds into an artwork of a new sort: a work that not only builds upon existing limits, namely, determinate borders, but itself comes to constitute a boundary of a new sort. Such double-edging is no longer confined to the option of inner versus outer framing but now entails the transmutation of borders into boundaries (or, alternately, of one kind of boundary into another), which occurs constantly in the creation of art, even though we rarely recognize it as such or in just these terms. But recognize it we must if we are to appreciate the formative immanence of edges in the creation and experience of art.

IV

Art is itself an edge. It is an ultimate edgework. It exists, moreover, at the edge of our lives: it is our own personal or collective avant-garde. This is not only because it takes us out of our accustomed ways and solicits the imagination of new things, the renewed remembrance of past things, and the freely varied perception of existing things ("things" here including both the artwork itself and that to which it leads by implication or resonance). It also takes us to visual (and auditory and felt) extremities—out there on the edge of our usual sensory pathways. It edges us out of habitual patterns of experience. Even if not essential to our livelihood or sheer physical survival, it is basic to soul and spirit, both of which are nourished from the differences that edges make. And the edges of artworks make a considerable difference in our sense of how the lifeworld we know could be very different, thanks to an ever more nuanced grasp of landscape and the built environment. Artworks afford altered states—not only states of mind, but states of the world, including the detailed setups of surfaces that act to affirm or disrupt our ongoing lives.

Every edge, as I have contended, gives us privileged access to the novel and the surprising—thanks to its inherent occlusive properties: the most effective and moving disclosures come from the opaque edges in our own immediate environs. Opaque, that is, until we turn the edge, and see what lies just beyond—or better, let it come to us. Then what I have called its "openness" occurs: Heidegger would doubtless say "the openness of the Open." Art is an enhanced experience of edges in their paradigmatic power to conceal things from plain or full vision, yet then suddenly to disclose what had been barred from our seeing or hearing or touching. All edges, even those of the most banal daily perceptions, adumbrate what is to come; but the edges of art do this in a particularly challenging and thematic manner. They invite us to imagine actively what lies on their other side, not from a motive of fear or self-defense but from sheer wonderment at what *may* be found on the undisclosed far side of any given work of art. At one quite literal level, this leads us to ask: What is the Spiral Jetty like in its underwater foundations, normally concealed from our sight? How might Cézanne have represented the *other* side of Mt. Sainte Victoire, whose abrupt outer edge he presents in so many canvases? At another level, still other questions arise: Toward what overall vision of the perceived world does the Jetty reach out? What sort of Mountain—what way of being mountainous—do Cézanne's images of Mt. St. Victoire portend?

Cézanne: Mt. St. Victoire

In the end, the issue of edge is not only that of what happens when material surfaces run out, even if such ending is emblematic of all edges. The issue concerns any and all such enclosing and occlusive structures, both borders and boundaries, including those of imagination and memory and thought: what do these structures indicate even as they conceal or at least complicate determinate visions of this "what"? Edge magic and edge mystery bear on nothing else—whether the edges themselves are resolutely physical or subtly psychical. The artist is someone who plays with this magic and engages this mystery in an especially poignant way: a way from which witnesses of his or her work have much to learn each time they are in its presence.

V

The celebrated "visual cliff" experiments of Eleanor J. Gibson and R. D. Walk[7] confirm and extend the remarks I have been making. Young infants and certain animals will freeze and fail to walk over a transparent but sturdy glass surface if, under that surface, a significant downward descent is to be observed. The haptic information reaching feet and hands is reassuring, but the optical information is disturbing. Given this conflict, the child or animal will pause at the edge of the cliff, refusing to continue walking or crawling even though there is no chance of falling. Here the visual edge is a genuine brink, beyond which motion is proscribed—in contrast with the side edge of a wall, around which one can move freely, or with a door in the same wall, through which one can also move with impunity.[8] Such a brinkish edge is nothing other than a *border*: a limit which one will not voluntarily trespass, given the strong fear of injury from possible falling. To consider it a *boundary* over which one might move—or around which one might just explore—is to court disaster. True, it is a purely *visual* boundary (it is a border only as haptic): one is free to look it over as something that offers a band's width of information in its optical display. But the inconsistency between what is seen with what is being touched leaves the organism up short in a form of virtual motor paralysis.

J. J. Gibson, reflecting on this same experiment two decades later, describes the visual cliff experience as one in which "one perceives the affordance of [the] edge."[9] Affordances are conceived by Gibson as what the environment offers the individual animal in relation to its perception and movement: "what [this environment] *provides* or *furnishes*, either for good or ill."[10] Thus, an edge that is a brink of the sort at stake in the visual cliff situation affords physical support for the body even as it gives negative affordance at the level of vision. Affordances, like edges themselves, can offer conflicting evidence and point to differing lines of action. Just as an occluding edge "both separates and connects the hidden and the unhidden surface, both divides and unites them,"[11] so the same edge can solicit contrary directions of action—being both inviting (e.g., when there is no conflict between haptic and visual data) and repelling (when such a conflict is present). Either "potential passage" is suggested—when the data are consonant—or else "potential conflict" ensues: conflict as to what to do with one's lived body on the brink.[12]

Affordance is crucial here, for it can be asked of any perceptual phenomenon, including an edge: What does it *afford* the viewer? What does it actively allow this viewer to do, or inhibit him from doing? What Gibson says more generally of the "layout of surfaces" that constitute any given visual (or other sensory) field can also be said of edges considered as affordances: "To perceive them is to perceive what they can afford."[13] Edges afford important things: entry to what is not now available to sight or touch or hearing *and* what will be given to these sensory systems, once we move around the edges that obstruct our current view or motion or touch. This lets us say that edges deliver to us both what is hidden and what is surprising *as such*: what is manifest within the arc of the edge and yet not yet accessible as lying just beyond it. The bivalency of edges is again confirmed. No wonder we are so ambivalent toward them, and so often neglect them in most accounts of perception, including the perception of art.

Beyond "information" (Gibson's preferred term for the content conveyed by affordances), edges offer opportunities for fitting action. When the information relays danger to the organism—as in the visual cliff situation—the impulse to move forward is checkmated. But when an organism is out of the bodily danger, the range of opportunity is considerably broadened. This is particularly the case with art. Rather than affording safety in the environment—as do most supportive surfaces—artworks afford something else: in particular, various ways of seeing and looking and moving (this latter especially in the case of architecture and sculpture) and hearing (e.g., in poetry or music) that are not otherwise so easily available in a comparatively risk-free environment. They encourage our bodies to look and move freely in their presence, whether actually (as when we draw back to see a painting better, or walk around a piece of sculpture) or virtually (as so often happens when we listen to music or poetry, accompanied by inner or psychical motions of mind or soul).[14] Out of danger in the actual layout of surfaces, we are drawn to a level of responsiveness that reflects our experience of the art work as (in Merleau-Ponty's words) an "in-itself for us." Being something in itself—some kind of "thing"—an art work is *afforded* to us, and in this respect is for us. Even as it turns away from us in its density, it turns its edges toward us, offering them to us as its special gift.

There is a complemental series at work in the role of edges in art. On the one hand, in the *other* side or surface of any given edge, there is room for surprise but not for the threatening (this latter would distract and disable the experience from the start, as sublimity in art *almost* does in the displeasure of its pleasure); on the other hand, in the side or surface directed *toward* me as appreciator or witness, there is something alluring even if greatly complex in given cases. In artworks, edges deliver more of the surprising and less of the demanding, leading us to be: more responsive than merely reactive. Not the altogether shocking or upsetting—not even the farthest out avant-garde delivers this up, despite its repeated effort to *épater les bourgeois*—but the intriguing and inviting, that which takes me in (however repellent its content may be) even as it takes me out (out of my accustomed rituals of vision and motion). Not the visual cliff but the visual spectacle, not the whole visible world but the immediately appealing visual field, not the requisite but the volitional, not necessity (or even, altogether, chance) but something freely entered into: this is *art as giving edge at the edge of our lives*.[15]

VI

Hard-edged or soft in its presentation or style, art is always open-edged in experience or effect. The convexity of its angles signifies its open embrace: its generous solicitation of our regard or gesture, its powerful draw if not its outright seduction, the attraction that does not abate with time or repetition. It presents us with open arms if only we respond to the nuance of its edged surfaces, attending to it with aesthetic care. Even the most rebarbative art work calls us to come to it—to encounter its edges and to savor their layout: both the external edges of its contours and the inner edges of its composition.

If corners close us in (they no longer give access to the other side of things), edges ask us to come in—to join them in mutual embrace. Not that this is always easy, and it is certainly never a matter of indifference (we must not confuse Kant's insistence on "disinterest" with aesthetic not-caring). We need to feel intensely that the work of art wants us to join it at the level of perception or action—no matter how off-putting, strange, or unaccustomed it may seem at first. But above all we must (in Wallace Stevens's dictum) "let be be finale of seem"[16] we have to enter the work on its own terms, its discrete ontology, its *idios cosmos*; we have to expose its site (and the aspects and sides that structure this site) rather than imposing our wishes or our need for pleasure upon it (pleasure as "amusement," as Collingwood insists, has nothing to do with art: the disruption of that which does not fit our expectations has to be allowed if we are to experience the edges of the work with the right patience and passion).[17]

Its edges hold open the future of the work: they hold this future in trust by gesturing toward what lies just beyond the visibility or tangibility of its presented surfaces. Merleau-Ponty said that artworks "have almost their entire lives [still] before them,"[18] and if so this is due in no small measure to their possessing the right edges. This future—not just of the physical work but more importantly that of our own and others' looking and moving, hearing and touching—is in a condition of *Parathaltung* (in Ingarden's term): a readiness to be activated at any time—any time we ourselves are ready to enter the edges of the work and to engage them openly.

Hovering around the edges of any artwork lie possibilities other than those we thought we knew about before we dared to take these edges up: in short, virtualities held in the penumbra of the possible. This is the opposite of Gadamer's *Horizontsverschmelzung*: it is not a matter of fusing horizons but of letting them stand out in the visible from the invisibility guarded by their edges.[19] Horizons, too, are edges and need to be respected as such. They are the outermost edges of anything (including artworks) and represent the transition from the invisible to the visible and back again, being the basis of the dialectic of the hidden and the unhidden, the known and the unknown—a dialectic that is the crux, the hinge, of every work of art. Following out this dialectic, we edge forward and back along the principal axes of the work, which is at once before us and beyond us.

Art and edge converge in the work: their twain meets: artwork is edge-work. Thanks to what its edges afford, a work of art breaks out of the sclerosis into which the history to which it belongs confines it: the history of convention, of style, of art itself. But thanks to the work, edges that might otherwise be nothing but dispersive or occlusive congeal and cohere into art that renews by its power to surprise, reinvigorates by its sudden turns toward the unexpected. We need to come to the edge of the work—to the work of its edges—to have such an experience, as intensive as it is ecstatic, as incoming as it is outgoing, as invasive as it is exhilarating.

NOTES

1. See J. J. Gibson, *The Ecological Approach to Visual Perception* (Hillsdale, NJ: Erlbaum Associates, 1986 [1979]), 308.

2. See the remarkable study by Gary Shapiro, *Earthwards* (Berkeley: University of California Press, 1995).

3. Robert Smithson, statement at symposium entitled "Earth," cited in Robert Smithson, *Collected Writings*, ed. J. Flam (Berkeley: University of California Press, 1996), 185. See also Smithson's statement that "I feel that you have to set your own limits [in art] . . ." (Interview with Anthony Robbin, in *The Writings of Robert Smithson: Essays with Illustrations*, ed. N. Holt (New York: New York University Press, 1979), 159.

4. Igor Stravinsky, *Poetics of Music* (New York: Random House, 1960), 68.

5. The first part of this citation comes from "Earth," *Collected Writings*, 181; the second from the essay, "Spiral Jetty," ibid., 146.

6. "Toward the Development of an Air Terminal Site" (1967) in *Collected Writings*, 60; his italics.

7. The classical statement is found in E. J. Gibson and R. D. Walk, "The Visual Cliff," *Scientific American* 202 (1960), 64–71.

8. For a discussion of "brink" and a comparison of horizontal versus vertical surfaces in the environment, see Gibson, *The Ecological Approach to Visual Perception*, 230.

9. Ibid., 157.

10. Ibid., 127. His italics.

11. Ibid., 308.

12. These two phrases come from ibid., 230; they form part of the first epigraph to this paper.

13. Ibid., 127. On the layout of surfaces, see ibid., 33–43.

14. On such virtual bodily motions, see R. G. Collingwood, *Principles of Art* (Oxford: Oxford University Press, 1938), e.g., 151: "an imaginative experience of total bodily activity."

15. For a rigorous distinction between visual field and visual world, see Gibson, *The Ecological Approach to Visual Perception*, 206–207. Cf. Merleau-Ponty's comparable distinction between "phenomenal field" and physical world: *Phenomenology of Perception*, Introduction, chapter 4.

16. Wallace Stevens, "The Emperor of Ice-Cream."

17. See Collingwood, *Principles of Art*, 78–104.

18. Maurice Merleau-Ponty, "Eye and Mind," tr. Michael B. Smith in *The Merleau-Ponty Aesthetics Reader: Philosophy and Painting*, ed. Galen A. Johnson (Evanston: Northwestern University Press, 1993), 149. These are the last words in this remarkable essay.

19. See Véronique Fóti, *Visions's Invisibles: Philosophical Explorations* (Albany: State University of New York Press, 2003).

13

Existence Authoritarian

Compulsion, Facticity, and the Philosophy of Identity

NAMITA GOSWAMI

> To begin with, for you to be here now trillions of drifting atoms had somehow to assemble in an intricate and curiously obliging manner to create you. It's an arrangement so specialized and particular that it has never been tried before and will only exist this once. For the next many years (we hope) these tiny particles will uncomplainingly engage in all the billions of deft, co-operative efforts necessary to keep you intact and let you experience the supremely agreeable but generally under appreciated state known as existence.
>
> —Bill Bryson, *A Short History of Nearly Everything*

> No reckoning allowed
> save the marvelous arithmetics
> of distance.
>
> —Audre Lorde, "Smelling the Wind"

WITH-OUT THE WITH-WORLD

Asha Varadharajan asks, "If . . . the unity and self-sufficiency of th[e] subject is possible only at the expense of the racial, ethnic, and feminine object, why has this perception not produced the emancipation and self-acceptance of the object?"[1] The humbled subject must pay attention to the failure of ideological production in the moment of its "consumption" in order to "*prepare the ground* for the profession of the object's political desire."[2] Varadharajan is interested in locating a discursive regime that will no longer render an object that cannot speak, except perhaps as an automaton to the ostensibly neurotic and pushy western scholar.

Varadharajan resuscitates Adorno "as the figure who incorporates the insights of poststructuralism without succumbing to its weaknesses,"[3] such as inertia, unsuspended suspension, and political ineptitude. Yet, Varadharajan's account of the object whose account of itself to the subject is always in abeyance or whose impenetrability is the sign and mark of its strategic resistance does not suffice to undermine the very crises of the object that she elucidates. Despite her attempt to shift attention from the perennial process of self-discovery undertaken by the subject at the expense of the object, even while trying to render it subject, she merely reinterprets silence as resistance, strategic or otherwise. The ethical import of that silence and impenetrability, therefore, remains ontologically bound to the object: It "*is*" silent; therefore, it "*is*" an object. It "*is*" an object; therefore, it "*is*" silent. This dialectic between subject and object removes the very history that she seeks to interrupt because the subject, plagued by "epistemology *as* violation, representation *as* colonization,"[4] is centered through de-centering while the object, as "insubstantial,"[5] is present through absence, that is, bound to its particularity and hence its difference. Both subject and object, therefore, are ontologically determinate.

In this paper, I question "how far" ontology is "capable of crisis in its concepts,"[6] arguing that certain strands of postcolonial feminist theorizing privilege gender, race, class, nationality, and sexuality, among other categories, to arrive at ontology by a more tortuous route. This strategy of what I term "particularizations" intervenes within purportedly universal claims about the world and the human being. However, a feminist *and* philosophical project must enable, along with political and social activism, a space-clearing gesture; the determinate question is not one of fixing identities and thereby existence to categories that are themselves historical. Existence beyond categories of identity cannot simply be what Adorno terms the "remainder." Instead, a feminist philosophical project must contend with existence as something we are both beyond and to which we belong. Particularity, however, does not account for historicality. Thus, "working out the conditions on which the possibility of an ontological investigation depends" (BT, 62) becomes necessarily both a philosophical ("a universal phenomenological ontology" as Heidegger notes) *and* a feminist project.

In this respect, Heidegger's hermeneutics of facticity, "in each case our own Dasein in its being-there for a while at the particular time,"[7] as a formal indication of facticity discloses Dasein as in each case specific, distinctive, and detailed. And yet, we "must face the Being of the whole man, who is customarily taken as a unity of body, soul, and spirit" (BT, 74).[8] For Heidegger, however, Dasein is "already determined in its metaphysical neutrality" insofar as gendered or raced being is "factical." Even prior to sex or race determination, the "with-one-another" of Dasein necessitates this neutrality. Indeed, "only with reference to this neutrality is the rupture of neutrality itself possible" and this "broken neutrality of its essence belongs to the essence of the human."[9]

For example, Judith Butler points to the primary fallacy at the heart of feminism: sex is biological and natural while gender is cultural and socialized. For Butler, both sex and gender are cultural categories, coding male and female genitalia as men and women, respectively. More insidiously, our categories of sex betray our heterosexism. The binary is paradoxically a priori and cultural, making men and women complementary to each other. She goes on to demonstrate the various ways in which gender itself is a set of assumed performances, in particular times and spaces. These include bodily desires, postures, clothing, and sexual practices.[10] However, on what *grounds* does Butler make her critique? In other words, *what* allows her to look *toward* a *prior* nonheterosexist horizon *as* she attempts to *return* to it?

I argue that despite the "essential" (in a Heideggerian sense) contributions of feminist and postcolonial theory to particularizing the universal and universalizing the particular, a simultaneously opaque *and* transparent facticity does not render the object more than a placeholder for the subject, and thus more than an object; or, concomitantly, more than a placeholder for the ideologically determinate status quo, and thus more than a subject qua object.[11] As Heidegger notes, while the " 'subject-object' relationship must be pre-supposed" and is "unimpeachable," the very *grounds* of the question and of the questioning, "its ontological necessity and especially its ontological meaning," should not *remain* accounted for as the *remains* on which the question and the questioning ensues (BT, 86).

The critical import of facticity lies, instead, in the fact that as "thrown" and "fallen" Dasein, facticity is marked by the hermeneutic and existential-phenomenological endeavor of "being-wakeful"; it is a "how" of the "*being-on-the-way* of itself to *itself*" such that "factical Dasein critically confronts itself and explicates itself" (OHF, 13, 56, emphases original). Thus, categories of identity such as gender, race, and class can function as limit-situations insofar as they disclose irreducibility. They do not, however, house existentiality and they do not individualize even though they particularize. Rather, they are the embodiment of self-consciousness concerned with what is "merely 'actual' " (BT, 239).

In other words, categories of identity do not necessarily reveal *who* or *what* we *are* and *where* we dwell. As conditioned conditions they inevitably lead to recoil and oscillate between the metaphysical and the systemic at the same time. This form of self-consciousness, however, is "being" "forgetful" of the "world 'wherein' Dasein . . . already *was*" such that ontologically "cognition" is inherently "a *founded* mode of Being-in-the-world" (BT, 262, 107, 101). I argue, however, that this self-consciousness may lead to speechlessness in the event of announcing one's *whoness*. Facticity is "being-wakeful" of itself such that "it brings itself to itself" in order to "let one encounter what *has presence* environmentally." Precisely this capacity of "making present," that is, "letting itself be encountered undisguisedly" within "authentic potentiality-for-Being-a-whole" and hence the "indefiniteness of its 'limit-situation' " (BT, 357, 374, 356) that stands in question within what has come to be called the metaphysics of presence and the politics of recognition.

For example, Hegel's Master and Servant dialectic may be understood as that "factical life" which is the "advance appearance of the factical life of others" such that "what is being encountered" is "*in a with-world*" (BT, 76). This "encounter" occurs insofar as others "bring with them the 'one-self' . . . one-self is therewith what one pursues." This "advance availability of what we encounter and the advance appearance of those whom we encounter" are the "wherein in which *one* . . . knows one's way around, one self" (OHF, 77). What Agamben recuperates as "the passion of facticity," that is, "the most radical experience of possibility," which has "both *potentiality* and *impotentiality*,"[12] and what others configure as Dasein's embodiment, becomes man "ek-sistent." This "open region" clears the " 'between' within which a 'relation' of subject to object can 'be.' "[13] Varadharajan recognizes this moment as a "failure" because (im)proper articulation by the object must be accompanied by a space-clearing gesture that "prepare[s] the ground" for the object to speak in what Spivak emphasizes as a completed speech-act. However, as I contend later in this chapter, particularization through categories of identity rather than enabling speech may in fact further the condition of speechlessness and homelessness.

This "between" is marked by "*Falling*," that is, "fugitive Self-concealments" that deny that "[f]actically one's own Dasein is dying already"; death is, instead, "just a 'case of death' in Others" and " 'oneself' is still 'living.' " Thus, *"the 'they' does not permit us the courage for anxiety in the face of death."* In "being-wakeful" of itself as *"being* the thrown basis of nullity" or as the "possibility of the *im*possibility of existence," Dasein's "Being toward death" is "that possibility which is one's ownmost, non-relational, not to be outstripped, certain, and yet indefinite." However, because Dasein comes "face to face with itself" only insofar as "anticipatory resoluteness" follows "the call of conscience" and "frees for death the possibility of acquiring *power* over Dasein's *existence,"* singularity and temporality, facticity's "present" ("ecstases") and "futural" aspect ("having been"), acquire Hegelian overtones of self-recognition because Dasein's "authentic future" is "existing as the possibility of nullity" such that in "time reckoning" Dasein "uses itself up" (BT, 298, 354–57, 373–79, 381). This "nothing" is revealed to us in anxiety (*es ist einem unheimlich*) as the ground for (im)possibility of any kind. Anxiety, for Heidegger, often elicits "compulsive talk" which, in turn, makes all "utterance of the 'is' fall silent" (BW, 101). Without nothing, beings as a whole cannot be revealed. Being must be "held out into the nothing" in order for a relation to Beings as a whole to be such that we interpret not just beings in relation to beings but in relation to the whole being of beings. This "transcendence" or "surpassing" is "metaphysics" (BW, 103, 106).

Heidegger's analysis of "spatiality" and "temporality," however, neglects the configuration and topography of "familiarity" or "publicness" on the basis of which it is (im)possible for "something *'strange'* [to] come forth within the initial givens of the there of the world." Indeed, the object " 'stands in the way,' 'comes at an inconvenient time,' 'is uncomfortable,' 'disturbing,' 'awkward,' 'hindering' " (OHF, 77) only insofar as Dasein's "Being alongside entities within-the-world" (BT, 263) is "ek-sistence" to which we both belong and are beyond (BW, 228–30, 252). If man is "the 'there' [*das "Da"*]" who takes "the *Da"* into "care," then this "fateful sending" is "not only the ground of the possibility of reason, ratio," (BW, 229, 231, 228) but is also the *ground(ing) of* or the "ontico-ontological condition *for* the possibility of any ontologies" (OHF, 34, my emphasis).

If the " 'essence' of man—lies in his ek-sistence" (BW, 229) or the " 'essence' of Dasein lies in its existence" (BT, 42), then Dasein is also "truth of Being as the clearing itself," and this "clearing" is "that in which the essence of man preserves the source that determines him" (BW, 235, 228). In this respect, "being wakeful" constitutes not only Dasein's "ontological foundations" of "always 'there' already" (BT, 75) but is also "properly" the manner in which Dasein "experience[s] and take[s] over this dwelling" and makes of it a "homeland" (BW, 241).

Despite Jean-Luc Nancy's and François Raffoul's work on homecoming as recognition of homelessness and authenticity as recognition of inauthenticity, I maintain that the "pronounced oppressiveness, a heightened 'there' " (OHF, 77) presupposes what has yet to be (perhaps "having been") brought into "true safekeeping." The most significant aspect of Dasein ("being") "already both in truth and in untruth" (BT, 58, 265) is that there is no " *'outside-of-itself' in and for itself*" of temporality and singularity. Dasein does *not* traverse space and time in order to "meet up with" those entities that "show" themselves "within a *world*" (BT, 377, 84, emphases original). I argue that the only space and time that exist are those that it creates.[14] Although Dasein "is always 'outside' alongside entities which it encounters and which belong to a world already discovered" (BT, 89), it is precisely the "aroundness of the environment" or the "worldhood of the world" that prevents this encounter in the first instance.

For example, while the term *Western* all too easily applies to demarcate boundaries of concern it has also become a truism that assumes transparency without clarification of its own premises and terms of engagement that effectively conflate both being and time with the "European" or the "Western." This "Europe" or "West" remains removed from the rest of the world, which it is in the midst of colonizing and appropriating, and includes those within its bounds (the poor, slaves, migrants, and women) who do not come to presence within its destiny.

While "Europe" and the "West" may be provincialized and rendered relative to "the rest" this does not begin to address the way in which this "Europe" and this "West" so constructed and obstructed "belongs" also to those others who would like to have a say in the *about-which* and *how* of its imagining and its destiny. Indeed, "Europe" or the "West" cannot be known or even rendered comprehensible as a category without looking not only to the invisible "within" but also to those through whom and with whom it is constructing its own self-image and identity. Those colonies are not passively receiving the knowledge that is being created about them nor is "Europe" or the "West" simply taking a self-standing identity to its colonial adventures and occupation.

This bias is not simply perpetuated by the presupposition of the male subject of knowledge and thus ontologically foreclosing women as irrational and recipients rather than creators of knowledge. It is also achieved by circumscribing this "Western" male who is the (only) subject of philosophy through disavowal of this subject's relationship with particular men and women not only "within" "European" and "North

American" borders but also particular men and women "within" the colonies that are politely referred to as the developing "world."

Consequently, such circumscription reinforces the notion, as Gayatri Spivak has repeatedly pointed out, that "Europe" or the "West" are self-contained and, I would add, homogenous entities. This demarcation also retains the subject as a self-contained and homogenous entity who is *not* in relation with those "within" the borders of his "homeland" as well as those "without" with whom he nonetheless has, in a Heideggerian sense, a shared destiny. In this, the "Western" philosophical tradition no longer remains the (natural) possession of certain individuals marked perhaps by race, class, or citizenship but becomes a vocabulary (among many others) that enables certain kinds of questions to be asked.

Such a reconceptualization also demands steadfast diagnosis, to borrow Adorno's term, as to what precisely is meant by our common usage of the term *Western*, and why. Through this complacent but self-deceiving apparent self-possession," the "West" not only renders itself transparent (the metaphysics of presence is not the only knowledge system the "West" has to offer) and empties itself of its own history (a sustained look at which, as Heidegger notes, cannot be precluded), but also withholds precisely those discourses of normativity and hegemony that emerged in the context of relationships and were not sui generis. In this respect, "Western" and "European," boundary markers often used to sustain particularity and curtail normative universals, do not themselves undergo critical scrutiny. In Heideggerian terms, the lack of clarity prevents us from asking the very questions most in need of being asked.

Thus, subsuming the encounter with others within the "ready-to-hand" premised on "involvement in [*bei*] a region," despite the profound implications of Heidegger's *kairological* moments, indeed "presupposes not too much, but *too little*" (BT, 145, 363). We do not, in fact, come upon others "otherwise than one thought" in their "*unpredictability, incalculability*" (OHF, 77) because our basic orientation, the "ready-to-hand" (*not* necessarily reducible to the "they"), does not demand of many that this encounter even take place. The cost of "familiarity" is that the "hither" and "thither" within the possible "whither" ("referential totality") constitutes our essential sense of "belongingness" (*Gehörigkeit*) ("significance") and does not necessitate "involvement" with others; these others simply do not come to presence "within" the "region" ("as having been placed") in which we conduct our "circumspective-concernful discovering" (BT, 145, 360). The "encounter" is in fact a non-moment moment (in a Hegelian sense) because the "ready-to-hand" does not require that this "involvement" take place even though it always already "is." Heidegger's emphasis on "my having the responsibility for the Other's becoming endangered in his existence, led astray, or even ruined," which is the "formal conception of 'Being-guilty,' " becomes instead a conscious choice or act of will rather than "*Being-the-basis* for the lack of something in the Dasein of an Other" (BT, 327–28).

Precisely at this moment Theodor Adorno makes his assertion that "ontology is apologetical": what Heidegger "promotes" by neglecting ideology, that is, "the pure principle of being-for-something else, of being merchandise," is, in fact, "slave thinking."[15] The "ideological function" of "Being," that "nonsubjective, nonobjective third," through "repetition" and the "pathos of its invocation," is to serve as the "*quid pro quo*" of the "objective interest" that "abstract[s] from the dehumanization that has made subjects what they are."[16] The "de-subjectifying process" prohibits "social consciousness, which precisely in the ontologies of Antiquity was inseparable from the philosophical one."[17] Thus, entity, "once called upon to bear witness against the sanctity of the man made idea"[18] is robbed of its capacity, of its "ownmost" possibilities, perhaps, to elicit an ethos.

While Adorno does not refer explicitly to value-thinking, Heidegger is explicit, for example in his Nietzsche lectures, in his critique insofar as an ethos or originary ethos is at stake. For Nietzsche, in order for something like a value to exist, we must already presuppose a will to power, that is, the preservation and enhancement of life. Thus, in order for life to be enhanced or preserved, we must take for granted a relation between life and the world, that is, truth. What we value, therefore, enhances life and helps us understand our relation to ourselves as a part of beings as a whole. Heidegger states,

> Do values therefore arise from will to power? Certainly. But we would be committing another error in thought if we now wished to understand values as if they were something "alongside" the will to power, as if there were at first the latter, which then posited "values" that would from time to time be pressed into service by it. Values, as *conditions* of preservation and enhancement of power exist only as something conditioned by the one absolute, will to power. Values are *essentially conditioned conditions*.[19]

Values are conditioned conditions but we know the truth only in thinking being; our understanding of the truth is metaphysical. Furthermore, values emerge in relation to becoming and not through appearance. The thinking of truth is purely metaphysical even as it involves relation to beings around us. In addition, due to the movement of history, what we assume to be true is constantly being destroyed. Values are particular and being is interpreted in relation to beings but not in relation to the whole being of beings.[20]

> When do "conditions" come to be what is evaluated and valued; that is, come to be values? Only when the representing of beings as such comes to be that representing which absolutely posits itself on itself and has to constitute of itself and for itself all the conditions of Being; only when the basic character of beings has become the sort of essence that itself demands reckoning and estimating as an essential requirement for the Being of beings.[21]

Adorno is indeed "in earnest about the difficulty involved" (OHF, 85) in discerning the "essence common to all men" such that "this universal can be neither imagined nor even conceived otherwise than in particularization." Yet, if the "history of thought has been a dialectic of enlightenment," that is, to discern what it may mean to think freely, then to "decipher the human essence by the way it is now would sabotage its possibility." To recuperate the immaculate particular from "the rationalized form of reality with which every possible consciousness is entwined" (Adorno 1990, 118, 124) is to perhaps "deny oneself the ideological misuse of one's own existence."[22] In spite of "the mutilations" borne by the subject "every cognition that seriously resists reification . . . bring[s] the petrified things in flux and thus make[s] us aware of history" (Adorno 1990, 124, 130). This "*wakeful* intensification of the difficulty" (OHF, 85) involved here is not brought about by what Adorno calls the "empty thesis" as Heidegger's "man is open" is almost always accompanied by "an invidious side glance at the animal." Instead, "real history" is "stored up in the core of each possible object of cognition." According to Adorno, therefore, Heidegger's "ascetic" philosophy, characterized by its "nihility," becomes the very relativism it was solicited to counter (Adorno 1990, 124, 130,115).

THE SUBJECT OF POSTCOLONIAL REASON

I would like to introduce, at this moment in the text, Spivak's remarkable interjection that the subaltern cannot speak within the bounds of Adorno's ethos of "missed chances" (Adorno 1990, 95) and Heidegger's ethos of "primordial 'truth' " as "the 'locus' of assertion" (BT, 269).

This subject of postcolonial reason, the subaltern, cannot be arrived at through the strategy of "particularizations." Indeed, Spivak answers her rhetorical question in the negative *for* the ontologically constituted subaltern qua a who or a what or a she or a he who cannot do something, that is, speak, thus ontologically determining the subject qua a proper name who can do something, that is, speak. The subaltern's silence is her performance but this silence, in fact, renders her non-subject(ive). The impossibility of performance (speech) names the subject (ontology) such that the (im)possibility of doing has bearing on the (im)possibility of "being" in a manner that matters (subaltern).

For example, the figuration of the feminist and postcolonial subject through the discourse of rights and autonomy, premised on the inviolability of the individual, can be "appropriated" without *necessary* ethical consequences. The form of personhood and the freedom imagined therefore becomes critical. In addition, the discourse of rights foregrounds the "right" subject who can invoke and inhabit these rights. This entails the assumption of particular forms of personhood, or status of the subject, in order to render oneself intelligible in the public domain. At this moment, however, Spivak notoriously interrupts that the subaltern cannot speak.

In terms of the available forms of personhood and place, the subaltern has no subject position from which to make her voice intelligible to us, that is, the fellow inhabitants of the public sphere to whose temporality and spatiality her experience must be translated and made comprehensible. For her to become the subject of rights she must inhabit a particular subject position, indeed be allowed to "dwell" in a particular vision of "being," and in this respect the subaltern remains perennially in another place and of another time. The subaltern thus belongs to no place and no time; that is, within this neo-Kantian framework, the subaltern cannot be apprehended through the a priori intuitions of the mind, that is, *our* time and *our* space.

For Spivak, the "association of 'consciousness' with 'knowledge' omits the crucial middle term of 'ideological production.' "[23] She criticizes the "positivist inclusion of a monolithic collectivity of 'women' in the list of the oppressed whose unfractured subjectivity allows them to speak for themselves."[24] In such a view, representation becomes simply the enabling or the transmitting of the authentic voice and needs of those who are excluded from certain circuits of power and communication. Through this strategy, the "Subject of desire and power" becomes an "irreducible methodological presupposition." Concomitantly, the "self-proximate, if not self-identical, subject of the oppressed"[25] becomes his constituency on behalf of whom the Subject intervenes. Yet, this "S/

subject, curiously sewn together into a transparency by denegations, belongs to the exploiters' side of the international division of labor."[26]

In the dichotomy between the authentic subaltern and the subject of desire and power, as Spivak points out, the "theoretical problems only relate to the person who knows. The person who knows has all the problems of selfhood. The person who is known somehow seems not to have a problematic self."[27] The subaltern, therefore, is not a privileged subject. Just as Adorno regards the subject's capacitation as his further debasement, Spivak posits her "privilege" as her "loss" because it prevents her from accessing another form of knowledge or another horizon of meaning and subjectivity. She states, "[T]he postcolonial intellectual *systematically* 'unlearns' female privilege" (Spivak 1988, 295, emphasis original). This process involves a radical refusal to reduce the subaltern to symbolic status, that is, as the static and transparent reminder of the failings of theory to speak for the subaltern, or as the remainder that is, in fact, the law of theory's limit. What is critical to her own account and what Spivak does not explicitly state in this text is the "gynocentrism" that often marks certain feminist positions; gynocentrism entails that one has already entered economic imperialism and has a subject position. Indeed, particular vocabularies for particular forms of female victimization are a mode of problematization, to borrow Foucault's phrase, which (our) temporality and spatiality, as products of economic imperialism, do allow.

A radical revision of the "investigating subject" forms the space of intervention, and not, I emphasize, the subaltern. She invokes and calls upon "the female intellectual *as* intellectual" (emphasis added) rather than the female intellectual qua female or even qua postcolonial, a privilege she indeed asks us to forego. I argue that in certain strands of current critical feminism the failure to represent is resolved through an identitarian move whereby the (transparent) identity and (transparent) politics of the researcher are often invoked in order to bridge the gap, where a slippage between politics and identity occurs. In what is often a reductive move, this identity of the researcher is represented through race, class, gender, or a myriad of other constellations—what I earlier termed as "particularizations." Through a curious elision, however, the recognition of representational failure is displaced by a proprietary relationship. Race, class, and gender often become markers for the researcher to elucidate his authority and concomitantly for others to refuse, through a remarkable perversion, the diligence and labor required for thorough and authoritative scholarship on the basis of his perceived race, class, gender handicap (read: lack) as opposed to, what is, ironically, his privilege.

I believe that Spivak points to a manner in which experience "lives by consuming the standpoint" (Adorno 1990, 30) and provides a basis for discerning the mechanisms through which we gain knowledge and inhabit the subject-function such that we remain perpetually capacitated to render ourselves the object of our own scrutiny in a manner that really matters. Spivak has been charged with rendering herself voiced and relevant because the subaltern's silence becomes the precondition and occasion for the postcolonial feminist intellectual to establish her own voice and agenda, by filling in the blanks so to speak. She has also been charged with ignoring the manifold ways that agency manifests itself thereby challenging our preconceptions.[28]

I disagree with these criticisms simply because they are based on notions of authentic representation. Instead, I argue that to charge Spivak with inadequately representing the subaltern, or founding her "voice" on the premise that the "voice" or the subjectivity of the subaltern cannot be retrieved, recreates the fallacy of presuming that there is a form of representation that is methodologically adequate. This fallacy presupposes, moreover, the centrality of the representative enterprise as opposed to the intersubjective encounter that I argue, through Hegel's Master and Servant dialectic, and Adorno's call for "felt contact" (Adorno 1978, 247) with the object, is critical.

In this respect, the "relationship" of the intellectual to subject made object is not a question of adequate representation of the object through the privilege one has of being in (im)"proper" space and (im)"proper time," and thus a voiced and materialized self-consciousness (subject). Rather, "felt contact" evokes the poignant moment of mediation. Proper self-consciousness cannot occur (the subject cannot become subject) without the intersubjective encounter. This does not entail abdicating one's self but allowing the mediation of self by another and thus subjecting ourselves to the meaning another makes of us, and enabling those meanings to matter.

I believe that Hegel extends the implications of Kant's modernity farther. If, as Kant states, the object in-itself cannot be known and is only accessed under description, a premise that Adorno acknowledges (Adorno 1990, 3–4), what are the ramifications when man takes himself and his society as object? For Hegel, this becomes the "moment" of self-consciousness in the subject; the subject finds himself or recognizes himself in the world that he has created. This recognition enables the subject to will his reconciliation with his actual existence since his world holds a place for him. In Heideggerian terms, this "world" "is" "his" "place." A subject that matters for Hegel is one that can achieve the true unity of form and content, universal and particular, objective and subjective, and actual and immediate. The subject reconciles his object status by making his objectivity his own; his objectivity is, in fact, his subjectivity. The subject, therefore, does not feel alienated in the world but through his "activity" makes it "his" own.

While Hegel refers to specific events in European history and Christianity, I focus on what I perceive to be the essential kernel of what forms a human capable of working on the world and working in the world. The capacity of mind to be free, and the ability of reason to actualize, constitute Hegel's vision of belonging or of being of/with/in the world. It is freedom qua mind qua reason that allows the thinking being qua subject qua individual qua universal qua *Spirit* to cohere with his time and space. Do personhood and place reflect one another such that the latter embodies the best of the former? Or, can the subject think freely and attain enlightenment given that in Hegel's schema the subject materializes insofar as personhood reconciles with place?

Self-knowledge and self-recognition are not possible until we are able to negotiate and bring back to ourselves the mediation of who we are by another. Hegel designates this capacity sublation, which is that which creates the *ground* or the *place* of and for consciousness in the midst of others. The Master does not simply nullify or disable the capacity of the other consciousness to render him another. He takes up and holds onto this moment of recognition of himself as also another for another. The power of mediation enables this moment to be overreached; what one is for another is incorporated into what one is for self with the latter as the superior moment. In sublation all moments are taken up and held together rather than completely dissolved or annihilated. Consciousness escapes "thinghood" because it preserves for itself and is also for another "absolute mediation." In order to "mutually give and receive one another back from each other" they cannot "let one another go quite indifferently, like things." This would only be "abstract negation" because it does not entail confrontation of concrete content by consciousness. Instead, consciousness "preserves and maintains what is sublated, and thereby survives its being sublated."[29] I argue that because the superior moment is being-for self, how we understand this process stands in question.

While Hegel's dialectic upholds what one is for another and allows for a moment when this can be fused with what one is for self, this moment has been corrupted within what can be termed inauthentic moments of recognition. What one is for another, and this is I believe Adorno's critique of Enlightenment dialectics, no longer has to be considered or incorporated into what one is for self. The other is simply an instrument or object. It necessarily follows, as per Hegel's view, that since the purported Servant is a dependent consciousness, the purported Master is also a dependent consciousness since this is how the latter's consciousness is objectified and made manifest in the world.

Spivak, therefore, does not take her criticism far enough. Even though she points to the excluded middle term of "ideological production" she does not examine the ideologies that infuse the impetus for, or the centrality of, the representative enterprise, primarily as it relates to and identifies the intellectual's self-consciousness, which, in turn, becomes centralized through "transparency" and "denegations." Ironically, the intellectual becomes knowable through the ideological investments that constitute "dealings" (BT, 96, 102) without the moment of mediation by another that would allow the recognition of these ideological investments, and thus self-consciousness, to be known in the first place.

Spivak undermines the critical and radical force of the subaltern by neglecting what I perceive to be the specifically intersubjective, and necessarily global, element of the dialectic. Thus, I argue that we cannot learn to represent ourselves because the crucial element of recognizing our own mediation by the subaltern does not take place, even if we are acutely aware of the ideologies that invest and determine our own representations of the subaltern. This is constitutive of the subaltern qua subaltern. In this respect, as mentioned earlier, Adorno's ethos of "missed chances" (Adorno 1990, 95) and Heidegger's ethos of "primordial 'truth' " as "the 'locus' of assertion" (BT, 269) become relevant. Race, class, gender, and sexuality are not *necessarily* a corrective nor necessarily *better* able to account for the dynamics that enable the constitution of the knowing subject. The emphasis on particularization often renders the subject more "ideologically functional" as it renders him more transparent; the subject becomes ontologically bound to categories of identity that are themselves historical and thus inherently relational.

For instance, Spivak is unclear about what she specifically means when she refers to "female privilege." Perhaps she is referring to the sex/gender binary that has been criticized by feminist theory or perhaps she is making an allusion to Sara Suleri's criticism of the racially coded female body as a synonym for the good. She may also be invoking any possibility of establishing a relationship of identity with the subaltern through the category of gender, in this case the "woman" who is the ostensible subject of discourses of widow-burning. The process nonetheless involves a radical refusal to reduce the subaltern to symbolic status, that is, as mentioned earlier, as the static and transparent reminder of the failings of theory to speak for the subaltern, or as the remainder that is, in fact, the law of theory's limit.

Scholars such as Sara Suleri have, however, carried the criticism farther. Suleri argues against the disturbing trend within postcolonial and multicultural feminism whereby personal experience does the work of epistemology and ethics.

> The embarrassed privilege granted to racially encoded feminism does indeed suggest a rectitude that could be its own theoretical undoing. The concept of the postcolonial itself is too frequently robbed of historical specificity in order to function as a pre-approved allegory for any mode of discursive contestation. The coupling of *postcolonial* with *woman*, however, almost inevitably leads to the simplicities that underlie unthinking celebrations of oppression, elevating the racially female voice into a metaphor for the "good."[30]

In other words, is there a way to argue and theorize marginality without recourse to identity politics and "the hidden and unnecessary desire to resuscitate the self"?[31]

Suleri investigates certain key postcolonial and African-American feminist texts and the strategies employed by their authors. She points to the ways in which scholars such as Trinh T. Min-ha, bell hooks, and Chandra Mohanty establish their own authenticity, that is, give themselves a voice, although she is often mistaken in her characterization of the work of these scholars. Their identity, according to Suleri, bolstered through the category of lived experience, not only gives them the ability to represent African-American or postcolonial women accurately but also grants them ownership of these particular emerging knowledges and discourses. Her indictment of the increasing "parochialism and professionalism"[32] of raced feminism challenges a simple biological reading of race. For Suleri, feminist discourses that justify lived experience as realism serve only to mistake the latter for autobiography. Feminism and the category of "woman" remain skin deep in that "identity [is raised] to the power of theory."[33]

This recognition demands, indeed even makes necessary, a form of intellectual honesty that I perceive, like Suleri, to be lacking in certain strands of contemporary academic feminism. Suleri attempts to recuperate lived experience in feminist discourse through "the third person narrative known as the law."[34] She, therefore, "proffer[s] life in Pakistan as an example" of lived experience that does not "achieve its articulation through autobiography."[35] She relates the effects of the

Hudood ordinances on the Pakistani female body whereby, for example, child abuse could be blamed on the victim rather than on the perpetrator. Citing the work of Asma Jahangir, a Pakistani feminist lawyer, she relates the experience of a "fifteen-year-old woman [*sic*] Jehan Mina" who was raped and impregnated by a relative. Mina's testimony led her to be convicted for fornication, which carries a punishment of one hundred public lashes. For Suleri, the law provides access to the concrete manner in which the category of woman is created. She concurs, therefore, with Fraser and Nicholson's emphasis on the "social object" that, in turn, generates gendered categories and hierarchies, that is, "the law of the limit."[36]

Child abuse and rape demand urgent response and action by feminists and by the communities in which they are occurring, locally and globally. The lack of protection that this girl experienced, both at home and by the state, evokes outrage and compassion. Jehan Mina's experience, however, and the meanings of that experience, whether to us or to her, are not the same and not altogether obvious. For Suleri, her experiences have become a means to shame postcolonial feminism, or more importantly, postcolonial feminists who seem all too concerned to talk about themselves. We are assuming, however, that we know what justice is in this situation; we are assuming that right and wrong are transparent.

Suleri broadens the scope of analysis to include U.S. foreign policy and economic interest in the region, among other avenues of research that one can take. I maintain, however, that she does not consider the concrete epistemological and ethical dilemmas involved in speaking about or narrating the experiences of someone else—especially if one is using these experiences to bolster or to prove one's own discourses and methodologies. Suleri's "law of the limit"[37] entails the refusal to make the subjects of our knowledge processes speak our politics. It also entails the recognition that the meanings of our own experiences and those of others are ambiguous and not transparent.

The merits of cross-cultural research cannot be minimized, particularly for feminist theories that focus mainly on white middle-class Western experiences. More importantly, if we seek to create a world where Jehan Mina can experience the childhood that she deserves then, regardless of the personal response scholars may have to her, she cannot be equated or reduced to the experience of her rape. Suleri's critique foregrounds how the "subject" woman is created in the discourse of the law, in a manner that has little or nothing to do with (auto)biography. Feminist theory must, therefore, radically investigate the limits of using other people's (and one's own) experiences in its discourse, the "law of the limit" that refuses to deduce personhood from a particular experience or from a particular gender.

Spivak's call for global politics centralizes the international division of labor, what Adorno terms the "barter relationship" (Adorno 1990, 75), and asks the researcher to critically examine the freedom envisioned and demanded—lest it be premised on the annihilation of other ways of life and at the cost of other subjects who are so located, and thus denied audience, that neither their lives nor their thoughts matter. The "right" subjects, therefore, are not those who can provide the "right" answers but those who have the capacity to ask the "right" questions. The very possibility of both transcendence of the status quo through its negation, and the recognition of limitations in the given present depends upon the inculcation of critical thinking. This requires self-knowledge and self-recognition, the awareness of oneself as a subject that matters, in order to discern the conditions of possibility for who we are today and what we may hope for tomorrow.

For Adorno, however, the subject has lost the critical and argumentative capacity to take himself as object in a manner that really matters. Enlightenment rationality is, at once, both mediation and appropriation. In other words, what the subject takes as the faculty that capacitates him to negate the threat of otherness that is the world, in fact, incapacitates him. He is "lulled" into a belief that technology, bureaucracy, and the destruction of nature and the consumption of human and animal life enable him to objectify the world without being objectified in return. Rather than the unity of objectivity (actual existence) and subjectivity (freedom to choose a content), the subject is further and further objectified. The *sensus communis* creates subjects that do not, in fact, speak. They reflect the status quo; they are always already defined by the status quo. They will themselves to continually negate the possibility of a genuine "encounter" with the object through the descriptions of it that are already in place. A relationship does not materialize and is, in fact, preempted by the manner in which the subject comes to know and recognize himself qua subject.

This relationship of "docility-utility"[38] indeed anticipated and articulated by Adorno, prevents the possibility of what Heidegger terms authentic "disclosedness." Dasein's facticity is, therefore, to be "closed off" from its "double possibility" of "full existential-ontological meaning." The "*a priori* character of the factical subject" is that "it is in the truth and in untruth equiprimordially." Thus, "λόγος is that way of Being in which Dasein can *either* uncover *or* cover up." Because "Being-in-untruth makes up an essential characteristic of Being-in-the-world" it is incumbent upon Dasein that it "assure itself of its uncoveredness again and again." I take Heidegger's assertion that Dasein "remains in a Being-towards these entities," even though "uncoveredness gets appropriated not by one's own uncovering" but rather by "hearsay," "idle talk," "everydayness," "lost hearing," "obviousness," the " 'hubbub' of the manifold ambiguity" that discourages "curiosity," further (BT, 233, 266–68, 296, 316) by arguing that only intersubjectivity yields this assurance. Yet, this intersubjectivity is spatial and temporal insofar as singularity, our individual *whoness*, does not, as mentioned earlier, traverse space and time; the only space and time that exist are those that it creates.

Certain strands of both postcolonial feminist theory and philosophy, therefore, undermine notions of community and belonging that are premised simply on singular aspects deemed common and thereby noteworthy, such as, to use Hegel's example, ownership of property, because they exclude other forms of interpersonal engagement and self-recognition. Instead, the "world" provides many opportunities through which to learn more about the ways in which personhood and place has been imagined and created.

I read "Can the Subaltern Speak?" through the Master and Servant allegory in order to emphasize, as Heidegger does, that what is "absent too, cannot be as such unless it presences in the *free space of the clearing*" (BT, 444, emphasis original). Thus, Spivak's text alludes to the beginnings of a pragmatics of scholarship that will prevent the "encroachment" of the "unacknowledged Subject" by "selectively defining an Other" or by becoming "the absent nonrepresenter who lets the oppressed speak for themselves." More critically, however, I locate Spivak's project within the purview of a Heideggerian existential phenomenology precisely because the possibilities of the intersubjective relationship undertaken by the intellectual and her subject matter, when "[s]een from the point of view of questionableness," represent a "*being-possible* [that] become[s] visible as something autonomously and concretely existential" (OHF, 3). And this existentiality is "essentially determined by facticity" (BT, 236).

ODDS AND ENDS

The emphasis on "particularizations" leads to the "leveling off of Dasein's possibilities " such that "what is proximally at its everyday disposal also results in a dimming down of the possible as such" (BT, 239). The task of assuming a relationship with oneself and with other human and animal life is profoundly harder than our categories of identity and our knowledges have allowed us to presuppose. Rather than privileged access, what emerges in Spivak and Adorno is precisely what Heidegger terms the "call of conscience" to which "there corresponds a possible hearing. Our understanding of the appeal unveils itself as our *wanting to have a conscience* [*Gewissenhabenwollen*]"; this involves an "existentiell choosing," that is, "*resoluteness*" (BT, 315).

If the subaltern cannot speak, then this absence is presence in the "*free space of clearing*"; if the subaltern cannot speak, then this "locus of assertion" does not constitute "discourse" or "calling" (which presume "intelligibility") (BT, 316). Instead, "Dasein fails to hear itself and listens away to the 'they' " (BT, 316); it is "smitten" with its "alienation from itself" (OHF, 12); it is marked by a "peculiar insensitivity to difference"; "*the* 'no-one' . . . haunts it like a specter" and is "a how of the fateful undoing of facticity to which the factical life of each pays tribute" (OHF, 26). And yet, I argue that what Heidegger terms "the innocuous initial 'givens' of the day which are closest to us and these givens as a for-the-most-part and for-most-of-us" is precisely what stands in question. *Whose* "givens" are these? *How* do these "givens" determine "publicness" or "averageness" that is normative and ideological? *Who* does not materialize in the "there"? Who *assumes* that "every-one has said it"? If "no one takes responsibility for it," then why? *What* enables "them" not to?

At this moment Adorno interjects his criticism that even though Heidegger emphasizes that " 'life' is something that one cannot go back 'behind' " (BT, 253), the concept itself is "indefinite, that as a concept, it lacks precisely what is meant by it," and this is "supposed to be why all light is cast on its form." Heidegger's Dasein lacks "the miseries of real human history to this day . . . dispense[s] with the memory of those miseries . . . [and is] cold to the infamy and fallibility of historic reality as that reality is sanctioned as immutable." Thus, "an ontology in accordance with the basic state of facts . . . would be pure horror. . . . Good would be nothing but what had escaped from ontology" (Adorno 1990, 119, 121–22). According to Adorno, "objective interest" does not constitute "a hidden ontology" (Adorno 1990, 66); Dasein "functions, in secret as the model of a life that is arranged so no measure of mechanical progress—the equivalent of a concept—may ever, under any circumstances, do away with poverty" (Adorno 1990, 121).

I would like, at this moment, to recuperate Heidegger after this scathing critique to foreground the "assertion" that the concept of the subaltern does indeed make, and the work that must be done, to prepare the ground, as mentioned earlier, for this "assertion" to matter.

For Heidegger, "assertion is grounded in Dasein's uncovering, or rather in its *disclosedness*; it is the ontological condition for the possibility that assertions can be either true or false—that they may uncover or cover things up" (BT, 269). The concept of the subaltern locates a "cogitative aporia" (Adorno 1990, 76); it is precisely, however, "within" the aporia that "something" slips "through." Spivak underscores "unlearning one's privilege as one's loss"; negative dialectics confront the cost of subject-formation, the cogitative function that is not capacitated with "mystical mediation as [it is with] the distress of a thinking that seeks its otherness and cannot make a move without fearing to lose what it claims" (Adorno 1990, 78). If the subaltern cannot speak, and if, as per Heidegger's view, "vocal utterance . . . is not essential for discourse, and therefore not for the call either," then

> one is not so much thinking of an utterance (for this is something which factically one never comes across); the "voice" is taken rather as a giving-to-understand. In the tendency to disclosure . . . lies the momentum of a push—of an abrupt arousal. The call is from afar unto afar. It reaches him who wants to be brought back.

More importantly, however, "one [is] called *to one's own Self*" (BT, 316–17). Heidegger emphasizes Dasein as a "possibility of its becoming and being for itself in the manner of an *understanding* of itself . . . not a comportment toward . . . (intentionality) in any sense, but rather a *how* of Dasein itself . . . the *wakefulness* of Dasein for itself" (OHF, 12). In this respect,

> "everyone" is precisely . . . historical consciousness . . . history and philosophy . . . are modes *of the being-there* of Dasein, paths which are held open and preserved in it itself, on which *it is underway and finds itself* in its characteristic manner (of falling away), i.e., on which it *is taking possession of itself*, i.e., *making itself certain and secure* about itself. . . . Historical consciousness lets Dasein be encountered in the entire wealth of the objective being of its *having-been*, while philosophy lets it be encountered in the immutability of its *always-being-in-such-a-manner*. Both directions of interpretation bring Dasein itself before its highest and pure *present* (OHF, 51).

I suggest that this can only take place through the intersubjective encounter such that a space-clearing gesture occurs whereby "anxiety" is manifest and "familiarity" can indeed be rendered "disturbable" (BT, 77). While the "ready-to-hand is always understood in terms of a totality of involvements" (BT, 191), that "in the face of which anxiety is anxious is nothing ready-to-hand within-the-world." Rather than "tranquilized self-assurance" (BT, 233), Dasein is "individualized *as* Being-in-the-world" such that "Being enters into the existential 'mode' of the *'not-at-home'* " (BT, 231).

The intersubjective encounter must take place in a manner that really matters if we are to become subjects that matter. If "uncanniness" also means "not-being-at-home" (BT, 233), then this requires a basic reorientation on our parts such that we no longer flee "*into* the 'at home' of publicness" or "flee *in the face of* the 'not-at-home.' " Thus, as Heidegger emphasizes, "*[f]rom an existential-ontological point of view, the "not-at-home" must be conceived as the more primordial phenomenon*" (BT, 234). I argue that "the contingent 'otherwise than one thought' " cannot "come down to us like a storm" through "the recalcitrant sense of its there" (BT, 77) unless we bring back to ourselves what we are for another; this, in turn, can only occur if our world is so ordered that we encounter those others in the first place.

Precisely in terms of this ordering, the neo-Kantian and neo-Hegelian impulse of postcolonial feminist theorizing emerges. Sojourning, tarrying, care, and concern are spatial and temporal insofar as the "being-there which is being encountered, . . . is there as not yet, as to be . . . for the first time, as already, as approaching, as until now, as for the time being, as finally." In spatiality is "found a familiarity with its references which prevails for a while at the particular time." Spatiality and temporality, infused with caring, are what "put" the "world" in "place" (BT, 79, 84).

If "its own past" is not "something which *follows along after* Dasein, but something which goes ahead of it" and facticity "implies . . . Being-in-the-world in such a way that it can understand itself as bound up in its 'destiny' with the Being of those entities which it encounters within its own world," then this can only "be" possible if we travel away from "what lies within the range of the familiar, the attainable, the respectable—that which is fitting and proper" (BT, 41, 82, 239).

Categories of identity, as conditioned conditions of speech, or of will to power, may no longer be the ready-to-hand in so far as they are also limit-situations. How is one rendered speechless and homeless when the will to power recoils and when it no longer makes sense to relate to oneself and to others on the basis of these categories? How does one speak when the conditions that make one's speech meaningful and audible are themselves destabilized as an event of redefinition and creation of one's relationship to oneself? How does one then announce something like one's individuality and one's *whoness*?

We cannot glean what lies on the "hither" side of the "world." In this respect, traversing the distance to "meet up" with the other does not involve traveling a road perhaps less traveled than it ought to be. There is no "outside" of singularity; the only space and time that exist are those that it creates. In addition, the actualization of a response to suffering seems to be our responsibility and at the core of our intellectual labors. Our criticisms, however, assume rather than establish the predisposition among practitioners of feminism, postcolonialism, and philosophy for justice and equity. Perhaps this is a faulty assumption. Despite Adorno's call that "the need to lend a voice to suffering is the condition of all truth," (Adorno 1990, 18) we do not know at the outset of our critical practices what justice, in fact, entails in the particular situation at hand. Rather than "posturing as metaphysically homeless and nothing-ness bound," which leads to "anticipatory consent to an oppression" such that "freedom has largely remained an ideology," perhaps enlightenment lies in the ability to ask questions that truly matter.

In the movement from not-knowing to knowing, however, how do we recuperate the ethical and epistemological force of not-knowing? Feminism strives to bring those experiences to the forefront that have hitherto been invisible and discounted in the world of ideas and experiences. What do we stand to lose by humbly placing uncertainty and inevitable "failure" as the explicit or implicit premise of feminist work? Is this a subversion of the teleological bias of knowledge processes, that to know is better than not to know?

A privileged few have their being-in-the-world accompanied by recognition, who do not need to confront what they are for another and who live in a world that presents them with their own presence as the one that matters. The capacities and the forms of personhood and place that our knowledge enables thereby place the subject in question. If "humanism" is "that man be human and not inhumane, 'inhuman,' that is, outside his essence" and if "humanism differs according to one's conception of the 'freedom' and 'nature' of man" (BW, 224, 225), then our task as readers is to see what Heidegger "does not *have* to see" to "spot" his "unthought."[39] With the passing of each human life (and perhaps one day we will learn to respect the animal life that exists *alongside* rather than *for* us), passes another story that may provide another glimmer of our existence; it is our common humanity that remains proximally and for the most part the farthest away.

NOTES

1. Asha Varadharajan, *Exotic Parodies: Subjectivity in Adorno, Said, and Spivak* (Minneapolis: University of Minnesota Press, 1995), xi.

2. Ibid., 29, my emphasis.
3. Ibid., 28.
4. Ibid., xvii, emphasis original.
5. Ibid., xxiv.
6. Martin Heidegger, *Being and Time*, trans. John Macquarrie and Edward Robinson (San Francisco: Harper, 1962), 29. Hereafter cited as BT.
7. Martin Heidegger, *Ontology—The Hermeneutics of Facticity*, trans. John van Buren (Indianapolis and Bloomington: Indiana University Press, 1999), 17. Hereafter cited as OHF.
8. I have chosen to retain the masculine pronoun in this chapter for the following reasons: (1) Norma Alarcón argues that feminist philosophy has often failed to dismantle the terms of discourse that only enable particular subjects as the creators of and as the centers of knowledge but instead replaces this subject with its female mimic. Citing Gayatri Spivak's analyses of the subject of feminist theory who "articulates herself in shifting relation to . . . the constitution and interpellation of the subject not only as individual but as individualist," she insists that "the most popular subject of Anglo-American feminism is an autonomous, self-making, self-determining subject who first proceeds according to the *logic of identification* with regard to the subject of consciousness, a notion usually viewed as the purview of man, but now claimed for women" (Gloria Anzaldúa, ed., *Making Face, Making Soul/Haciendo Caras: Creative and Critical Perspectives by Feminists of Color*. 1st ed. [San Francisco: Aunt Lute Books, 1990], 357). I do not, therefore, simply replace all masculine nouns and pronouns with feminine nouns and pronouns; (2) I also attempt to foreground the masculine bias of the ostensibly "Western" philosophical tradition while also making it "mine."
9. Martin Heidegger, *Einleitung in die Philosophie (1928/29), Gesamtausgabe* Volume 27 (Frankfurt: Klostermann, 2001), 146–47.
10. In *Gender Trouble: Feminism and the Subversion of Identity* (New York: Routledge, 1990), Butler refers to the prior or prediscursive naturalizing of heterosexuality whereby the signification of biological sex comes to have meaning, "Can we refer to a 'given' sex or a 'given' gender without first inquiring into how sex and/or gender is given, and through what means?" Butler emphasizes the scientific and political interests that rely upon the binary of male or female sex. She goes on to state, "If the immutable character of sex is contested, perhaps this construct called 'sex' is as culturally constructed as gender; indeed perhaps it was always already gender, with the consequence that the distinction between sex and gender turns out to be no distinction at all" (ibid., 6–7). Butler deploys the ramifications of "sex itself as a gendered category" (ibid., 7) to examine the heterosexual matrix that is reinforced and maintained by this obfuscation. Both sex and heterosexuality, in this schema, amount to a "politically neutral surface on *which* culture acts" (ibid., 7, emphasis in original). Butler furthers her argument through a spatial analysis, similar to Irigaray, in which the realm of the "outside" serves as both a dislocation and elision of power relations while also as a gesture that underscores and perpetuates existing structures. In addition, Butler dismantles the

notion of sexual essence that manifests as gender by locating "gender" as performative rather than ontological. She states, "In other words, acts and gestures, articulated and enacted desires create the illusion of an interior and organizing gender core, an illusion discursively maintained for the purposes of the regulation of sexuality within the obligatory frame of reproductive heterosexuality" (ibid., 136). This illusory cohesion comes from the fact that the "subject is not *determined* by the rules through which it is generated because signification *is not a founding act, but rather a regulated process of repetition* that both conceals itself and enforces its rules precisely through the production of substantializing effects. In a sense, all signification takes place within the orbit of the compulsion to repeat; 'agency,' then, is to be located within the possibility of a variation on that repetition" (ibid., 145, emphasis original). Thus, "imitative practices" and "parody" (ibid., 138) emphasize the "failure to become the 'real' and to embody the 'natural.' " This, Butler, argues, is the "constitutive failure of all gender enactments for the very reason that these ontological locales are fundamentally uninhabitable" (ibid., 146).

11. Iris Marion Young states that the "culturally dominated undergo a paradoxical oppression, in that they are both marked out by stereotypes and at the same time rendered invisible" in *Justice and the Politics of Difference* (Princeton: Princeton University Press, 1990), 59. Predominant feminist responses to this simultaneous hypervisibility and invisibility have been: (1) Reveal the particularity of what has hitherto been universal, or rather, universal-ized. Discourses that speak of the human condition stem from contingent white, male, upper-class perspectives that have been normalized through specific but elided and often-elusive power structures. These concrete power structures are in turn mystified and naturalized. (2) Reveal how certain forms of contingency are elided in order to maintain historical and material inequities while others are made hypervisible yet profoundly invisible. Feminists argue that nonwhite peoples have been relegated to nonexistence and insubstantiality. The former in that they are considered incapable of meaning-making and the latter in that they are unable to objectify the world. They are of the world and of the same substance as the world because they cannot enter into a relationship of objectification with it. They are one with nature and immune from the burdens and triumphs of rational being. Rational existence and rational being may bring the pleasures of progress and conquest. They also plague us, however, with isolation, alienation, and fragmentation. And (3) Intervene through either additive or transformative methods: One can maintain existing structures and attempt to add more and more hitherto disadvantaged people into the system of opportunities and privileges. Or, attempt to dismantle existing structures and formulate progressive and revolutionary concepts of personhood, opportunity, and success. At best, one already does a bit of both.

12. Giorgio Agamben, Infra, 105.

13. Martin Heidegger, *Basic Writings*, ed. David F. Krell (San Francisco: Harper, 1993), 252. Hereafter cited as BW.

14. I am indebted here to Bill Bryson's opening chapter "How to build a universe" in *A Short History of Nearly Everything* (London: Black Swan, 2004).

Bryson explains: "A proton is an infinitesimal part of an atom, which is itself of course an insubstantial thing. Protons are so small that a little dib of an ink like the dot on this 'i' can hold something in the region of 500, 000, 000, 000 of them, or rather more than the number of seconds it takes to make half a million years. . . . Now imagine if you can (and of course you can't) shrinking one of those protons down to a billionth of its normal size into a space so small that it would make a proton look enormous. Now pack into that tiny, tiny space about an ounce of matter. . . . If you'd prefer instead to build a more old-fashioned, standard Big Bang universe, you'll need additional materials. In fact, you will need to gather up everything there is—every last mote and particle of matter between here and the edge of creation—and squeeze it into a spot so infinitesimally compact that it has no dimensions at all. It is known as singularity. In either case, get ready for a really big bang. Naturally, you will wish to retire to a safe place to observe the spectacle. Unfortunately, there is nowhere to retire to because outside the singularity there is nowhere. When the universe begins to expand, it won't be spreading out to fill a larger emptiness. The only space that exists is the space it creates as it goes. . . . The singularity has no around it. There is no space for it to occupy, no place for it to be. We can't even ask how long it has been there—whether it has just lately popped into being, like a good idea, or whether it has been there forever, quietly awaiting the right moment. Time doesn't exist. There is no past for it to emerge from. And so, from nothing, our universe begins" (Bryson 2004, 27–28).

15. Theodor W. Adorno, *Negative Dialectics*, trans. E. B. Ashton (New York: Continuum, 1990), 61, 89, 94.

16. Ibid., 104, 95, 96, 75, 66, 124.

17. Ibid., 124, 74.

18. Ibid., 128.

19. Martin Heidegger, *Nietzsche: Volumes Three and Four*, trans. David F. Krell (San Francisco: Harper and Row, 1979), 67.

20. Heidegger also states: "Now the essence of *idea* changes from visuality and presence to representedness for and through the one who is representing. Representedness as beingness makes what is represented possible as the being. Representedness (Being) becomes the condition of the possibility of what is represented and presented-to and thus comes to stand; that is, the condition of the possibility of the object. Being—Idea—becomes a condition over which the one representing, the subject, has disposal and must have disposal if objects are going to be able to stand over against him. . . . Only through the metaphysics of subjectivity is the at first largely veiled and reserved essential trait of *idea*—the trait of being something that makes possible and conditions—transposed into the free region and then put into uninhibited play" (ibid., 174).

21. Ibid., 177.

22. Theodor W. Adorno, *Minima Moralia: Reflections from Damaged Life*, trans. E. F. Jephcott (London: Verso, 1978), 27.

23. Gayatri Chakravorty Spivak, "Can the subaltern speak?" in *Marxism and the Interpretation of Culture*, ed. C. Nelson and L. Grossberg (Urbana: University of Illinois Press, 1988), 286.

24. Ibid., 278.

25. Ibid., 279.

26. Ibid., 280.

27. Gayatri Chakravorty Spivak and Sarah Harasym, ed. *The Post-Colonial Critic: Interviews, Strategies, Dialogues* (New York: Routledge, 1990), 66.

28. For Spivak, poststructuralism and postcolonialism must bear the press of material conditions rather than put the economic "under erasure." In addition, the aim of a truly deconstructive enterprise must be to examine "how an explanation and narrative or reality was established as the normative one." The direction of the critique thus changes from "rendering vocal the individual" to "rendering visible the mechanism." Spivak emphasizes that those whom we presume to speak for and speak about are, in many ways, the products and the creations of our own ideological investments. Rather than seeking "pure forms of consciousness" our emphasis should be "moments of productive bafflement" and the "task of 'measuring silences.' "

Spivak uses the example of widow immolation in India to examine its particular textual and ideological production as a site of imperialist intervention. Despite careful and critical scrutiny of the various textual, cultural, political, legislative, and literary sites where the discourse on widow-burning occurred, there is "no itinerary we can retrace here." She cannot encounter the "voice" or the subjectivity of the women who were burned. She states, "Such a testimony would not be ideology-transcendent or 'fully' subjective, of course, but it would have constituted the ingredients for producing a counter sentence." These sites of discourse, moreover, create widow-burning as it is spoken about. In this, the "narrow epistemic violence of imperialism gives us an imperfect allegory of the general violence that is the possibility of an *epistemé*."

Spivak's text alludes to the beginnings of a pragmatics of scholarship that will prevent the "encroachment" of the "unacknowledged Subject of the West." In this respect, the question becomes the ability to prevent the "ethnographic Subject from establishing itself by selectively defining an Other" or from becoming "the absent nonrepresenter who lets the oppressed speak for themselves." I read Spivak's "Can the Subaltern Speak" through Hegel's dialectic of recognition in the *Phenomenology*. While Spivak outlines the impossibility of tracing a "counter-sentence" through her case study of *sati*, I argue that she ultimately ignores the ethical import of the silence of the subaltern.

29. Georg Wilhelm Friedrich Hegel, *Phenomenology of Spirit*, trans. A. V. Miller (Oxford: Oxford University Press, 1977), 233–34.

30. Sara Suleri, "Woman Skin Deep: Feminism and the Postcolonial Condition," *Critical Inquiry* 18 (1992): 757–69, 759, emphasis original.

31. Ibid., 762.

32. Ibid., 768.

33. Ibid., 762.

34. Ibid., 766.

35. Ibid.

36. Ibid., 769.

37. Ibid.

38. Michel Foucault, *Discipline and Punish: The Birth of the Prison*, trans. A. Sheridan. 2nd ed. (New York: Vintage Books, 1995), 25.

39. Rudi Visker, "Philosophy and Pluralism," *Philosophy Today* 48, no. 2 (Summer 2004): 115–27, 123.

14

Primordial Attunement, Hardening, and Bearing

Patricia Huntington

"Dasein *can* comport itself towards its possibilities, even *unwillingly*."

I believe that learning to bear one's life journey well is a lived precondition of bearing-with others well. I think this holds for all relations of *Mitsein*, the parent-child relation being no exception. And I take it to be an extension of Heidegger's claim in *Being and Time* that becoming individualized by anxiety is key to becoming authentically related to others.[1] Ontologically speaking, all human beings "bear-with" one another in one way or another simply because *Mitsein* is an existential structure of being-in-the-world. Nevertheless, with the language of "bearing" I wish to emphasize the existentiell dynamic of human comportment, the moment of decision involved in determining the fundamental *pathos* or attunement out of which one bears life and its travails. Understood as a modality of *Mitsein*, inauthenticity pertains not solely to idle chatter and acquired beliefs. It points to the primordial question of whether I am truly willing to bear-with another in openness and not merely go forth unwilling, partly closed, resistant, or hardened. In lived reality people can and do break with one another, even where they still interact. Because breaking with, hardening against, and closing off to another are deficient ontological modes of *Mitsein* (BT, 124), I believe that refusing to bear-with another in openness is a failure of bearing of a primordial kind.

In this chapter, I want to think about factical existence (BT, 56, 174), the reality that we always operate out of a finite mode of concernful engagement with people and world, as delivering us to a unique ethical task of bearing all things well. For Heidegger, facticity denotes existence as a thrown transcendence. As Dasein, we are thrownness (*Geworfenheit*); we are "delivered over" to existence in such a manner that we find ourselves always already engaged concernfully in existing. One's self, others, life, and things matter to us (BT, S, 29). To say that, as thrown, we nevertheless are transcendence does not mean that we can ever abstract from concern. Concernful existence can deteriorate into deficient modes, such that we can suffer existence and bear the possibilities availed in our particular lives *utterly unwillingly*. Or, by virtue of our transcending reach toward authentic possibility (BT, 2, 69), we can take over existing in such a manner that we win through to full engagement in the situation and in our manner of bearing-with others.

Contrary to the view that Heidegger's study of factical or finite existence contains no ethics, I endeavor to show that *how I comport myself toward others* carries its own ethical culpability, even if what I do is not morally egregious by all appearances. I wish to claim *that failure to live out of the full openness of one's ontological being-in-the-world is an ethical failure in its own right*, for it introduces harm into the way I bear-with or refuse to bear-with others.[2] A special violence inheres in hardening and closing off. It is no accident that children are sensitive to this basic ontological datum of bearing, of whether the person who acts toward them is closed off or open. Similarly, many classic misunderstandings between lovers center on this question of being-attuned. Many men cannot tolerate harshness in women or shrillness of voice, each of which is symptomatic of hardening. Hardening is the beginning of conflict, of the plunge into negative and distorted modes of being-with others. Many are the ways that hardening infects *Mitsein*.

Here I adopt a limited focus, for I shall discuss only the most elemental effects that hardening in women can have on children. I address my comments to women because they are traditionally considered the ones who impart life-feeling to children by a kind of native instinct. Such a view overlooks the struggle for authentic bearing that women, like all people, must face. Hardening is a grave temptation women face before the task of learning to embrace life with steadfast openness (anticipatory resolution). Many people, male and female, exhibit an ontological erraticness before the prospect of authentic choice.[3] Though I do not develop a rich examination of sex difference as a dimension of facticity, I believe erraticness arises for many women because they undergo being turned transparently upon themselves as a "being-exposed." With profound concern, I want to say that any woman who has not learned the art of resolutely bearing life well, an art that entails quieting this erraticness, simply cannot be a model of true living and life-giving force for others.[4]

BEARING LIFE WILLINGLY AS PRIMORDIAL ATTUNEMENT

My thesis is that bearing one's own life well is an existentiell precondition of bearing-with-others well.[5] Learning the art of embracing life is no small order. It means that one must become *steadfast in willingness* to meet each and every situation with *the full openness of one's being*. I want to name willingness an attunement more primordial than anxiety because it prepares one to meet unanticipated anxiety or any disposition without bolting or collapsing beneath it. I understand willingness to be an ontologically founded virtue of constancy of heart rooted in greeting every life situation—whether hard or easy, whether it brings wounding or reception—as an equal occasion for growth. Cultivation of constancy of heart is the primordial way to become life-embracing and life-giving. It thus denotes no disposition automatically realized by nature or acquired habit, but rather an attunement that must be renewed abidingly and dynamically even as it alone readies one for the unexpected. What Heidegger calls readiness for anxiety entails, on this view, cultivation of steadfastness in bearing life.[6]

To be life-embracing is neither to face life's travails naively in a tranquilized inauthentic existence, incorrigibly unprepared to meet what comes with an eye toward its essential possibility. Nor is it to become hardened and uniformly braced against the future pain that life might bring, with at best a grudging willingness to muscle one's way through. It is, rather, to know life as pain and nevertheless be willing to bear that order of pain requisite to serve the essential possibility latently gathered in the situation for meeting self and others in a fully human, albeit finite, way. To bear life well impregnates one with a robust yet sober joy, a full willingness to greet what comes that refuses to take its point of reference from those orders of joy or sorrow that aim to ward off, regulate, limit, and constrain—rather than give oneself wholly to—what comes.[7] Part of the ongoing, day to day chatter of inauthenticity unfolds around the constant complaint that one is not ready for either a particular, impending circumstance or what in general impends. This chatter expresses a prejudicial resistance to living life. In other words, we like to pick and choose, modify and control what happens to us. Yet all such resistance to what happens makes me too slow to apprehend let alone resolve upon the timely act in the moment. It reveals a lack of primordial willingness to go with the venture of life. And it ill prepares me to discern what is essential and unique in a circumstance because I refuse to be open for a full and essential engagement with the new, with what is unpredictable in a situation. I can hardly bear well what happens when I harden against life from the start. To have heart is to enjoy, on pain of much growth, a sober, constructive disposition rooted in knowing that the art of life is decided *in media res*. I wish, in effect, to name "anticipatory resolution" this steadfast, vulnerable openness to and readiness for life.

This portrait of the need to embrace life presupposes Heidegger's understanding of facticity as being-thrown in such a manner that I am affected by what arises in the world (BT, S, 29). It further relies upon his distinction between being-attuned in the primal sense by basic moods such as anxiety or boredom and all the volatile moodiness that can come over us emotionally (BT, 138; S, 40). Heidegger notes that our inauthentic ways of being-attuned evince a fitful, unstable moodiness. One day I wake up in a blue funk, the next I am elated; one hour I feel open, the next closed and disgruntled.[8] Yet Heidegger clearly asserts that one must learn to master one's moods. Mastery here does not denote control but rather points to the possibility of becoming ready to bear the phenomenon of being-attuned (moved, affected) well. We cannot, Heidegger says, simply be given over to the uncontrollable "disclosive submission to the world" characteristic of the everyday modality of attunement (BT, 138). The random feeling-open and feeling-closed characteristic of fitful moodiness presupposes a more basic decision to close off and turn away from the possibility of turning toward anxiety. Anxiety, as a primal form of being-attuned, is the basis out of which I can give myself over to random moodiness (BT, 251–52). Heidegger's analysis calls us to differentiate between the fitful feeling that being open or closed lies outside our decision and cultivation of primordial openness in and for anxiety.[9] There are two layers within any attunement, the primal and the nonprimal, the root call to face anxiety and the mere feeling of being bandied about affectively by atmospheric changes in circumstance.

Yet I wish to underscore that anxiety is not the final word. Willingness to face and win through anxiety, without closing down, bolting, or fleeing is necessary if one is to be freed to bear well what occurs and how it disposes me. However difficult it may be for people to cultivate an increasingly stable primordial openness to life that exceeds (and thus enables one to meet) anxious concern, it is possible. Echoes of this can be heard in Heidegger's notion of "being-ready for anxiety" (BT, S, 60 and 62). It may well be the case that none can predict in advance how one's mood, in the sense of feeling-tone, might suddenly be affected by a given situation, but one can be "at the ready" to see the truth of one's fitful moods in transparency. The same could be said for one's disposition to meet that most uninvited of guests, the return of anxiety triggered by something one believed had been mastered! Heidegger takes pains to depict anticipation as a qualitative modification of how I am disposed to meet the situation. Anticipation is no random mood, he says; anticipation is not an occasional attitude. I believe that anticipatory resolution can best be depicted as a distinctive fundamental pathos, a robust willingness more basic than any random moodiness or particularized will to do this or that, that prepares one essentially for the task to bear well what arises. While none can predict whether he or she will renounce fallenness and the lure toward inauthenticity, willingness alone prepares one to confront whatever might impede that decision. Unwillingness, because it forms a conflicted predisposition toward life, necessarily gives rise to conflict. For resistance to life adversely affects how the interpersonal dynamic unfolds by unduly restricting what can occur to fall short of its radical prospects. Even worse, it can lead me to enforce my obstinate particular will simply because I am *unwilling*. I can simply refuse to bear life and others well.

NAIVETE AND TRANSITION

Before I can speak directly to hardening in women, I must make a comment about growth and transition. Times of transition are times of crisis. But what is the nature of this crisis? In order to answer this question, I believe we must distinguish between two distinct orders of possible change latent within every transition. I want to call these the developmental and the radical orders. Moments of transition occasion not simply developmental alterations but radical personal transformation. I thus distinguish a developmental "change in" disposition from a radical "change of" disposition. Whereas psychological processes of development can account for marked changes in behavior as well as for the ongoing process of character formation, a change of heart must be likened much more dramatically to the breaking of habit, to a radical and primordial change of attunement. A radical change entirely reorients the compass by which I navigate life passage, firms up my primordial willingness to greet life, and frees me from reified narratives and force of habit to meet the new with freshness. Radical change endows me with a definitive sense that what is at stake in each moment of decision exceeds what I do and penetrates to the level of how

I fare. It teaches me that how I bear a situation impacts my becoming and that of others in a decisive manner.

I understand the Heideggerian notion of authenticity to delineate the possibility of the second, more radical kind of change, namely a change *of disposition*, a change of primordial attunement toward life's passage in the moment of decision. What is ontologically first we often discover last in our existentiell mode of bearing life; for this reason times of transition are fraught with the danger that one may fail to get to the root of decision.[10] Every moment contains within it the structure of transition, even though critical stages of development mark off the difficulty of transition in a distinctly tangible and visible manner. Heidegger did not theorize stages of development from birth to early childhood through adolescence into young adulthood and ultimately into midlife crisis and the realities of old age. Nevertheless, his philosophy reveals what developmental psychology typically does not, namely, that a qualitative change of heart avails itself in the moment of transparency to one's being-in-the-world. And this radical change of heart is key to living well.

We must, then, differentiate mere developmental growth from transformation proper. Early development may well be a process that brings into formation differentiated forms of consciousness and capacities requisite to being-in-the-world in an adult, autonomous fashion. Still, it would be fundamentally mistaken to think that psychic development automatically promotes growth in the order of willingness to bear existence well. Common wisdom holds that the transition from adolescence into young adulthood proves so very fragile because it is the time when we lose innocence. But what truly is loss of innocence? One might ask instead how hardening can be the danger faced in development when aging alone never decides the question. Acquiring a differentiated view of the world with age is the occasion for, but never the cause of, deciding whether to harden or not. The essential nature of crisis is not, as custom holds, a simple effect of discovering that the world is a calloused, competitive, and nonideal place. To the contrary, the grave danger lies in how I will respond to such a discovery at the ontological level of my mode of bearing.

Common wisdom confuses loss of naivete with loss of innocence. It might be extremely painful to awaken to the fact that not all is as it seems (Being dissembles) and that even my closest friends can lie to me (people can disappoint). Yet the ontological dimension of pain lies not in the acquisition of this knowledge, but in the fundamental reality that this knowledge places a new order of existentiell burden on me. It turns me upon the truth that bearing my own existence and bearing-with others calls for a distinct intensification of pathos. For every time I awaken to a new order of seeing what people and the world are capable of, I encounter the problem that realizing a repeat performance is more difficult on the basis of this newfound perception. Where I once naively acted from constructive willingness to meet life and people without prejudice, I am now challenged to reclaim willingness to live openly though no longer naively in this world and with these same people. Now this same bearing in open reception requires a new intensity of pathos. The greater one's awareness not simply of the world's questionable ways but of all that is (Being's aletheiac character), the more intense becomes the task of winning authenticity.[11]

Knowledge of the duplicity of people and the fact that reality dissembles tempts me to distrust my openness to life and lose my essential bearings. While a developmental change "in" disposition certainly allows one to adjust to a non-naive view of world, it never reaches the fundamental question whether one undergoes a change "of" heart in the right as opposed to wrong direction. Failure to pierce to the transparent groundless ground of the self and intensify one's pathos or willingness to live authentically will give rise to the shadow of a death incompletely undergone. A change ensues that touches the primordial, but not for the better. For that shadow will color one's *primordial attunement* with an unresolved negativity and a profound, though misguided, sense of irremediable loss: one hardens, one loses trust in people, one lapses into cynicism, one grows deeply saddened in a primordial sense. One suffers a blow, it is true. Yet the difficulty arises not because the blow steals something once held to be "mine." It arises because one loses heart and thus the way. One stops short and does not bear the blow all the way through to its essential potential to strengthen, rather than crush, to give back willingness to live openly in a newer, richer, more aware realization. And so one begins to live *a radical lie*: one claims that life snatched one's innocence and not merely one's naivete. One draws the self-deceptive, surface conclusion that one lost faith in oneself at the primordial level because others, God, cosmos, or life betrayed one. In truth, one gambles away trust in the free presencing of the self *in freedom*. Loss of faith in one's willingness to bear well life and its travails is never caused but only occasioned in and by the tests of freedom that life delivers.

There is no shame in naivete. Naive is what we remain even having been made richly sober in awareness, for naivete operates whenever we venture new realms and new people in life. If innocence names vulnerable openness to being, to others, and to life's venture, then in whatever way we think children enjoy innocence, it is not as something steadfastly won. Innocence is a task. Loss is the test. Much will be stripped from us in life—naivete, a merely immediate mode of being, any and every illusion I entertain about another, about a situation, about the future, about life and things. Much tragic loss could be visited upon us. Innocence comes to birth on pain of bearing every order of loss well. It is the child of a fundamental resolution to rise up and meet the abiding reality of loss rather than suffer loss in an unresolved manner that makes the weight of life unbearable. The birth of innocence is won on pain of bearing adversity through to its strange, if unpleasant, power to strengthen me by teaching me what possibilities to renounce. For what I must freely renounce is the power to engender the unspeakable harm that hardening necessarily delivers in relation to others.

WOMEN, FICKLENESS, AND HARDENING

Failure to impart a free and total embrace of life to the child deprives it of a healthy model for how to live well in freedom and sets it adrift in the groundless sea of change without bearings in life. This model cannot be given merely in word, for it must encompass one's full being-in-the-world. It must be a quality of one's presencing reach toward and within the field of action as it arrives. Lack of such a prototype, a living model in the parent, is no neutral phenomenon. It imparts a primordial sense that there is no resolution to life. Here I do not refer to any particular resolution to the various blows life sends but to life itself as something suffered insofar as one has to contend with blows in the first place. Dasein undergoes existence—the facticity of being born, existing without ground, and being-thrown into a body, a sex, a family, a time and place—as an ontological burden. A parent's failure to find healing in her primordial disposal toward life will impart to the child an exaggerated sense that living entails meaningless loss and unnecessary suffering, that existence itself is but a weighty burden that can only disappoint, a faulty cosmic design that only a spiritless trickster could invent. The killjoy negativity of disappointment in life casts a shadow of ontological distrust over the child's basic sense of being-there.

I refuse the notion that women, by virtue of native disposition, find it easy to impart a life-embracing legacy to children. In response to the question, are women more life-giving than men, we could at best give a qualified yes and no. At the level of immediate being-with, many women do enjoy a wonderful first-order willingness to engage with children in a dance of tactile game and early social attunement. I do not doubt the immense importance of women's capacity to give themselves over to this first form of attunement, a form aptly fitting to the child's immediate needs and its greater immediacy of being-in-the-world. Yet this ontic willingness does not, in itself, evince a radical ontological confrontation with one's being-there. Nor does it depend upon the fundamental order of resolution requisite to give birth to primordial constancy in being radically open to the child, and neither simply open in immediacy nor merely open on the surface.[12] That is why it does not prepare mothers for anxiety separation any more than it provides the model for assisting the child with its own anxiety before freedom. It is a hard task for any person, male or female, to become a prototype in action of a life-embracing and life-imparting mode of being-there. None automatically becomes such a prototype by force of nature, immediacy, or habit; for none comes to terms with life passage short of winning radical openness and the perspective that sustains it on pain of trial.

One tremendous impediment to becoming such a prototype is that factical existence confronts us with ontological nakedness. Without delving deeply into sex difference, I wish to note that many women undergo a tremendous struggle with the question of being-vulnerable and without felt-protection. These women suffer the facticity of being delivered to the "there" of existence as "being-exposed" (BT, S, 29).[13] We have yet to meditate on how an *irresolute disposition* toward life stems from an erratic response to anxiety before exposure, and, further, on how resistance to being denuded may be the ontological (not psychological or ontical) source of women's struggle with felt-shame. Yet it is a pervasive phenomenon that women *indiscriminately* undergo exposure as violent. Being-thrown presents women with the peculiar difficulty of having to learn to distinguish between healthy and unhealthy, innocent and non-innocent exposure. By non-innocent, I mean any form of exposure that is ethically objectionable because obtained by manipulation and designed to humiliate.

The very facticity of "being-thrown" means that existence itself is designed to expose us transparently to ourselves so that the choice in anxiety to "turn away" or "turn toward" authentic bearing can arise. Yet existence is no sadistic and humiliating tormentor. In denuding us, thrownness provides the occasion to choose naked vulnerability as a decided, rather than accidental and occasional, mode of bearing. Two things merit mention. First, facticity can only avail me the possibility of growth in authentic bearing if it gives me the occasion to see all the petty desires and impulses I harbor in order to decide how I become; that is to say, whether I am willing to renounce them or whether I wish them to come to birth as distinct qualities of my present bearing. Second, I can only become weaned of cradle and crib, and all false dependency upon mother or father, lover or friend, if existence bids me learn to trust it—life—as my true teacher. If I am to become free to embrace life's journey, then I must trust into the mystery and gentleness of being-exposed, through no humiliation, for exposure provides the occasion that bids me choose proper love of self, love of the fundamental growth that heals and enlivens, love of freedom in self-becoming, and love of the journey, travails and all, as the necessary medium for my strengthening.

Fickleness, then, has an ontological source; it is a more primal phenomenon and harder to quiet than we typically admit. Ontically, fickleness may pertain to a particular actuality. I have ambivalent feelings toward this person, activity, or thing. But its ontological significance points to the need to find a genuine counterpoise to the tendency to respond erratically to anxiety over life's character as thrown exposure.[14] Psychologically, interpretatively, and in lived actuality, we often use ontic ambivalence to explain away ontological fickleness. Yet seemingly ontic phenomena—such as a marked inability to resolve one's feelings toward another person or a pronounced negative resistance to a specific activity—may well rest upon ontological erraticness. Taking refuge in ontic particulars can mask a desire to hide from the very travail of having to see the truth of what one is or is not able to bear in an authentic and open way. After all, one can accept the finitude of what is and is not possible with a given person, and harbor no ontological fickleness or confusion about it. Fickleness means, in part, that people feel shame before their very finitude. Transparency might reveal small motives. Yet most fundamentally, it might reveal that I lack heart—I know not why—for some things at some times.

Instead of fleeing such truth in shame, one must learn to bear it if one is to do justice to others. For example, even if not all has been made clear about a person, one can discover that one has the heart to venture life with that person, flaws and all, and never renege on the choice. Conversely, one can decide to leave a marriage cleanly and without false blame. Or one can discover that one lacks heart to take on certain orders of difficulty in another person without blaming him or her for "making me" choose against relationship (as if there was some intrinsic manipulation in this finite aspect of the current situation). Even where another person exhibits severe flaws, there is no need to blame that person for my decision that these are not something I am ontically willing to bear in life, though I bear them ontologically in the manner of my decision. It is possible to have full, compassionate openness toward the other and nevertheless make a sound decision to accept one's finitude without shame and without erratically casting false blame.[15]

My key concern, however, is with hardening. Hardening seeks false resolution to the ontological difficulty of fickleness, for in hardening I decide against being-there as exposure by issuing a *blanket refusal* to allow life to turn me upon myself and work for my radical growth. In hardening hatefully against factical existence (life), I fall away from seeing the essential possibility contained in particular dynamic of a situation. The difficulty inherent in facing exposure stems from the fact that the two dimensions, ontic and ontological, intertwine in a given circumstance. This means that all the forces in that circumstance—human and nonhuman—mirror me to myself in a distinctive way that only these people and bodies could, and yet the phenomenon of being-exposed in a particular light exceeds their motives and wills. People in general, but I am concerned with women, tend to blame the other participants in the situation for this exposure rather than accept it as the very structure of being-situated. The task of becoming life-embracing entails meeting the occasion for growth latent in each situation, rather than settling for mere ontic resolution (e.g., doing what someone asks). Furthermore, it requires me to learn that apprehension of a truly productive solution hinges upon my ontological mode of bearing.

Without setting my sights by the fundamental possibility of my own genuine self-becoming, I won't be properly disposed toward others and the circumstance. Even where all other people in a given circumstance act from utterly despicable motives, the very structure of the circumstance may reveal something about me or the other that I must come to see if I am to find an open and fitting response. Their faults and actions are no excuse for my failure of bearing. To see circumstance narrowly as a competition over whose will may prevail altogether neglects the hidden lessons it holds. To believe that exposing others and being exposed manipulatively form the core ethical battle is to refuse life as teacher. For this belief allows me to skirt the essential task to win a rich, human comportment toward one another, even though we must find a genuine way to do difficult things, such as leave a marriage or turn another upon truth in the face of pain.

Unless a woman comes to terms with the tendency to respond erratically to "being-exposed," she will incline either to develop hardened strategies of defensive posturing before life circumstance or to volatilize in defensiveness on the spot. Each sex must do battle to see potentiality as potentiality as a distinct dimension hidden within the otherwise objectionable wills of men and women. Nevertheless, how women customarily enter into situations differs from men based upon the relational posture. By virtue of their greater comfort with and tendency uniformly to adopt a relational approach to *Mitsein*, many women lack the distance that men have on the field of action. The relational approach exhibits greater immediacy and thus leaves women unprepared to do battle for essential possibility. Women tend to consent on a naively sympathetic basis to whatever another person shares only belatedly to realize either that they were manipulated or that surface agreement neglected some crucial reality that called for attention and cultivation.

In order to combat being-given over to such naive seductions, women typically display two equally deficient and questionable modal possibilities for being-in-the-world. They either persist in a sympathetic openness that is unprepared for authenticity or they develop calculated strategies to gain greater distance on the field of action. The former cries innocence, while the latter insists that the world's brutal violation of her innocence justifies hardening. Much needs to be pondered about why women feel the need to train themselves to close off and build protective, harshly conditional barriers as if this could encourage a sound form of being-with-others. There is a highly questionable genealogy that women bequeath to women. Common it is to be told by more seasoned women, in the aftermath of a failed relationship, that one should learn to hold back and not give of oneself except on condition that the other, especially a guy other, prove himself. I take all such counsel to be part of *das Man*. Hardening at the ontological level never makes one free. It never delivers one to the willingness to trust oneself to live fully and openly. It aborts love.

Both false options—persistence for life in believing oneself to be innocent and the acquisition of distance on the field by building barriers, cognitive and emotional—exhibit flight from anxiety before "being-thrown/exposed." One can achieve reflective distance by closing off emotionally and learning patterns of acquired behavior. But such closure has dire consequences for oneself, for others, and for the legacy one passes on to children. I believe that women betray themselves when they do not find a way to come to terms with vulnerability. Many women persist in conflating naivete and innocence for a lifetime. Their concept of self dictates that they must always appear sympathetic. One woman flees into the immediacy of sympathetic identification for want of being seen as understanding; the other flees from having valorized sympathy uniformly and naively, after discovering the horror of her complicity. While custom holds the former to remain naive and the latter to be worldly wise, in truth each remains naive in relation to her ontological refusal to grow the capacity for authentically open and vulnerable bearing. The former hides from her entangled freedom, for she can be open and sympathetic only where she is not tested. The moment she feels exposed, she will defensively assign blame to the other for having violated her innocent being. She will be incorrigibly offended by the other's ability to see through her fake innocence; and the fact that she quite non-innocently harbors hidden conditions for how one should approach her will be painfully made known. The latter flees into entangled freedom by deliberately regulating how events unfold, rather than trust herself to meet what arrives from out of the primordial attunement of openness. Neither loves freely.

The truly distinguished woman becomes capable of compassion by contending with her self-naivete rather than fixating on her naivete about others. Instead of protesting her innocence or defending its alleged loss, she faces the lessons of exposure in order to divest herself of naivete. For sympathy does not always benefit the other and there never is justification for the hardened refusal to receive another as an open, if limited, human being. The true woman wins through to stability of heart to receive what comes, whether what arrives is an act of transgression or not. She ceases to fear wounding and blows from life but instead meets what comes with the same, open graciousness that is ready to seek the humanizing possibility that latently avails itself within the nexus of forces that obtain. She no longer prefers sympathy above all else. She consents to be released into the situation in its full compass and wholly "at the ready" to discern the finite yet fitting expression of compassion it commands.

In this light, I wish to say that there is, sadly, a profound difference between first and second naivete in women. To the extent that a given woman does not come to terms with her first wholesale disappointment in life, she chooses willfully to give birth to second-order naivete about herself. The first wholesale disappointment for many young women is the first romantic relationship. A guy turns out to be a cad, so she protects herself with the strategic assumption that all men are cads. Meanwhile her hate grows, not her innocence, for she unjustly makes men the fodder for her hardening against life. Such a posture is a form of deliberate or willed naivete, for it persists in being naive about one's growing hate while trying to resolve the crisis of loss of naivete purely through others. This defensive posture aims to make me invulnerable to life, to being affected by others, to the pathos-filled reality that people move me. Ironically, by making me unaffected, such posturing renders me like the cad, deficiently human, immune to my own harmful denial of genuine response to others. Defensive hardening flees the true lesson, namely, that in order to preserve my own essential potentiality for being, I must learn how to bear being-thrown (exposure) and being-attuned (affected) freely. It takes pain to bear affect and give birth to genuine response. I must cultivate proper self-care if I am to impart it to the young. Choosing to persist in willed naivete makes me ethically culpable, for it inevitably leads me to pass on the objectionable female legacy of teaching children and others the wrong lessons in the "how-to" of bearing-with others. These are the lessons of stunted growth and hateful hardening. This is the solicitude of deprivation, the care that dampens youth's free spirit to greet life with open arms.

IMPARTING THE SHADOWY LEGACY OF IRRESOLUTE BEARING TO CHILDREN

There are, then, at least two key stumbling blocks to undergoing the radical change of heart necessary to become life-embracing. The first is loss of faith in possibility as possibility. To lose faith in loving openly because the first love did not work out is never merely a matter of the other; it is a matter of one's own mode of being-in-the-world. I sell off trust in my own possibility to become life-giving because I decide that I must build barriers against others—against men—as a form of self-protection. The second, related issue is pain. Failure to intensify trust in open presencing actually amasses false orders of pain by leaving pain unresolved. Allowing myself to sink into disappointment in life, in men, in parents, in people gives pain a cumulative effect that it need not have. This cumulative effect haunts my life as the shadow of not bearing well and makes me unbearable for others. Here I provide three portraits of the harmful effects that the shadow of willed naivete, with its hidden refusal of life, has on youth and children.

Frozenness and the Destruction of Youthfulness

Failure to resolve the fundamental conflict catalyzed by the transition out of naive being-in-the-world yields a split subjectivity: the ontological root of one's primal disposition is severed from the self I present to the world. This means that self-suppression is a modality of being that must be distinguished from the state of being-repressed in the psychological sense. Willed naivete, as a form of combating felt-lack of control over vulnerable openness, develops an aggravated pattern of self-suppression. It makes me non-innocent because it entails adopting manipulative or possessive control over the phenomenon of presencing. I control both what I present to the world and what remains hidden. A manipulative relation to self-presencing affects both the dimension of presencing and that of absencing. Insofar as I indulge self-suppression, I am unwilling to bear the world and to bear-with others with the fullness of my self.

Self-possession introduces a wedge between the primal level of being-attuned (which I protectively suppress) and the presentable level at which I allow myself to be affected. I split off the primordial, ontological level at which I comport myself toward life from the habituated and learned ways I "carry" the ontical worlds I inhabit. But such carriage is never full or true bearing. By all appearances, I could seem like the most bubbly of girls, yet secretly hidden away harbor a stubborn closure, a hardened anger at life. I might even convince myself I am this bubbly girl in order to remain naive about the hidden hardening, the ugliness festering beneath the surface. Still, at a fundamental, albeit suppressed level, I do not bear well. I cannot entirely escape the shadow of self-suppression. A dark cloud hangs over my existence. A primordial depression qualifies my bearing, a postadolescent acquisition that I keep safe as my cold comfort, for in a perverse way I can grow accustomed to such unhappy acquisitions and even derive a hidden glee from the fact that I give myself to life and to others in a gingerly, petty, and deliberately withholding manner.

To make a bedfellow of the pain that recalls my fundamental failure to rise up to life makes my primordial comportment altogether devoid of gracious generosity. Instead of modeling how to face and bear pain, I use the story of pain to legitimate utter lack of magnanimity. For in order to position myself as unwilling to undergo a radical change "of" heart, I must freeze growth at the level of personal transformation. I may adjust my behavior here and there in small ways, but never radically carry the day for others. Yet in order to freeze growth I must valorize my pain above that of others. The story of how life pained *me* forms the childish ditty, the security blanket I won't give up. A change "in" but not "of" disposition prepares me for the wrong battle, viz., to defend my hardness and inauthenticity. Anxiety over "being-exposed" gives way to the settled want of protecting my pain rather than being transformed by it. There is a qualitative difference between speaking of pain within a comportment that seeks to come to terms with it and one that makes of it a special and prized negative comfort. The truly special lies in how one bears pain and not in the ostensible uniqueness of the particular occasions that caused pain. All people suffer; many suffer terrible, terrible burdens. How one bears and not solely what one bears ultimately distinguishes one.

Self-suppression freezes open presencing and truthful engagement with all things. I am never justified in freezing my ownmost possibility for being. In so doing, I at best may impart to my child the complete absence of a model of true willing, engagement in life. At worst, I will impart hardening and the resentful model of prizing one's pain above that of others. I will thereby make the child's struggle in life all the more difficult than it could have been. Although many people do reasonably well at parenting without having truly resolved their pain, I still hold that lack of a genuine resolution to life as a form of suffering cannot impart to the child a model for how to live well. As a mother, I might learn quickly that I must keep my secret darkness, my loss of faith in self and others, firmly hidden from sight precisely because it can harm the child. But this order of hiddenness, because it is unnatural and lacks a genuine resolution to life as crisis, cannot fully succeed. In unexpected moments, events conjure forth this hidden anger and depressiveness into view. The child intuits it one way or another; exposure simply confirms its horrific intuition.

This suppressed and yet valorized relation to pain conjures a great fear in children and adolescents. I speak of the fear that they must sell off their youthful vibrancy and openness to the new in order to become a weighted-down, if not broken adult. It teaches the confusion that maturity entails having to become broken by life. But aging alone never makes me mature in the fundamental sense. For the adult, in this case the mother, who seeks to repeat the ditty of personal sorrow as a barrier to life remains immature; worse, she prepares herself for the wrong thing, namely, to be disappointed in all future people. After all, they, too, will eventually fail her! Cold comfort, indeed. A failed solution to being hurt yields defensive readiness for disappointment rather than for one's true potentiality for being. It prepares the child to find disappointment where none need be.

By contrast, a radical change "of" heart preserves youthfulness. It is an attunement that becomes constructively oriented like the child even with the eyes of the adult. One simply must get over the psychic tendency to feel stupid and ashamed because one appears naive by worldly standards when one chooses to preserve essential potentiality in oneself and hold out for it in others. That is what I call the primal ethical task, never to let people sell off their deepest humanizing choice without notice and because it can be so readily justified by all ordinary standards. One can do many right things even where one fervently refuses ever to become open and vulnerable. How sad for all humanity this reality is. How we need the children to remind us that this never suffices, for the child gets something right, namely, vulnerability. The task of becoming life-embracing is that of preserving the elasticity and creative adaptability to what arises that are the hallmarks of youth. It is to gain youthfulness as an essential and no longer merely developmental trait. Youthful willingness to meet whatever may arise, the feared, the not feared, the good, the bad is what I am calling the capacity to be a source of life for the child. We should be painfully leery of teaching children to abandon their open willingness to venture forth in life.

Sleep and the Maternal Seduction to False Embrace

A woman's desire to stay in a sleeping relation to existence, like the lovely Sleeping Beauty, overburdens child and youth. To live in a sleeping mode means that I refuse to be made transparent to myself by the events that arise, even by innocent questions or actions that a child or friend might pose. But sleep is death of the wrong order. It engenders an unbearable passivity, a sinking that none can cure, save oneself. It creates a zone that cannot be touched, addressed, called out, made intelligible. It withholds unnaturally and thus engenders unnecessary anxiety, exaggerated fears, and excessively cautionary behavior on the part of the child who seeks to avoid provoking a volatile response from out of this dark zone of hiddenness. None likes to see that at heart she is culpable simply because she is unwilling. So hard is it for us to accept this truth that we constantly rationalize sinking into the vortex of negativity and blame life, time's passage, the world for how we are. Yet at root, any failure to receive the child openly with one's whole being, even though one may have to deny the child what it demands, establishes a dynamic of reactive fear and frustration. The child will forever manipulate for what it demands as the means to be received, embraced ontologically at root. In becoming habituated in this struggle for the maternal embrace, the child will misapprehend itself. It will confuse how with what, the object of demand with the fact that it cannot bear the mother's hidden hardness. Clearly, such confusion will later infect its approach to love and its disposition toward women, for its desperation for a free reception may grow pronounced, even to the point of seeking it by force.

This is why I earlier remarked that we can at best give a qualified yes and no to the question whether women by nature are lifegiving. To the extent that women, indeed all humans, do not battle to win the most primordial form of open attunement, they cannot receive people freely let alone impart a life- and people-embracing disposition to children. To the contrary, there is a specifically female form of plunging into the abyss of negativity. The bonds of early social attunement, when not tempered by the mother's weaning herself of false dependency upon the child as a substitute for her inability to engender in herself a life-embracing primordial disposition, will burden the child with felt-responsibility for her unhappiness. In extreme cases, the mother will lull the child into a death-like vortex of negative bonding that isolates it from life and rich relations with others. In its desperation for free, open reception, it will plunge into achieving this maternal connection at any price.

So many women exhibit pronounced anxiety before felt- loss of connection, even where such loss is essential to the realization of a genuinely richer possibility in relationship. This threat is symptomatic of a refusal to realize open embrace in the fundamental ontological sense. Open embrace is more primordial than the question whether one must bear a time of separation or a time of togetherness. It determines both how I bear-with another when together and how I bear-with another during times apart. Open reception imbues times of togetherness with an unfettered and nonpossessive differentiation necessary to sustain genuine intimacy. It suffers no fear of losing the other to freedom. Women have a tendency to valorize life and connection over death and separation. Yet the very notion that one can separate death from life proves illusory. No person, not least the mother, can escape the role that death claims in giving birth to authentic meeting. Death is an integral part of intimacy, for in intimacy the other is always departing to him or herself, even as he or she comes toward me. Many women truly undergo loss of an immediate sense of connection as the most horrific abyss. Yet terror before loss of immediate connection (fusion) overwhelms me only where I have not learned to bear the pain that enables intimacy. I mean the pain of that imbues being-with-the-other with the quality of free release, the pain of abiding the tension inherent in a coming-toward that is also a departing. We do not own others any more than we can possess self-presencing. Meeting another well requires that I die to want of forcing an immediate and total connection to the other at the expense of genuine intimacy.

To die existentially means many things. These include that I must divest myself of burdening others with responsibility for my well-being in life journey. My well-being when apart and my well-being when together. For failure to disburden others inevitably means that death operates as the shadow of my inauthentic existence. Just when my child needs to cut the umbilical cord, I won't be able to assist him to drop disbelief in his potentiality. The mother who cannot bear death as an integral part of life cannot wean. She is hopelessly unprepared to release the child to what life bids him or her face. Out of anxiety over loss of connection, I can, as a mother, indulge the selfish vortex of sympathy carried to the point of imparting paralysis to my child. I can indulge a long two-hour phone conversation with my son about how horrible it is that others treat him so badly and how only I understand his travail. What, then, do I teach? Instead of giving him over to his sense of potentiality, I seduce him into fitful moodiness and the cold comforts of negative complaint. And I impart a dangerous model of false love. For I prize his bonding with me over his need to be turned upon freedom to venture his potentiality for being. I teach the false lesson that love is antithetical to freedom rather than rooted in it. I teach that he and I have an intimacy so special that it cannot be found anywhere else in life. I lull my boy into a deep sleep with me by calling him to prize the feeling of connection over genuine intimacy. True intimacy involves rather than denies risk. It takes great pathos. For there are times when sympathy cannot afford complicity in the child's anxious flight from risk. And I, myself, must be willing to impart this lesson to youth, on pain of bearing alone. I myself must be a living model of this truth.

Deficient Solicitude and the Clash of Wills

Earlier I said that I consider willingness an ontological precondition of ethical action. First, it denotes operating awarely and with full consent to one's vulnerable presencing within and reception of what happens. Such nonprejudicial readiness to engage the full field is the ground of ethical action. For openness is the sole basis out of which I can receive others freshly available to what might be new in them now, no matter their past transgressions. Second, it is the sole disposition out of which I avail myself the discovery of the fitting action in the moment. Willingness entails setting one's sights on the preservation of potentiality as potentiality. This perspective alone wins free from the narrow-sightedness of having a planned agenda, a hardened willfulness to press through an agenda and outcome.

When hardened, my bearings are off the mark and my solicitude proves deficient. The colloquial expression "I lose sight" does not mean that my sights are not set. It means, rather, that I fail to set my sights on preserving each in her or his open potentiality for being. I prize what over how, a calculable outcome over the matter of how the other bears its situation. I want to say that, in the parent-child relation, narrow-sightedness means that I lapse into a distinct failure to assist the child in learning how to care for itself as a free, potentiality for being. There are many, many reasons why one understandably might lose sight of the essential, the most obvious being anxious fixation on the particularities of an actual circumstance. Nevertheless, I believe that loss of proper sighting entails closing off to being affected by the rich, latent possibilities in the finite circumstance for the child or any person to find a way to be true and open. Simply put, to be without heart means that I am not willing to venture an outcome that exceeds my forced personal agenda to have my way. This narrow, one-sided aim, is an inevitable outcome of closing off to being-disclosed transparently to myself. It involves loss of trust in the possibility that a judicious outcome might assume a different shape than the preconceived goal I have in mind. Or, in the case of a child, it entails the denial that his or her venture might have import over and beyond all that I anxiously resist and fear.

The task of the parent to help the child preserve its potentiality as potentiality is no merely formal affair. Holding open its own potentially is no abstraction, but rather the fundamental comportment and perspective out of which a budding youth:

1. can learn what is trustworthy in him or herself;
2. can venture life with the clear sense that he or she can fall back upon the virtue of open attunement, however else his or her actions might prove inadequate; and
3. can cultivate fundamental, ethical reception of others.

The purely constructive, complete willingness to give of oneself, to seek something true, just, and fitting is the trustworthy in each of us.

Much in even the child's motivational life is not trustworthy. Learned habits can always be questioned. Yet even with its undifferentiated awareness, a child can gain a beginning sense that its native presencing as open reception is the only trusted mode in which to go forth. To fortify an awareness of venturing forth in openness is perhaps the one crucial way parents can prepare the child for all that lies outside their control. Openness does not guarantee that one does not make mistakes in action. But it does mean that one goes forth without prejudice, wholly willing to meet what arises and with complete readiness to give oneself over with concern to find a fitting way for all parties involved. To eliminate this basic level of culpability in one's bearing is not simply to live life truly but to enter the situation without calculated withholding or reserve. The nature of the true engagement cannot be predicted in advance. It centers not on having one's agenda fulfilled but rather on finding a way that holds open the potential as that which avails each of the possibility to choose openness in how he or she bears-with others. Whatever else the situation demands in terms of what must be done, people cannot afford ultimately to ignore the fact that every situation contains within it this ultimate possibility, not as a future eventuality but as a present possibility.

Failure to renounce hardening leads me to enforce my personal agenda out of anxiety and fear. It establishes a contest of wills between me, the parent, and the child at the expense of teaching the child to attend first and always to its primordial willingness to venture. By valuing personal conflict above essential possibility, this clash of wills threatens to occlude the child's basic attunement even to itself. It is hard for parents to entrust children to the venture. Yet being distracted into a conflict of wills may be a surefire way to catalyze reaction behaviors in the child that ill-prepare it for the venture. Assisting youth to venture well is thus a mode of being-with that differs from imparting absolute resistance to and anxious fear of venture proper. The latter engenders either overanxious regard or undue disregard for the dangers of venture because it teaches the child or youth that you, the parent, distrust its fundamental willingness. It infects youth with disbelief at the primordial level.

This returns me briefly to the effect that a mother's refusal of a radical change of heart can have on her interaction with a child's exercise of choice. A change in attitude can be expressed as tolerance. On that basis, the mother can allow a child to do something with which she wholly disagrees. Nevertheless, such tolerance does not deliver a primordial change of her modality of being but stays within a preexisting disposition. It does not free her fundamentally to carry the decision all the way through. Short of winning through to authenticity, a finite disposition may allow a range of flexibility toward what happens, yet this range will always be bound by a hidden, outer limit that will sneak up unexpectedly. Typically, we claim that one hardens or breaks at that limit. But what is most typical is that a latent hardening against an unwanted possibility merely makes itself manifest at the point that one feels one can bear the decision no more.

There is, then, a difference between radically squaring off with finitude at the moment of decision and merely negotiating the space between oneself as parent and one's lack of control over the child. A compromise of wills never in itself frees one radically from the inherent clash of wills, but only suppresses and modifies the expression of that entangled clash. A radical change of disposition is the ultimate compass requisite to fare well in relation to finitude in all its facets: the finitude of one's decision, the finitude of the child, and the finitude of the situation. Radical acceptance of finitude involves knowing one cannot predict all outcomes and overcoming the felt-need to root one's decision in being able to predict and ward off unwanted outcomes. By contrast, an act of unwilling tolerance carries within it the danger that a negative pull from the past, a backlash effect, will violently emerge when the choice exercised by the child does not pan out in a positive sense. Truthfully, it can emerge even where a positive outcome prevails. The shadow of unresolved resistance to the child's choice can reveal itself in numerous ways: as an "I told you so," as resentment, as falsely burdening the child with guilt, or as the incessant need to edit and criticize the child's course of action as it evolves. All such forms of incessant nagging and harsh judgment are symptomatic of the mother's not having become divested in a radical way of anxious concern at the moment of decision.

We cannot get around anxiety before death. Failure to undergo complete death to the clash of wills pulls mother and child into an unbearable and ultimately meaningless battle, for no one wins. Neither does the mother find loving reception nor does the child win free of hate. Not so ironically, the mother's willful rejection of life venture establishes confusion of will in the child as well as the felt-need to protect itself from those who claim to love it by becoming itself willful. And the clash winds up protecting none from risk. For it teaches the child not how to risk well but rather that it is unable to risk, may as well give up, and return to the mother's false and deathlike escape from venture.

LIFE AND LOVE BEGIN BEYOND HARDENING

Life need not be feared, neither as venture nor insofar as it delivers the stimuli to awaken and grow in love. Life is not like a merciless father who sends jolts of death and loss for cruel pleasure. Life is not the false allure of a mad mother who lulls one to sleep in an endless deathlike slumber forever and ever. Awakening through jolts of exposure to the possibility of receptive open bearing promises love. Love begins beyond hardening. I believe there is a decisive link between bearing life well and loving well. Primordial active receptivity to life is the font out of which unconditional modes of being-with arise. That is why we must not harden in and against life but instead bear-with all people, things, and events completely willingly. Mutual growth depends upon such bearing. To give reception freely without condition avails the other of the possibility of bearing with greater ease and without misunderstanding whatever difficulty the situation might hold. For it is far easier to accept, you and I, that we must depart where you do not absolutely reject me, nor I you, by violating the fundamentally open nature of being-with. And far easier, too, is it not to draw the mistaken conclusion that my mother has no faith in me, although she denies me a desire, when she receives me without anxious hardening. Unless we impart this basic ontological openness to children, I believe we do not prepare them for freedom and love, for proper care of self and others. Instead we perpetuate that horrid cycle of defensive valorization of my pain against your pain that leads people to harden and refuse to bear-with one another primordially, however much they persist in limping alongside one another even for a lifetime.

NOTES

1. I follow John Macquarrie and Edward Robinson's translation of *Sein und Zeit*, *Being and Time* (San Francisco: Harper and Row, 1962). Hereafter cited as BT.

2. The claim that breaking with, hardening against, and closing off to another are deficient modes of *Mitsein* holds double significance (BT, 124). Thematically understood, it has ethically neutral meaning; it simply points to the reality that "Dasein is essentially Being-with" (BT, 120). Breaking with another would then be a mode of Being-with. Nevertheless, whenever I bear-with or refuse to bear-with in a hardened manner, I tacitly reject the other from the human race. My act of closing off rejects that person's very existence at an ontological level, insofar as that existence calls me out to receive him or her as Dasein.

3. Heidegger's discussions of "bewildered making-present" and "bewildered awaiting" suggest as much (BT, 342).

4. I intend no disregard for men. Like women, men also face a fierce battle in order to become a source of life to others. While addressed to women, this analysis could, strictly speaking apply to any person, for, as Heidegger held, there is a crucial gender neutrality in human existence even though each exists factically as sexed. Men and women alike are fully defined by the same, basic structures of being-there. Nevertheless, I believe we still need to undertake a phenomenology of our sexed modalities of everyday and inauthentic being-in-the-world in the way Heidegger's philosophy promises, viz., not merely as acquired habitus but as flight from anxiety. Yet even where we can note how women might tend to identify with certain poles of being-there (life,

connection, the past) in distinction from men (death, individuation, the future), a dualistic view of such native tendencies would prove misguided. I believe dualism is Irigaray's mistake; and I believe the immediate and anxiety-driven preferences of each sex impede living out of the full possibilities of Dasein for authentic forms of *Mitsein*. Thus, I fully agree with Heidegger when he says, "If each Dasein, which is factically in each case male or female, were not essentially with-one-another, then the sexual relation as something human would be absolutely impossible" (*Introduction to Philosophy*, forthcoming translation by Eric Sean Nelson and Virginia Lyle Jennings; *Einleitung in die Philosophie* (1928–29), GA 27 [Frankfurt am Main: Vittorio Klostermann, 1996], 146–47). Heidegger also mentions the sex and gender neutrality of Dasein in his Marburg lecture, *Metaphysiche Anfangsgründe der Logik im Ausgang von Leibniz*, GA 26 (Frankfurt am Main: Vittorio Klostermann, 1978), 171–75. Cf. *The Metaphysical Foundations of Logic*, trans. Michael Heim (Bloomington: Indiana University Press, 1984), 136–39. For a discussion of the few but various places where Heidegger mentions *Geschlecht*, see Jacques Derrida, "Geschlecht: Sexual Difference, Ontological Difference," *Research in Phenomenology* 13 (1983): 65–83. See also, his "*Geschlecht* II: Heidegger's Hand," trans. John P. Leavey Jr., *Deconstruction and Philosophy: The Texts of Jacques Derrida*, ed. John Sallis (Chicago: University of Chicago Press, 1987), 161–96; and "Heidegger's Ear: Philopolemology (*Geschlecht* IV)," trans. John P. Leavey, Jr., *Reading Heidegger: Commemorations*, ed. John Sallis (Bloomington: Indiana University Press, 1993), 163–218.

5. Despite the fact that Heidegger calls Being-alone "a deficient mode of Being-with" (BT, 120–21), his full analysis of authenticity places a radical and total burden upon the individual to become entirely responsible for the quality of his or her attunement toward life passage. While Being-alone, in the sense of not being with others, does not dissolve the ontological structure of human existence as *Mitsein*; nevertheless, how I bear-with others hinges dramatically, in my view, on whether I am willing to bear up under what occurs alone; that is, for my part all by myself or independently of how badly others behave. I would reserve the term *alone* to signal authentic bearing whether with another or not.

6. There is a question whether willingness can be called an attunement proper or that which prepares one to stay with, bear up under, and hold into a primal attunement (anxiety, boredom) until primordial disclosure is granted. I assume it to be both essentially preparatory and formative of a new unique capacity to avail oneself of meaningful existence. As preparatory, willingness enables one to meet any attunement, for example, sorrow, in such a way that it can deliver one to an essential disclosure about existence. If, in the face of sorrow, one collapses into a sentimental, emotional attachment to personal pain, then one allows sorrow to devolve into mere sentiment and thereby deprives pain of its function to attune one to a full and essential disclosure that exceeds one's particular life set-up. Typically, we are not prepared to bear with and be carried through the full movement of a primal attunement. We are impatient to ascribe rather than receive meaning. But this impatience fails

to realize that the personal significance one can give to pain is horridly limited to one's finite narrative of life. Worse, it traps one in that narrative with no essential and richly universal meaning to be found. Essential meaning can never be manufactured out of the limited repertoire of my psyche's bitter complaint about who did what to me and all the bad things that happened to me in life. If I fail to allow pain its basic potential to reveal something meaningful that exceeds my personal narrative, then I deprive myself of that which could free me up to bear the circumstance with an eye toward ultimate growth for me and all involved. My point here is that this willingness denotes a unique disposition in that it prepares me to bear well all the unanticipated ways I may be affected by a circumstance (anxiously, sorrowfully, boringly). Yet cultivating such willingness enables me to grow a specific life-embracing strength that may be properly called a primordial attunement.

7. The idea that there is an enduring form of joy is of Kierkegaardian vintage. See his *Christian Discourses: Kierkegaard's Writings, Vol. 17,* trans. Howard and Edna Hong (Princeton: Princeton University Press, 1997). Some of what I say anticipates turns in Heidegger's thinking that come later. William McNeill's recent presentation to the Heidegger conference (New Orleans, 2004) shows that what I name enduring joy, Heidegger calls festivity in *Hölderlins Hymne "Andenken"* GA 52, ed. Curd Ochwadt. (Frankfurt am Main: Vittorio Klostermann, 1982). Heidegger's reflections on pain in "Die Sprache," his 1950 discussion of Trakl's "Ein Winterabend" (Unterwegs zur Sprache [Pfullingen: Günther Neske, 1965]) also form the backdrop for my thoughts on pain in human relations. There he discusses pain as the rift that separates and joins world and thing to one another. So thought, pain is not subjective but instead the between, the dimension that allows intimacy by letting things to "bear world" and world to "grant things" (*Poetry, Language, Thought*, trans. Albert Hofstadter [New York: Harper and Row, 1971]: 202; US 24). We have yet to think of bitter complaint, incessant nagging, and collapse into negativity as debased forms of lamentation in woman's tonal bearing that reflect unwillingness to cease coveting subjective pain and turn it upon the Open.

8. Those of us who have dated artists who are attached to their emotional lives know well this distorted phenomenon: Today my artist lover feels emotionally divorced from life, so s/he says s/he does not love me; tomorrow s/he feels connected, so s/he loves me.

9. This question of opening and closing instinctively or emotively calls for exploration in relation to sex difference. Although any person can be given over to fitful moodiness, many women enjoy a primary identification with the "feminine" energy of opening and closing. If "stimulus," here understood as penetration by a person or environment, has masculine connotations, then "being opened and closed" under stimulus has typically been associated with feminine responsiveness. Part of the struggle for authenticity that women face entails distinguishing between the genuine spontaneous presencing afforded by primordial openness and the mistaken belief that how a person, in particular a man, comports himself toward a woman determines whether she closes

or opens. The latter, instinctive or habituated response is not true spontaneity, for it has not won the freedom to be open, even where transgression may arise. Transgression does penetrate one's being, male or female. Still, it is not necessary to harden in order to meet transgression firmly. The ethical implications of this issue pertain to men and women alike. It might simply be the case that women give us a look into a problem that plagues Dasein.

10. Ontologically understood, the possibility of undergoing the change from inauthenticity to authenticity marks the fundamental basis out of which any "change"—in or of—can arise (cf. BT, 259). The transcendental method of *Being and Time* has its formal character in that it delineates conditions for the possible intelligibility of beings and how Dasein can theorize that intelligibility on the basis of authenticity. Although the theoretical aim of *Being and Time* does not include developing a rich existential philosophy, I nevertheless hold that rich existential implications can be found therein. Fundamental ontology, so understood, not only delineates formal conditions for the possibility of developmental growth but also thematizes how it is possible to undergo a modal qualification of being-in-the-world that radically transforms one's comportment and understanding (how one sets one's sights and avails oneself of disclosure).

11. For example, it is harder to love once someone transgresses against me. Nevertheless, facing the task of intensifying one's pathos enables one to come alive in life. The stakes are supposed to grow intense. Each time that a new intensity of burden (of knowledge or ultimate insight) is placed upon me by life, a new crisis ensues and yet greater intensity required in winning through to authenticity. In this discussion, I gloss over the vital issue of trust because I wish to focus on hardening. The vital issue centers on the discovery that Being dissembles or has an aletheiac form. Awakening to naivete about a person or the world catapults one into awareness that Being lacks a stable and fixed ground, and refuses to be grasped in an easy, final transparency. Much could be said about how this discovery cuts short the youthful, heroic dream to get truth once and for all time. This awakening—which can be refused if I fixate solely on people and historical events—begins to draw me into both the possibility of authentic existence and the journey into ever greater horizons of depth perception. By making me aware of absentiality, it avails me authentic choice. But it also confronts me with the factical reality that the outer aspects of a being's presencing are no necessary sign of either its truth or falsity. *Aletheia* thus requires that I learn to differentiate operatively, and not by prejudging characteristics of a thing as if it is fixedly present, between disingenuous and genuine forms of withholding (absentiality) as intrinsic to a being's mode of presencing. All the basis crises of trust are built into the aletheiac structure of Being. Trust has an ontological and not solely psychological root. How can a child be weaned of dependency upon parents and grown into the freedom to trust that Being's withholding is no ill-conceived trick designed solely to inflict pain? How can I apprehend when another person's withholding is essential to my own growth and not a strategy for duping me? How can I learn that my own self-presencing cannot be willfully

manipulated but must be freely trusted? I do not advance a rich exploration of these basic matters of trust, let alone develop the kind of parental maieutics they demand. Yet I do suggest that unwillingness to trust Being, here thought as life, impacts adversely my capacity to parent. Heidegger's comments in *Being and Time* on semblance and seeming (BT, 29) and on untruth (BT, 222, 256, 298) merit much thought in this regard, as does his later, more sustained exploration of errancy. in *Parmenides*, GA 54 (Frankfurt am Main: Vittorio Klostermann, 1992 (English trans. André Schuwer and Richard Rojcewicz [Bloomington: Indiana University Press, 1992]). Because I do not develop a model of child rearing, I do not address explicitly Heidegger's eminently suggestive comments on leaping in and leaping ahead as improper and proper modes of solicitude (BT, 122–23).

12. Multiple issues call for exploration here. Some mothers are available only on the surface immediacy of being, but withhold their true presencing from the child. I will speak to this shortly. Yet it is also a widespread phenomenon, among mothers and fathers alike, that the child's vulnerable presencing stimulates the parent's openness. My concern is that, even in the latter case, vulnerable openness to the child arises out of dependency upon external stimulus, at least in some measure. For this reason, it is no necessary signal that a constancy in ontological willingness to meet hardship with the child, and not simply the gentle times, has been cultivated.

13. These comments invite discussion of the different attitudes among those women, such as supermodels, who enjoy a decided love affair with being denuded by the camera and those who shy away from and bolt in the face of the possibility of existential (rather than physical) denuding.

14. Note, however, that "feeling-exposed" as a random mood is not the same thing as being-exposed. One can feel violently exposed even where no violent exposure has occurred. This discussion begs us to think of kinesis, the dynamical nature of being thrown and attuned, as something we must grow capable of bearing in its full sway in order that it can free us. Aborted movement, always aborted through mortal will, deprives us of growth in understanding and necessarily yields erratic, volatile, and destructive outcomes.

15. The same comments hold for deciding to stay with the beloved without bemoaning and exacting a price for the decision.

15

Re:Thinking Facticity

GREGORY SCHUFREIDER

Facticity may well be the hardest thing for thinking to hold on to; perhaps, because it is, in some cases, quite literally hard—like a book in the hands of a reader. In fact, while "the book" will eventually make Heidegger's short list of "things," the question immediately arises: Can facticity be contained in a book; especially in what remains of it at its presumed end, after the age of the text? Can we be confronted with facticity in a text or must we be struck (perhaps, dumb) by the brute fact of the book itself, as if it (and not the text) might hit us over the head and strike us senseless in our thinking?

To be more specific: Is *this* book (or any book) bound to undermine facticity in the very act of reading? Is its "poetic" operation a (sure) sign of transcendence—of "Being" or "the Text"—or can a book underline facticity, and not simply by highlighting the word but by concretely outlining the end of language itself? Or does "literature" create an endless problem for facticity, and precisely because it confounds or at least compounds the modern distinction between fact and fiction, leaving us, at best, with a choice between fiction and nonfiction? In short, is a "writing" that takes its standard from fiction bound to virtualize facticity: to "fictionalize" it in a modern literacy that assumes the form of the text/book? And, if so, what about Heidegger's own, presumably, nonfiction work, which claims to face the ultimate end (of facticity) in a book called *Being and Time*, designed to mark the demise of the modern subject through a reading of the death of Dasein that occurs in a text without a proper ending?

THE OPENING (OF THE BOOK)

> I would rather die a natural death than be prepared for it at the university . . .
>
> —Vincent van Gogh

We know that Heidegger, even before the writing of *Being and Time*, would like to think that he is thinking in terms of facticity: in a thinking that is founded on its factical situation and acts in the face of it. In his university lecture courses of the early '20s, he sites the hermeneutical situation of his own thinking as the university itself; including in the class entitled *Ontology: The Hermeneutics of Facticity*, in which the above quotation from van Gogh is cited Admittedly, at this point Heidegger's thought is insufficiently historical, factically speaking. While he will be thinking in terms of instrumentality and of the concrete thinking (in action) that is required in "factical life," he does not think in terms of the textual apparatus of the modern book or of the material role that it played in the development of the university—let alone of the transformation in the nature of reading that took place in the historic movement of the center(s) of learning from the monastery to the university. Nor, for that matter, does he trace the creation of the very discipline of hermeneutics to the need to control the proliferation of interpretations of the text (namely, the "Bible") as a result of its distribution in the book, thanks to the printing press. And while we will not presume to be in a position to show how these historical "facts" determined the character of modern existence, we would like to address the question of facticity with respect to the book at the historic point at which we are told that the age of the book has come to an end, presumably, at the beginning of the text. For the book may well mark the facticity of the text itself, and the point at which reading has come to a close, if only in the corner of a dog-eared page.

In that case, we would have to think, not just in terms of the hermeneutics of facticity but of the facticity of hermeneutics, and of the ergonomics of an understanding that turns the opening of the book into a historical breach: a concrete opening to freedom that is created through a new apparatus of thinking. This is not just a matter of university professors tracing their own history back to Greek philosophy, let alone through the late Middle Ages and the movement of Scholasticism (when the discipline of ontology first received its proper name) or to the system of modern education created by a Humanism that thinks through the book.[1] Nor is the thought of a textual instruction designed to reduce thinking to a matter of "writing." Instead, it is a question of reading and of a freedom that is bound to the book—including in the historical assignment of a textbook named *Sein und Zeit*, which, as a matter of fact, had to be published in an incomplete form when its author wanted to keep his job at the university.

But what kind of a book is *Being and Time* and how is it to be read; especially now, in our time, when we need to deal not only with the transition from a monastic to a scholastic reading but are, perhaps, still reeling from the movement of a modern to a postmodern thinking? Are we "reading for revelations" or for "information," and is a book to be "studied for action" or is it a text that is to be read for the sheer "pleasure of reading"?[2] Put in its own terms, are we to read *Sein und Zeit* as a theoretical work or as an existential manual: a "how-to" book in the field of phenomenological ontology, as a set of instructions (which are, presumably, to be followed) on how to become an authentic ontologist?

We do not have the time to attend to the details of the fundamental ontology of Dasein that is said to precede all other ontological thinking insofar as it is bound to the facticity of the questioner, originally raising the question of (its own) being not only in the concrete setting of a practical life but in a specific historical situation. Instead, we would like to leap to the end of the story, keeping in mind that the original talk of facticity is designed to bind thinking to action; in our case, to a sign of the end of ontology in Heidegger's *corpus* that marks the facticity of Dasein in a historic reading of (its) "being" in a time of nihilism. To interpret this sign of the times in an age of literacy, we would have to outline our own facticity in a hermeneutics that is bound to the opening of the book as a historical act of thinking; in point of fact, to a book that (like *Being and Time*) is designed to free us to act. Clearly, a certain type of freedom is contained in the printed book, a freedom that is created through the type; although not altogether unlike the freedom that is captured in the frame of modern painting. In fact, what we would write as the text/book marks the design of a framework of freedom that can be traced through the topology of the space of painting, including in the material structure of the picture/frame.

The documentation of this modern framework would require us to view the book as a revolutionary institution: in terms of a freedom that is, quite literally, created out of print; even if it would demand the analysis of a Dasein that put its life on the line in an act of signing.[3] Let us just say that, in Heidegger's case, in an academic setting organized around theory and, as such, having lost sight (or hold) of concrete existence as it is actually lived, the appeal of and to death is designed to bring thinking back to life. Of course, as a textbook, *Sein und Zeit* is bound to "theorize" death: to make (a certain) sense of it by turning the brute fact into a "being-toward-death" which with we can live. As such, its script of selfhood effectively neutralizes the brutality of death, fictionalizing the fact by turning it into a histrionic act. In this respect, we might say that Heidegger does not take death seriously (enough); in part, because he takes it personally and, in part, because there is a body buried in *Being and Time* that would need to be exhumed. In any case, the book is able to bind facticity to a virtual death in the text, which involves a kind of double ending. For the ultimate (in) facticity is the end of Dasein, which brings facticity itself to an end. To resolve this double bind, the text must project a fictional end in which Dasein stands alone, "before" death and without a friend.

If a textual thinking is bound to fictionalize facticity, perhaps, this is why philosophy must appeal to a preliterate thinker, historically speaking, to characterize the fact of death; to a preacademic philosopher who, according to Heidegger (and others), stands at the brink of a thinking that has not yet entered into "literature" (let alone "theory") but is factically designed by one who defines himself in the act of dying.[4] To put it in writing, "Socrates" becomes the proper name of the one who dies in fact and not just in fiction: whose death is an act of thinking; in fact, a political act. This is to say that "the purest thinker in the West" finds a way to turn the fact of death into a free act before others, so as to secure a thinking that acts in the face of the facticity of a freedom that is bound to death and freed by it.

As if in the name of the one "who does not write," we are looking for a sign in the text that is directly connected to death; a mark of the fact that Dasein is inevitably engaged in "The Art of Dying," to appeal to the title of a late medieval blockbook. The *Ars moriendi* was a bestseller in the fifteenth century, not only because it addresses a topic in which everyone has an interest but because its xylographic printing was designed to accommodate the literate and the illiterate alike—a book whose lesson is clear: there is no cure for death; in which case, we all need a friend in the end.

THE F/ACT (OF FREEDOM)

> If it is not possible here to attempt to go further in this determination of the political, we will at least posit that the political does not primarily consist in the composition and dynamics of power

> (with which it has been identified in the modern age to the point of slipping into a pure mechanics of power that would be alien even to power as such, or to the point of a "political technology," according to Foucault's expression) but in the opening of a space. This space is opened by freedom—initial, inaugural, arising—and freedom there presents itself in action. Freedom does not come to produce anything, but only comes to produce itself there (it is not *poiesis*, but *praxis*), in the sense that an actor, in order to be the actor he is, produces himself on stage. Freedom (equality, fraternity, justice) thus produces itself as existence in accordance with relation. The opening of this scene (and the dis-tension of this relation) supposes a breaking open, a strike, a decision: it is also as the political that freedom *is* the leap. It supposes the strike, the cut, the decision, and the leap onto the scene (but the leap itself is what opens the scene) of that which cannot be received from elsewhere or reproduced from any model, since it is always beginning, "each time."
>
> A politics—if it is one—of initial freedom would be a politics putting freedom at the surface of beginning, of allowing to arise, in the sense of allowing to be realized—since it is realized in arising and in its breaking open—*what cannot be finished*. Like sharing, freedom cannot be finished.[5]

If it is true that, in Modernism, the walls of the monastery were turned inside out—especially, we would insist, of the *scriptorium*—then a more than radical hermeneutics would turn on a revolutionary reading that turns the book itself around, topologically speaking: not simply returning to the roots of the text but to a hole in the ground, like a grave in the page, through which the book may be opened from the inside out. Such an opening would mark a type of decision that puts freedom right *there*, if not on the line then on the surface of the page. This is not necessarily achieved by delving more deeply into the text; especially if, in the end, a book is designed to describe a freedom that cannot be contained within it. No doubt, it may help to attend to the history of writing if we are to appreciate how the distribution of the text through printing creates a sense (including of "freedom") that is out of control in the modern world, thanks to a book that it is no longer chained to the rostrum but is free to circulate in a pseudoanonymous community. This is not the collectivity that Heidegger grammatically dubs "*das Man*," since it not a question of an unsigned social contract. Instead, it involves a community of readers marking the advent of a collective sense in a modern literature that is a literal binding of letters; indeed, a virtual Republic of Letters, which attempts a liberation through literacy that would put us all in an alphabetical order.

To mark the fact of a freedom that is bound to death as well as to the book, we would have to turn to another page in Heidegger's thinking; to a passage that describes the free space of a breach in the text, designed as the marker of a hole in the ground of "being": a concrete opening, marked with an ×. In so doing, we would like to begin our own commonplace book, as if to create a book of "quotable quotes" by taking his × utterly out of context. As we know, it was a standard practice of modern reading to extract a striking passage from a text and enter it into a notebook, so as to gather citations from one's favorite authors to create a book of one's own, "lifted" from the work of others.[6] Of course, as a result of such commonplacing, we run the risk of turning those extraordinary passages into commonplaces. And there is just such a striking passage in Heidegger's *corpus*—the most striking in all of his work, I would say—which has, as a matter of fact, become a commonplace, at least of deconstruction.

I am thinking of the passage in *Zur Seinsfrage* that strikes "being" itself from the text: writes it as "being."[7] This citation is harder to make out, more difficult to extract from the text, not only because we are beginning at the end (of ontology) but because it is marked with an ×. This is not the alphabetic X (although it has been compared to the Greek χ); nor, for that matter, the Roman numeral. Instead, it is an act that raises the question of reading: literally raises it off the page in the creation of a three-dimensional sign or de-sign, through which Heidegger makes his mark, not just in but on the text: with the signature mark of *Sein*.

At the same time, the × is inclined (if not designed) to lose its meaning in its extraction from the (con)text, and all the more so if we attempt to think it without "being," that is, to free the × from Heidegger's text. It is not altogether clear how to extract a deletion without it simply disappearing—especially one that is designed to turn being itself into nothing. Of course, if *Zur Seinsfrage* is also assigned the task of addressing the question of the relation between "Dasein" and "*Sein*," then we are, presumably, free to read the act of the × back into the text of *Being and Time* (as if these two lines of thought form the bookends of Heidegger's ontology), as a redesigning of the "being" of Dasein. In that event, it might well be taken as the sign of a "Dasein" that is marked for deletion: bound to a vanishing point as the ultimate fact(icity) of its own being, in a death, however, that binds it to others insofar as the × creates the common place of an open space where a community of "mortals" is bound to the *Geviert*.

While the most well-known account of "~~*Sein*~~" quite literally underreads it, as a reading (of being) "under (*sous*) erasure," it not only overlooks the fact that the X is a sign of Heidegger's Fourfold (of earth, sky, divinities and mortals) but that it is signed as a nihilating act: as a literal auto-graph of nothing in the text, designed to mark the end of ontology in the nihilation of writing.[8] No doubt, the X is a commonplace for writers, as an editorial sign marking the withdrawal of words. In this case, however, it operates as a polygraphic de-sign that marks the historical opening of a free space through a crossing of the line: as if the X marks a "spot" that is more than an ink blot, let alone an accidental spill.[9] As an autograph of nothing, signed by the hand of Dasein, it is not only a mark of the deletion of a word but a sign of death that puts Dasein on the spot; or, to be precise: on the map of a topology of ~~being~~. For we must insist that in a topographical reading (for action), the critical point is the one that is often marked with an X, as a formal indication that "You Are Here (X)"; or, more simply put, that: You ~~Are~~ Here.

To mark this open space as a concrete place, we would like to connect what Nancy calls an "initial" freedom to an act that comes before the word in a double stroke of genius on Heidegger's part: a mark that comes before "being" as what comes after it in the signing of the X over (*über*) it. This topotypographical sign defines a "sharing" that is depicted by a literal doublecrossing of the line; in fact, in a kind of double reading. If we are on the lookout for a type of decision ("the strike," "the cut," "the leap") that puts freedom on the line (and, in fact, in that order), literally "places" it on the surface of the page, then we would have to treat the graphic de-sign of ~~*Sein*~~ as a mark of the facticity of Dasein: the free sign(ing) of an act that creates itself in fact thanks to a fact that is created in an act. In that event, what we would write as the f/act of freedom must be signed in a signature act; in the case in point, with the act of the X as the mark(er) of an open place in the text.

We know that the "Da" of Heidegger's "Dasein" is neither here nor there insofar as it is "placed" in an open space (of freedom): in a "t/here" that can only find itself by doubling back through a facticity that is doubled back on it. Dasein can only locate its own "being" by coming back to a "here" that is always already "there," where it finds itself bound to others (*Mitsein*) as well as to beings (*das Seiende*) in its being-t/here (*Da-sein*). In that case, the drawing of the line, that is, of the slash in "t/here", is not only a convenient way to mark the "here" in "there" but to sign the space between the "fact" and the "act": to mark the "act" in "fact" as our own design of the f/act of a freedom that only exists as a fact in act and only acts in fact. Of course, thinking along another line, Heidegger will himself remark on the opening of Da-sein though the creation of a space in the word that quite literally spells it out; thanks, that is, to the inclusion of a hyphen in its very name, which we might well regard as a sign, not just of its being-there (as the there of being) but of its t/here-being.[10] In any event, if facticity is the fact of a freedom that is bound to act, then what we are describing as a "f/act" binds freedom to (an) act as well as to (the) fact(s); just as Dasein's "here" is bound to its (being) "there." This is to insist that freedom is not free to act before it does, since it does not exist as a fact until it acts; at least, not as an initial freedom, which initiates itself through factical action. Only in the act does freedom become a fact; in which case, we might say that the free act takes place after the fact, *ex post facto*, shall we say, according to the "law" of freedom.

If we are inclined to double up on the *Da*, to multiply it (exponentially), as it were, with an × that cuts both ways in a double drawing of the line, it is to mark a collective signing that is tied to an initial act; in fact, to a double act of freedom that will eventually require a rendering of the × in the design of a double slash. Initially, however, we would like to read the space that is de-signed by the × as a sign of the f/act(icity) of freedom; in point of fact, as a signing of Heidegger's own Dasein, in which he has designed a passage between "*Sein*" and the "*Geviert*" in an act of thinking that can only be thought (including by Heidegger himself) in a literal reading of Jünger's proposal to cross *Over the Line* (*Über die Linie*). As its initial title would indicate, *Zur Seinsfrage* is originally written *On "The Line"* (*Über "Die Linie"*), that is, "over" Jünger's initial design(s). As such, our own doublecrossing of the line would have to mark a freedom that is bound to death as well as to others in the writing of "Da~~sein~~" by crossing out its own "being" as the sign of a true nihilism.

To write the × in the name of Dasein would not only be a shorthand way of signing the f/act of freedom but a sign that every signature is a mark of death—which is to say that if the *Da* points to the facticity of existence, then Da~~sein~~ is never simply a question of being but of nothing as well. It is this "nothing" that is topographically marked by the commonplace of the × as a crossing "over" the line: a *koinos topos* that is a sign of the partial deletion of "Dasein" in its signing on to what we would be inclined to call the democracy of death.[11] For death creates a common place by admitting it into Da~~sein~~, not only as the collective name of "mortals" but in the sharing of a sign that puts being itself on the line.

THE SIGNING (OF THE TEXT)

> The essence of nihilism directs us to a domain that would call for another language. If a turning-over-to belongs to "being," and such that the latter rests on the former, then "being" is dispensed in its allocation. This now renders it questionable how being, which has reverted and is exposed to its essence, may from that point come to be thought. Correspondingly, a thoughtful foresight into this domain could only write "being" in the following way: ~~being~~.
>
> . . . The sign of the crossing can, to be sure, according to what has been said, be no merely negative sign of a crossing out. Instead, it points to the four regions of the Fourfold and their gathering at the site of the crossing (cf. *Vorträge und Aufsätze*, 1954, pp. 145–204).[12]

As far as we are concerned, Heidegger gets closest to the book in his thinking about being when he crosses the word out in the text: in a graphic design that crosses the line and, in so doing, marks a textual thinking at its vanishing point; marks it, without (a) question (mark), not simply through the apparatus of writing (editing) but in a literal "drawing" of the line. For the × does not just mark a space of deletion or even the space between "writings"—between the ontological language of "being" and the mythopoetic thought of the "*Geviert*"—but between semiotic systems: between an alphabetic and a pictographic script, in fact, crossing the two in a superimposition that creates a type of hypersign or, indeed, a trademark. If the ×™ is read as a pictograph of the Fourfold, then its intersection marks the vanishing point of being into nothing at the collective opening of an interchange between earth, sky, divinities, and mortals; in which case, "~~*Sein*~~" provides a corporate logo for Heidegger's thinking as whole—or, dare we say, as a hole, if the signature mark of the × is treated as the de-sign of an opening between (his) writings.[13]

While the figure of the × may be viewed as a sign of convergence in (and of) Heidegger's text(s), we would, at the same time, have to read it as a mark of divergence: as a sign of the space between vocabularies, if only insofar as "being" vanishes into nothing at the opening of an abysmal exchange between earth, sky, divinities, and mortals. In effect, the × must be submitted to a double reading, in a *Gestalt*-switch in which the crossing of lines marks a breach of the sign, as the two lines break into four (quadrants) at their intersection. Of course, if we do not limit our reading of the × to a pictograph of the *Geviert* but treat it as a sign of the cross between writings in

Heidegger's own *corpus*, then the question remains: What becomes of "Dasein" when "*Sein*" is crossed off the page? Presumably, our own name would have to be written with an X; written off the page, as it were, in the re(de)signing of what we have signed, for short, as Da~~sein~~.

In so designing our own signature mark, we would like to regard the X as a sign of facticity in the text, signed in the name of Dasein: a "determinative" that, while turning a common noun into a proper name, retains its neutral or, as Heidegger would insist, its neuter status (*das*), including as neither male (*der*) nor female (*die*).[14] If we may speak, in this regard, of the hieroglyphic writing of Da~~sein~~, it is not only to mark the X as a sign of death or to indicate its association with the divine (in the *Geviert*) but to characterize the complexity of the sign itself, as both phono- and picto-graphic; in our case, as the crossing of an alphabetic script ("*Sein*") with a literal drawing of the line (X), as a graphic portrait of the sign. Strictly speaking, the X is not simply an index but an icon of the line in its semiological design: a direct depiction of the act of drawing the line; outlining, as it were, the initial design of the sign itself as a mark of Dasein's own signing onto a system of signs. So read, its crossing of the line is clearly not ("merely") a sign of deletion; and not only because it points to the Fourfold but because the *Da* remains: is, in effect, doubled, if not underlined, in a partial deletion of "Dasein" that marks a contraction of the sign, reducing it to its "initials" in a literal drawing of the line(s) that is designed to sketch the out-line of a Dasein without being. As such, the X marks the de-sign of a double bind in the name of Da~~sein~~, not only as a crossing of *Sein* with the *Geviert* but as a sign of the finest line that can be drawn: the fine line between being and nothing.

In the act of signing our common name with an X, we would like to mark an original facticity that is written into the design of Dasein by drawing on a preontological line; a primitive line, as it were, that is tied to death and on which we would, in fact, like to remark. In this re-markable facticity, "being" comes to an end in the initialization of Da~~sein~~ with a collective X that is literally signed in the text. Here we would have to show that, in its polygraphic design, the X is not only an autograph of nothing or a pictograph of the *Geviert* but, as the signature of the illiterate, is the mark of a collective act: the sign of a freedom that is marked by the democracy of death and signs on to it in the hieroglyphic de-sign of a defaced "Da~~sein~~." This is to say that rather than posing "the question of the meaning of being" or proposing a "poetic dwelling" in the Fourfold, we are more inclined to wonder what it would be like to remain lodged in the rift between writings, in fact, between semiotic systems: to follow a pre-scription that is marked by a primitive f/acticity; marked for death and "initialed" in the name of the X as the sign of a complete nihilism. If we, in effect, double up on the *Da* with an X, it is as the mark of a collective signing that is tied to the initial act of a double f/act of freedom: to a facticity that acts insofar as it is bound to nothing as well as to others—which is simply a shorthand way of noting that the crossing of the line would not only affect "being" or "Dasein" but all of the "ontological" categories and "existentials" in *Being and Time*: would infect (or at least inflect) all signs of "*Sein*," from "*~~Sein~~-zum-Tode*" to "*Mit~~sein~~*" to each and every "*~~Seiende~~*."[15]

At the present time, however, we would prefer to concentrate on the X, in its extraction from the text, as a signature mark of Da~~sein~~. As a pure extract of nothing, this autograph is designed to bind us to one another through the marking of a collective grave in the page. Like a cenotaph or cenograph, as the empty sign of a proper name, the commonplace of the X marks an aboriginal space in the text that is open to the f/acticity of a freedom committed to death through an initial de-sign: as if initial(iz)ing the bottom line of a contract that is created in an act of signing. This is why, if we are on the lookout for a thinking in action—a thinking whose practice, quite literally, *makes* sense—then we might well look to the signing of a signature as the design of a binding freedom: the de-ontological mark(er) of a semiotic facticity that creates a (common) sense of responsibility, which may be binding unto death when signed in the face of others. While, in one respect, death is the bottom line, in another—which may well, in effect, be the same respect (for death)—there is no bottom line without action; even if the "act" involves a drawing of the graphic line that "in fact" creates the signature as a distinctive mark of Dasein. For only Dasein "signs" in this signature sense, and precisely because it is marked for death in the design of a finite sense for which it may assume responsibility in so signing. At the same time, as a sign of the withdrawal of the sign, the X is designed to mark the contraction of sense to its vanishing point in the text; such that, if we are to make sense of ourselves, it can only be in a common sense(lessness) that is marked by a collective commitment to the bottom(less) line of sense itself: that there is no sense but the sense that we make to each other.

If we may think in terms of a double bind of freedom in its concrete creation, then we would like to take an initial clue from the X as a sign of sense in the making. Here we would have to think of the double bind both literally and figuratively: not just in a (double) crossing of the line(s) but in the cosigning of the text ("with" others) as the graphic design of a common bind(ing) of freedom. No doubt, a signature must be freely signed to be binding; in which case, it is not simply a semiotic fact but an existential act. As a binding sign, however, the f/act of the X de-scribes the initial design of a common sense that is marked by a profound illiteracy. Like sense itself, the X is a sign of freedom in the making: a collective freedom that must be signed with a proper name, through which we are, in effect, assigned to one another. In this (common) sense of a democracy of death, what we might call the X-factor involves a structure that is bound to freedom (and vice versa) as it marks the initialization of a framework that is tied to the signature as a creative act: a commonplace through which a transfer of freedom literally takes place in the "sharing" of a collective free space. As a sign of commitment, the X marks the bottom line of a contract that is binding as a consignment of freedom, in which we are all free to sign with the same common proper name.

THE MARK (OF DA~~SEIN~~)

> The human race has adopted four main methods of making records or communicating information: pictograms, word-signs, syllabic signs and the alphabet. As we shall see, two or more of these could function together within the same system. This list is not meant to imply a hierarchy, with the alphabetic at the culminating point. So-called "primitive" societies using pictographs may be just as complex in their modes of thought as users of other methods but it is a different order of complexity. Pictographs have been used chiefly by hunting or farming communities, the best-documented examples being those of the North American Indians. The other methods have evolved in more complex economies with more advanced technology—usually therefore in an urban environment. There is a further, crucial difference between the pictographic method and the rest. Pictographs have no linguistic reference of any kind; they depict an event, or convey a message, by means of a series of drawings. Such a medium can hardly be called writing.[16]

It is a long way from *Sein und Zeit* to *Zur Seinsfrage*, especially if we go by way of the *Geviert*. This is why we would like to trace a shortcut through the signature, along which it is, admittedly, easy to get lost. Of course, in this, as in other cases of what Heidegger calls "thinking," the point is not to retrace a route that is already known (like a sightseeing tour) but to cut a trace on which we are free to roam; in the case in point, by following a sign through which we can get lost together in what the lecture "On the Essence of Truth" refers to as "the mystery of the *Da-sein* in man," or as we might write it: human ~~being~~.[17]

If we are to create a shortcut in the text, it will be by tracing the complex crossing that we have marked with an × as a sign of (the doublecrossing of) Dasein: the signature mark of a signing that must be made with a graphic de-sign, when all that is left is the *Da* of Da~~sein~~. As we have indicated, this is not simply a deletion of "Dasein," but the sign of a concrete opening in the text that marks the design of a free space, signed with a common proper name; in our case, as the signing of a commonplace in the name of the ×. For every proper name is a pseudonym of Dasein, marked by the f/act of freedom: a signing onto the *Da* by admitting facticity into the act—including the fact(icity) of language itself, in Da~~sein~~'s own signing off on a system of signs.

This is simply to insist that, after the writing of ~~being~~, freedom can no longer be thought of as a prehistoric event or as an ontological condition. If anything, we would have to cross the two in a paleontology of freedom, tracing its creative evolution across our f/actical history in the concrete structures that create it and that it, in turn, creates. No doubt, some of the spadework would involve a paleography that excavates the "prehistory" of a writing that is the origin of "history," including of the recent "history of being," which clearly accounts for another phase of freedom. If freedom is something that we bring upon ourselves in fact and in act—in an act that is the creation of freedom (in its double sense)—then the ×, as a signature, would be the mark of this f/act as an act that cuts both ways, as if to double back on itself. For the signature is a free signing (of a semiotic facticity) that binds itself to others; perhaps, most obviously when it is marked with an ×, which creates the design of a collective sign: an act that marks the creation of an initial freedom by initialing (or initializing) a bottom line that would not exist without the signing.

Although it need not occur in words, even when it does, a signature depends upon a certain crossing of the line between the sign and the mark; especially in a world that has come to be designed through written contracts. Legally speaking, it is the signing of the mark that gives the signature its warrant: the drawing of the line or the placing of the sign or seal by the hand of the signer on an item in the world, which we, consequently, refer to (and in a number of senses) as "making one's mark." Here it must be clear that the × that serves as the autograph of the illiterate is neither the alphabetic letter "x" nor its graph, whether upper or lower case. Instead, it is the holographic marking of the hand drawn line as a sign of signing: a literal mark of commitment that holds the hand of the signer to a contract thanks to a profound illiteracy. For what distinguishes the signature from the proper name—even among the literate—is the graphological character of the free-hand line as an indexical sign that a particular signer has been there: a chirographic sign(ing), as it were, that is written into the facticity of writing itself.[18] It is the idiographic character of the handwritten signature that allows it to function as a sign, to speak with Heidegger, of Dasein; or, to put it in broken English: as the mark of a *Da*-sign. As such, the ✗ is sufficient to serve as both the proper and common name of every human being; as if each and every one of us, whether we could read or write, had the right to mark the autographic site of a semiotic being-in-the-world, and to do so with a sign of our being there that crosses at least certain linguistic barriers.

This is, of course, only one indication of the worldly character of the ×, which, as a kind of all-purpose sign, is employed to make a great many marks on the world, and often at sites at which action is to be or has been taken. In the present case, this common sign becomes a signature only when it is performed by hand. As such, we might say that the written signature is a cross not only between the sign and the mark but between a semiotic and an ergonomic account of sense. If we may think in terms of the ergonomics of the sign (in §17 of *Being and Time*), it is not only to underline the chirographic ✗ in view of the manual labor of writing but to describe the capacity of Dasein to sign as the mark of its existential character: a sign of the fact that Dasein defines its signs, like all of its designs, in its factical engagement with the world.

As we have indicated, in the drawing of the line(s) as a (signature) mark of Da~~sein~~, the crossing out of "*Sein*" is not only an abbreviation of its name, as if to its initials, but the sign of a shortcut in the text: an exit, as it were, to a free space that originates in the f/act of a signing that comes before the letter. To follow this shortcut through the signature, as a "leap" of thinking to its origin (*Ur-sprung*), it would have to be clear that there are at least two ways to read the ✗ as an autograph of *Dasein*: as a logogram that stands for a proper name or as a common mark that allows it to stand without a name. Needless to say, the × will incline us toward a double reading: that we view this signature as operating between the name and the nameless. In so doing, its signing traces the entire history of writing in the simplicity of its initial design: as a mark of the original act that first creates the sign, in fact.

We will not pretend that the × can take us back to the beginning, let alone to a time before writing; although we would insist that it marks the design of a suspended sign—including as a sign that is literally suspended between semiotic systems. In the case in point, namely, of writing, it can operate as a pictographic mark, a logographic sign or an alphabetic letter, crossing them with and against one another to create Heidegger's own logogriphic de-sign.[19] As such, it makes the transition, right before our very eyes, from a pictographic writing that draws on the world, to the logogram as the sign of a word, through an alphabetic system that is fully "phono-graphic," to the puzzle of a typographical act that creates an unpronounceable name. In two quick strokes, the × cuts across the history of writing, as if its signing could take us from its opening line to the end of the text: not just point ahead ("beyond" being) but direct us back to a "preliterate" existence that runs along a broken line into and through the age of literacy, in a concrete history of freedom that is preserved in the chirographic f/act of the ✗ as a distinguishing mark of Dasein. In this respect, we might say that facticity always returns (us) to the beginning of thinking, which was not in Greece.[20]

Instead, the unspeakable character of the × takes us back to a time before speech and writing were conjoined: to a writing that exceeds speech in a prephonological inscription. This is not to assume that writing precedes speech, any more than we would assume that speech precedes writing. If we would go so far as to say that the × marks a writing that is prelinguistic, it is to offset the prejudice that an alphabetic script inevitably invites: to emphasize the fact that speech and writing, as independent systems, must be brought together in the invention of a phonetic "alphabet" (as its Greek "initials" would have it). At the level of pictography, speech and writing are independent of one another; which is simply to say that writing may, in fact, operate as a system of inscription that has no phonological component. The written marks that are inscribed, in the first instance, quite literally on the world, are not, properly speaking, "linguistic"; just as pictographic signs have nothing to do with the tongue (*lingua*). Of course, as at least one version of the story goes, we could trace a transition in the history of writing from a pure pictography through the logogram to the syllabic systems that render even a nonalphabetic script phonetic. But this movement—reading backward, as it were, to the beginning (as if phonetic writing were the ultimate end), including through mixed systems—would only serve to make it clear that the mark of the × is not, first and foremost, a linguistic character.

While the × may well serve as a simple sign of the original separation between speech and writing, as the signature of the illiterate it would have to be regarded as a rather more complex design. Not only is the X a letter of the alphabet, it has, in fact, been taken as a proper name by those who can write (Malcolm X), and is often used as a common name of the unknown (Mr. X); although, in either case, it retains something of its nonlinguistic character, assuming that it is designed to hold open a blank in the line of letters. We might say that the × operates at the end of language, marking the point at which thinking runs into and out of the alphabet (or at least at which writing runs out of letters[21])—especially, if this would help us to explain why it took on the character of a signature; that is, why this particular character came to mark the design of an autograph of the illiterate. If we would presume to trace it back to the beginning in its own ergonomic formation, read the × like some semiotic fossil whose remains are left in the text, as the record of a prehistoric "writing" that still survives today, then we must imagine it as a primitive sign originally designed to mark a site in the world. In that event, while the signature is a performative act of writing that marks the design of a rather sophisticated linguistic operation, we will assume that the × is used as an autograph of Dasein to sign one's own facticity as a mark of our being-t/here—as if the ✗ marks the spot (in the text) where the illiterate signer announces: X was here (×).

As such, the performative ✗ is not simply a sign of signing or, for that matter, a mark of the mark. In crossing the two, it is a mark of the marker: a mark(er) of Dasein itself, making its mark in an act of signing. In that event, the ✗ is not just a sign of the facticity of language but a mark of facticity in writing, through which "Dasein" marks its "being-there" in a system of signs. It is as if Dasein locates itself through a sign that it has not just appropriated from the world but signed in an act that is designed to signify it as the signer. In the case in point, for example, the inscription of Dasein, in its hieroglyphic design, would serve as a formal indication of its (prior) determination in an alphabetic thinking. This includes the possibility of its signing as "being-t/here," if only as a reminder that such a script consists of more than just letters. In fact, not only is the "x" the only letter of the English alphabet that is a verb, but the word is named for the act that performs it, even if as a sign of deletion.

At the same time, if we analyze its own (graphic) design as a sign, it should be clear that the × marks a place by placing a mark in a place that first makes it a place: marks that "place" in the first place. This is not to pretend that the × is the first sign but to suggest something of the way in which its own ergonomic design functions by doubling up on the simplest of lines: draws a second line to secure the first, as a sign that points nowhere but *there*: to itself, as an initial mark that marks the spot precisely where it "is."[22] In the case of writing, as a signing of one's own name, we could say that the ✗ is designed as a mark of Dasein to sign its (being) t/here (*Da*) with an ink spot or, to be precise: a clot. So thought, as a signature mark, once the × becomes an official spot made on paper or parchment in the transition to a literate culture, we would have to view the formal signing of this mark on a contract ("making one's mark") as the direct counterpart to the medieval practice of attaching a clod of earth to a "deed" that was no longer executed on site.[23]

At this point, however, we would simply like to underline the precise way in which *Dasein* "finds itself" through the sign, as the ✗ marks the initialization of a certain "signing" in its double drawing of the line: as both the sign of a proper name and the mark of a primitive *Da*-sign. As the signature of the illiterate, it cuts both ways; cuts back, like a shortcut to the beginning, as it cuts across history: cuts a cross that marks our most recent ontological history as a history of the alphabetic writing of "being," which comes to an end in the re(de)signing of Dasein, albeit in a double ending.[24] For the × may be read as a logogram standing in place of the name—a sign, in other words, of other words—or it may be read as the mark of a more profound illiteracy. As an index of the act of signing that points directly to Dasein, the ✗ operates by breaking down the sign itself into its initial drawing of the line(s); "initials" that, in effect, doublecross one another as an icon of the line in its own inscription. As a concrete sign(ing) of one who cannot write *in writing*, we mark, without a word, the design of a primitive opening in (and of) language, described in the name of Dasein through a sign of (its own) self-deletion: a disappearing sign, to say the least, given that, as an editorial mark, the × crosses itself off the page in the final version of the text, vanishing without a trace along with the sign that it marks for deletion.

Of course, Heidegger's × is left in the text, not only as an autograph of nothing but as a logogram of the *Geviert*: as the sign of another writing (to which he, in fact, refers) or, so one might insist, as a mark of the "intertextuality" of his own thinking and its freedom to move in the space between an onto-logical and a mytho-poetic thought. In either case, it operates as a grave marker in the name of Dasein, when the latter is read along the lines of a community of mortals. At the same time, *Zur Seinsfrage* concludes that, in crossing over the line, the × de-scribes the drawing of a vanishing sign: a self-deleting sign that withdraws itself from the text in an act of utter nihilation. In the thought of the withdrawal of the sign, the question (on the line) remains: How do we delete the ×, edit *it* from the text; delete the sign (of deletion) without doubling up on it? How, in other words (or, to be precise, without words), are we to mark the deletion of Heidegger's × unless we sign over it, as if resigning ourselves to it; in which case, we do not accomplish its extraction from the text but merely solidify the lines of his thinking with (yet) another ✗?

Are we caught in a double bind or, in tracing the sign to a literal drawing of the line, would we have to think in terms of double "initials," neither of which comes first: of a double crossing "over" the line(s), as each must cross the other, not only to create but to doublecross the sign? Is there, in effect, a drawing of the line that frees the sign in a doubling that makes a difference, even when it is signed on the same line or, in fact, in the same space, as if written over the name of another? In that case, a topological reading of the line would be designed to trace the × to an exit from the text by signing it, as Heidegger did not, through a double lining in the name of Dasein.

THE END (OF PRINT)

> Reading, like other acts of consumption—like eating, looking, or listening—seems to deny its material presence. Once we have finished holding a book in our hands, we remove our body from the act and the event vanishes without a trace. To construct a history of reading might seem then a nearly impossible task: we read by ourselves; we read lying in bed or in the bath; we read in studies, offices, or libraries; we read passively, privately, and silently. But the early modern reader was likely none of these, and we can begin to gather a sense of that reader equipped for reading, "studied for action," surrounded by books, contemplating and marking texts. . . . Perhaps most revealing of all is the material evidence left by readers themselves, for the early modern reader was an epitome of material action—studious, attentive, and composed. Armed with pen and penknife; with ink and inkhorn; with sand and sandbox; with letter cases and paper; with table books, journals, and commonplace books, early modern readers left their traces everywhere: on the covers of books, on their title pages, on flyleaves and pastedowns, all over the margins of books, even between lines of print.[25]

If what we would write (not so long after Heidegger) as Dasein only "exists" after the f/act, if its "freedom" is tied to a signature act, then we would be inclined to sign our name with an × not only as a mark of death or even as a formal indication of Dasein as the "placeholder" of nothing (which it "is"), but to mark the facticity of our assignment to a structure of signs in which we are free to act; in fact, as a sign of the nameless site at which various semiotic systems interact, marking the point at which they are connected to one another and through which a collective free space is initially designed. For the signing of Da~~sein~~ is a mark of its commitment to the system in which it becomes a sign, freely admitting its consignment to the fact(icity) of language itself, whether alphabetic, pictographic, hieroglyphic or logogriphic. This is why, if we think of the × as an initial, it is not simply as the first letter of a proper name but in the original act(s) of the drawing of the line(s) that creates the sign itself in the f/act of a double stroke of freedom. Like a paraph, whose free design can be traced in the signing of any name, the ✗ is the sign of an existential character, in our case, de-signed to mark a graceful exit from the text.

As the signature of the illiterate, the chirographic ✗ is not only the logogram of a proper name but the pseudonym of a nameless *Da*: a pure paraph that is signed without a word to mark a double ending. For Da~~sein~~ is the sign of as a pseudo(ano)nymous freedom that must make a name for itself. This is why we would have to distinguish between the singularity of the *Da*, as a (primitive) facticity that we mark with a common ×, and the individuality of the self, which is assigned a proper name. "Dasein" is not who we are (the proper name) but how we are (the open place); which is to say that, technically speaking, the self is not what we are but whom we happen to become—an event that occurs to Da~~sein~~, as a matter of f/act. Consequently, if we stress the impersonal character of the *Da*, would properly write our own name with an ×, it is not only because what *Being and Time* calls Dasein becomes a "person" in the intimacy of its being-with-others-in-the-midst-of-things (not just in its "self-relation") or because Heidegger will later treat the naming of "being" as a feature of our historical determination, but to endorse—or at least initial—the deletion of "*Sein*" so as to mark the design of Da~~sein~~ as an empty sign: a cenograph, as we have put it, like an open grave in the page, such that the × is treated not only as an epitaph to the end of "Dasein" but as the trace of a space where freedom collects in Heidegger's text.

If we attend to the performative edge of Heidegger's ×, as an act of "nihilation" in the text, then we would have to distinguish between saying and *doing* nothing. As the sign of a breach in writing, the literal "crossing of the line" is not a metaphor but the semaphore of a free space that is "cleared" in an act of thinking; a concrete opening that connects us to one another through a collective freedom that precedes (or, to be more accurate, concedes) politics or any social contract. And yet, there is a "signing" involved here that marks the fact of Dasein's existence in a concrete (historical) structure as well as its own (primitive) need to act.

This is simply to insist that, in an age of literacy (and thought in terms of its original title), *Zur Seinsfrage* would have to be read as an instruction manual; such that the × is treated as a command or imperative, marking directions that have to be followed. As a manual instruction, it is the sign of a chirographic act that must be performed on the text *in fact*. In a (double) reading of ~~being~~, not simply "under (*sous*) erasure" but, as Heidegger would have it, as a crossing "over (*über*) the line," it is as if we were directed to sign by tracing a de-sign between the lines of the ×, extracting it from a text that requires us to act, so as to provide the book with a proper ending. If, in short, we follow Heidegger's thinking to the end of the line, then the reader would have to complete the sketch of the "destruction" of the history of ontology that is begun in *Being and Time* by providing the outline of a second act, designed to create the portrait of a Dasein that comes after "being," if this can be thought: a "*Da*" that (once) came before and (now) comes after "*Sein*," and which we have already marked with an × in the text—in the partial deletion of "Dasein" that, in effect, parts the word, and more decidedly than Heidegger himself does when he writes it with a hyphen. For we would like the × to direct us not only to a textual spacing but to an abysmal opening in the name of Da~~sein~~, as we trace it, through the shortcut of the signature, to an actual space in the page that must be staged in a collective signing.

This is why ("Dear Reader") we must put an address at the end of the book to mark its closing, as if addressing an envelope that remains to be opened; an epilogue or postmark designed to inscribe our Dedication after "The End" of the text—like a Foreword that comes at the end, after every word, as was once the practice, when both the title page and colophon came last, to name the book as well as its printer. For we "moderns" would have to regard the × not just as a proofreader's sign of deletion or as the drawing of a pictographic design or, for that matter, as the mark of an illiterate writer, but as a printer's signature, addressed to the binder: a disappearing sign on the direction line, cut off without a trace in the text and yet designed to align the sheets with a registry mark, repeatedly resigned to collate the pages in the complexity of the folds, so as to secure the proper order of their opening.[26] This is, of course, why the modern book must be read with a penknife: to open the fold of the paper along a cutting edge that invisibly marks the collective creation of the page as a manual event.

If it takes a reader and a writer to create a text, it takes a printer and a binder to produce a book. In the end, however, it is the reader alone who makes the final cut, including in the material opening of the page that creates the free space of reading; at least in the case of the initial reader, who comes (at) last.[27] But is there a place, in our time, for the reader to sign on what should, perhaps, be printed as a dotted line or, to be precise, as the hyphenated de-sign of Dasein? How, in other words, do we propose to bring the book to a close—not just any book, but *this* book; "we," who not only come after "Dasein" (as the fictional hero of *Being and Time*) but after Postmodernism and its endless attachment(s) to the text, as if caught in a 1∞p of language? How are *we* to end a book on facticity if not by proposing that the reader act in fact?

Needless to say, if we treat the X as marking a place to sign on the bottom line (as if on a contract), it is to trace the point at which reading comes to an end in a time and space that calls for action. And yet, while we have presumed to take a shortcut through the signature, it is obvious that Heidegger's X is merely printed in the text (although not in the holographic version); just as our own recreation of the sign, including with a broken line, would not be the mark of a handwritten signing. It is as if the best a writer can do these days is a printed ><, if he wants to secure the mass distribution of the text. But the reader is in a rather different position; especially if we can treat the broken sign as instructions for the signing of an abysmal line: a sign, after the signature, that the (presumably, solid) letter is not simply sealed with a kiss (***XXX***) but must be unsealed by holding the hand of the reader to a book whose future she holds in her hands.

If readers once read with a knife, perhaps we can still appeal to such an instrument to mark the opening of the book from the inside out—to release the freedom that modern printing has created in the complex folding and binding of the page and which is still contained in the Postmodern text. As collectively signed and aligned with an ><, we would have to contrast the virtual openness of the text with the actual opening of the book; although, strictly speaking, the text has a beginning and an ending, while it is the book that opens and closes. In fact, as a matter of bibliography, the "front" of the book is the edge that opens (even if it hinges on its "backing"); in which case, we might say that the end of the text that we have in view is not a question of an endless erasure but of an open embrasure. In effect, we would like to attach an opening to the text: a concrete space, in the name of Dasein, designed to make our mark at the close of the book, as the sign of a facticity that remains bound to it for its freedom. In so doing, we are not interested in the resurfacing of a space that makes room for (more) writing but in the widening of an opening that creates a material breach in the structure of the page. This is why we have left a common place for the reader to sign by cutting along a broken line (✂------), designed to trace the extraction of the >< from the text as a sign that is acted on. The instructions, as it were, for the creation of a commonplace must be signed on the dotted line by those readers who come after the writer—in the case in point, with a knife—if only to ensure that "the death of the author" is not being faked.

In this second signing, as the over- and under-writing of a double bind, the shortcut through the signature would create an open space in the commonplacing of a striking passage that is literally cut from the text to secure a common place in the book; as if the >< in Da~~sein~~ is de-signed to align the opening(s) between the reader and the writer: registered to doublecross their (k)nots, as Nancy would write it, so as to free them from the bind of modern printing. Of course, a good knot is not only designed to provide a strong bond but to be easy to open; like a good book or, for that matter, a good Dasein, which is bound at one end so that it is free to open at the other. In that event, we would want to contrast the textual n∞se with a knot that is always coming loose—which is why it must be secured with a double (k)not that does not simply revert to the positive but operates "nihilistically." For we might well wonder whether the binding of letters has become so tight that it can only be opened with a knife. If nothing else, we know that while there is always a hole through which the multiple bands are drawn together, the tighter the knot, the more its opening closes.

This is why we are taking a shortcut through the signature, and taking it literally: as a final cut that contracts thinking to a vanishing point that cuts the text short through the extraction of the >< in two quick strokes of the knife. Without exactly connecting the dots, this short cut would demand the drawing of the penknife along the face of the page, in effect, retracing the printed lines of the × by, quite literally, cutting it out of the text. As the point of the knife crosses "over" the line, its incisive design would (in)visibly mark the decision to exit from the text through a concrete opening in the book. By creating a free space in which neither reading nor writing can take place, the signing of the >< with a pen/knife is designed to line a clear-cut break in the page, through which the text is exposed to (its own) facticity. In effect, the re(as)signing of the × is registered as a remarkable operation, de-signed to create an open lining in the book that is secured through a paper embrasure—at least when the flaps are folded back to line a hole in the surface of the page as a concrete opening in the name of Da~~sein~~®.

In the commonplace of an open book, we (re)trace not just a modern reading or a postmodern writing but a primitive drawing (of the knife) between the lines of the ×, extracting it from the text to create an envelope of nothing in the face of the page. This is not just to register the copyright of the >< ® but to extend it to the reader, assuming that they buy a book of their own.[28] Only the collective crossing of the line(s) creates a common place in which we are free to trace an open passage that marks the end of writing in the middle of the page; not in the margin of the text or even in the space between letters or lines but at the end of language, where it is exposed not only to the world but to its own nihilation. As a sign of the times, marked through a de-faced Da~~sein~~, our prescriptive signing of the line signs off on the age of literacy in a type of philosophical suicide. Like a *pharmakon* that is, at first, hard to swallow, this homeopathic preparation is designed to stage the final act of Western ontology; assuming, of course, that the "leap" takes place at the point at which philosophy comes to the end of the line, to be precise, in a complete nihilism. As if reciting an epitaph without saying a word—as is, perhaps, befitting a silent reader—the freeing of the × from the text marks the *Ur-sprung* to an abysmal "origin" through an empty sign that is de-signed as a staging ground for the defense of nihilism, not as an axiological condition but as an existential position that is sufficiently refined to face the fact that death ~~is~~ (absolutely) nothing.

EPILOGUE

If the point of the penknife is to create an opening (to facticity) in the name of Dasein, then in tracing a primitive line through the sign, we mark a certain facing of the book at the end of the textual history of philosophy.[29] This prototype of a groundless space is designed to place Da~~sein~~ on an insecure footing; assuming that "the strike" and "the cut" are to prepare us for "the leap" through a hole in the page: a paper opening at the close of the book that turns the surface of the text quite literally into nothing.

Admittedly, it is not easy for a thinker to write nothing; especially not as an abstraction but as an extraction or, at the very least, a contraction to the vanishing point that is initialed in marking our own name with the ×, so as to create an "open place" in the very sign of Da~~sein~~. It is as if "Dasein" must cut itself open, in fact, fold itself back through the sign (in its own "*Sein*") to keep itself free; in the case in point, by performing a type of semiological surgery, required to save its "factical life." In the striking act of signing with a knife that draws on (*über*) the lines of print, the cutting of the >< out of the text would turn ~~*Sein*~~ into a free sign, and precisely along those lines that are designed to open. Topologically speaking, not only would the twofold

(*Zweifalt*) of the ontological difference (*Sein/Seiende*) break into four at the crossing of the × (as a mark of the *Geviert*) but a more incisive design would create a chorographic line, which is literally spaced and figuratively displaced in the re(as)signing of the >< as an open sign. For the de-cision that slashes the sign open would create new lines, on which the folding of the four flaps hinges and thanks to which they are free to open and close. If we may think of this free fold in terms of the flaps of an empty envelope that is inscribed in the face of Da~~sein~~, then if the dotted line is the sign of a cutting edge, the fourfold opening of the page, when folded back on itself, would create the out-line of a *Da* without *Sein*—which we might, these days, iconically (and ironically) sign as *Da*✉, as if to attach a memo to the *Da* that remains to be opened: an attachment to ourselves, as a *memorandum* designed to remind us—if we may put it in (im)proper English—not to forget nothing.[30]

Who would have thought that, in *Rethinking Facticity*, we would be referred (Re:) to nothing (as the ultimate in facticity) through a bottomless hole in the book, as if a clear de-sign of our own abysmal opening (to the f/act of freedom) through an act of "signing" that marks the end of the line in a thinking that is finally out of print? Obviously, the point has been to put a certain pressure on Heidegger's × to see what *we* can make of it in the face of our own f/acticity by returning to the original as an act of thinking that cannot be repeated but can only be re-marked on. In the cutting of the × from the text, the free design of Da~~sein~~ would create an empty space in the page whose rectangular outline does not describe the periphery of a static frame but the edge of a fold that opens: the point or line along which the flaps of the envelope are free to double back to define an open place that can never altogether close.[31]

To be exact, the signing of the >< with a knife would invite what we can only write as a 4fold hole in the text, to distinguish it from Heidegger's own Fourfold: a clear opening in the book, as a free space that could not "be" more clearly "there." The embrasure of this open space, created in the crossing of a double stroke of freedom that is braced and faced in a literal 4folding of the page, is designed to line an abysmal hole in the name of Da~~sein~~. As the re(de)signing of an aboriginal place, this nominal opening must be (in)secured on the surface of the page in a thinking that is freely bound to facticity through an open passage. For the direction lines leave the reader free to sign, since their instructions need not be followed. If they are, the act of in(de)cision would not only mark an attachment to Heidegger's Dasein but would, at least in part, cut us off from his writings. By extracting the × from the text, turning it into nothing, we free Dasein from the structure of "being" thanks to a f/actical opening that does not simply insert the reader into the *Geviert* but holds our place in a 4fold free space—like the self-insertion of a dog-eared page, through which a book is kept open even when it is closed.[32]

NOTES

1. For a sense of Heidegger's "plan" for a history of the university, see his *Phenomenological Interpretations of Aristotle*, trans. Richard Rojcewicz (Bloomington: Indiana University Press, 2001), 47–58, especially 54–55. In this respect, one should also see E. Grassi's study of *Heidegger and the Question of Renaissance Humanism* (Center for Medieval and Early Renaissance Studies, SUNY at Binghamton, 1983). At the time of these "phenomenological interpretations" (Winter Semester, 1921–22), however, far from a "poetic" thinking, Heidegger warns: "It is easy to run away from the university. But the university does not thereby change, and we ourselves, along with our affairs, are then—Nietzsche is a typical example—sacrificed on the altar of literature" (50). A few pages later, he speaks of "literatuers, and those philosophers who would rather gush with enthusiasm than think . . . " (61). Needless to say, there is no little irony in the fact that Heidegger will himself, soon enough, be sacrificing philosophy on the altar of Hölderlin's (presumably, divine) poetry.

2. For some discussion of these differences, see my *Confessions of a Rational Mystic: Anselm's Early Writings* (West LaFayette: Purdue University Press, 1994); 7–25. For a treatment of the difference between scholastic and monastic reading practices, see J. Leclercq's *The Love of Learning and the Desire for God* (New York: Fordham University Press, 1982). For a survey of the development of modern theories of interpretation, see *The Hermeneutics Reader*, ed. Kurt Mueller-Vollmer (New York: Continuum, 1994). And for a postmodern buffet, I would recommend *Modern Criticism and Theory*, ed. David Lodge and Nigel Wood (London: Longman, 2000).

3. We might well think of our own "John Hancock" as a figure of the signature: as the (con)signing of (a) freedom that binds the hand of the signer to others in a performative act that takes writing as seriously as death.

4. Heidegger remarks on this historic moment, when philosophy enters into literature, in *What Is Called Thinking?*, trans. Fred D. Wieck and J. Glenn Gray (New York: Harper and Row, 1972) as does E. A. Havelock in his *Preface to Plato* (Cambridge: Harvard University Press, 1963), whose thesis (about the transition from orality to literacy in Greek culture) has, in effect, been taken up and applied to the Middle Ages by Brian Stock. See his *The Implications of Literacy* (Princeton: Princeton University Press, 1983).

5. J.-L. Nancy, *The Experience of Freedom*, trans. Bridget McDonald (Stanford: Stanford University Press, 1993), 78–80. These comments follow a citation from Heidegger's *Grundbegriffe* (a lecture course from 1941[GA 51,

16]): "The beginning as the beginning of history is found only where there is freedom, that is, where a human group (*Menschentum*) comports itself resolutely toward beings and their truth."

6. See Mary Thomas Crane's *Framing Authority: Sayings, Self, and Society in Sixteenth-Century England* (Princeton: Princeton University Press, 1993). She concludes: "The commonplace book and its attendant practices of gathering and framing thus shaped the theory of discourse in this period; as we shall see, through its role in education, it shaped human subjects as well" (52).

7. "On the Question of Being" is most easily accessible in English, these days, in Heidegger's *Pathmarks*, trans. W. McNeil (Cambridge: Cambridge University Press, 1998), 291–322.

8. We would not want to underestimate the significance of Derrida's reading of Heidegger's ×. We might say that he was the first to take it seriously; in fact, to extract it from Heidegger's text, so as to make use of it in his own thinking—even if he twists it into an emblem of deconstruction that turns it back into the text in a trick (*tour*) of writing. See *Of Grammatology*, trans. G. C. Spivak (Baltimore: Johns Hopkins University Press, 1997), 24.

9. We refer here to Nancy's thought of "Exscription," whose spilling of the ink, nonetheless, remains attached to writing (*e(x)criture*).

10. Let us be clear that in *Being and Time*, "Da-sein" is not hyphenated to underline its "being" but to outline the "*Da*," namely, in chapter 5, which addresses the "existential constitution of the *Da*" and its "everyday *Sein*."

11. This is, in part, to remind us of Lefort's claim that "the revolutionary and unprecedented character of democracy" is that "[t]he locus of power becomes *an empty place*" (*Democracy and Political Theory*, trans. David Macey [Minneapolis: University of Minnesota Press, 1988]; 17; see also 225ff); although it is not to suggest that he shows any understanding of Heidegger's "politics." We are, however, sympathetic with his contention that, at the critical moment of decision (in democracy), the "individual" become numerical, in the counting of the ballots. In that case, we might read the × as Heidegger's casting of the initial vote in what we would regard as the calling of the question of being.

Let us just say, for our part, that if we must (re)turn, as Heidegger did, to the *topos* of the "*polis*," it is not the result of some presumed priority of the political in "a politics of being," as Heidegger's thought is often (mis)thought to be (not only in the face of his Nazism but under the mistaken assumption that he is "the thinker of being"). Instead, it is to address the question of the × as a sign of "collectivity" in Heidegger's text, if only insofar as its inscription over "being" points to the *Geviert*, in which "mortals" are bound to one another, not as a "people" (*Volk*) but in a community from which no one is excluded so long as they are willing to die.

12. *Pathmarks*, 310. The translation is my own.

13. See my "Heidegger's Hole: The Space of Thinking," *Research in Phenomenology* XXXI (2001): 203–29. Needless to say, the Earth names the site of a new facticity in Heidegger's thought, beginning in the early '30s, which

is initially described in the original version of "The Origin of the Work of Art." Admittedly, this is a somewhat different "earth" than the one at issue in the later thought of the *Geviert*, which is a more domesticated place ("the building bearer") than the one that is characterized in topographical terms of the rift/design (*Riß*). To follow these developments, however, we would have to trace the convoluted relation between the poetic and the plastic arts in "Origin" itself and across its various versions; a text that, while beginning from a model drawn from architecture, sculpture, and painting, doublecrosses them in the end in favor of the priority of poetry, so as to connect the latter to philosophy (through language) as "a work of the word." In fact, one would have to think this relation all the way through to the very late "Art and Space"; the only place, to my knowledge, at which Heidegger discusses the "plastic" arts by name, and which suffers from the same "poetic" problems, even though it is written in stone.

14. In a hieroglyphic script, a "determinative" is a mark "placed at the end of words to assist in establishing their meaning, where otherwise there might be uncertainty" (*Reading the Past: Ancient Writing from Cuneiform to the Alphabet* [Berkeley: University of California Press/British Museum, 1990]. 105). Thus, the same logogram (which I cannot reproduce here, given the limitation of an alphabetic typography) means "scribe" when it is followed by a determinative depicting a man while it means "writing" when it is followed by a determinative depicting a book-roll. Perhaps even more to the point, in Egyptian inscriptions, "name determinatives" are typically used in the form of male or female figures to distinguish the name of a man or a woman. This is particularly important, given that, as W. V. Davies puts it: "The name of a person, inscribed in hieroglyphs, was believed to embody the person's unique identity. If the representation of a person lacked a name, it lacked also the means to ensure his continued existence in the after-life. To destroy the name(s) of the person was to deprive him of his identity and render him non-existent" (89). In that event, given Heidegger's comments in *The Metaphysical Foundations of Logic*, the ✕, as a determinative of Dasein, could be regarded as the sign of a sexual determination that remains to be decided.

15. It would, of course, be quite an assignment to go back to *Being and Time* with the aim of crossing out every sign of "*Sein*" in the text, in effect, creating a book full of ✕s. Nonetheless, in this respect—and with all due respect—I would have to disagree with Nancy (the undisputed mastermind of *Mitsein*) in his call for an "ontology" of being-with, as the design of a (re)new(ed) First Philosophy. See his *Being Singular Plural*, trans. R. D. Richardson and Anne E. O'Byrne (Stanford: Stanford University Press, 2000). Let us just say that the trouble with "First Philosophy" is that it always puts philosophy first.

At the same time, for the discussion of another crossing of the line (in the barring of the sign) and of yet another hole, see Nancy and Lacoue-Labarthe's reading of Lacan in *The Title of the Letter*, trans. François Raffoul and David Pettigrew (Albany: State University of New York Press, 1992).

16. J. T. Hooker, "Introduction" to *Reading the Past*, 6.

17. See *Pathmarks*, 148ff; although we should note that the hyphen in "*Da-sein*" does not occur in the 1930 version of the lecture (at least not in the typescript to which I have had access).

18. In graphology, all handwriting can be read for its "hidden" meaning. The signature, however, holds a special place as an act of the creation of a writer's own self-image.

19. While written initials are logograms in an alphabetic system, a logogram need not be a letter but can be any sign or mark, figure, or symbol that stands for a word. We might also mention that, according to the OED, "logogram," "logograph," and "logogriph" have been con-fused with one another in English. Strictly speaking, a logogriph is a word-puzzle, while "logograph" is a synonym for "logogram." Apparently, the phonographic similarity between "logograph" and "logogriph" led to their confusion; in which case, in a further confusion (by association and, perhaps, in connection with "anagram") "logogram" is also sometimes used as the name of a word-puzzle. We might also mention, in passing, that "logography" is a form of stenography in which multiple writers, in turn, transcribe in sequence (in our case, however, by signing over another's signing).

20. Without pretending to know exactly what it means, let us just note that the oldest human "art(ifact)" that we currently possess is a piece of polished ochre on which a set of Xs is inscribed. For an illustration, see David Lewis-Williams, *The Mind in the Cave* (New York: Thames and Hudson, 2002), 116 (Ill. 6) or simply google "Blombos."

21. In fact, at the time of Cicero, X was the last letter of the Roman alphabet. Y and Z were included to capture Greek sounds. (*Reading the Past*, 11). As we know, Heidegger's view of Cicero's distortion of Greek thought is critical to his account of the history of being (the "rootless" of Western thinking begins with its "translation" into Latin); although he is, apparently, less concerned about what Greek did to Latin.

22. Would it surprise anyone to find that one of the original marks was the line or that cuneiform writing was itself the formalization of an aboriginal operation? In that event, it would not be altogether unlike the way the (Arabic) number 1 would appear to be a sign created from the mark of a counting line, as the initial Roman numerals would also suggest: in a stylized pictography of lines (I, II, III, IV, V . . . X, where one side of the V marks the crossing line that groups the other four; just as the X sums up the initial group), which are clearly designed, let us admit, on the ten "digits" that we all learn to count on so much (assuming that the facticity of our fingers produces the base 10 system of counting).

In any case, as the crossing of the line in a sign that secures itself, is it any wonder that the X would form a figure of community as a design in which neither line comes first in the formation of a common sign: one whose meaning is created only once the lines cross, that is, at the point at which two lines become one sign? It should be clear, then, why we have insisted upon breaking down the sign along its initial lines.

23. In the early stages of our own textualization, in the legal history of the "documentation" of private property in Europe, we still needed a material sign, as a kind of proof of purchase. In those days, a clod of earth was attached to the contract from the land that was being sold. Ironically, this attachment of (and, presumably, to) the Earth marked a certain transcendence of it: a departure from the actual on-site negotiation of agreements in favor of the virtuality of written contracts. Needless to say, as we approach the end of that historic development, in its all but complete consummation, there is a certain irony in the current need to face the fact(icity) of our own virtualization. In this respect, for a High-Tech appropriation of the X, see Thomas Langan's *Surviving the Age of Virtual Reality* (Columbia: University of Missouri Press, 2000).

24. That the signature of the × is nonalphabetic is indicated by the fact that the cross (+) was also used "to make one's mark." On the checkered history of chirographic signatures (and many other relevant points), see Henri Martin's *The History and Power of Writing*, trans. Lydia Cochrane (Chicago: University of Chicago Press, 1994).

25. Steven N. Zwicker, "The Reader Revealed," in *The Reader Revealed*, catalogue of an exhibition at the Folger Shakespeare Library (Sept. 4, 2001–Jan 19. 2002), compiled and edited by Sabrina Alcorn Baron and distributed by the University of Washington Press, 11–12. See also Kevin Sharpe, *Reading Revolutions* (New Haven: Yale University Press, 2000).

26. For a quick anatomy lesson in the material creation of the book as well as a sense of the significance of historical bibliography, see Douglas McMurtrie's *The Book: The Story of Printing and Bookmaking* (Oxford: Oxford University Press, 1943) and John Feather's *A Dictionary of Book History* (Oxford: Oxford University Press, 1986).

27. Readers once had more of a hand in the actual creation of the book, since pages were not sold bound but simply printed and folded (the uncut version, as it were). Thus, the reader was free not only to choose the binder but could include inserts of their own before the final binding of the book.

28. In this regard, we must postpone the question of the modern library, which, while guaranteeing a free circulation of the text, involves a sharing of the book that stops us from writing in it—either that, or the signing of the X would entitle our text to the name of *Being and Crime*.

29. This textual history has been conveniently collected for us in a recent volume of Philosophical Classics, appropriately entitled: *From Plato to Derrida* (Englewood Cliffs: Prentice-Hall, 2000). The book ends with (the bookend of) Derrida's own (reprinted) "signature," from his "Signature, Event, Context" (1198).

30. There is an obvious irony in the fact that the act I am proposing we perform on the text could not be accomplished in a so-called "ebook" (even if, on my computer screen, an ☒ marks the exit, while a stylized × is the icon of deletion), since the precise operation requires a paper page. Let us just add, then, that we cannot say enough about paper and the role that it played in the creation of the modern world: not only in relation to printing (and not just the

book but paper money) or to the university, but as a model of what is valued for its valuelessness. Eventually, paper is cheap (which is what makes the mass distribution of the text economically viable); even if, early on, it was not.

31. On the (double) opening of the envelope, see, again, my "Heidegger's Hole," 222ff. Let us just note that the literal point of the flaps directs us to a three-dimensional space that is not contained in the page, but is a "sitation" or sampling of the open—not altogether unlike the enclosing of an (original) opening in the initial folding of an envelope. In that case, we would have to think in terms of a continuous opening that cuts through the page.

32. If this all seems a bit childish (or, to be kind, child-like), we can only hope that such a regressive analysis will serve as a reminder of the way in which some of us were seduced into the book in the first place. In works such as *The Very Hungry Caterpillar* (New York: Philomel Books, 1987) and (my personal favorite) *Barney and BabyBop Follow That Cat* (Allen: The Lyons Group, 1994), the original en-trance into the written word (read to us, of course, by others) is not only surrounded by pictures but comes through a hole in the page.

In this respect, I would like to dedicate the (future) opening of the book to my granddaughter Sydney, who has recently exposed me to those initial readings that are the first stage of the drama (if not the trauma) of literacy. To spell it out (silliabically): in the "in-no-sense" of her ~~being~~ t/here, the wonder is absolutely clear.

Contributors

Giorgio Agamben is professor of philosophy at the University of Verona. English translations of his many works include: *Homo Sacer* (1998), *Potentialities: Collected Essays in Philosophy* (1999), *The Man without Content* (1999), *The End of the Poem* (1999), and *The Open* (2004).

Robert Bernasconi is the Moss Professor of Philosophy at the University of Memphis. He is the author of two books on Heidegger and, more recently, of *How to Read Sartre*. He has written numerous articles on various aspects of continental philosophy and race theory. He has edited *Race* and, with Tommy Lott, *The Idea of Race*. He has also edited a number of collections of reprints documenting the history of race thinking, the most recent of which is the three-volume *Race, Hybridity, and Miscegenation* which he co-edited with Kristie Dotson.

Ed Casey is Distinguished Professor at the State University of New York at Stony Brook, where he teaches as well as at the New School for Social Research and at Pacifica Graduate Institute. He was chairman of the philosophy department at Stony Brook from 1991–2001. His books include *Spirit and Soul: Essays in Philosophical Psychology, Imagining, Remembering, Getting Back into Place, Representing Place in Landscape Painting and Maps,* and (most recently) *Earth-Mapping: Artists Reshaping Landscape.* He has just completed a new book, *The World at a Glance* (Indiana, 2007). His new research bears on the role of edge in human experience.

Bernard Flynn is professor of philosophy at the State University of New York, Empire State College, and an adjunct faculty in the philosophy department of the Graduate Faculty of the New School for Social Research. He is the author of *The Philosophy of Claude Lefort: Interpreting the Political* (Northwestern University Press, 2006) and *Political Philosophy at the Closure of Metaphysics* (Humanities Press, 1992) as well as the co-editor of a collection of writings on the philosophy of Merleau-

Ponty, *Renewing the Tradition, Merleau-Ponty and the Possibilities of Philosophy* (State University of New York Press, 2007). In addition he is author of numerous articles on political philosophy, phenomenology, and the history of philosophy.

NAMITA GOSWAMI is assistant professor of philosophy at DePaul University. She is interested in nineteenth and twentieth century Continental Philosophy, Postcolonial, Critical Race, and Feminist Theory. She is currently writing a book concerning issues of identity and the subject of feminism and postcolonialism.

PATRICIA HUNTINGTON, associate professor of philosophy at Loyola University of Chicago, dedicates her current thought to questions of loneliness and hardening of heart. Her teaching concentrates on philosophy of religion, existentialism and phenomenology, and Asian philosophies. Past initiatives led her to author *Ecstatic Subjects, Utopia, and Recognition: Kristeva, Heidegger, Irigaray* (State University of New York Press, 1998) and edit *Feminist Interpretations of Martin Heidegger* (Penn State University Press, 2001). Presently, she is writing a book entitled *Joy Wandering Alone: A Philosophy of Solitude.*

THEODORE KISIEL is Distinguished Research Professor emeritus of philosophy at Northern Illinois University. He has translated Heidegger's course of Summer 1925 as *History of the Concept of Time: Prolegomena* and coedited *Reading Heidegger From The Start: Essays in His Earliest Thought* and *Becoming Heidegger: On The Trail of His Early Occasional Writings, 1910–1927.* Books include *Phenomenology and the Natural Sciences* (with Joseph Kockelmans), *The Genesis of Heidegger's Being and Time,* and *Heidegger's Way of Thought: Critical and Interpretative Essays.* He has published numerous articles on Heidegger's development from the vantage of unpublished archival manuscripts.

JEAN-LUC NANCY has recently retired as professor of philosophy at the University of Strasbourg. Among his many books are: *The Inoperative Community* (1991), *The Title of the Letter* (1992, with Philippe Lacoue-Labarthe), *The Experience of Freedom* (1993), *The Birth to Presence* (1993), *The Muses* (1996), *The Gravity of Thought* (1997), *The Sense of the World* (1998), *Being Singular Plural* (2000), *The Speculative Remark* (2001), *Hegel: The Restlessness of the Negative* (2002), and *A Finite Thinking* (2003).

ERIC SEAN NELSON is assistant professor of philosophy at the University of Massachusetts-Lowell and has taught at the Universities of Memphis and Toledo. He has published articles on Kant, Schleiermacher, Dilthey, Levinas, and Heidegger. He is the co-editor of *Addressing Levinas* (Northwestern University Press, 2005).

DAVID PETTIGREW is professor of philosophy at Southern Connecticut State University. He has co-edited or co-translated several books concerning Heidegger or Lacan, including *Heidegger and Practical Philosophy* (State University of New York Press, 2002), and Jean-Luc Nancy and Philippe Lacoue-Labarthe's *The Title of the Letter: A Reading of Lacan* (State University of New York Press, 1992). He has co-translated (with François Raffoul) two books by J.-D. Nasio, including *The Book of Love and Pain: Thinking at the Limit with Freud and Lacan* (State University of New York Press, 2004). He has published essays on the work of Derrida, Merleau-Ponty, Freud, and Lacan. He is co-editor of a book series at State University of New York Press entitled Contemporary French Thought.

FRANÇOIS RAFFOUL is associate professor of philosophy at Louisiana State University. He is the author of *Heidegger and the Subject* (Prometheus, 1999). *A Chaque Fois Mien* (Paris: Galilee, 2004), and is currently preparing a book tentatively entitled "The Origins of Responsibility." He has edited and co-edited several volumes on Heidegger and Lacan, including *Disseminating Lacan* (1996), *Heidegger and Practical Philosophy* (State University of New York Press, 2002), and *French Interpretations of Heidegger* (forthcoming State University of New York Press). He has co-translated numerous works of French philosophers into English, such as Jean-Luc Nancy, Philippe Lacoue-Labarthe, and Françoise Dastur, as well as Heidegger's last seminars, *Four Seminars* (Indiana University Press, 2004). He is co-editor of a book series at State University of New York Press entitled Contemporary French Thought.

JACOB ROGOZINSKI is professor of metaphysics at the University of Strasbourg, where he succeeded J. L. Nancy in 2002. His current research is focusing on contemporary French philosophy, phenomenological thinking of the Body, and the work of Artaud. He published recently in French *Faire part—cryptes de Derrida* (Paris: Ed. Lignes—Léo Scheer, 2005) and *Le moi et la chair* (Paris: Ed du Cerf, 2006). Some of his essays have been published in English in the collections: *Radical Evil* (Verso Press, 1996), *Bodies of Resistance* (Northwestern University Press, 2001), and *Heidegger and Practical Philosophy* (State University of New York Press, 2002).

GREGORY SCHUFRIEDER is a professor of philosophy at Louisiana State University. He has authored a number of books and articles on Anselm and Heidegger as well as in the philosophy of art. He was the founding director of the Program for the Study of the Audiovisual Arts at LSU and is currently associate chair for Philosophy. The essay here is drawn from a work in progress entitled *Heidegger's Hole.*

ANTHONY J. STEINBOCK is professor of philosophy at Southern Illinois University at Carbondale. His books include *Verticality and Idolatry: On a Phenomenology of Religious Experience* (Indiana, 2007), and *Home and Beyond: Generative Phenomenology after Husserl* (Northwestern, 1995). He is the translator of the critical English edition of Edmund Husserl, *Analyses Concerning Passive and Active Synthesis: Lectures on Transcendental Logic* (Kluwer, 2001). He is the general editor of the Northwestern University Press series "Studies in Phenomenology and Existential Philosophy" (SPEP), and editor-in-chief of *Continental Philosophy Review.*

RUDI VISKER is professor of philosophy at the Catholic University at Leuven in Belgium. Visker has authored numerous articles and books, including *Michel Foucault: Genealogy as Critique; Truth and Singularity*, a response to critics of Foucault, and most recently, *Inhuman Condition.*

Index